Everything You
Need to Know About

COLLEGE
WRITING

Lynne Drury Lerych
Grays Harbor College

Allison DeBoer Criswell
Grays Harbor College

Bedford/St.Martin's
A Macmillan Education Imprint

Boston • New York

For Bedford/St. Martin's

Vice President, Editorial, Macmillan Higher Education
   Humanities: Edwin Hill
Editorial Director, English and Music: Karen S. Henry
Senior Publisher for Composition, Business and Technical Writing,
   Developmental Writing: Leasa Burton
Executive Developmental Manager for English: Maura Shea
Executive Editor: Molly Parke
Senior Developmental Editor: Joelle Hann
Editorial Assistant: Evelyn Denham
Production Editor: Kendra LeFleur
Production Assistant: Erica Zhang
Production Supervisor: Robert Cherry
Marketing Manager: Emily Rowin
Copy Editor: Arthur Johnson
Director of Rights and Permissions: Hilary Newman
Senior Art Director: Anna Palchik
Text Design: Marsha Cohen
Cover Design: John Callahan
Cover Art: Blue Delliquanti
Composition: Jouve
Printing and Binding: LSC Communications

Manufactured in the United States of America.

1   0   9   8   7
f   e   d   c   b

For information, write: Bedford/St. Martin's, 75 Arlington Street, Boston, MA
   02116   (617-399-4000)

ISBN: 978-1-319-08807-1 (Student Edition)
ISBN: 978–1–319–03582–2 (Instructor's Edition)

Introduction for Students

Don't skip this part —
it's important!

What you're reading right now is a good book. In this age of the magical Internet machine, you might not grasp the significance of a good book so let us explain. Back in olden days, when your faithful authors were growing up — without handheld devices that could shoot video, chart the stars, scan barcodes, translate multiple languages, and advise the quickest route to Grandma's house — people relied on books as primary sources of information. Why, back then we would check them out of libraries or buy them in bookstores, because e-books did not exist. Isn't that adorable?

Nowadays, of course, we love the Internet. Who doesn't? It has everything. If we need to know something, or even just *want* to know something, we can ask our friend the Internet. *Which bands were central in creating punk rock? How many aquatic mammalian species are there? What's the best way to braise carrots?* No matter what we ask it, the Internet has the answer.

Actually, it has many answers. Many, many answers. Sometimes it gives us so many answers that we literally don't know what to do with them. The prospect of narrowing them down and sorting them out and evaluating them all in order to find the answer we were actually looking for can be exhausting.

And this brings us to the reason we still like a good book. See, we could ask the Internet, *What do I need to know about college writing?* and we would get about 652 million answers in about 0.52 seconds. (Seriously. We just googled that question and got that exact result.) This happens because the Internet knows everything about everything, all at once; it really doesn't understand what we *need* to know, no matter how nicely we ask. But a book on the other hand — a book is a *focused* presentation of ideas and an *organized* collection of information. Doesn't that sound more efficient?

We called this book *Everything You Need to Know About College Writing* because it's the most accurate name we could think of. This book is truly designed to provide you with everything that you will genuinely need to know in order to write successfully in college.

Academic writing is a fairly complex process, and academic papers are usually rather sophisticated pieces of writing. Neither the process nor the product of writing occurs magically — which is a bummer, we know.

But the good news is that breaking that complex process into bite-sized chunks makes writing completely manageable. The central philosophy of this book is that college writing is do-able, and even enjoyable, as long as the writer (that's you!) approaches the task one piece at a time. To encourage that approach, we've organized this book around those bite-sized chunks, also known as steps in the writing process:

Part 1.   Reading and Writing Basics
Part 2.   Prewriting
Part 3.   Drafting
Part 4.   Revising and Editing
Part 5.   Writing Effective Arguments
Part 6.   Researching Effectively
Part 7.   Fine-Tuning the Text

Within those bite-sized chunks, we offer explanations and advice, of course.

But that's just the beginning. To get you moving toward Happy Writerville, we've created some special features that we think you'll like:

▶ **A three-step process** to learn and master what you really need to know:

- *Let Us Show You*   Models and examples of good writing and research processes brought to you by our students, Casey and Mara, and by us, your tireless instructor friends.

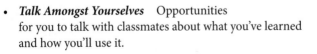

- *Talk Amongst Yourselves*   Opportunities for you to talk with classmates about what you've learned and how you'll use it.

- *Now You Try*!   Focused, manageable assignments to help you confirm what you've learned.

▶ *Reality Check!* Very handy checklists to help you focus on the most important concepts in each chapter.

We brought Casey, Mara, and our friend Grammster along on this journey because in our experience, the best way to learn new skills is by trying, making mistakes, and learning from those mistakes. What better way to ensure that *you* achieve that level of learning than by having a couple of courageous classmates who are willing to take one for the team in every chapter? And every step of the way, we're here with you. Just open the book, and there we'll be: your very own personal writing coaches, just itching to help.

We'd like you to think of this book as the one tool you'll need for conquering academic writing tasks large and small. It is designed to give you the tools you need to respond with competence, confidence, and style (yes, style!) whenever you need to write out your understanding of — or opinions on — the great and not-so-great ideas you'll encounter in your college career.

Writing doesn't have to be scary or otherwise intimidating. Just remember to breathe, and to approach each individual task as it comes. Who knows? You might even find yourself having fun. We certainly had fun writing this book. One student even told us, "My husband looks at me funny when I'm doing my homework reading, but only because I'm laughing." We'll take it!

Our goal in writing this text was for you to experience some genuine enlightenment as well as at least a few moments of amusement. You, of course, will be the ultimate judge of whether we've succeeded.

Lynne Drury Lerych
Allison DeBoer Criswell

Aberdeen, Washington
Spring 2015

Preface for Instructors

Psst, students— you can read this too!

We wrote our first version of this book in 2006 for our own freshman composition and pre-college writing students. Since we both run lively classrooms, we knew we had lots of material to draw from to make a better book than the ones our students were lugging around. We wanted to deliver serious writing instruction in a friendly and entertaining way, presenting concepts that aren't hard to understand and delivering them in language that avoided unnecessary complexity. We knew that if we could help students see themselves as writers, they would feel writing was something they could do and we wanted to bring our playful approach to life in the book as effectively as we do in our classrooms. Which is why we've included ourselves and students as characters.

> Ultimately, we wrote this book to lighten our students' loads.

> Serious writing can also be serious fun. It just depends on how you look at it.

What We Set Out to Do

Whether in person or in book form, we aim to provide practical, engaging instruction that helps students to become confident writers of expository and argumentative prose. We want to appeal to the sensibilities of today's students, who live in a fragmented, media-driven culture (like the rest of us). We're writing for students who depend on tweets, memes, and wall posts for information, for students who rely on irony and pastiche without knowing it, and for students who are inherently trusting of authority, even as they are also inherently skeptical of it, too. In short, we're writing for postmodern students who don't often realize their own postmodernity.

Our guiding principles have been straightforward, and we believe this direct approach is where our material shines (aside from our entertaining asides, of course):

▶ **We keep it simple.** Only the most necessary and appropriate topics and explanations are included. We do think Aristotle was right about rhetoric, but instead of unpacking all of the words in our lexical storage unit, we *show* theoretical constructs and explain them as clearly and simply as possible. When we've finished what needs to be said, we respectfully shut up. Well, okay — we sometimes go on for a sentence or two for the sake of fun. But *then* we shut up.

▶ **We keep it practical.** Our goal in structuring this book has been to honor writing as both process and product, and to honor students' need for meaningful engagement with both. For this reason, each chapter is focused on a specific, functional component of that process and product. Each chapter also contains a balance of theory, examples, discussion, and practice. We've made considerable effort to maintain a sense of timelessness and immediacy through a fresh approach to universal topics in both our examples and the student's practice opportunities.

▶ **We keep it lively.** If students genuinely want to turn the next page because they're interested, engaged, or entertained by what they're reading, they might actually *do their assignments.* This is refreshing for both students and faculty. In fact, students who have worked with this text over the past several years have regularly been caught smiling while doing their homework — and, hand to heart, the most frequent comment we see in end-of-term course evaluations is some variation on, "Who knew college textbooks could be *fun?*"

What's in the Book

We have aimed to create a text that offers a unique way of untangling the toughest writing tasks and helps students to learn from their mistakes. While poking light fun at ourselves — and general fears of academic writing — we deliver a carefully sequenced, hands-on approach to rhetorical skills that help students develop their writing and research skills. We have found that plenty of grammar and mechanics coverage, plus tips all along the way, help even the most reluctant writers stay on track. We are delighted to present such robust support for all elements of a writing course in such a small package and in a way that does not overwhelm students. Here's what we present in the book:

▶ **A sequenced approach to applying concepts and learning skills.** Our three-part approach helps students get past their frustrations with the writing process so they can become better writers in a stress-free way.

  • **Show.** Theory gets students only so far, of course, and so we follow up each brief theoretical discussion with a clear demonstration that writing isn't just a concept, it's also an artifact. Most chapters include a feature called *Let Us Show You*, in which we walk our model students, Mara and Casey, through specific, engaging scenarios that demonstrate the practical application of the concept.

  • **Talk.** We find that in-class small-group discussions help our students digest the material that they are learning, so most chapters include a feature called *Talk Amongst Yourselves . . .* which suggests exercises and topics meant for class discussion.

  • **Try.** In our experience, once students have read the theory, thought it through, seen the sample, and talked to each other, they're ready to give it a whirl for themselves. So each chapter includes a feature called *Now You Try*, which presents the student with opportunities to engage in tasks relevant to sample assignments that highlight a craftsmanlike approach to the processes and products of writing.

▶ **Additional review and practice features for mastering essential skills.** We present *Reality Check!* boxes throughout the book that outline key skills concisely for easy reference. With *Practice!* exercises we offer short quizzes on key issues in mechanics and style that help students to internalize what they are learning.

▶ **Sample student and professional writing throughout.** Our two student characters, Mara and Casey, whom you met above, engage in everything from prewriting to final drafts, asking questions, finding solutions, and gaining confidence just the way our own real-life students do. In discussions and assignments throughout, we refer you (and your students) to seven full professional readings at the back of the book. We also have excerpts from eleven more professional texts that act as models of good rhetorical strategies in action.

▶ **Grammar coverage, practical advice, tips, and encouragement.** Sprinkled throughout the discussion of concepts are encouraging hints — nuggets of focused, relevant advice — often delivered by one of us (as characters) or by Grammster, the Grammar Hamster. The book's final section, Part 7: Fine-Tuning the Text, is a mini-handbook where we teach students about the most common issues in grammar, usage, mechanics, and style that they are likely to encounter. We also include more basic grammar and punctuation material in Appendix A in a reference format.

▶ **A fun, approachable tone makes academic writing engaging and relevant to students.** We also appear as characters throughout, teaching material, discussing common issues, and commenting helpfully — we hope — on professional and student work, including the work of our student characters, Casey and Mara.

All of these elements — theory, examples, tips, characters, exercises, and assignments — have been created based on our years of working with actual student writers and responding to genuine student writing. We have learned from our own students — their successes and failures, their frustrations and triumphs. What you read here is *our* advice, based on *their* needs.

Options for teaching. We understand that instructors with various levels of teaching experience will be working with this book — and with various challenges in their classrooms.

▶ **Instructor's Manual.** In the Instructor's Manual (free with the instructor's edition of the book, and downloadable as a PDF from **macmillanhighered .com/everythingwriting/catalog**) we give ideas for how to use this book for different lengths of academic terms. We believe our approach — a principle-based chronological organization that exploits process to create product — is intuitive and flexible enough to suit any class whether it's a fifteen-week semester or a ten-week quarter.

The Instructor's Manual also contains chapter-by-chapter notes that give a broad overview of the aims of each chapter, followed by a description of each exercise and a discussion of how to use the exercise best with students. We point out where students tend to struggle and how you can help them, indicate when to prioritize teaching one skill over another, and give you answers to *Practice!* exercises from the book.

Get the Most Out of Your Course with *Everything You Need to Know About College Writing*

Bedford/St. Martin's offers resources and format choices that help you and your students get even more out of your book and course. To learn more or to order any of the following products, contact your Bedford/St. Martin's sales representative, e-mail sales support (**sales_support@bfwpub.com**), or visit the Web site at **macmillanhighered.com/everythingwriting/catalog**.

Choose from Alternative Formats of *Everything You Need to Know About College Writing*. Bedford/St. Martin's offers an e-Book format of this text, allowing students to choose the one that works best for them. For details, visit **macmillanhighered.com/everythingwriting/catalog**.

Select Value Packages. Add value by packaging one of the following resources with *Everything You Need to Know About College Writing*. To learn more about package options for any of the following products, contact your Bedford/St. Martin's sales representative or visit **macmillanhighered.com/everythingwriting /catalog**.

▶ **LaunchPad Solo for Readers and Writers.** Allows students to work on whatever they need help with the most. At home or in class, students learn at their own pace, with instruction tailored to each student's unique needs. *LaunchPad Solo for Readers and Writers* features:

▶ **Pre-built units that support a learning arc.** Each easy-to-assign unit is comprised of a pre-test check, multimedia instruction and assessment, and a post-test that assesses what students have learned about critical reading, writing process, using sources, grammar, style, mechanics, and help for multilingual writers.

▶ **A video introduction to many topics.** Introductions offer an overview of the unit's topic, and many include a brief, accessible video to illustrate the concepts at hand.

▶ **Adaptive quizzing for targeted learning.** Most units include LearningCurve, game-like adaptive quizzing that focuses on the areas in which each student needs the most help.

▶ **The ability to monitor student progress.** Use our gradebook to see which students are on track and which need additional help with specific topics.

LaunchPad Solo for Readers and Writers can be **packaged at a significant discount**. Please contact your Macmillan sales representative for a package ISBN to ensure your students can take full advantage. Visit **macmillanhighered .com/catalog/readwrite** for more information.

Writer's Help 2.0 is a powerful online writing resource that helps students find answers whether they are searching for writing advice on their own or as part of an assignment.

▶ **Smart search.** Built on research with more than 1,600 student writers, the smart search in *Writer's Help* provides reliable results even when students use novice terms, such as *flow* and *unstuck*.

▶ **Trusted content from our best-selling handbooks.** Choose *Writer's Help 2.0 for Hacker Handbooks* or *Writer's Help 2.0 for Lunsford Handbooks* and ensure that students have clear advice and examples for all of their writing questions.

▶ **Adaptive exercises that engage students.** *Writer's Help* includes *LearningCurve*, game-like online quizzing that adapts to what students already know and helps them focus on what they need to learn.

Student access is packaged with *Everything You Need to Know About College Writing* at a significant discount. Please contact your Macmillan sales representative for a package ISBN to ensure your students have easy access to online writing support. Students who rent a book or buy a used book can purchase access to *Writer's Help 2.0* at **macmillanhighered.com/writershelp2**.

Instructors may request free access by registering as an instructor at **macmillanhighered.com/writershelp2**.
Visit **macmillanhighered.com/getsupport** for technical support.

Portfolio Keeping, **Third Edition, by Nedra Reynolds and Elizabeth Davis**, provides all the information students need to use the portfolio method successfully in a writing course. *Portfolio Teaching*, a companion guide for instructors, provides the practical information instructors and writing program administrators need to use the portfolio method successfully in a writing course. To order *Portfolio Keeping* packaged with this text, contact your sale representative for a package ISBN.

Make learning fun with *Re:Writing 3*
bedfordstmartins.com/rewriting
Bedford's free and open online resource includes videos and interactive elements to engage students in new ways of writing. You'll find tutorials about using common digital writing tools, an interactive peer review game, Extreme Paragraph Makeover, and more. Visit **bedfordstmartins.com/rewriting**.

Instructor resources
macmillanhighered.com/everythingwriting/catalog
You have a lot to do in your course. Bedford/St. Martin's wants to make it easy for you to find the support you need — and to get it quickly.

▶ **Teaching Central** offers the entire list of Bedford/St. Martin's print and online professional resources in one place. You'll find landmark reference works, sourcebooks on pedagogical issues, award-winning collections, and practical advice for the classroom — all free for instructors. Visit **macmillanhighered.com/teachingcentral**.

▶ **Bedford Bits** collects creative ideas for teaching a range of composition topics in a frequently updated blog. A community of teachers — leading scholars, authors, and editors such as Andrea Lunsford, Elizabeth Losh, Jack Solomon, and Elizabeth Wardle — discuss assignments, activities, revision, research, grammar and style, multimodal composition, technology, peer review, and much more. Take, use, adapt, and pass the ideas around. Then, come back to the site to comment or share your own suggestions. Visit **bedfordbits.com**.

Acknowledgments

We hope that you — and your students — will have as much fun reading this book as we've had writing it. But we would be remiss if we didn't acknowledge all of the people who have helped us along the way, beginning with several of our colleagues on the faculty at Grays Harbor College, where we both teach, who gave us excellent advice: Darby Cavin, Brad Duffy, Diane Muir, James Neiworth, Bob Richardson and Adrienne Roush.

Throughout the process of writing and revising (and revising and revising), we have consistently had the support of our college, particularly our awesome vice president for instruction, Laurie Clary, and the Grays Harbor College board of trustees. Our colleague Jeff Koskela, who introduced us to the incomparable "Mick Bourbaki," has earned our undying admiration and gratitude.

People we haven't had the pleasure of meeting in person also helped us immeasurably to refine our material and our approach. Reviewers on campuses across the country who offered their insights include: A. Mara Beckett, Glendale Community College and Los Angeles City College; Mark Blaauw-Hara, North Central Michigan College; Elizabeth Brewer, Central Connecticut State University; Louise Brown, Salt Lake Community College; Maury Elizabeth Brown, Germanna Community College; Kristin Brunnemer, Pierce College; Carolyn Calhoon-Dillahunt, Yakima Valley Community College; Ron Christiansen, Salt Lake Community College; Beth Dobry, Redlands Community College; Jason Dockter, Lincoln Land Community College; Holly French-Hart, Bossier Parish Community College; Elizabeth Genovise, Roane State Community College; Michael Johnson, Muskegon Community College; Melinda G. Kramer, Prince George's Community College; Walter Lowe, Green River Community College; and Ann Smith, Modesto Junior College.

We owe a special thanks to the entire team at Bedford/St. Martin's, starting with Publisher for Composition, Business and Technical Writing Leasa Burton, who shepherded this book through several incarnations over four years. We have also worked closely for nearly as long with the apparently inexhaustible Senior Developmental Editor Joelle Hann, who always had *just one more* good idea for us. We're grateful also for the excellent judgment of Molly Parke (Executive Editor) and Maura Shea (Executive Developmental Manager for English); the patient and precise work of Kendra LeFleur (Production Editor); the diligence and creativity of Anna Palchik (Senior Art Director); book designer Marsha Cohen and illustrator Blue Delliquanti; and the invaluable support of editorial assistants Rachel Childs and Evelyn Dunham.

Although she is no longer with Bedford/St. Martin's, we'd like to thank Sophia Snyder, whose voice on those initial East-Coast-to-West-Coast conference calls put us at ease and made us look forward to the next call. And we'd like to offer a special shout-out to our former Bedford/St. Martin's sales rep, Kristina Yesley, who "discovered" us and our book, eventually introducing us to Leasa Burton and the rest of the exceptional Bedford team.

Thanks aren't enough for Jacek Lerych and Jared Criswell, whose patience, humor, and brilliance provided us excellent space and time to write — and for Bysshe Lerych and Oliver Criswell, whose existence gives us joy.

Finally, our most heartfelt thanks to all of the students we've worked with over the years. *Much* of what we've written we learned from you.

Lynne Drury Lerych
Allison DeBoer Criswell

Aberdeen, Washington
Spring 2015

WPA CORRELATION GRID

macmillanhighered.com/wpa

Everything
you need
to know about
College
Writing

Lynne Drury Lerych
Allison DeBoer Criswell

Everything You Need to Know About College Writing (print)

macmillanhighered.com/everythingwriting/catalog

Everything You Need to Know About College Writing (PDF e-Book)

macmillanhighered.com/everythingwriting/catalog

by Lynne Drury Lerych and Allison DeBoer Criswell

AVAILABLE FORMATS:

Everything You Need to Know About College Writing (print and PDF e-book)
Each version comes with integrated media — **LaunchPad Solo for *Everything You Need to Know About College Writing*** — that includes 10 multimodal guided readings (e.g. films, presentation, a digital map) and 27 dynamic thematic readings (on identity, the body, the environment, and heroes and villains), plus tools for working with these contents.

Note: You don't need to be an experienced writing instructor to teach with this book. Our **instructor's manual** (available as a PDF) offers sample syllabi, lesson plans, answers to practice activities, and — perhaps most important — chapter-by-chapter notes to help you plan and teach your class.

If you are an experienced instructor, the instructor's manual has handy ideas for how to use the lessons and exercises with your students.

How *Everything You Need to Know About College Writing* Supports WPA Outcomes for First-Year Composition

WPA Desired Outcomes	Bedford/St. Martin's Relevant Features of *Everything You Need to Know About College Writing*
Rhetorical Knowledge	
Learn and use key rhetorical concepts through analyzing and composing a variety of texts.	• *Everything You Need to Know About College Writing* helps students identify the appropriate audience, purpose, and mode they are reading and composing at both the paragraph level in **Part 3: Drafting** and at the essay level in **Part 4: Revising and Editing.**

Note: This chart aligns with the latest WPA Outcomes Statement, ratified in July 17, 2014.

- A sequenced approach to instruction gives students lots of models and hands-on support for drafting, composing, revising, and giving feedback. This approach begins with a model (***Let Us Show You***) and is followed by peer discussion (***Talk Amongst Yourselves . . .***), before students receive an assignment for practice (***Now You Try***). Whether students are learning to analyze or compose texts, they go through the same sequential, step-by-step process to increase their understanding and facility.

- Reflective notes from student characters Casey and Mara identify rhetorical moves in student essays and paragraphs throughout **Parts 1–5** and model student feedback.

- Authors model the **communication triangle** (beginning in Ch. 2) to show how meaning is made among the writer, the audience, and the text and return to this model when other issues of audience come up, such as in Ch. 3 on the reading/writing relationship; Ch. 7: From Topic to Written Product; Ch. 10: Analytical Paragraphs; Ch. 11: Modes of Rhetoric; Ch. 16: Making an Argument, Ch. 17: Supporting an Argument; Ch. 19 Engaging the Reader.

- In **Part 3: Drafting, Ch. 11** contains excerpts from professional writers such as Malcolm Gladwell, Stephen King, and Ta-Nehisi Coates to demonstrate rhetorical moves involved in narration, description, definition, examples and illustration, comparison, contrast, causal analysis, effect analysis, process analysis, classification, and division.

- The **mini-reader in Appendix C: Readings for Writers** contains several full-length professional readings that exemplify the modes at the paragraph and essay level from authors such as Brent Staples, Jessica Pishko, and Neil deGrasse Tyson. Students are assigned to read and analyze these essays **throughout Parts 1–5**.

Gain experience reading and composing in several genres to understand how genre conventions shape and are shaped by readers' and writers' practices and purposes.	- As noted above, **Parts 1–5** contain student and instructor examples of genre conventions as well as examples of how readers' and writers' intentions shape texts with the most specific being Ch. 11: Modes of Rhetoric. - **Reflective annotations** from student characters Casey and Mara identify where student essays contain paragraphs in the various modes and give feedback on the effective use of those modes. - At the same time, instructor characters Allison and Lynne are teaching students about the effect of conventions especially in **Ch. 2: The Writing Situation; Ch. 3: Reading and Writing; Ch. 9: Successful Paragraphs; Ch. 11: Modes of Rhetoric; Ch. 19: Engaging the Reader.**

(continued)

	• **Exercises throughout** model context, audience, intention and modes and then offer assignments for students to practice these key skills.
Develop facility in responding to a variety of situations and contexts, calling for purposeful shifts in voice, tone, level of formality, design, medium, and/or structure.	• **Ch. 2: The Writing Situation** specifically discusses the importance of context in creating texts, showing that different **rhetorical situations** will require different responses.
	• From the outset (Ch. 2) the authors model the **communication triangle**, a model that asks students to think about how meaning is made among the writer, the audience, and the text. The authors return — and send students back to — the communication triangle throughout the book, especially when other issues of audience come up, such as in Ch. 3 on the reading/writing relationship, Ch. 7: From Topic to Written Product; Ch. 10: Analytical Paragraphs; Ch. 11: Modes of Rhetoric; Ch. 16: Making an Argument, Ch. 17: Supporting an Argument; Ch. 19 Engaging the Reader.
	• **Ch. 24: Grammar and Usage** specifically addresses errors in voice, mood, and form.
	• **The text follows the student character Casey** as he develops a full draft of an essay on plagiarism (full draft given in Ch. 8). He then revises for voice, form, and audience in Ch. 12 (peer review), Ch. 13 (content-level revision), Ch. 14 (structural revision), Ch. 15 (revising for coherence and tone).
	• **We also follow student character Mara** as she drafts and revises her research essay. She specifically revises to keep the reader's needs in mind (Ch. 19: Engaging the Reader) as well as to choose the sources that best support her thesis and present a coherent argument before presenting her final draft in Ch. 22: Research and *Ethos*.
Understand and use a variety of technologies to address a range of audiences.	• This book assumes that students are working across platforms — with print texts, e-mail, text messages, and also possibly with classroom management systems. It incorporates references seamlessly into the instruction throughout.
	• Certain chapters and exercises send students online (to Google, Google Scholar, Dictionary.com, for example) and to read specific essays or watch videos that explain concepts in more detail; the book warns students (more than once — but specifically in a ***Reality Check!* box in Ch. 3**) about the dangers of researching online and explains how to evaluate information and sources students find through online research.

- It alerts students to the differences between voice in different platforms, specifically in **Ch. 23: Writing with Style**, which addresses, among other things, the issue of when and how to use Standard English, what tone and words to use when writing to an instructor in an e-mail versus to a friend in a text message, and so on.

- In **Ch. 10: Analytical Paragraphs**, the authors analyze a cartoon by Roz Chast as they analyze an effective claim, sending the message that even **visuals can be viable texts**.

Match the capacities of different environments (e.g., print and electronic) to varying rhetorical situations.	• Attention to rhetorical situations is a principle that underlies this book and is introduced right at the beginning in **Part 1**. Rhetorical situation and the communications triangle emphasize that every audience has specific needs, and these include how content is delivered to the audience (in what medium), in what voice, and in what format.
	• See **Ch. 2: The Writing Situation** for specific introduction to "rhetorical situation" and the "communications triangle." Students are reminded of these core concepts throughout the book.
	• Later chapters in the book lead students through making appropriate choices to suit their purposes, audiences, and use of rhetorical appeals (*ethos, pathos, logos*). See **Ch. 16: Making an Argument** (*logos*), **Ch. 18: Faulty Reasoning** (fallacies), **Ch. 19: Engaging the Reader** (*pathos*).

Critical Thinking, Reading, and Composing

Use composing and reading for inquiry, learning, thinking, and communicating in various rhetorical contexts.	• The purpose of this book is **to help students read, analyze, and compose in any mode, genre, or classroom setting and in any context**. The authors provide a framework that students can use when reading and analyzing the works of others and in composing their own texts.
	• **Ch. 2: The Writing Situation** introduces the idea of a writer's purpose, the context he or she is writing in, and the audience. These fundamental concepts underpin the thinking and communicating skills that students learn to employ in *Everything You Need to Know About College Writing*, no matter what the rhetorical context. **Ch. 3: Reading and Writing** discusses explicitly how learning to read well reinforces the skills of composing and vice versa. And **Ch. 10: Analytical Paragraphs** shows how claims, context, evidence, analysis, and synthesis work together to create successful academic exercises.
	• **Annotated student drafts** throughout the book as well as **conversations between student characters,** and between student and instructor characters, model critical thinking and writing for students reading the book.

(continued)

Read a diverse range of texts, attending especially to relationships between assertion and evidence, to patterns of organization, to interplay between verbal and nonverbal elements, and to how these features function for different audiences and situations.	• **Ch. 9: Successful Paragraphs** introduces the idea of a relationship between texts' organizations and their assertions. This is further developed in **Ch. 10: Analytical Paragraphs** and **Ch. 14: Structural Revision**, in which students address their bias (if they have one) toward five-paragraph essays and consider instead the relationship between the organizational options open to them and the idea they wish to convey. • An explicit connection between evidence, claims and purpose in different rhetorical situations is made in **Ch. 16: Making an Argument; Ch. 17: Supporting an Argument**; and **Ch. 20: Research and Sources**. All of these chapters go into detail on how evidence relates to different audiences, rhetorical situations, arguments being created, and sources being used as support, if any. • See the **mini-reader in Appendix C** as well as **Readings by Rhetorical Purpose** (beginning on p. xlv) for a list of diverse authors and subjects addressed by the text in this book. See also **Ch. 11: Modes of Rhetoric** for coverage of the patterns of organization.
Locate and evaluate primary and secondary research materials, including journal articles, essays, books, databases, and informal Internet sources.	• Students get a preview of working with sources in Ch. 3 where they are instructed to do light research as they hone in on an idea to write about. A key *Reality Check!* box on Web domains and reliability helps orient students early in the book to the idea of locating various primary and secondary sources, and evaluating which ones are worth further reading. • **Part 6: Researching Effectively** is dedicated to locating and evaluating primary and secondary research materials and contains three chapters that elucidate these important skills. • **Ch. 20: Research and Sources** defines what primary and secondary sources are and shows how to formulate a strong research question, find reliable sources, and narrow research results. **Ch. 21: Choosing and Using Sources** gives deeper coverage on evaluating sources; understanding them; and paraphrasing, analyzing, and summarizing them. This includes taking good notes, integrating them into an essay, and quoting effectively. **Ch. 22: Research and *Ethos*** covers avoiding plagiarism, avoiding using sources in misleading ways, and citing sources correctly.
Use strategies — such as interpretation, synthesis, response, critique, and design/redesign — to compose texts that integrate the writer's ideas with those from appropriate sources.	• In **Part 6: Researching Effectively**, the author characters Lynne and Allison work with the student characters, Casey and Mara, to formulate an **effective research question**, **find sources** to support the question, **narrow and choose the best sources for the essay** — including watching for bias in sources and finding the most relevant sources — **take notes, analyze the sources**, and **integrate the sources** into a college-level essay. • We see students Casey and Mara analyzing their sources, deciding how to use them, annotating their list of sources,

and using them in their writing. This modeling effectively gives students visual instruction on working with sources to complement the book's textual instruction.

- The three chapters that compose this section of the book also cover essential skills such as paraphrasing sources, summarizing source material, quoting effectively, making an annotated bibliography, and keeping track of publication data for a future Works Cited or References list.

- **Appendix B: Writing and Citing Across the Curriculum** guides students in integrating and citing sources in the MLA, APA, and Chicago formats. It offers sample Works Cited/References as well as some foundational principles for each citation style.

Processes

Develop a writing project through multiple drafts.	• In this book, **student characters Casey and Mara go through the stages of prewriting, drafting, and revising** for two essays, giving student readers a realistic sense of the steps of composing and self-editing college-level essays. Readers see the student characters thinking, questioning, and changing their writing in response to feedback. They also see the skills the characters are learning, in the form of initial ideas, brainstorming, initial drafts, annotated drafts of paragraphs and essays, and in illustrated conversations with the instructors and the Grammster character.
	• **Part 2: Prewriting** includes three key chapters to help students get initial ideas down on paper and make the leap from the inkling of an insight to a topic or thesis sentence: **Ch. 5: Prewriting; Ch. 6: From Brainstorm to Topic;** and **Ch. 7: From Topic to Written Product.**
	• **Part 3: Drafting** contains four full chapters to guide students through the process of drafting college-level paragraphs and essays. Specifically, **Ch. 8: Draft and Draft Again** gives students specific instruction in revision and how to overcome writer's block when students don't know where to begin or how to troubleshoot their revising, and **Ch. 9: Successful Paragraphs** leads students through drafting and revising topic sentences, body paragraphs, and conclusions.
	• **Part 4: Revising and Editing** is dedicated to the process of revision. **Ch. 12: Levels of Revision** introduces students to the idea that they will want to revise for content, structure, coherence, and precision. It also prepares students to revise with feedback from peers as well as instructors. Chs. 13, 14, and 15 lead students through these steps in revision.
	• **Part 7: Fine-Tuning the Text** is dedicated to helping students learn the essentials of grammar and mechanics — a well as Standard English and college-level language use — that will

(continued)

	allow them to effectively proofread their own work. This part includes **Ch. 23: Writing with Style**; **Ch. 24: Grammar and Usage**; **Ch. 25: Solving Sentence Structure Problems**; and **Ch. 26: Solving Problems with Punctuation**. These chapters cover the errors most students will encounter in their papers. For more coverage, students can refer to **Appendix A: Basic Grammar and Punctuation Reference**.
Develop flexible strategies for reading, drafting, reviewing, collaborating, revising, rewriting, rereading, and editing.	• Instruction in **Part 2: Prewriting**, **Part 3: Drafting**, and **Part 4: Revising and Editing** emphasizes understanding unique rhetorical situations and the relationships in each individual text's communication triangle. This foundation prepares students to think flexibly about what they are reading as well as what they are writing and revising.
	• In addition, the instruction takes a growth mind-set approach to learning, allowing students to see a skill modeled (*Let Us Show You*), then discuss it (*Talk Amongst Yourselves . . .*) before they try it out (*Now You Try*). In later chapters, students return to earlier exercises to revise and expand them — and to learn from previous mistakes. This gives them the opportunity to see that their learning is not a fixed thing but something that is continually growing.
	• **Ch. 3: Reading and Writing** discusses how the processes of reading and writing are intricately related, while the premise of **Ch. 4: How to Read?** is that texts need to be read several times, at different levels, to be truly understood and engaged, in much the same way that texts must be revised in order to truly develop and support their ideas.
	• As a part of getting feedback during the revising process, students are encouraged to do **peer reviews of their work** (Ch. 12); they are also encouraged to collaborate with each other with **collaborative activities** called *Talk Amongst Yourselves . . .* that appear in each chapter. These activities ask students to work together either to understand a text, to review a student draft (from a character in the book or from a peer in their class), or to come up with their own understanding of a rhetorical situation.
	• Editing and revising are addressed on several levels from content and structural revisions to the fine details of grammar and mechanics. These are covered in detail in **Part 4: Revising and Editing**.
Use composing processes and tools as a means to discover and reconsider ideas.	• **Ch. 3: Reading and Writing** introduces the idea of using "light research" to discover and test ideas, being careful to draw from reliable sources. It shows Casey and Mara in conversation about what acceptable searches accomplish and how to carry them out.

- **Part 2: Prewriting** focuses on the preliminary processes involved in discovering one's own ideas, from prewriting (Ch. 5) and brainstorming (Ch. 6), to understanding a controlling idea (Ch. 7) and narrowing down the options to get to a workable topic sentence or thesis statement. *Reality Check!* boxes such as "Topic Orientation," "Focused Freewriting," "Stay on Track with Your Topic," and "The Working Thesis" help students find their way through the discovery process toward a working idea.

- **Drafting and revision** are central teachings of this text and are covered extensively in **Part 4: Revising and Editing** and **Part 5: Writing Effective Arguments**. Over eight chapters, we follow Casey and Mara as they learn to identify and narrow down their ideas for college paragraphs and essays, begin the composition process, and then return to their ideas in the revising stages to make sure they are working effectively.

- **Part 6: Researching Effectively** contains three chapters that help students form good research questions (Ch. 20) and evaluate and choose sources as well as learn to paraphrase and summarize them, thereby discovering how well sources serve their main ideas and support points (Ch. 21). This section also asks students to be honest with themselves and their readers about how they represent their sources (Ch. 22), a lesson that will require some students to re-evaluate their main ideas.

Experience the collaborative and social aspects of writing processes.

- The idea of **collaboration informs the entire approach of this book.** Throughout, visuals show Casey and Mara collaborating on coming up with ideas for paragraphs and essays, refining drafts and research, commenting on exercises, and reminding each other of good writing techniques. **The instructor characters, Lynne and Allison,** also appear as guides for the students' collaboration process, and the Grammster appears regularly to help shape student work.

- **Collaborative activities,** called *Talk Amongst Yourselves . . .* appear in almost every chapter, sometimes more than once. These activities ask students to work together to reflect either on a process just given, or on one of the student characters modeling that process or skill (given in the preceding *Let Us Show You* section). These activities reinforce the idea that students can benefit from bouncing ideas off their peers, and sets them up well for activities like peer reviewing.

- **Ch. 12: Levels of Revision** contains a section that explains peer review, what to expect, what to comment on (big things vs. small things), and how it's different from feedback from instructors. This section shows Casey getting feedback from Mara on a draft of his essay on plagiarism.

(continued)

Learn to give and act on productive feedback to works in progress.	• As discussed above, visuals throughout show Casey and Mara coming up with ideas together, refining drafts and research in discussion, commenting on each other's exercises, and reminding each other of good writing techniques.
	• **Peer review** is specifically addressed in **Ch. 12: Levels of Revision**, in a section that explains what to expect, what to comment on (big things vs. small things), and how peer review is different from feedback from instructors.
Adapt composing processes for a variety of technologies and modalities.	• The approach of this book prepares students to compose any kind of text. From **Ch. 2: The Writing Situation**, the authors emphasize applying a basic framework: (1) Look at the rhetorical situation first. (What do you want to say? Who is your audience? etc.) (2) Identify the players in the communication triangle of any rhetorical situation (reader, writer, text — or, speaker, message, audience) and (3) Think critically and creatively about which genre(s) (and modalities) would work best in that situation. This framework can be applied regardless of a student's access to electronic technology.
Reflect on the development of composing practices and how those practices influence writers' work.	• **Activities** called *Now You Try* appear in every chapter, sometimes more than once, and encourage students to both apply the skills they are learning — and that they see modeled in the preceding Let Us Show You sections — as well as to reflect on their composing processes. How successful were their composing processes and what might they change in their next attempts?
	• **Peer review exercises** in the form of *Talk Amongst Yourselves . . .* **activities** allow students to work together to reinforce each other's composing practices — and to point out what they might do better next time. Students can take inspiration from the way that student characters Casey and Mara do this work throughout the book in the visuals.

Knowledge of Conventions

Develop knowledge of linguistic structures, including grammar, punctuation, and spelling, through practice in composing and revising.	• **Part 7: Fine-Tuning the Text** is dedicated to helping students learn the essentials of grammar and mechanics — as well as Standard English and college-level language use — that will allow them to effectively proofread their own work.
	• This part includes **Ch. 23: Writing with Style; Ch. 24: Grammar and Usage; Ch. 25: Solving Sentence Structure Problems; and Ch. 26: Solving Problems with Punctuation.** These chapters cover the errors most students will encounter in their papers. For more coverage — especially for developmental students who might need more guidance with the basics, students can refer to **Appendix A: Basic Grammar and Punctuation Reference.**

Understand why genre conventions for structure, paragraphing, tone, and mechanics vary.	• In **Part 3: Drafting, Ch. 11** contains excerpts from professional writers such as Malcolm Gladwell, Stephen King, and Ta-Nehisi Coates to demonstrate that writers use different structures, tones, paragraph sequences and mechanics depending on their rhetorical situation. These important examples are offered with a lot of context — and after students already have a good idea of what an effective draft of a college-level paragraph or essay requires. • The mini-reader in **Appendix C: Readings for Writers** contains several full-length professional readings that exemplify the modes at the paragraph and essay level from authors such as Brent Staples, Jessica Pishko and Neil deGrasse Tyson. Students are assigned to read and analyze these essays **in Parts 1–5.** • A helpful list following the table of contents helps readers to locate readings of different genres in the book, including readings that contain different modes of rhetoric. • Student characters **Casey and Mara give feedback on professional essays** as they read and reread them, identifying rhetorical moves and speculating on what the author had in mind in using particular modes, mechanics, tones, and paragraph sequences. They also give this kind of feedback to each other when they do peer reviews of their own work **throughout Parts 1–5.**
Gain experience negotiating variations in genre conventions.	• See above. • In **Part 2: Prewriting, Part 3: Drafting** and **Part 4: Revising and Editing**, students get lots of practice navigating idea creation, creating paragraph structure, appropriate tone, and a relationship with their readers, as well as an overall set of rhetorical conditions to best express their ideas. • **In sequenced activities** (*Let Us Show You, Talk Amongst Yourselves. . . , Now You Try*) student readers are led through the processes of understanding rhetorical moves in their own work and applying the skills they see modeled. • Students refine their first attempts and initial drafts with the help of **peer review** and by following the growth mind-set approach modeled by the book's student characters, Casey and Mara, who rather than being set back when they make mistakes or don't understand a concept the first time around, instead use discussion and peer feedback as a learning opportunity before trying again, perhaps a different way.
Learn common formats and/or design features for different kinds of texts.	• **Appendix B: Writing and Citing Across the Curriculum** guides students to understand the different requirements of courses in the arts and humanities, the social sciences, and the natural sciences, including the nature of essays and written reports for each.

(continued)

Explore the concepts of intellectual property (such as fair use and copyright) that motivate documentation conventions.	• In **Part 6: Researching Effectively**, the author characters Lynne and Allison help student characters Casey and Mara understand how to **take notes, analyze,** and **integrate** sources into their college-level essays — Casey's on what constitutes plagiarism and Mara's on academic doping. This section of the book also covers important skills such as paraphrasing sources, summarizing source material, quoting effectively, and making an annotated bibliography, keeping track of publication data for a future Works Cited or References list in the service of respecting intellectual copyright and to promote ethical use of sources.
	• **Appendix B: Writing and Citing Across the Curriculum** guides students in integrating and citing sources in the MLA, APA, and Chicago formats. It offers brief sample Works Cited/References as well as foundational principles for each citation style and examples based on giving credit to others' works and ideas.
Practice applying citation conventions systematically in students' own work.	• See above.
	• **Part 6: Researching Effectively** contains three chapters dedicated to finding, using, and citing sources effectively and ethically. Specifically:
	▪ **Ch. 21: Choosing and Using Sources** covers the essentials of integrating sources into essays, including summarizing, paraphrasing, quoting, and keeping track of sources so that they can be accurately cited later in the drafting and revising process.
	▪ **Ch. 22: Research and *Ethos*** contains discussion and exercises about avoiding plagiarism, including patchwork plagiarism and other unintentional forms of unethical source use. Also covered are how to cite sources so that writers are being clear about where their information is coming from.
	• **Appendix B: Writing and Citing Across the Curriculum** guides students in integrating and citing sources in the MLA, APA, and Chicago formats. It offers brief sample Works Cited/References as well as foundational principles for each citation style and examples.

Contents

PART I   Reading and Writing Basics   1

PART 6   Researching Effectively   303

20   Research and Sources: The Intellectual Treasure Hunt   305

Readings by Rhetorical Purpose

General Rhetorical Purpose (Full Essays Only)

Specific Rhetorical Mode (Essays and Excerpts)

Lynne Drury Lerych teaches English and film at Grays Harbor College, where she is chair of the humanities and communications division, and teaches everything from developmental writing to film interpretation to playwriting. She earned both her B.A. and her M.F.A. from Western Michigan University. The only thing she enjoys as much as watching her students learn is watching her original plays brought to life on the stage. Most recently, her first musical, *Back in the World*, about soldiers returning from war in Iraq and Afghanistan, had its world premiere at the Bishop Center for Performing Arts in Aberdeen, Washington.

Allison DeBoer Criswell teaches composition, American literature, women's literature, and philosophy at Grays Harbor College. She earned her B.A. from Western Washington University and her M.A. from The University of British Columbia. In 2010, students at GHC awarded her Faculty of the Year. She lives in Aberdeen, Washington, with her husband and son.

PART I

Reading and Writing Basics

Chapter I

The Writing Process: It's a Journey *and* a Destination

> If all difficulties were known at the outset of a long journey, most of us would never start out at all.
> — Dan Rather

Contrary to popular belief (or plain old wishful thinking), good writing doesn't just happen. Good writers aren't magical; they aren't imbued by the universe with a special literary Spidey-sense. They do, however, share a few characteristics, one of which is courage.

Courage? you may ask.

Well, yes. It takes courage to shape the ideas floating around in your head. It may feel like a risk to even begin the process of organizing your thoughts — somehow, the very act of arranging the elements of your knowledge about a topic is a commitment to follow through. It's a contract you make with yourself in which you agree to be the Writer, which means it's your responsibility to create a Text. What sort of text? As a college student you'll write paragraphs, journal entries, responses, reports, and even memos. But most often the text that you create is going to be the benchmark of college writing: the essay.

Did You Know That *Essay* Means "To Try"?

Before we go any further, we'd like to say a little something about the word *essay*. Most English speakers recognize this word as the label for a piece of writing that has a purpose; it's a word that is used interchangeably with the word *paper* when college students are talking about the written work they need to do in the course of their academic careers. But what you may not realize is that the word *essay* comes from the French verb *essayer*, which means "to try" or "to attempt."

As you're gathering up your courage before diving into the creation of a text, keep in mind that an essay isn't carved in stone. It's not the final statement made on a topic or the sum total of a writer's worth. It's an attempt. When you sit down to write an essay for a college class, just remember that what you're really doing is deciding to *take a shot at it*. You can handle that, right?

3

Fun fact! Other acceptable translations of *essayer* include "to have a go," and my personal favorite, "to give it a whirl."

SET YOUR MIND ON "GROW"

What we're talking about here is an attitude — a *mind-set*, really — that says, "New knowledge? Improved skills? Sure, I can do that!" Here's the key: instead of thinking of your brain as something that has finite intelligence, think of it as something that's always growing.

Why is adopting this perspective important? Recent research has shown that students who worry about how smart they are tend to believe that they have a limited amount of intelligence. If they think they weren't born with enough smarts, then they have little hope that they'll master difficult subjects — or improve what they already know.

On the other hand, students who recognize that learning requires time and effort — and sometimes failure, at least at first — are more likely to persevere through challenges to their learning until their skills and understanding improve.

Learning and growth never stop. What makes this possible? Just being dedicated and persistent. You can do that, right?

In other words, if you *think* you can do it — and if you behave accordingly — then you *can* do it!

Thinking flexibly about your intelligence not only will help you succeed in your writing classes but also will help you stay engaged with any college subject that challenges you. You'll find ways to understand instead of giving up.

Speaking of dedication and persistence, research psychologist Carol Dweck has studied student motivation for more than thirty-five years. What has she learned? Quite a lot, as it turns out:

- ▶ Successful students aren't afraid to fail — instead, they understand that the only way to learn is through making mistakes.
- ▶ Successful students understand that ability is increased through effort, and that they're not simply "stuck" with the smarts they started out with.
- ▶ Successful students recover from setbacks, increasing their efforts after a failure instead of giving up.

Take a look at a couple of examples Dweck presents in her article "The Perils and Promises of Praise":

> Let's get inside the head of a student with a fixed mind-set as he sits in his class-room, confronted with algebra for the first time. Up until then, he has breezed through math. Even when he barely paid attention in class and skimped on his homework, he always got As. But this is different. It's hard. The student feels anxious and thinks, "What if I'm not as good at math as I thought? What if other kids understand it and I don't?" At some level, he realizes that he has two choices: try hard, or turn off. His interest in math begins to wane, and his attention wanders. He tells himself, "Who cares about this stuff? It's for nerds. I could do it if I wanted to, but it's so boring. You don't see CEOs and sports stars solving for x and y." . . .
>
> Let's look at another student — one who has a growth mind-set — having her first encounter with algebra. She finds it new, hard, and confusing, unlike anything else she has ever learned. But she's determined to understand it. She listens to everything the teacher says, asks the teacher questions after class, and takes her textbook home and reads the chapter over twice. As she begins to get it, she feels exhilarated. A new world of math opens up for her.

Sure, Dweck's examples are about students in a math class, but it's really no different in a writing class or a foreign language class or a psychology class: going into the challenge of a college class with an attitude that says, "Yeah, it's hard, but I'm up for the task!" is the difference between miserable frustration and hard-won success.

▶ **Talk Amongst Yourselves . . .**

In a small group of classmates, discuss your ideas about your intelligence. Is your intelligence limited or unlimited? What is required for you to master difficult subjects? Do you think you can keep learning throughout your life? Why or why not? Imagine how a challenging subject might become easier if you were to adopt a flexible approach to thinking about it. What would you gain? What would you lose? How might you change your perspective on what kind of learner you are?

Writing Is a Process — But One Size Does Not Fit All

So now you know that successful student writers tend to be both courageous and flexible. In addition to having these attributes, good writers tend to accept that writing, like all meaningful endeavors, is a process — that is, it's a systematic activity that takes place over time. *Mm-hmm,* you're thinking. *What does that mean?*

Well, for one thing, it means there are steps involved in writing — it really *doesn't* just happen all at once, as if by magic or divine intervention. If you've ever procrastinated on a writing assignment, only to get it done at the very last moment, you may be tempted to believe that your writing doesn't have a process. However, you would be mistaken. Perhaps your process went something like this:

The Procrastinator's Process
1. Receive the assignment.
2. Ignore it for hours/days.
3. Realize it's due.
4. Panic.
5. Load up on caffeine.
6. Stare at the computer.
7. Think of many things unrelated to your assigned task.
8. Fall asleep.
9. Wake up and type something.
10. Drag yourself to class and turn it in.

> THE PROCRASTINATOR'S PROCESS
>
> **WARNING:**
>
> This is technically a writing process, but it is an exceptionally unhealthy writing process. Please do not try this at home.

> Hey, that "procrastinator's process" sounds familiar. . . . I wonder if that's bad.

Whether or not it seems like it, writing *is* a process. Throughout this book, we will work our way through the major steps in that process — and we'll provide you with a useful, reliable, *manageable* series of steps that we promise will be infinitely healthier and more productive than the procrastinator's process above.

And because writing is a process, it can be broken down into parts and analyzed (if you're so inclined), or at least separated into chunks that can then be sorted into what's easy, what's hard, what takes a lot of time, what can be accomplished fairly quickly, what you can do alone, and what you'll need help to accomplish.

Finally, it's important to note that writing is not simply a product. When you write, you should be aware that every stage of writing is at least as important as what ultimately emerges from the printer, whether it's a report, an essay, a poem, a book, or whatever.

VARIATIONS IN THE WRITING PROCESS

We must also point out that the fact that not all writers make use of exactly the same process.

For example, some writers begin writing as soon as they settle on an idea they'd like to explore; these writers are typically willing to sit for stretches of time, waiting for words to come with fingers poised above the keyboard or with pen hovering over paper. Other writers have to toss their ideas around, either in their own heads or in discussion with others, before they're ready to commit words to screen or paper.

Some writers like to put actual pencil (or pen) to actual paper and write everything in longhand, while others do everything at the keyboard. Some do their initial brainstorming and note taking by hand but then move to the computer when the time comes to start crafting complete sentences and paragraphs. When structuring their writing, some writers create formal outlines to use in organizing their thoughts prior to drafting; others jot down informal organizational notes on cocktail napkins and shopping receipts. Still others do all of their organizing in their heads — but we're not quite sure how that actually works. (Note: Keeping everything in your head is not recommended!)

Differences among writers account for some of the variations in the writing process — but those variations are also tied to differences among writing *tasks* (also known as assignments). And variations in assignments are often directly linked to the specific discipline (or subject matter) of each class. Writing assignments in literature classes are different from those in psychology, physics, economics, or business classes. These differences are discussed in detail in Appendix B at the end of this book.

Many College Classes Require Writing

Casey assumes that math and science classes never assign students to write. He'll find out soon enough whether that assumption is correct. In the meantime, though, what he needs to know — and what *you*, dear reader, need to know — is that writing for college is essentially always the same process, no matter which class you're writing for.

STAGES OF THE WRITING PROCESS

Regardless of the assignment or the class, there are certain stages in the writing process that you always need to engage in if you want to be successful. We've listed all of them below, in a handy feature we call a *Reality Check!* These *Reality Check!* boxes are sprinkled throughout the book, at every step of the writing process, just to make sure you're . . . you know . . . *checking in with reality* every now and then.

Reality Check! The Writing Process

Before you're finished writing any college paper, here's what you'll do:

▶ understand the task you've been given
▶ explore your own preconceived notions
▶ gather new information and ideas
▶ evaluate ideas both old and new
▶ focus on a main point
▶ organize your ideas into a draft that makes sense to you
▶ revise your draft so that it will make sense to your audience
▶ edit your draft for clarity and precision of expression
▶ prepare a final manuscript for public consumption

Like most meaningful processes that are broken down into their components, the writing process can be pretty daunting at the outset.

It helps to remember that each stage in the process is important and deserves your attention — don't rush through or skip any of them. You'll get there, we promise! And if you're nervous about the final stage of the process, just remember that, in academic writing, having your manuscript ready for public consumption simply means that your essay is ready to be submitted to your professor as a final draft, a draft you can take pride in because you've successfully navigated the entire writing process.

And hey! Come to think of it, those stages sound an awful lot like the categories of writing concerns around which the entire structure of this book is built—wow, what an amazing coincidence. Just to recap, here's what we think successful writers do throughout the writing process:

Reality Check! Using This Book

The Writer's Task	Where to Learn About It
▶ Figure out the context of the assignment	▶ Part 1: Reading and Writing Basics
▶ Engage in meaningful prewriting	▶ Part 2: Prewriting
▶ Prepare a first draft	▶ Part 3: Drafting
▶ Revise and edit the draft	▶ Part 4: Revising and Editing
▶ Build an argument for your reader	▶ Part 5: Writing Effective Arguments
▶ Make good use of research sources	▶ Part 6: Researching Effectively
▶ Proofread the final manuscript	▶ Part 7: Fine-Tuning the Text

Stages in the writing process will not always happen in the ways we've listed.

For example, when you're assigned to write a research paper, you'll almost certainly make use of Part 6 before diving into Part 3 or 4, right?

As you become a more competent and confident writer, you'll play around with the stages in your own writing process, emphasizing some elements and subordinating others, perhaps even shifting the order around. After all, who says that you can't delay focusing on your main point until after you've created your first draft, or that you can't gather new information prior to exploring your own ideas?

So as you're exploring this book, please keep in mind that we're presenting the process of writing as it makes sense to us. We happen to think it's the best process, of course, and if you are a beginning writer or an otherwise nervous or unhappy writer, you might want to take our advice literally and follow the steps like a paint-by-number kit until you get more comfortable with your own process.

If, however, you're an experienced, relaxed, and happy writer, congratulations! You might wish to pick and choose which parts of our process you'll use and then organize them as you see fit. In other words, feel free to add to, omit, or modify the stages in our process. We'll try not to be offended.

Chapter 2

The Writing Situation: Context Is Everything

Context is worth 80 IQ points.
—Alan Kay

Writing exists for a variety of purposes — to inform, to entertain, to please, to conduct business, to express emotion — but its primary function over the past four or five millennia has been to argue. That is, writing has been used to assert that something is true or that it is good or bad, or to urge our fellow humans to follow a particular course of action. This type of writing — whose purpose is meaningful discussion and consideration of ideas — is known as **rhetoric**. People often use the term *rhetoric* pejoratively, as in "Oh, that's just more rhetoric," implying that someone's words are empty or don't mean much. But in fact, *rhetoric* comes from the Greek *rhetor*, meaning "orator," "lecturer," or "teacher."

> *Rhetoric* simply means talking, teaching, or making a point through argument.

Most arguments are written out of a sense of need, a desire to explain to others how we interpret the world around us and to ask others to agree with us or join us in our causes. It is that sense of individual and shared need that creates the **rhetorical situation**, the environment in which the argument is made — also known as the **writing context**.

To gain true understanding of a text — and indeed, to create a text that can be understood — one must always consider its context. It's tempting to think of writing simply as a text, when in reality writing is a Text-Plus. *Plus what*, you ask? Well, plus the writer, for one thing. And the reader. And the context — the time, place, and situation in which the writer creates the text and the reader encounters the text.

> The word *context* comes from the Latin *con* ("together") and *texere* ("to weave"). It means "weaving together."

So the environment in which the writer, text, and reader exist — the writing context — is a weaving together of attitudes, needs, values, ideas, and events.

The Communication Triangle

The diagram to the right illustrates the key players involved in any piece of writing. It's called the **communication triangle**, and its meaning is essentially this: writer, reader, and text — the three components represented by the points of the triangle — are required players any time written communication occurs. If any of these components is missing, communication does not happen.

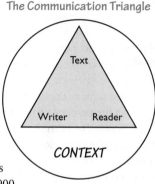

The Communication Triangle

The circle that surrounds the triangle — i.e., the context — is not a player in the same way that the writer, reader, and text are players. Rather, context is like the air we breathe. Because context is the time, place, and situation surrounding the communication, it's just there. For example, when L. Frank Baum published his novel *The Wonderful Wizard of Oz* in the year 1900, his intent was to provide a fantasy story for children. But by the time Victor Fleming made Baum's novel into the film *The Wizard of Oz* in 1939, Americans were in the depths of the Great Depression, and the story had come to be seen as a commentary on wealth and power as compared to poverty and powerlessness. In this way, the same story can take on a different meaning because its context — as well as its audience — has changed.

Note that the story's title changed, too — the word *wonderful* is missing from the name of the film. Why might that be?

The three points of the communication triangle — and the context that surrounds them — are not only necessary for communication to occur; they are also crucial to the creation of meaning. Words on a page have no meaning without a reader because meaning is something that exists only in the mind of the reader.

Here, try it yourself: The sentence "Art is a lie that reveals the truth," attributed to the artist Pablo Picasso, could mean many different things to many different people. In fact, it could even mean many different things to one person. How many ways can you think of to interpret that sentence? The more interpretations you can imagine, the more you'll start to realize that a text can certainly exist without a reader, but the *meaning* of that text is dependent on the reader.

In other words, written communication doesn't exist unless a reader exists. Writing is often an intensely personal thing — born of strong emotion and created in response to significant individual experiences — but it is ultimately a social phenomenon. It is a means of connection between humans. It is, to date, our most permanent method of communication. It's how we understand those who have come before us and how we leave word for those who will come after us.

Good writers are aware of the dynamic nature of communication, so they get into the practice of thinking not just about their topics, or about their own ideas about those topics, but also about their readers. The reader, after all, plays an important role in determining the meaning of the text that the writer has written.

What we mean is this: different readers may interpret a writer's statement in different ways. For example, if you heard someone say, "There's no time like the present," how would you interpret that?

Different Readers Read Texts Differently

See? The speaker and the message are the same each time, but a different audience (or reader) changes the meaning of the message.

▶ *Talk Amongst Yourselves . . .*

Now is a good time to get together with a partner or a group of classmates for a discussion of "There's no time like the present." How might this statement mean different things to different audiences in different situations? Can you think of other audiences whose interpretations would be different from the interpretations given above? See if you can come up with your own example of a sentence that could mean different things in different contexts.

▶ *Now You Try:* **The Communication Triangle**

Using the handy chart on page 16, mix and match the various speakers, messages, and audiences. Thinking carefully about what the speaker might be **implying** (hinting or suggesting) as well as what the audience might be **inferring** (deducing or assuming), try to imagine how each message might end up communicating different meanings. *Note:* This exercise might be even more fun in groups!

The Communication Triangle: Speaker, Message, Audience

Speaker	Message	Audience
you	Be careful — there's rough road ahead.	a bartender
a US senator	I regret nothing.	a newspaper reporter
the authors of this book	There is a time and a place for everything.	your mom
Spider-Man	A rose by any other name would smell as sweet.	a group of firefighters
a washed-up TV star from decades ago	The woods are lovely, dark, and deep, but I have promises to keep, and miles to go before I sleep.	a group of Olympic athletes

The Rhetorical Situation:
Who, What, When, Where, How, Why

The late-twentieth-century rhetorician Lloyd F. Bitzer found it useful to discuss context as the *rhetorical situation*. In other words, he looked at all the players involved in creating meaning. Crucial to this situation was the *exigence*. (Big word, eh? Don't worry; we'll walk you through this.) The exigence is the precise moment at which something special happens, or fails to happen, prompting the arguer to make an argument.

The term *exigence* comes from the Latin verb *exigere*, meaning "to demand." So an exigence is an event or a circumstance that demands an argument, compelling the arguer to make it.

Consider an example of an exigence: Imagine that a senator is holding a public meeting at which he advocates going to war. Attending the senator's speech is the parent of a soldier killed in action. It's not hard to imagine that the parent might feel compelled to speak out at the meeting.

In his best-known essay, rather unsurprisingly titled "The Rhetorical Situation," Bitzer describes the rhetorical situation as containing the following elements:

Elements of the Rhetorical Situation

EXIGENCE	What happens to compel the argument?
PEOPLE	Who is involved in the exigence? What are their roles?
RELATIONS	What are the connections or power relationships among the people involved?
LOCATION	Where does the discourse occur?
SPEAKER	Who is compelled to make an argument?
AUDIENCE	Whom does the speaker address? Why?
METHOD	How does the speaker address the audience?
INSTITUTIONS	What are "the rules" governing all of the above elements?

And here's how those elements might be identified and described in the hypothetical situation we introduced in the previous paragraph:

▶ The **exigence** is really twofold: both the senator's announcement and the threat of impending war compel the parent to speak.

▶ The **people** involved are many, but for our purposes, let's say they are the senator and the parent who is compelled to speak.

▶ The **relations** between these two people are interesting: they ostensibly have a public-servant-to-constituent relationship, but in many ways the public servant (the senator) is much more powerful than the constituent (the parent).

▶ The **location** is a public meeting, likely populated by the parent's fellow citizens as well as the senator's staff members and, perhaps, the media.

▶ We know that the **speaker** is the parent of a soldier killed in action, and we are probably safe in making some assumptions based on what we know (the parent likely feels grief, for example), but we are not safe in assuming much beyond that (we can't assume, for example, that the parent is opposed to war).

▶ The **audience** is certainly the senator as well as those whom the senator symbolically represents (other senators, the president). However, the audience also includes the other citizens attending the meeting and, if the media are present, the population at large as well.

▶ Because we're creating a hypothetical situation, we don't know the **method** of the speaker's communication. But given the circumstances described here, we can develop some ideas about what might succeed and what might fail rhetorically: Should the parent be loud? Quiet? Logical? Passionate? Brief? Thorough? Personal? Detached? Should the parent address only the senator or the citizens as well? How about TV cameras — should the parent directly address the larger population via technology? Should this parent shout? Cry? Use humor? Be sarcastic? The questions to consider go on and on.

▶ The **institutions** involved in this situation are both simple and complex, both large and small. The parent is speaking in a representative democracy, for one thing, which means that the right to self-expression is guaranteed, as is the right to question government officials. These are "the rules." But other rules are at play as well. There are community standards — is this a town or city in which the citizens are typically politically active? What difference might this make in the parent's decision-making process regarding means of communication?

By now you've probably realized that much of what we have just examined is, in fact, what we consider naturally, if unconsciously, whenever we encounter a communicated argument.

What we're asking you to do now is to be more conscious and deliberate in your consideration of the elements of any rhetorical situation. Consider how these elements affect communication — both in your role as the creator of an argument and in your role as the audience for an argument. Sometimes — often, actually — the difference between a pretty good argument and a civilization-changing rhetorical event is purely a matter of the speaker choosing the right words at the right time for the right audience.

▶ *Let Us Show You:* Analyzing the Rhetorical Situation

For her US history class, Mara has been assigned to read and discuss Abraham Lincoln's Gettysburg Address, after which she will write an analysis of its rhetorical situation. The Gettysburg Address can be found in its entirety at a number of locations around the Web. We recommend a site called **ourdocuments. gov,** which is an official collection of important documents chronicling US history, with useful contextual information also provided. Or you can simply turn to Appendix C, Readings for Writers on page 483 of this book and read the address.

We now join Mara's analysis of the rhetorical situation of the Gettysburg Address, with an assist from Casey, already in progress:

Analyzing the Rhetorical Situation

▶ *Talk Amongst Yourselves . . .*

Turn to page 483 and read the Gettysburg Address. Then find a partner and critique Casey and Mara's analysis. What would you change? What is missing? What do you disagree with, and why?

▶ *Now You Try:* **Analyzing the Rhetorical Situation**

We're so excited about the rhetorical analysis of President Lincoln's Gettysburg Address — nice job, Mara and Casey! — that we'd like you to take a look at another speech in order to examine the argument's context and evaluate the effect of the point of attack.

Here's your assignment: Watch or listen to one of the following speeches:

▶   "Amazing Grace," the Clementa Pinckney eulogy by President Barack Obama

▶   "This Is Water," the 2005 Kenyon College commencement address by David Foster Wallace

Each speech is easily found on YouTube, but make sure you find a video of the entire speech and not just an excerpt: Obama's speech is about ten minutes long, while Wallace's is about twenty-two minutes long. Both speeches are worth every second of your time.

As you're watching and listening, pay attention to the elements of the rhetorical situation. Specifically, see if you can answer the following questions, and then use your answers to provide a framework within which you can begin to evaluate the effectiveness of the speech.

▶   What is the exigence? In other words, what compels the speaker to speak?

▶   Who is involved in the exigence? What are their roles?

▶   What are the relationships/power dynamics between the speaker and others involved?

- ▶ Where and when was the speech delivered?
- ▶ Who is the speaker? What do you know about him that is relevant to the context of the text?
- ▶ Who is the intended audience? Is it the same as the actual audience?
- ▶ What can you say about the speaker's methods of communication?
- ▶ What can you say about the institutions governing all of the above?

Audience Awareness in College Writing

In the examples and assignments above, we have explored the rhetorical situation of public, professional texts. When writers and speakers like Abraham Lincoln, Barack Obama, and David Foster Wallace create their texts, they need to spend quality time thinking about their audience. Successful writers always need to think about their readers in order to communicate their messages clearly and engagingly.

So how does a writer think about the reader? Who is the reader, anyway? How can a writer ever really know who's reading his or her ideas? These questions were especially challenging for Lincoln and Obama, who were addressing large and diverse audiences, but perhaps less of a challenge for Wallace, who was addressing the graduating class of Kenyon College — a much smaller audience than that of Lincoln or Obama (whose audiences were the American people).

If the idea of figuring out who your audience is seems daunting, well, it is. But there's good news. As a college writer, you may sometimes be assigned to write for a specific audience — for example, you may be asked to write a proposal for your college administration or city council to consider — but even when no particular audience is identified, your reader is, in reality, fairly well defined. In general terms, your audience is made up of your classmates — assuming you share your work through peer review or other collaborative learning activities. But in specific terms, your reader is always your professor. Does that mean that you need to know everything about your professor? No.

I certainly hope not. That would be weird.

But you *do* know plenty of important things about your reader. You know that your reader values the subject matter you've been assigned to write about, and also that your reader is most likely fairly well informed about your writing topic, even when you've been allowed to choose your own. These may seem like simple things to know — and they are — but that simplicity doesn't diminish their importance.

You've heard people talk about college in comparison to the "real world," right? We happen to think college *is* the real world, but at the same time, we understand why some people might make a distinction between the two. When it comes to writing for an audience, college is a controlled environment. You won't need to spend an inordinate amount of time trying to figure out *who* your reader is because your readership has been determined for you. So instead you can spend your time figuring out how best to address that reader.

APPLY WHAT YOU KNOW . . . RIGHT NOW

You can apply what you're learning about the writing process, context, and the rhetorical situation — the fundamentals of good writing — to your academic life right now. Don't worry about not being an expert yet. We'll get to that very soon.

For now, even if it's early in the term, you may already have a writing assignment in one of your classes. Using the *Reality Check!* below — as well as all the information in this chapter — figure out the rhetorical situation of your writing assignment. Then get together with a partner or a small group to talk about what you've discovered.

You can do this exercise on your own — just 'cause. It's a super handy way to understand assignments for any class, for your entire college career, and maybe in your life beyond college!

Reality Check! The Rhetorical Situation

1. What is the exigence? In other words, what compels you to write?
2. Who is involved in the exigence? What are their roles?
3. What are the relationships/power dynamics between you and others involved?
4. Where and when are you creating your writing?
5. Who are you in relation to the context of your writing?
6. Who is your intended audience? Is it the same as your actual audience?
7. What decisions will you make regarding methods of communication?
8. What can you say about the institutions governing all of the above?

Chapter 3

Reading and Writing: Two Sides of the Same Coin

> The more that you read, the more things you'll know. The more that you learn, the more places you'll go.
> —Theodor Geisel (Dr. Seuss)

Readin' and writin' and 'rithmetic: the three *R*s are what we learn in grade school, and for good reason — they're absolutely crucial skills to have in order to be educated. *But why are they crucial,* you ask?

Because they're all variations on the one skill that's so important we sometimes forget to mention it: thinking.

That's right: reading and writing and arithmetic are simply different manifestations of the act of thinking, which is something all intelligent people should do as often as possible. In this book, we'll focus on the first two skills, giving special emphasis to the second one (writing). In other words, we'll be talking about the two *verbal* aspects — as opposed to the *numerical* aspect — of thinking.

> Fun fact:
> *Verbal* doesn't mean "spoken." It means "using words." So it can refer to either speaking or writing. Most people don't know that. But now *you* do.

The Reading-Writing Relationship

Let's pause for a second and think about this: reading and writing are the two varieties of textual communication. How do they differ? Well, reading is perceptive (we perceive it) and receptive (we receive it), whereas writing is active (we make it) and creative (we generate ideas). When we read, we perceive a text and receive its meaning. When we write, we act on ideas and create a text.

Perhaps this sounds so simple that you're asking yourself, *Why are they bothering to tell me this?* We bother because we care about you, but also because it's impossible to talk about writing — which means it's impossible to *teach* writing — without talking about reading. The two activities, reading and writing, can't exist without each other. Each activity is inextricably linked to the text. Without writing, of course, the text wouldn't exist; without reading, the text would have no *reason* to exist.

Ouroboros

The reading-writing relationship looks a bit like the guy on the right. This is the Ouroboros. He's a dragon-snake from Greek mythology. Isn't he pretty? As you might guess from looking at him, he represents an eternal cycle with no beginning and no end, which is pretty much what reading and writing are like.

In order to write well, you need to read well. Why? For the same reason that composers need to listen well, and painters need to look well, and chefs need to taste well: to improve your skills in a particular craft (and writing is indeed a craft), you must observe the work of others in the field.

Here it is again, in a nutshell: *Writers read. Good writers read well.*

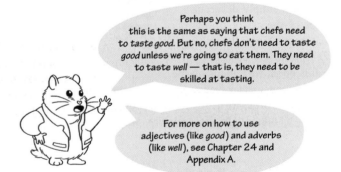

Perhaps you think this is the same as saying that chefs need to taste good. But no, chefs don't need to taste *good* unless we're going to eat them. They need to taste *well* — that is, they need to be skilled at tasting.

For more on how to use adjectives (like *good*) and adverbs (like *well*), see Chapter 24 and Appendix A.

Why Writers Read

At this point, we're guessing you have a decent understanding of the theory we've presented about reading. But perhaps you'd like some more practical reasons for writers to read. Okey-dokey. Because you've been such a good sport about the whole Ouroboros thing, here you go.

First, **reading provides models** to learn from. That is, written text is a code that already exists, which means that there are examples of it everywhere. If you can't decode the model — that is, if you want to learn to write but you can't read — then you can't learn from the model. And so we read texts — good and bad, entertaining and dull, reasonable and crazy — in order to learn what to do and what not to do.

We also **get our ideas for writing from reading** — both in terms of *what* to write and in terms of *how* to write. When we read, we engage in a series of mental activities that we're not always consciously aware of: we absorb, we react, we question, we agree or disagree, we smile or frown, and, perhaps most important, we respond by seeking additional sources of information. If we're reading a new text critically, we often respond by seeking confirmation or validation of what we've read. (*Can that be true?* we ask, and then we set out to answer our own question.) In short, reading makes us think — about what the text says, yes, but also about *how* the text says it. We learn to think (that's the *what* part) and we learn to write (that's the *how* part).

Finally, **reading quite literally leads to writing**. Most writing that's more sophisticated than a grocery list is created out of a mix of the writer's thoughts and the texts that the writer has read, either as models or as sources of information. And most writing that's more sophisticated than a grocery list is either academic or professional in nature, which means (you guessed it) it's the kind of writing we're going to be discussing for the next — well, gosh, for the rest of this book, actually.

Reading for Context

In short, reading gives us **context**. And in case you were wondering, this fact explains why your professors keep insisting that you read stuff as a central component of their classes. Philosophically speaking, reading contributes to your development as an idea factory: the more you read, the more you know, and the more you know, the more likely you are to come up with new ways of thinking.

Now just hold on a minute. "New ways of thinking"? How is that even possible? Hasn't pretty much every idea already been thought?

While it may be impossible to come up with a completely original idea, you can still be original in the way you deal with an idea. We read in order to fill up the libraries we have in our heads, packing them with concepts and information and opinions and odd details, and then we develop our own perspective on all that stuff and decide for ourselves how we might best present our ideas.

Later in this book — in Part 6, to be exact — we'll discuss in detail how to gather information to use in your writing. We'll also discuss academic research — why we do it, how we do it, and how we make sure we're doing it with integrity. For now, though, it makes sense to engage in a little reality check of what you've read so far before you use it as a path for writing.

Reality Check! Reading for Context

Before reading any text, answer a couple of questions:

▶ What did you already *know* about the topic before you started reading?
▶ What did you already *think* about the topic before you started reading?

After reading the text, answer another pair of questions:

▶ How did your reading change your knowledge?
▶ How did your reading change your opinions?

As long as you're honest with yourself about the answers to these questions — as long as you're paying attention to the difference between what you already knew and what you're learning as you read — your writing will benefit greatly from the reading that you do. And when you find that you need to understand more specifically what's okay and what's not okay as far as using what you've read in your writing . . . well, the research section (Part 6) will be there waiting for you.

▶ *Let Us Show You:* Searching for Context

You may recall that back in Chapter 2, Casey and Mara were analyzing the rhetorical situation of the Gettysburg Address in order to better understand the context of Lincoln's great speech. While that analysis was fairly successful, it was also an *innocent* analysis — meaning that it was the result of responding to questions without first having done any background reading about the speech or its context. An innocent analysis tends to be subjective — that is, it's more about the reader than the text.

Now it's time for a more informed, or objective, approach to the text. An objective analysis is one that is more about the object (the text) itself and less about the reader. To help the students achieve a greater degree of informed objectivity, Mara and Casey's professor has assigned their US history class to do some light research on the Web in order to discover some contextual details that might result in a more authoritative analysis of the speech.

Use Caution When Researching Online

Ah, the Internet — or, as we fondly refer to it, *the ultimate collection of everything*. Although the Internet in its current form didn't exist when we were wee tykes (hard to imagine, isn't it?), we have become so accustomed to it that we really have no idea how we would survive without it. Our guess is that you feel the same, dear reader.

In Part 6 of this book, we will discuss at length various tactics and strategies for using the Web in academic research. For now, though, we thought we'd provide just some bare-bones advice for finding *usable* information on the Internet.

Mara is on the right track. If you go to **scholar.google.com** instead of just **google.com**, you limit your search results to academic publications only. This will save you a lot of time that might otherwise be spent wading through long lists of whatever silliness might show up in a general Google search.

Remember that the Internet is huge, so you have to be specific when you ask it a question. For example, be precise about the terms you type into the search bar. If you want to learn about the context of the Gettysburg Address, don't just type "Gettysburg Address," because then Google doesn't really know what you're interested in learning. All it knows is that it should show you everything on the Internet that refers to the Gettysburg Address. And that's a whole lot of stuff, even in Google Scholar.

Narrowing Search Results

One more thing to try is to limit the site domain. The domain of a Web site tells you in very general terms what type of site it is. Some Web site types are more appropriate than others for certain purposes. You can limit your Web search to a particular domain type simply by typing your search term and then **site:** followed by the domain extension, which is the period and the three letters (such as **.gov** or **.edu**) that come at the end of a basic Web address.

Reality Check! Web Domains and Reliability

.com	**Commercial** Most Web sites with a .com domain extension are for-profit businesses, although nonprofits, schools, and other organizations and individuals are registering .com sites with increasing frequency. The odds that information found on a .com site is unreliable for academic purposes are fairly high.
.net	**Network** Anybody can post anything on a .net site, so reliability is definitely not assured.
.org	**Organization** This extension was once reserved for nonprofit organizations, which are often a good source of academic information; now anyone can register a .org domain, however, so exercise caution when using .org sites as academic sources.
.edu	**Education** Used almost exclusively by American colleges and universities, .edu domains are relatively reliable. But be aware that students can also post on .edu sites, so not all of the information on these sites will have come from qualified professionals.
.gov	**Government** All .gov sites are registered and controlled by US government offices and agencies. If you need information that's related to government, these are great sources.

Government documents might be the most reliable sources of factual context for a presidential speech. Let's see what happens when Mara limits the search for Gettysburg Address context to .gov sites:

How do I limit my search again?

In the *Google Scholar* search bar, type your search terms. And don't forget the quotation marks! Then add *site:.gov* to limit your results to government Web sites.

Excellent! Just thirty-two results, and several of them look useful.

▶ *Talk Amongst Yourselves . . .*

With a partner or two, talk about the advice Casey has given Mara about how to search the Internet for contextual information. Why isn't *Wikipedia* good for academic research? What specifically is *Wikipedia* good for? How might it be the springboard for valid research? What about SparkNotes and other study tools? Are they the same as *Wikipedia*, or are they different? What, if anything, are they good for, and when and why do you think they should be avoided?

▶ *Now You Try:* **Searching for Context**

To get yourself thinking about the relationship between reading and writing, do some informal research into the context of the speech you watched in Chapter 2 (either "Amazing Grace" by President Barack Obama or "This Is Water" by David Foster Wallace). You did that assignment, right? Good! Now read some reliable sources that will provide you with important factual details surrounding the writing and delivery of the speech.

Keep in mind that, as Mara and Casey have discovered, there are responsible ways to use the Internet even for the fairly light, surface-level research needed to uncover basic contextual information. If you're going to use Google, try limiting the search domain to an appropriate one for your purposes. Be sure to use the handy list of the most prevalent domain extensions and what they mean, provided above in the *Reality Check!* box on page 29.

It probably goes without saying, but we'll say it anyway, just for fun: once you've found some basic contextual information through your *responsible* Web search, you'll need to make use of that context to increase your understanding of the original text you're exploring. Here, we'll let Mara show you.

▶ *Let Us Show You:* Exploring Context

And off Mara goes to read some contextual information about the Gettysburg Address at the Web site of the United States National Archives before writing responses to the Reading for Context questions we presented in the *Reality Check!* box on page 26. Here's how her writing turns out:

Reading the Context of the Gettysburg Address from the National Archives

- **What did I already know before I started reading?** Well, I knew that it was during the Civil War, and that Lincoln was trying to end the war. And that he was dedicating the battlefield to honor the dead soldiers.

- **What did I already think before I started reading?** Honestly, I hadn't thought too much about it. I thought the address was nicely written, and I liked that it was short. I thought it was sad and very somber, and it seemed to me that the main point was to lay the soldiers to rest. I admired the way Lincoln used the most hopeful ideas from the Declaration of Independence.

- **How did my reading change my knowledge?** I learned that the Battle of Gettysburg took place around the Fourth of July, which might be what made Lincoln decide to use the Declaration of Independence to remind his audience of important national values. I also learned that 51,000 soldiers died in the battle, and that the battle marked a turning

---

(continued)

point in the war—the Union started winning. And I learned that Lincoln wasn't the main speaker at the ceremony to dedicate the military cemetery at Gettysburg: the governor of Pennsylvania delivered the main speech (2 hours long) before Lincoln's speech (2 minutes long).

- **How did my reading change my opinions?** It didn't change my opinions so much as it helped me to develop some. I think it was a very strategic speech — he used time and place and the authority of the Founding Fathers (and brevity!) to remind us that the US is one country.

▶ *Talk Amongst Yourselves . . .*

Break into groups and critique Mara's answers. To what extent is the information she found relevant? What information might she still need to find? What justifies the new or revised opinions she shares in her response to the last question? What would you add?

▶ *Now You Try:* **Exploring Context**

Find a magazine, either in print or online, and flip/click through it until you run across an ad that catches your eye. Then:

1. Examine the ad and write down what you think about it: What is it saying? How do you respond to it?

2. Analyze the rhetorical situation of the ad. (Look back at Chapter 2 if you need a refresher on "rhetorical situation.")

3. Do some light Web research about the ad to learn more about the context. (Make sure to pay attention to where your information is coming from. If it's all coming from the advertiser or from Web sources affiliated with the advertiser, the information might be biased or incomplete.)

4. Finally, write down how your opinion of the ad and its central message has changed now that you have informed yourself about the context.

Chapter 4

How to Read?
Why, Recursively, of Course

If one cannot enjoy reading a book over and over again, there is no use in reading it at all.
— Oscar Wilde

Pop quiz: how many times do you need to read something before you fully understand it? If you said once, then you were probably not thinking about college texts. A greeting card? A Facebook post? Even a newspaper article? Sure, you can understand those texts in a single reading. But academic and literary texts are a little different.

If you're wondering how phrases like "A greeting card?" or "A Facebook post?" count as sentences — well, they don't! If written *unintentionally*, these are errors called SENTENCE FRAGMENTS (see Chapter 25).

It's okay for seasoned writers to use them when they know what they're doing. But while you're in college it's best to play by the rules — until you get the hang of things.

Academic and literary texts are different from greeting cards, social media, and newspapers because there's reading, and then there's *reading*. There's a difference between decoding the words on a page so you can walk away with "the gist" of it and actually sucking the sweet nectar of truth and beauty from a well-written text. Academic and literary texts must be read **recursively**.

It's a great word, *recursive*. It comes from the Latin *recurrere*, which, not surprisingly, means "to return" or "to come back." Originally the word was used in reference to people — as in a person returning home after an absence. But over time it came to refer primarily to thoughts and ideas — as in revisiting a thought or reconsidering an idea. And that's how serious reading happens: in a way that revisits the text and reconsiders its implications. If you think about it, you probably already knew that recursive reading is required to understand academic texts, those complex, sophisticated pieces of writing that your professors will ask you to read.

The problem is that, in the course of your time in school (especially in high school), you're often given a short piece of literature, such as a poem, and simply told to read it. If you don't understand it, the teacher tells you what it means, and you're supposed to nod and accept that interpretation. Is this sounding familiar yet?

Raise your hand if you've ever gotten into a fight with a poem and lost. We can show you our scars, too.

We'll let you in on a little secret: *the problem wasn't you.* It's not your fault that you didn't fully understand that poem after reading it just once. We'll let you in on a bigger secret: nobody gains full understanding of most serious literature or college-level texts after only one reading. Such texts must be read *recursively.* That is, they must be read over and over because their meaning may not be obvious the first time around.

So if once isn't enough, how many times do you need to read a text? Well, that depends on a variety of things — most notably on the complexity or sophistication of the text, but also on the text's density and length. As a general rule, however, we're going to advise that any time you want to gain a full understanding of a complex or sophisticated text, you should plan to read it a minimum of three times.

Why three? We're glad you asked!

The First Reading: Relax

When you encounter a challenging text, read it all the way through one time without stressing about what should be happening or what you should be getting out of it. Just relax and enjoy reading without an agenda. Let the text take you wherever it wants to. In the words of our favorite philosopher — Ty Webb in the movie *Caddyshack* — "There's a force in the universe that makes things happen. And all you have to do is get in touch with it, stop thinking, let things happen, and be the ball."

In the case of particularly artful writing (like poetry and other forms of literature), it's very helpful to listen to the text being read aloud — although we're big fans of listening to *all* forms of sophisticated writing being read aloud. If you're fortunate enough to have someone in your life who is willing to read out loud to you, we strongly encourage you to take advantage of that willingness as often as possible.

But if you don't have a generous and talented person on call to read to you whenever the mood strikes you, you can read aloud to yourself. Just make sure you also *listen* to yourself. There's something about hearing the sounds of the words, noticing the pauses, and perceiving bits of meaning in the tone of voice, whether it's your voice or someone else's. All of these things are crucial to the first reading because they're all part of having a visceral and emotional reaction to the text.

Your initial subjective response is crucial. It's important that you encounter writing naturally, allowing it to flow over you — and it's equally important that you allow yourself to react subjectively. In subsequent readings you'll move beyond the subjective and aim for a more objective consideration of the text; more information on those subsequent readings will come a little later in this chapter.

But the fact that you'll try to gain objective understanding doesn't mean you should dismiss the subjective. The objective doesn't *replace* the subjective; it *adds* to the subjective. To truly understand what you've read, you need to access both the subjective and the objective — the yin and yang of the mind — and allow them to coexist.

▶ *Let Us Show You:* The First Reading

Casey and Mara's English class has been assigned to read a very famous essay by Jonathan Swift called "A Modest Proposal." You can find it in the reader at the back of this book (see Appendix C, page 483) — and you should probably go read it now. If you choose not to read it, all we can say to introduce the following conversation is "spoiler alert!"

First Response to a Reading

If Casey and Mara's conversation about Swift's "A Modest Proposal" shocks you, that's only because you haven't read the essay yet — or you haven't read it closely enough. In fairness, we did issue a clear spoiler alert. So really, you have no one but yourself to blame.

▶ *Talk Amongst Yourselves . . .*

If you haven't yet read Swift's essay, do so now. Afterward, think about your first response to it and talk about the essay with other students in your class. What is your initial feeling about it? What does it remind you of? What do you think of it?

All of these subjective, human responses are important. Good writing — literature especially, perhaps, but really *all* good writing — should be experienced on a human scale before the reader attempts analysis. Which brings us to this:

▶ *Now You Try:* The First Reading

In the reader at the back of this book, you'll find an essay by Michael Byrne titled "The Deep Sadness of Elk That Don't Run" (see Appendix C, page 490). It's not very long. Your first reading of it will probably take about ten minutes.

*Go ahead.
We'll go check our e-mail or something
until you get back.*

Now that you've read the essay, sit down and write a first response. How does the essay make you feel? Does it remind you of anything or anyone? Are you drawn toward it, or does it push you away? What do you think it's really about? Can you articulate what you think its main point is?

The Second Reading: Engage

The most important thing for you to know about the second reading of a sophisticated text is that it's necessary — really necessary. That's what we mean by recursive: you have to go back again. One reading just won't cut it.

The most important step to take in achieving the second reading is to open up that book again or take that assignment back out and settle in for a second go-round. We know reading something again might feel foreign to you at first, but you'll get used to it. The second time you read a text, you should interact with it as you read. That is, you should begin to read actively.

How? you may be thinking. *I mean, am I supposed to tickle it or something? Should I do jumping jacks while I'm reading?*

To which our response is, *You're very funny, with your tickling and your jumping jacks.* But metaphorically speaking, yeah, that is sort of what we're asking you to do. We'd like you to reach out and nudge the essay, poke at and play with it, to see what it will do.

And while you're at it, we'd like you to get some exercise as you read. How? By reading *actively*.

READ ACTIVELY

You can exercise your brain by *thinking* while you're reading — and yes, we know you saw that one coming, but bear with us: we can't even count how many times we've heard a student say, "I read it, but I have no idea what it says."

Unless the text is written in Swahili, there's no good reason for you to have "no idea" what it says — at least, not if you bring your brain along with you when you read. When students say that they have "no idea" what a text means, it generally indicates that something in the reading confuses them — so they've decided that they don't understand *any* of it. They stop trying. They shut down. They quit.

But don't quit, okay?
It's lazy, and it doesn't get you
anywhere. And you just end up
feeling bad about it.

But sometimes the reading is difficult, you say. *It has words I don't understand. It's all tricky with its hidden meanings and such. Why* shouldn't *I just quit?*

To which our response is: *Time to put on the big-girl pants, Tina.* Sophisticated texts will often have words you don't understand. Fortunately for you, there's this thing called a dictionary that you can use to look up words and find out what they mean. An added benefit of using a dictionary is that it provides at least a modicum of actual physical exercise — either you walk across the room and pull that big old *American Heritage Dictionary* off the shelf and then carry it back to your desk, or, at the very least, you exercise your fingers by typing the URL for **dictionary .com** into your browser.

Now, about those tricky "hidden meanings" — our response to that is: the meanings aren't hidden. They're right there for you to see. That's right: they're there in black and white, ready for the taking.

The only tricky thing about meaning is that you, the reader, are expected to participate in the process of creating it. Remember the communication triangle?

The implication of this triangle is that you, as a reader, are just as responsible for the meaning of the text as the writer and even the text itself are. So how do you meet that responsibility? One good way is to get even more exercise by using a pencil in the course of interacting with the text.

Remember when we said you should nudge that essay, poke at it, and play with it? Well, the best way to do that is to write notes in your books. Yes, right on the pages! It's okay.

And what should you write? Anything that seems relevant. Questions, observations and reactions, challenges, things you learn from your professor in class or through research that you've done because you think maybe you're missing something — whatever might be useful to you later in reconsidering the text is a valid thing to write on its pages. *Sure,* you're thinking, *but how do I know what's relevant or useful?* Here are three simple steps to help you start taking notes on a reading assignment:

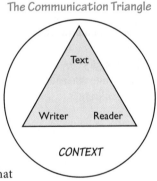

The Communication Triangle

Text

Writer   Reader

CONTEXT

It's *not* okay to write in a book if you've checked it out of a library or borrowed it from someone who wants it back. But if it's your book, write all you want!

Reality Check! Active Reading

► As you read, write down the main idea or purpose of each paragraph in the margin of your reading assignment.

► Underline words and references you don't know, look them up, and write their definitions in the margins so you will remember what they mean.

► Underline or highlight passages that are interesting to you or that seem important — but *don't* overdo this: if everything is important, then nothing is important. Never highlight something *instead of* thinking about it; rather, highlight it *because* you're thinking about it.

► *Let Us Show You:* The Second Reading

Now that Casey and Mara have discussed active reading, they've come to realize that "A Modest Proposal" contains many passages that they didn't understand very well on first reading. This happened because they glossed over the more confusing bits rather than working to understand them.

Remember that when your professors assign you to read something, they don't mean *look at all of the words and then close the book.* Professors expect you to make sense of what you're reading, to develop an understanding of it so that you will be prepared to talk or write about it. In short, they expect you to think about what you're reading.

Okay. Challenge accepted. I'll read it again, more carefully this time.

Here's what Swift's first paragraph looks like to Casey when he reads it a second time, actively.

It is a melancholy object to those, who walk through this great town, or travel in the country, when they see the streets, the roads and cabin-doors crowded with beggars of the female sex, followed by three, four, or six children, all in rags, and importuning every passenger for an <u>alms.</u> <u>These mothers instead of being able to work for their honest livelihood, are forced to employ all their time in strolling to beg sustenance for their helpless infants who, as they grow up, either turn thieves for want of work, or leave their dear native country,</u> to fight for the <u>Pretender in Spain</u>, or sell themselves to the <u>Barbadoes.</u>	First impression: poverty, over-population, desperation
	alms: "something, as money or food, given freely to relieve the poor"
	This seems important because it shows that whatever country these people are in, the wide-spread poverty is affecting them pretty dramatically.
	Pretender in Spain — the son of James II, who lost the English throne in 1688
	Barbadoes — an island in the former British West Indies. Poor Irishmen were selling themselves as indentured servants to go there.

▶ *Talk Amongst Yourselves . . .*

Find a partner in the class and critique Casey's notes. How useful and appropriate are they? What questions would you have asked the text? Take note of how you might have approached this task similarly or differently.

You've probably realized by now that the second reading will take longer than the first. That's okay; take your time. You're analyzing at this point — breaking the text down into its components in order to better understand them. During the second reading, you should mine the text for all of its riches. By the time you complete your second reading, you should have a clear understanding of what the text says, and a fairly good idea of what it means. The second reading provides you with a more considered, objective, analytical response to the text.

▶ *Now You Try:* **The Second Reading**

Read "The Deep Sadness of Elk That Don't Run" again, this time actively. Use the *Reality Check!* box on page 39 as a springboard to real engagement with the text: question the text, respond to it, challenge it, mark it up in places that require further investigation, and research anything that feels like it's just outside your grasp. Wrestle with the text until you have explored each line meaningfully. What is its argument?

The Third Reading: Achieve Harmony

On your first reading, you were all about your own subjective feelings, right? And your second reading focused on close analysis of the text and note taking. On the third reading, you need to think about what the text accomplishes as a whole and how it does that. Important to this type of analysis is the relationship between a text's *form* and its *content*.

Content is *what* a text says, and form is *how* the text says it. Jonathan Swift's essay "A Modest Proposal" is about the dire situation in eighteenth-century Ireland and what should be done about it (that is the essay's content), but it is written as a satire (that is its form). Swift could have used a variety of different forms to make the same argument (for instance, he could have written a formal research paper, a play, or a newspaper article), but all forms are not created equal: certain forms are better suited to certain types of content, depending on who your audience is.

For example, if you were writing a physics textbook, your audience would be high school or college students and the content would be physics (*duh*), so it might be weird if you wrote it using the same form as "A Modest Proposal" (satire). On the other hand, Swift's audience was the general public of England and Ireland in the eighteenth century — people who loved satire the way we love watching videos of cats on the Internet today. But they would not necessarily have considered a textbook to be pleasure reading. So it might have been just as weird if Swift had tried to make his argument in the form of a textbook. In evaluating Swift's or any author's strategy for making an argument, it is important to consider whether the form that the author has chosen is suited to his or her purposes.

Canadian theorist Marshall McLuhan famously coined the phrase "the medium is the message," and he went on to tweak that idea in a small, artsy book called *The Medium Is the Massage* (check it out some time — lots of pictures, some of them mildly creepy). His message was much the same in the book, but the way he worded it evokes a stronger image: all media "massage" or "sculpt" their content as they transmit it. Watching the DVD of a Broadway musical is not the same thing as seeing a live performance of the musical in a theater, for a variety of reasons: at the theater you don't have scene selections as an option, and the way that you experience the show will be shaped in part by the rest of the audience — not to mention the fact that with the DVD you're watching digitized light and color on a machine and in the theater you're watching real live humans.

To put this concept back into our terms (content and form, the *what* and the *how*): there is no such thing as form that does not affect its content. The *way* we see something shapes *what* we end up seeing. Likewise, the way we *say* something shapes what we end up saying.

That's why sometimes in this book we use images of ourselves to talk to you. It adds a personal touch, don't you think?

Admit it — you read these dialogues differently from the rest of the text.

Keeping all of this in mind, after your third reading of a text you are ready to support your notion of *what the text means* (the essential truth it lays bare) by describing both what it says and the way it tells this truth (the author's *rhetorical strategy*). This kind of analysis involves both *subjective* and *objective* judgments — both opinions and facts, in other words — about what you've read. The articulation of what a text means is an opinion (it's your point of view, an arguable statement, meaning that a person who had read the same text could reasonably disagree with you about its meaning). And what's the best thing to do with an opinion? In an academic setting at least, we state our reasons for having the opinion. This is where your objective analysis of the text comes into play: you can support your interpretation of the meaning of the text by using the text itself as evidence.

▶ *Let Us Show You:* **The Third Reading**

We now return to our regularly scheduled program, *Recursively Reading:* "A Modest Proposal." In the previous episode, Casey and Mara engaged Swift's text by asking questions, looking up definitions of words, and taking notes that would prompt more objective thought about the essay. Now it's time for them to complete their third reading and make informed statements about the essay's meaning.

First, Casey and Mara offer up a couple of clear opinions about Swift's essay. But having just read the preceding section about the need to support opinions with evidence from the text, they've also decided to try to find proof that their opinions are valid.

Third Response to a Reading

At this point, Mara and Casey need to take a step back and synthesize what they know now compared to what they knew after their first reading of the essay. Understanding how Swift uses satire causes Casey to reverse his previous position. Mara realizes that the essay is more complex than she had originally thought. Both Casey and Mara realize that there's a difference between the man who wrote the essay and the narrator he created in order to make a point.

▶ *Talk Amongst Yourselves ...*

Break into groups and discuss Mara and Casey's interpretations of "A Modest Proposal." Do Mara and Casey agree with each other? How can you tell? How is your opinion of the essay different from their opinions? What are the specific passages of the text that led you to your conclusion?

▶ *Now You Try:* The Third Reading

By now, you surely feel pretty familiar with Michael Byrne's "The Deep Sadness of Elk That Don't Run." Are you ready to achieve harmony through synthesis? Yes? Good!

Combine your first reading's subjective response and your second reading's objective analysis to arrive at a statement of meaning that you can back up with references to the text. Put your reading skills to the test and your opinion on the line:

1. What does the text mean?

2. How do you know that's what it means?

Note that these questions aren't designed to challenge (i.e., disagree with) your opinions. Instead, they're meant to challenge you to think about your opinions and about the proof that validates those opinions. In other words, they're meant to be challenging, but in a *good* way.

Reality Check! Recursive Reading

On your *first* reading of a college-level text:

- ▶ read through the text once without a specific agenda
- ▶ listen to it by reading aloud or having someone read aloud to you
- ▶ respond to it subjectively: What do you think? How do you feel?

On your *second* reading of a college-level text:

- ▶ read actively by taking notes and interacting with the text
- ▶ *think* about what you're reading and what it means
- ▶ look up unfamiliar words or phrases
- ▶ use the active reading tips on page 39
- ▶ respond to the text objectively: What does it say? How do you know?

On your *third* reading of a college-level text:
- ► read the text holistically by looking at the big picture
- ► observe the relationship between content (what the text says) and form (how the text says it)
- ► merge your subjective and objective responses to the text

Helpful Hint: Recording Your Results

When you've finished your three readings, answer the first question on page 44 (What does the text mean?) by writing a brief **summary** of the text, and then answer the second question (How do you know that's what it means?) by writing a brief **review** of your analysis of the text's content and form.

Engaging in this summary/review process is a useful way to gain a deeper, more reliable understanding of the text. And the good news? You've already done all the work mentally. It's just a question of putting your thoughts into writing.

Here's Mara's attempt at writing a summary and review of "A Modest Proposal." It didn't take her long, and she thought the process was really helpful.

In "A Modest Proposal" Jonathan Swift presents a sarcastic solution to his country's poverty, hunger, and large population of paupers. He proposes that the poor begin raising their children to be sold as food after one year of age, which is a more worthwhile job than begging. Swift presents detailed calculations of how many breeders there will be, how many viable children will be born, how many will be reserved to become breeders themselves, and how many will be sold for food. He also includes an estimated cost to raise a child up to one year, and how much it can be sold for. Swift lists the advantages of his plan to be that it would reduce the number of papists, give poor tenants a source of income, increase the nation's stock, lower the costs of raising children, introduce a new dish in the dining industry, and encourage marriage and healthy pregnancies. He closes the essay by saying that he has no children young enough to contribute, and that his wife is too old to reproduce.

Swift's essay is an entertaining — if also disturbing — read that forces readers to consider the unthinkable. He does a good job of making the impossible seem completely possible with his well-calculated numbers. He offers a few alternative

(continued)

plans, such as raising kids until they are pre-teens before butchering them. But he also suggests that this might be seen as "cruel" — an ironic point, given that his plan is inhumane. If you can get over the fact that it is based on cannibalism, the benefits of his proposal are surprisingly well reasoned. His closing line highlights the sarcasm of the essay, since he himself would take no part in the absurd plan. Swift's ridiculous solution makes readers consider what a more realistic solution might look like. His barbaric proposal makes a simple and humane solution seem completely within reach.

PART 2
Prewriting

Chapter 5

Prewriting: Where on Earth Do I Begin?

> If you believe you can accomplish everything by "cramming" at the eleventh hour, by all means, don't lift a finger now. But you may think twice about beginning to build your ark once it has already started raining.
>
> — Max Brooks, *The Zombie Survival Guide*

In Chapter 1, we told you that writing is a process, and we provided you with some advice and a few examples. Now it's time to walk you through some of the steps involved in the very first stage of the writing process: prewriting.

The Intellectual Road Trip

In many ways, writing is a journey: a stroll out of the darkness and into the light, a trip from ignorance to wisdom, a strenuous hike up Knowledge Mountain — okay, we'll stop now. But you get the point: writing is a journey.

And why do you take that journey, that intellectual road trip — aside from the fact that you're enrolled in all these college classes with professors who expect you to write, that is? Why do any of us take that journey? We take it because humans are hardwired to *impose order on chaos*. The world around us is chaotic on any given Monday morning, right? And don't even get us started on Friday nights. Yes, the world is chaos — and as humans we are uniquely equipped to do two things in response to that chaos:

1. We notice it.
2. We try to make sense of it.

And this is where the journey of writing comes in. See, the tool we need to use to make sense of the chaos is the human brain — that amazing bit of evolutionary magic that just keeps getting bigger and more sophisticated over time, so that we're capable of noticing and attempting to understand increasingly complex examples of chaos. What our amazing brains cannot do, however, is retain every thought we've ever had. So several millennia ago we used our brains to develop a system that allows us to retain our thoughts *outside* of our brains, a system that allows for the observable, storable manifestation of thought: writing. Writing enables us to keep track of our thoughts and insights in the hope that we might convince others of their relevance.

> And yes, in case you were wondering, we *can* see you rolling your eyes. It's true: we get a little excited about writing.

> But you have to admit: writing was an invention of pure genius. I mean, come on.

Here's the difference between good writers and those who moan about how awful their writing is: good writers master a series of learnable skills that begins with something that actually *isn't writing.* That's right: a good writer will begin *not* by picking up a pen or sitting at a keyboard but by thinking.

Okay, you say. *What should I think about?*

We're glad you asked.

Understanding the Assignment

The first thing you need to do when you find yourself with a new writing assignment — the *very first* thing — is to understand the assignment. That is, you need to make sure you comprehend everything there is to know about the task you've been given before you start working on it. We sometimes refer to this stage in the writing process as **analyzing the writing situation**.

KNOW WHAT YOU ARE REQUIRED TO DO

As with most things worth knowing in life, understanding an assignment begins with you asking yourself a bunch of pertinent questions and paying attention to whether you actually know the answers.

Reality Check! **Understanding the Assignment**

1. What sort of text have you been asked to write? Is it a personal reflection essay? A letter? A report? A story? An argument?

2. Are there words in the assignment that give you a hint about what the ultimate purpose of the writing is? Note that words such as *explain* and *inform* are asking you to do something very different from what words like *evaluate* or *propose* are asking you to do. You can read much more about these distinctions in Chapter 16.

3. Has your specific, narrowed topic been assigned, or are you expected to find one yourself?

4. Are you supposed to offer your opinion, stick to a presentation of facts, or perhaps do both?

5. Have you been given a specific job to do in the text, like solving a problem or comparing two topics? These specific jobs, also known as "rhetorical modes," are discussed in detail in Chapter 11.

6. Are you required to do research? If so, do you know what kind or how much? And if you're *not* required to do research, are you still *allowed* to do research?

7. How long does the assignment say the text should be? Is this length a requirement or a suggestion?

8. How formal should the text be? What do you need to know about formatting issues?

9. What do you need to know about audience awareness and tone? Who's going to read this once you're done? Is there an intended audience beyond, or in addition to, your professor and/or classmates? You can read more about audience and tone in Chapters 11, 21, and 22.

10. When is it due? Are you required to submit work (notes, outlines, drafts) along the way to creating the final product? If not *required*, is the submission of these things for feedback invited or encouraged?

ASK QUESTIONS

If you're fortunate, your professor has given you a written assignment that should answer most of these questions. If the assignment is given orally, or if the written assignment doesn't provide clear answers to these questions, ask your professor to explain. Yes, even if you're shy. It's better to ask a potentially silly question than to spend hours writing something that ultimately doesn't fulfill the assignment. Adopting a conscientious approach to the terms of the assignment — whether those terms are presented in thoroughly articulated written instructions or determined through thoughtful questioning of your professor —

is the first, best way to ensure your eventual success in completing the writing project.

It's a good idea to treat a suggested length as a requirement — but one that you can sidestep if you have a really good reason.

We highly recommend that you begin every writing assignment throughout your college career by going through each of the questions above: first see how many you can answer on your own simply by reading the instructions carefully, and then take any remaining questions to your professor for clarification.

One question that probably won't be answered explicitly within the assignment guidelines is: what are the reader's expectations with respect to the values, qualities, and traditions of writing in this particular field?

Much of this book is devoted to answering that question when it comes to English classes — and we've included a section (Appendix B) that provides a brief overview of what professors in other subject areas expect — but the best way to answer it for yourself is to be an active participant in class: read, listen, ask questions . . . in short, learn how to write for the situation.

WHEN IS IT DUE?

Before we move on, we'd like to say just a few words about the last question in the *Reality Check!* box on page 51: *When is it due?*

We've had students who think we're kidding when we include this question as a part of the prewriting process, but we're not. It's an important question — not just because you should remember to turn your writing in on time, but because you should start working on it early enough to do a good job.

The number one cause of bad student writing is a failure to devote sufficient time to prewriting.

If you know your deadline, then you can reverse-engineer your finished product: start with the due date, figure out the steps you will need to take to create the final draft, and then work backwards, setting deadlines that will allow you to meet your goal. In addition to setting aside a chunk of time for the actual drafting (which we'll discuss in Chapter 8), be sure to allow plenty of time for prewriting (addressed in the activities throughout Part 2) as well as for revision (discussed in Chapters 12–15).

▶ *Let Us Show You:* Understanding the Assignment

It's time for the first writing assignment in Casey's Freshman Year Experience class:

CASEY'S ASSIGNMENT: FIRST YEAR EXPERIENCE (FYE)

Choose any of the fourteen examples of "prohibited conduct" in the Code of Conduct section of the college's student handbook, and write a brief essay (around three pages) that demonstrates your understanding of the rule as well as your opinion of its value and effectiveness. Due on the day of the midterm exam.

Being a good student — by which we simply mean one who understands that a student's job is to learn — Casey immediately springs into action, going through the list of Understanding the Assignment questions in the *Reality Check!* on pages 50–51. He gets through the first several questions fairly easily before running into some trouble with question 6:

---

1. **What sort of text have you been asked to write?** That's easy! A personal reflection. The words "your understanding" and "your opinion" are the clues.

2. **Are there words in the assignment that give you a hint about what the ultimate purpose of the writing is?** Yup, as noted above. Moving on!

3. **Has your specific topic been assigned, or are you expected to find one yourself?** Well, I've been given a list of fourteen possible topics, so that narrows it down a bit.

4. **Are you supposed to offer your opinion, stick to a presentation of facts, or perhaps do both?** Hmm, I'd say that "understanding" sounds as if what I write should be based on facts, while "opinion" sounds like I get to say what I think.

5. **Have you been given a specific job to do in the text, like solving a problem or comparing two topics?** Two specific jobs, I think: to show that I understand, and to explain my opinion.

6. **Are you required to do research?** I have no idea. Uh-oh.

(continued)

7. **How long does the assignment say the text should be?** About three pages. It's just a suggestion, but I know I should treat it like a requirement because that's what the ace students do.

8. **How formal should the text be?** I'd say medium-formal. It's academic writing, but it's also a personal reflection.

9. **What do you need to know about audience awareness and tone?** I think my audience will be the professor and maybe my classmates, so my tone should appeal to them.

10. **When is it due? Are you required to submit work (notes, outlines, drafts) along the way?** It's due at the midterm exam, which gives me plenty of time to get it done, and I don't think I have to turn in any of my work except the essay itself.

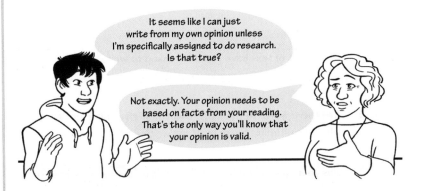

> It seems like I can just write from my own opinion unless I'm specifically assigned to do research. Is that true?

> Not exactly. Your opinion needs to be based on facts from your reading. That's the only way you'll know that your opinion is valid.

▶ *Talk Amongst Yourselves . . .*

Break into groups and discuss Casey's initial response to the assignment. How well has he understood it? What steps has he missed? What would you add to his process of understanding the assignment?

▶ *Now You Try:* Understanding the Assignment

Take a look around your workspace — your desk, your kitchen table, or wherever it is that you keep all of your schoolwork. Do you notice any writing assignments lying about? You should first look for an assignment from an English class, but you can also use an assignment from your Freshman Year Experience class or your history class. If by some chance you don't have a writing assignment handy, feel free to use the *Practice!* assignment on the next page.

Practice! Understanding the Assignment

Your task is to write a very brief essay (one to two pages) that responds to the following prompt: If you could somehow become, for one day, any character in any movie you've ever seen, who would you choose to be? Why? Due three days from now.

For whichever assignment you choose, try your hardest to answer the questions on pages 50–51. If you have trouble answering any of the questions, remember that your professor is the best person to ask for help. We think you'll find that answering these questions — or a similar set of questions that suits you better while still improving your understanding of the assignment — will give you a sense of confidence (even courage!) about moving forward with the next step in your prewriting process.

Generating Ideas

Okay, so you've come up with reasonably accurate answers to the ten questions presented earlier and have therefore figured out what your assigned task is. What's next? This paper's not going to just write itself, is it? The first thing you're going to need, now that you have a clear sense of your assignment, is a set of ideas.

Ideas? you say. *Those are exactly the problem! Where do I get some?*

BRAINSTORMING

If it were us — and it often is! — we'd start by brainstorming. Why? Well, primarily because most people can't just sit down and spit out great ideas. Generating ideas is hard work, and brainstorming is a terrific tool that will help you get the work done. Brainstorming is an activity that manifests itself in different ways, each with its own nickname: *listing*, *mind mapping*, and *clustering*, for example. If we were assigned to write an essay about — oh, let's say, the role of technology in daily life, we might make use of one or more of these techniques to generate some initial ideas for writing.

Listing
_____
The Role of Technology in Daily Life
  • at work
  • at home
  • at school
  • for entertainment
  • problems with technology
  • dependence on technology
  • constant upgrading
_____

Listing is exactly what it sounds like: making a list of ideas as they occur to you while you're thinking about your assignment. Note that it's helpful to sum-marize your assignment in a title at the top of your list, to remind yourself of the task so you don't get off track. Listing is a great way to increase the options that you'll have to choose from when you settle on a topic at the end of your brainstorm-ing. But it typically doesn't do much to help you generate a fresh, new idea.

Mind Mapping is a bit more useful when you need to zero in on a fairly precise or specific topic. It takes the basic idea of listing, but rather than simply writing down words or phrases as they occur to you in relation to the assignment, you start by writing the main idea of the assignment in the middle of a space that will represent your thought process. As each specific idea occurs to you, you connect it to your main idea by drawing a line — and you connect subsequent, more spe-cific ideas to the ideas that prompted them. In this way, you are creating a trail of mental breadcrumbs that eventually will reveal some interesting connections between and among ideas.

Mind Mapping

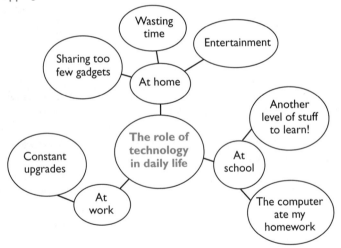

Clustering is very similar to mind mapping but takes the process a step further: once you've developed your mind map, you examine its outer edges (where the most specific ideas are presented) to see whether there are interesting connections between ideas that at first don't seem related to each other. For example, if you let your eyes wander over the ideas linked by circles and lines in the mind map above, you might come to the realization that the computer really *does* eat your homework sometimes, which makes for a colossal waste of time — and thus a potentially interesting new idea is born: the relationship between computer glitches and wasted time.

Clustering

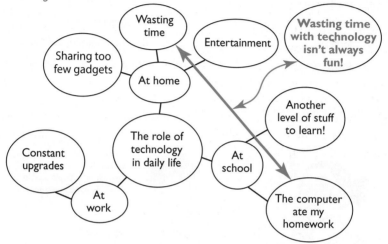

Although the specific techniques for each brainstorming strategy differ, the essential activity is the same each time: use a pencil or pen or a keyboard to scribble or jot or sketch or type some combination of words, images, and diagrams that will help you blow the dust out of your brain and shake loose a few potential starting points. You can think of it as **generative freewriting** — writing freely to generate an idea (or many ideas).

The initial focus of your brainstorming activity will depend on your answers to some of the ten Understanding the Assignment questions — for example, if the answer to the third question indicates that you need to find your own topic within a broadly defined territory, then your first brainstorm will almost certainly involve identifying a suitable and promising topic.

▶ *Let Us Show You:* **Brainstorming**

Casey is in precisely the situation described above: there are plenty of topics he could write about for the Freshman Year Experience assignment — fourteen topics, in fact — and so his immediate task is to list the possibilities and think them through in an effort to identify where a new or interesting idea might be.

Prohibited Conduct

1. smoking
2. drinking
3. use of controlled substances
4. lewd or obscene behavior
5. academic dishonesty
6. forgery
7. theft
8. vandalism
9. firearms possession
10. false alarms
11. computer hacking
12. sexual harassment
13. disorderly/abusive conduct
14. hazing

Brainstorming Possible Essay Topics

Note that Casey's brainstorming process begins with an old standby — listing — but then seems to take place without writing — that is, he brainstorms by thinking and talking about the assignment rather than through drawing, scribbling, or note taking. Some people can work well this way: they make a list, read it, think about it, and make a decision. But not everyone is equally suited to this style of learning, and relatively few people are at their most effective when they're keeping everything in their heads.

▶ *Talk Amongst Yourselves . . .*

Form a group with two or three of your classmates, and talk with them about your preferred ways to generate ideas. You might start by looking through your class notes or the notes you've taken for a writing assignment.

Are your notes made entirely of words, or do you draw or doodle as well? Do you make diagrams? Bullet lists? Do you circle certain things and put stars next to others? Do you draw arrows between ideas? Are your notes minimalist — that is, do you jot down individual words and expect yourself to remember what they mean? Or do you make more complete notes to ensure that you'll understand them later?

As you and your classmates compare and contrast brainstorming techniques, try to be mindful of how their processes differ from yours — and see if you can steal at least one good idea that you've never tried before.

▶ *Now You Try:* **Brainstorming**

Go back to the assignment that we started on page 54 and use one of the brainstorming techniques described earlier in the chapter — listing, mind mapping, or clustering — to generate a collection of ideas that will give you some options to pursue. Don't worry yet about which ideas are better than others. Your task at this point is not to *judge* your ideas but to *collect* them. This is also a chance to practice flexible thinking: don't worry if your ideas don't sound smart yet.

Just get them down on paper so that you have something — anything — to work with.

The first known usage of *brainstorm* — a very cool word — was in 1849. It's a metaphor. After all, you don't have a *real* storm in your brain. But a brainstorm is *essentially* a chaotic swirl of ideas. *Go* with it.

During this process, if one brainstorming method isn't working for you, switch to another one. Practice flexible thinking here. If listing doesn't work, try mind mapping. If drawing a mind map doesn't do it for you, talk about your ideas aloud, whether to yourself or to a patient and understanding friend. It's important that you make the brainstorming process a system of idea generation that works for *you*.

Remember, all you're doing at this point is generating some ideas, some thoughts, some tidbits of content. Don't expect too much for now — there will be plenty of time later for crafting your ideas into the fully formed, rational sentences that you'll eventually share with your reader. Right now, you're just gathering possible ideas *for yourself*.

Reality Check! **Where to Begin**

▶ Understand the type of assignment you've been given.
▶ Know whether you will choose a specific topic or whether one has been given to you.
▶ Make sure you know the due date, required length, and other logistical elements of the assignment.
▶ Brainstorm for appropriate and interesting ways to approach your assignment.
▶ Be aware of your own preferred learning style as you brainstorm.

Chapter 6

From Brainstorm to Topic: I Have Some Ideas . . . Now What?

Perfection has to do with the end product, but excellence has to do with the process.
— Jerry Moran

Once your brainstorming has brought you to a place where you have some ideas in front of you, it's time to narrow your focus to a single topic. If you've used one of the brainstorming activities described in Chapter 5, then you have already completed the most important step in identifying a suitable topic: you've given yourself options. Now it's time to evaluate those options by asking three important questions.

> ### *Reality Check!* From Brainstorm to Topic
> ► Which idea are *you* most interested in spending more time with?
> ► Which idea are *others* most likely to be interested in reading about?
> ► Which ideas in combination create the most interesting *new* idea?

The answers to these questions will potentially narrow your options down to a single idea, but more likely you will end up with a very short list of possible topics. To choose the idea you're going to pursue, go back to the original assignment: which idea best matches what you've been asked to write? That's your topic.

If you're fortunate enough to have more than one idea that meets all of these criteria, go with the one that most interests you. After all, you're the one who will be spending a ton of time with this topic, right?

Orient Yourself to Your Topic

Now that you have a topic you can get behind, you need to develop a sense of where you are in relation to your topic. And to get that sense, you need to answer a whole new set of questions designed to establish the initial relationship between you and your topic. So, ladies and gentlemen, we present to you:

Reality Check! **Topic Orientation**

- ▶ What do you already know about this topic?
- ▶ What are your gut feelings about it?
- ▶ What do you suspect is true or false?
- ▶ Where did you get these ideas?
- ▶ Are your ideas reasonable? Do you have a personal bias that might stand in the way of your ability to be reasonable?
- ▶ Are your ideas based on sound and verifiable information, or do you need to learn more?

You can answer these questions simply by thinking about them, but our advice is to write down at least some of your responses. Even if you're just writing down individual words and phrases — or doodling little pictures and diagrams — the act of getting some of your ideas down on paper (or on-screen, if you're not into writing by hand or using up valuable wood-based resources) is an important step on the way to creating the assigned piece of writing. It's always easier to write the *product* when you've already created concrete, reviewable evidence of at least some of the *process*.

▶ *Let Us Show You:* **Topic Orientation**

Casey's brainstorm ended with the selection of "academic dishonesty" for the general topic and "plagiarism" for the specific topic. Now he needs to step back and do an honest assessment of the ideas he already has about plagiarism by answering the questions in the *Reality Check!* box above.

Topic Orientation

- **What do you already know about this topic?** Not much, really. I mean, I've heard of academic dishonesty, but I've never been guilty of it — and neither has anyone I know. Well, except for that kid in tenth grade who copied a whole article off the Internet and tried to convince everyone he wrote it himself.

- **What are your gut feelings about it?** Well, it's lame. It's cheating. I don't have a lot of sympathy for someone who plagiarizes, just like I don't have much sympathy for someone who lies or steals.

- **What do you suspect is true or false?** I suspect it's pretty clear — either you plagiarized or you didn't. I don't see a whole lot of gray area with this topic.

- **Where did you get these ideas?** Umm . . . I really don't know. Personal experience, I guess? Or maybe from TV shows or movies? I've never really studied this topic or read about it.

- **Are your ideas reasonable? Do you have a personal bias that might stand in the way of your ability to be reasonable?** Well, *I* think my ideas are reasonable, but then again, I don't really have anything to compare them to. I'm open to the possibility that I could be wrong, but I don't think I'm actually *biased*.

- **Are your ideas based on sound and verifiable information, or do you need to learn more?** Umm . . . see above? I'm not sure.

> That question about whether my ideas are based on verifiable information is a really good one. Since I don't know where my ideas came from, it's possible, though unlikely, that I just made them up. Clearly I need to watch out for this!

▶ *Talk Amongst Yourselves . . .*

Break into groups and discuss Casey's answers to the Topic Orientation questions above. What useful pieces of information did that exercise generate, and how might these pieces of information be useful? Based on his answers to the questions, what do you think Casey should do first as he moves forward with this process, and why?

▶ *Now You Try:* Topic Orientation

Working from the brainstormed list of possible topics you created in Chapter 5 (see page 59), use the From Brainstorm to Topic questions in the *Reality Check!* box at the start of this chapter to identify a specific topic for your assignment. Then, with that topic in mind, work your way through the Topic Orientation questions from the *Reality Check!* box on page 62 that Casey has just answered. There's really only one rule for answering these questions: be honest.

Focused Freewriting

So now you've brainstormed a list of options, identified a single topic, and oriented yourself to what you already know, think, or believe about your topic. Good for you!

And just in case you're wondering — no, you're not done prewriting yet.

At this point, we'd like to introduce you to a sassy little technique called **focused freewriting**. It's another level of idea generation — one that's a step up from brainstorming, for two reasons: first, it's much more focused than brainstorming; and second, instead of generating individual words and phrases, freewriting will provide you with longer, more developed ideas. In other words, brainstorming is *jotting*, but freewriting is *writing*.

The basic idea behind freewriting is that you start with a single focused question from your brainstorming activities. With that question in mind, set a timer for, say, five minutes, and start writing everything that comes into your head. Our only guideline for freewriting is: Don't stop writing until the timer goes off. Once it does, take a moment to clear your head, get out a fresh sheet of paper (or scroll down to a new page), set the timer to five minutes again, and move on to the next question.

What you'll find is that after just a half hour, you will have recorded a wealth of raw material that you can potentially use as a starting point for the first draft of your written product. Note that we're *not* saying that your freewriting is your first draft. It's not. But it's likely to contain some nuggets of good, interesting writing that you can build on.

▶ *Let Us Show You:* Focused Freewriting

For his first attempt at freewriting, Casey has decided to use the six Topic Orientation questions as a springboard for generating fuller, more developed ideas. Here is the result of his first two five-minute freewrites, based on the first few orientation questions:

Casey's First Freewrite — Plagiarism Project

What do I already know about plagiarism? Well, I know that I would never do it. Copying somebody else's paper, or buying one of those ready-made papers

---

from a Web site, or maybe asking a friend to write your paper for you —
those things are all wrong. My gut feeling about plagiarism is that it's
a pretty pathetic thing to do (and also that it's hard to spell — why do I
always have to think about what letter comes after the "g"?). OK. Get back
on track. Plagiarism. It sounds like a disease. Not exactly back on track yet,
Casey. Focus. OK. What do I think is true about plagiarism? I think that
people who would turn in papers that they didn't write would probably
also cheat on tests. Maybe even steal. Or maybe not — that's different,
I think. And why would anyone need to plagiarize anyway, now that the
Internet is so readily available? I mean, you can find any information you
might ever possibly need any time of the day or night, and anywhere on
the planet that has a WiFi hotspot. There's just no excuse for stealing — or
buying — somebody else's paper that they wrote for school when you can
so easily borrow from people who have posted good stuff on the Web for
you to use.

And there you have it: a chunk of text related to the topic at hand. The beauty
of freewriting, truly, is that even writers who go all cold and clammy at the
thought of committing their words to paper can get through a freewrite without
hyperventilating — and as a bonus, they end up with some potentially good ideas
right there in front of them that they can read, think about, and use or ignore as
they see fit.

▶ *Talk Amongst Yourselves ...*

Find a partner in the class and discuss Casey's freewrite. In your view, what is the
most useful or interesting nugget of text? And what do you observe about the
freewriting *process* by observing Casey's freewriting *product*? What helped Casey
stay on task?

▶ *Now You Try:* **Focused Freewriting**

Using the orientation questions in the *Reality Check!* box on the next page as a
starting point, and adding other questions as they occur to you, create a freewrite, or three freewrites, or nine ... seriously, the more freewriting you do, the
more ideas you'll generate. Just remember that freewriting is a more structured
activity than its name suggests — while the *product* that you'll create through
freewriting will look and feel "free," the *process* of freewriting works best with a
few restrictions.

> ### *Reality Check!* **Focused Freewriting**
>
> ▶ Have your questions ready to go before you start.
> ▶ Set up your workspace so that there are as few distractions as possible.
> ▶ Set a timer for five minutes so you can focus on thinking about what you're writing rather than on how long you've been writing.
> ▶ Do *not* stop writing until the timer buzzes, even if you can't think of anything else to write about. It's okay to write "I can't think of anything else to say" until you think of something.
> ▶ When the timer buzzes, you can finish the thought you're on, but then you have to stop.
> ▶ Allow yourself at least a minute or two to clear your head between freewrites.

When you're done with your freewriting activity — and we recommend devoting a half hour to freewriting, allowing you to respond to five good prompt questions — make sure to read through everything that you've written. We think you'll find at least one sentence or phrase that jumps out at you for its originality or its importance, or for both of those qualities.

Original and important ideas are crucial to good writing, so make sure you hang on to any that arise from your freewriting.

Stay on Track with Your Topic

Before you get too involved in the sheer brilliance of your freewrite, though, remember that all of the good work you've done so far has been in response to a specific assignment. Now is the time to go back and remind yourself of the originally assigned task to make sure you're still on the right track.

If it's pretty clear that you're being asked to write a just-the-facts report, then you shouldn't spend too much time on your opinions about what's good or bad, beautiful or ugly, right or wrong about your topic — such opinions would be great in an essay that's supposed to be about what you think, but not in a paper in which you're supposed to avoid making any judgments. Likewise, don't travel too far down the path of developing solutions to problems inherent in your topic unless you've actually been assigned to write a proposal. (In Chapter 16 you will learn much more about these different purposes for writing.)

In other words: keep an eye on the original assignment. You will need to monitor the relationship between the product of your freewriting and what you've actually been asked to do. A central component of almost every college writing assignment will be to show what you know about the topic — to share your understanding of information and its significance. But students' initial attempts at freewriting in response to college writing assignments usually contain relatively little knowledge, information, or deeper understanding. Instead, they tend to be heavy on feelings and reactions. This is natural; human beings are subjective creatures. But because school isn't really about natural reactions to things (bummer, right?), you'll need to deal with the growing gulf between what you're prepared to write and what you've been assigned to write.

It's best just to face that gulf. In fact, it might be time for a reality check. A good way to start this process is to ask yourself questions like the following:

Reality Check! Stay on Track with Your Topic

▶ Are your ideas still relevant to the assignment you were given? Are you staying on task?

▶ Do you have valid information about this topic, or are you making things up?

▶ If you do have valid information, how do you know it's valid?

▶ Is the information you have enough, or should you become better informed?

▶ If you are making things up, where can you go to gain the necessary knowledge?

In most academic writing situations, the answers to the above questions will lead you to the inescapable conclusion that you just don't know enough yet. And that's really okay.

It's okay that you don't yet know enough *unless* you put off even thinking about your assignment until the last minute — that's not really okay, because then you're just avoiding the task. Got it?

Writing should be a discovery process — a big part of the point of academic writing is for you to learn as you write. No, really, it's true. We know that most students think writing assignments are all about being tested or punished or something, but in reality, teachers assign you to write because giving you a task that you can think about and then express your ideas about is an excellent way of helping you to figure out the world around you. No, no, don't thank us. We're just happy to help!

So now you're thinking, *Yes, okay, learning as I write is a great goal — but how do I do that?*

HOW TO STAY ON TRACK

There are plenty of good ways to become better informed and therefore make yourself better prepared to write. One of the best ways to accomplish this is to read, as we discussed in Chapters 3 and 4. Your particular assignment will determine what might be best for you to read, but here are some ideas:

▶ your class text(s) and/or lecture notes
▶ articles (print or electronic) written by people who know what they're talking about — for more on how to decide who qualifies, see Chapters 20 and 21
▶ books or sections of books relevant to the topic

Depending on your assignment, other means of gathering information might be more appropriate than reading. There are three good ways to gather information without reading:

▶ observation (of people, places, objects, artifacts — note that this might include things like asking questions and listening to answers)
▶ memory (reaching back for what's relevant in what you already know)
▶ experimentation (engaging in your own original research or survey)

> ### ▶ *Let Us Show You:* **Stay on Track with Your Topic**
> Now that Casey has finished his freewriting, he's concerned that his opinions don't sound terribly informed. He's wondering whether he should dig a bit deeper into his topic so that he really knows what he's talking about. He decides to go back to the student handbook to see how his college defines *plagiarism*.

Researching the Essay Topic

▶ *Talk Amongst Yourselves . . .*

Break into groups and discuss Casey's reality check. To what extent has it helped him stay on track? Which other reality-checking activities should he engage in at this point? Ultimately, the goal of reality checking at this stage is to ensure that you are armed with useful and appropriate information as you move ahead. How did this reality check force Casey to begin moving *away from* the purely subjective reactions to ideas that humans are so fond of having and *toward* a more focused, informed, academic exploration of the topic?

Stay on Track with Your Information

Before choosing your method of information gathering, be sure to go back to the original assignment and reality-check your options (see page 50):

- ▶ Are you required to do research? (Doing research typically means reading valid sources — there's more on this in Chapter 20.)
- ▶ Are you expected *not* to do research?
- ▶ Are you allowed to write about personal experience?
- ▶ Are any types of information off-limits for the assignment?

As for the information gathering itself, we have one very important piece of advice: *take notes*. Do not assume that you'll be able to remember what you read or saw or imagined when the time comes to include it in your paper, because you won't. And the really sad part is that you won't even know you've forgotten it.

If you're the kind of person who thinks taking notes is a waste of time and energy, we strongly encourage you to rethink that thought. Taking notes can actually *save* you time and energy. For example, when you're gathering information from a source (i.e., reading), making sure that your notes clearly state exactly where the information came from (e.g., the source's author and title, the facts of publication) will save you valuable time later when you need to acknowledge the source in your own writing.

Have you ever wondered when to use *i.e.* as opposed to *e.g.* (both used in this chapter)? They're the respective abbreviations for the Latin terms *id est* (meaning "that is" or "in other words") and *exemplia gratia* (meaning "example given" or "for example"). Now you know!

And please, when you're taking notes, make it a habit *never* to write down the exact words from what you're reading unless you put them in quotation marks. When you return to your notes later, you'll need to know what are your words and what is original text. Otherwise, guess what? You'll be plagiarizing. Chapter 21 includes plenty of good advice on the note-taking part of research.

Once you're better informed about the facts and perhaps some opinions relevant to your topic, it's time to figure out where you stand. A good way to do that is to answer questions like those in the following list, perhaps through another round of freewriting. (Oh, come on! It was fun last time, wasn't it?) Here's another reality check, just to help you out.

Reality Check! Stay on Track with Your Information

- ▶ What do you know now that you didn't know yesterday?
- ▶ What do you think, now that you're better informed?
- ▶ If others have ideas different from yours, why might that be?
- ▶ Is somebody being unreasonable, or are you perhaps both just thoughtful people who disagree?
- ▶ Are you perhaps tempted to reexamine your initial ideas in response to what you've learned?

▶ *Let Us Show You:* **Stay on Track with Your Information**

Casey's last round of questions made him decide to do another focused free-write. The results are in the box below.

Casey's Second Freewrite — Plagiarism Project

OK. What do I know now that I didn't know when I did my first freewrite? Well, I know quite a bit more about what plagiarism actually is. Turns out it's not just deciding you're not going to write your own paper and that you're going to buy or steal one instead. Based on reading the definition of plagiarism in the student handbook, I'd have to say that plagiarism can be as minor as reading an idea, liking it, and saying pretty much the same thing in your own paper without mentioning that it was somebody else's idea. This makes me think that plagiarism is a lot trickier than it seemed when they explained it to us in high school. Also, it seems like it's not enough to acknowledge the source when you use someone's exact words — you have to put them in quotation marks. I didn't know that either. So, for example, if I used the definition of plagiarism from the handbook (or maybe even just a part of the definition? I should check on that!), and if I used exact wording from that definition, I would not only have to say where it came from but also have to put any exact wording in quotation marks. That's a little scary. I mean, what if by the time I write my paper I don't remember anymore which words in my notes are mine and which words are from the handbook? Well, maybe that's what all that picky advice about note taking was trying to get at. Anyway, I guess it turns out that my original opinion (basically, that anyone who plagiarizes is a dishonest loser) might not be quite as solid as I thought.

▶ *Talk Amongst Yourselves . . .*

Break into groups and discuss Casey's freewrite. Note that when you are evaluating freewrites, it's a really good idea to compare later efforts to earlier ones. How is Casey's second freewrite different from his first? To what extent does the second freewrite incorporate more information or less information? Is it more general or more specific? Is it more open ended or more focused? As a rule, which direction do you think would be more productive in moving forward with a writing task: from specific and focused to general and open ended, or the other way around? Why do you think this?

▶ *Now You Try:* **Prewriting — the Whole Shebang**

Consider how you would approach the following assignment. Note that we're not asking you to *write* the assignment — at least not right now. No, we simply want you to think about how you would *approach* it. In other words, how might you go about prewriting this assignment?

PRACTICE ESSAY ASSIGNMENT # 1

Write a brief essay (around three pages) that summarizes and responds to one of the two essays listed below. Both essays are available in Appendix C at the back of this book. Your summary should demonstrate your understanding of the key points of the text; your response should present your reasoned view of what is most significant about the text. In other words, your essay will explain for your reader what you think your chosen text *says* and what it *means*, as well as what *you think* about it. Due in two weeks.

- ▶ "Bad Feminist" by Roxane Gay (see page 492)
- ▶ "Serving Life for Surviving Abuse" by Jessica Pishko (see page 501)

It's possible that your professor will choose which of these essays you will write about — or perhaps assign a different essay — so listen up in class!

Once you've read the essay, go through the steps of the prewriting process presented in this and the preceding chapter. Undertaking these steps should help you move forward in this assignment, or at least give you new ideas for how you might do so. We think you'll find *all* of the steps useful, so don't skip any — and make sure you adopt a meaningful approach to the process, okay?

As a reminder, those prewriting steps include:

1. understanding the assignment (pages 50–55)

2. brainstorming (pages 55–60)

3. orienting yourself to your topic (pages 61–63)

4. focused freewriting (pages 64–66)

5. checking whether you're still on track (pages 66–71)

If you're anything like us — and you probably are — the last step will cause you to realize something very important: you will need to read your selected essay more than once. In other words, you will need to read *recursively*, as we discussed in Chapter 4. Don't panic. It doesn't mean there's anything wrong with you. On the contrary, when you discover the need to read a text again in order to understand it, then you're doing something very right.

And if you're not sure exactly how to go about achieving that deeper understanding of the text, don't worry: you can always go back and review Chapter 4.

Reality Check! Focusing Your Ideas

▶ Orient yourself to your topic by asking and answering questions about your thoughts and feelings.

▶ Freewrite until you discover some promising bits of content to explore further.

▶ Review your freewriting to make sure your topic is still on task with your assignment.

▶ Reexamine your method of information gathering to ensure that it meets your assignment.

Chapter 7

From Topic to Written Product: You *Can* Get There from Here

> The most fatal illusion is the settled point
> of view. Since life is growth and motion,
> a fixed point of view kills anybody who
> has one.
> — Brooks Atkinson

As we pointed out in Chapter 5, the writing process is like a journey. And we are of the opinion that it's an important journey that all thinking humans should undertake. Writing is exciting and challenging and can generate all sorts of wonderful ideas that might not see the light of day otherwise. In short, we think that engaging in the writing process on a regular basis will make you a better, more interesting person.

But just as important as that journey, in our view, is its destination.

You see, the process of writing may simply be the process of thinking on paper (or on a screen), but the *product* of that thinking — the *something* that appears on paper or on-screen — is tangible. It's the result, and results matter.

The Products of Writing

And so, dear reader, it is now time to talk about the *products of writing*: the texts that are created when writers engage in their writing processes.

Uh-oh. Did we just hear you gulp? We think we did. And we understand: the thought of moving from a bunch of cool but disconnected and only partially formed ideas bouncing around in your head (or on the page) to a finished manuscript that you can hand to someone who will not only read it but also (gasp!) take it seriously — well, gosh, it's heady stuff, this being a writer, isn't it?

Yes, it is, in a way — but only if you're always thinking about the end point of your writing journey (i.e., the destination of the finished, beautiful, elegant text). What most accomplished writers understand, though, is that there are many destinations along the path of the writing journey. If you keep your focus consistently on the next landmark in your journey instead of squinting way down the road at your final stop, you'll likely find that the components of the writing process — which together add up to the written product — are bite-sized and therefore achievable.

So what exactly is the next delicious little mouthful of process? We're so glad you asked!

At this point, you've gathered all sorts of input that needs to become output. You've *downloaded* a bunch of ideas — from inside and outside your head — and stored those ideas in a folder in your consciousness called "the writing project I'm working on." So far, so good. Now you simply need to *upload* those ideas into a new space (your assigned paper) and a new format (an essay).

How do you start turning input into output, or uploading what you've downloaded? You probably won't be surprised to learn that you do it primarily by thinking in a couple of very specific ways. Essentially, in order to begin the trek from process to product — from journey to destination — the ideas you have gathered and stored throughout the prewriting process need to undergo two minor operations: selection and organization.

Make *Yes, No,* and *Maybe* Piles

Selection is all about making decisions regarding which ideas will most likely make the journey with you and which ideas will be better served by sitting this one out. Before you can select from your ideas, though, it's important that those ideas exist in a way that can be observed, considered, and evaluated. This is why writers engage in the prewriting activities we've discussed in the past few chapters: so that they will have ample documentation — in the form of brainstorms, freewrites, working thesis statements, and so on — that they can then review when it's time to select the content that will eventually become a draft essay.

And how do you select that content? Well, we think it's best at this point to just accept the clutter of prewriting. No, wait. Don't just *accept* the clutter — *glory* in it.

Gather together all those pieces of prewriting: the handwritten notes on loose-leaf paper, the typed and printed musings, the sticky notes and cocktail napkins. For longer pieces, such as freewrites, you might want to physically separate the distinctly different ideas so that, for example, a single freewrite becomes three or four or five pieces of prewriting, depending on how many ideas ended up in the freewrite. Spread all the pieces out in front of you on a desk or a table or whatever surface works best for you; then pick up each piece separately, read it, think about it, and place it in one of three piles: *Yes, No,* and *Maybe.*

Yes, No, and Maybe Piles

The *Yes* Pile	The *Maybe* Pile	The *No* Pile
The *Yes* pile is for ideas that you're certain you want to use in your essay. These are the ideas that leap right out at you, screaming "Pick me!" because they're *just exactly right*. Not too many ideas go straight to the *Yes* pile, in our experience.	The *Maybe* pile is for ideas that you can't quite figure out what to do with but that still make sense on some level. They're somehow relevant, even if you can't really prove it right now. These are ideas you want to keep handy because they *might* pay off.	The *No* pile is for ideas that seem absolutely nonsensical to you — ideas whose creation you cannot remember, whose relevance cannot be determined . . . in short, ideas that seem to have come from another (not very interesting) planet.

Once you've created your three piles of ideas, take the *No* pile and set it aside. Put it away somewhere, but don't throw it away.

> Be sure to save the notes in your *No* pile; you never know when you might wake up and suddenly remember what you were thinking when you wrote some of them. Consider keeping them in a folder labeled "Unused Ideas."

Then put the *Yes* and *Maybe* piles together in a single stack. Yes, really. See, the best way to figure out whether some of your *Maybe* ideas are *Yes* ideas is to throw them into the *Yes* pond to see whether they sink or swim. And by "sink or swim," we mean whether they will be good companions for your *Yes* ideas for the duration of the journey.

Bring More Order to the Chaos

The best way to figure out whether any of your *Maybe* stuff is actually *Yes* stuff is to put some thought into **organizing your ideas**. But before you start hyperventilating over painful memories of being forced to write balanced sentence outlines with Roman numerals and a dizzying array of capital and lowercase letters in a predetermined pattern, relax. We aren't talking about creating a formal outline — not that there's anything wrong with formal outlines (we'll discuss them in some detail in Chapter 13, actually). For now, we are talking about organizing in a more holistic and less formulaic way.

To organize your ideas, simply take the pieces of paper from your new *Yes-Maybe* pile and start sorting them into separate piles again, this time based on which ideas seem more closely related to each other. It's okay to let your *Yes* ideas mingle with your *Maybes* — in fact, if this is happening, then you are probably in the process of discovering that at least some of your *Maybe* ideas are good enough to join Team *Yes*.

> Organizing holistically just means looking at the big picture rather than individual parts. See? Big words aren't always complicated.

If you're like us, you will probably end up with several new piles based loosely around **subtopics** of your overall essay topic. Each pile will represent a single subtopic for further exploration, so that you can ultimately decide which subtopics will end up in your draft.

If your subtopic pile has . . .		then you are probably looking at . . .
. . . two or three ideas that fit together		. . . a subtopic that will belong in your draft.
. . . more than three ideas that fit together		. . . more than one subtopic — so consider splitting the subtopic into two piles based on which ideas are more closely related to each other.
. . . one lonely idea all by itself		. . . either an idea that doesn't really belong, or an idea that needs further thought before you can determine whether it stays or goes.

At this point, you have taken a giant step in the journey from process to product. You have reviewed and considered the ideas you generated through prewriting in order to choose which pieces you will take with you into the drafting process. Note that you're not drafting yet — that will come soon. Right now you're just staking out your territory. You're right on the boundary between process and product. Isn't it exciting?

▶ *Let Us Show You:* **Organizing Your Ideas**

You may recall that at the end of Chapter 6, Casey had completed all of the prewriting tasks related to the paper about plagiarism for his Freshman Year Experience class. Now it's time for him to start moving from process to product. He has all of his prewriting materials: his notes about the assignment; his brainstorm about topics; both of his focused freewrites, which he has broken down into chunks; and his notes from the reality check. He's ready to make *Yes*, *No*, and *Maybe* piles.

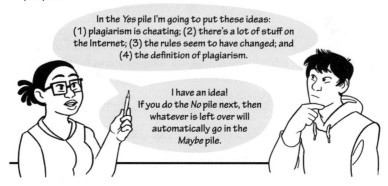

Mara's right. It's often easier, and more useful, to decide first what you definitely *do* want to use and then what you definitely *don't* want to use. After that, the remaining ideas automatically become your *Maybe* pile.

After sorting through his work this way, Casey realizes that at least two ideas belong in his *No* pile: the picky note-taking advice, and his discussion of how weird the word *plagiarism* is. Casey is left with a *Yes-Maybe* pile that includes eight ideas; with any luck, those ideas will make up the central content of his exploration into plagiarism.

Yes	Maybe
plagiarism is cheating	the difference between words and ideas
there's a lot of stuff on the Internet	the formal rules about quotation marks and such
the rules seem to have changed	the different types of plagiarism
the definition of plagiarism	how easy it is to plagiarize by accident

And now it's time to organize these ideas into subtopics, grouping together ideas that seem related. For one subtopic, Casey groups the definition of plagiarism with different types of plagiarism. For another, he puts the plagiarism-by-accident idea with his note about the difference between words and ideas, and for a third subtopic he groups the ideas about the Internet with the idea that the rules are changing. That just leaves the idea that plagiarism is cheating and the formal rules about quotation marks and such.

Organizing Ideas into Subtopics

The definition of plagiarism probably fits with the different types of plagiarism. And the plagiarism-by-accident stuff belongs with the words-vs.-ideas debate.

That leaves 3 ideas: that plagiarism is cheating, the Internet is changing and so are the formal rules.

They're all important. I'll keep them. The one about formal rules might be its own subtopic. But the cheating part seems to fit best with the definition section. Of course, the Internet changing relates to the rules changing.

Nice work, Casey! You've made it through the idea-organizing stage of the prewriting process. This means you've got several subtopics for your essay. Now it's time to —

▶ Talk Amongst Yourselves . . .

Find a partner in class and discuss Casey's decisions about selecting and organizing ideas for the draft plagiarism essay. How would you have sorted things differently into *Yes*, *No*, and *Maybe* piles? Once the ideas were sorted, how would you have grouped them differently?

▶ Now You Try: Organizing Your Ideas

Now it's your turn. Go back to the prewriting work you completed at the end of Chapter 6. Remember this assignment?

PRACTICE ESSAY ASSIGNMENT # 1

Write a brief essay (around three pages) that summarizes and responds to one of the two essays listed below. Both essays are available in Appendix C at the back of this book. Your summary should demonstrate your understanding of the key points of the text; your response should present your reasoned view of what is most significant about the text. In other words, your essay will explain for your reader what you think your chosen text *says* and what it *means*, as well as what *you think* about it. Due in two weeks.

- "Bad Feminist" by Roxane Gay (see page 492)
- "Serving Life for Surviving Abuse" by Jessica Pishko (see page 501)

You've already worked your way through understanding the assignment, brainstorming, freewriting, orienting yourself to your topic, and reality-checking your work. Now it's time for you to take the next step. Ready? Here goes:

1. Gather all of your prewriting materials for the assignment. Be sure to break your freewrites down into chunks based on separate ideas.

2. Spread your materials out in front of you on your desk.

3. Sort them into your three piles for *Yes, No,* and *Maybe* ideas.

4. Set aside the *No* pile, and combine the *Yes* and *Maybe* piles.

5. Sort the *Yes* and *Maybe* materials into new piles based on which pieces seem to fit together best.

When you're done, you'll have the makings of your first attempt at organizing subtopics for your draft essay. Congratulations!

What's that you say? You're not sure what to do with those makings? Don't worry! That's what the next section is all about.

The Controlling Idea

It will probably not surprise you to learn that between prewriting and drafting, there is a middle step. This middle step involves developing something called a controlling idea. *Wait,* you're thinking, *I need to do even more work before I can start drafting? Why, that's crazy talk!* Actually, no, it's not — and yes, you do.

See, the purpose of prewriting — that is, the purpose of all that talking and thinking and brainstorming and reading and note taking in preparation for writing — is to generate the ideas that you will need to have handy when you actually sit down to write. And ideas are great. But here's the thing: ideas, at least at first, tend to be cluttered and far ranging, even random. They don't always fit together in a systematic or rational way. Academic writing, on the other hand, *must* be both systematic *and* rational. So how do you corral your random, cluttered ideas into something that will ultimately lend itself to a single unified piece of writing? You do so by focusing those ideas around a plan, and that plan's success relies on a solid **controlling idea**, which is your sense of the main point you want to make in your essay.

The good news is that you're almost there already. Remember the work you did earlier in this chapter, sorting all of your ideas into *Yes, No,* and *Maybe* piles? That hard work has put you in a position where you are *this close* to articulating a working thesis. But first . . .

What *Is* a Thesis? And How Does It "Work"?

A thesis is a wonderful thing. Actually, it's a couple of wonderful things.

When we use the word *thesis,* we are generally referring to either a formal written argument in its entirety (as in a senior thesis or a master's thesis) or a single statement that articulates the central point of a piece of academic writing. In this chapter — and throughout this entire book, really — we are concerned with the definition of a thesis as a central point.

> Why does the word
> *thesis* mean "a central point?"
> Well, the Greek word *thesis* refers
> to soldiers marching, and more specifically to
> the motion of planting one's foot on the ground.
> So it's all about putting your foot down.

If we take the original meaning and implication of this term from classical Greek and apply them to our modern understanding of academic writing, we can see how the word *thesis* came to be used to identify the main point of an essay: a thesis is the place in the essay where you establish your step. It's where you take a stand. See how that works?

When you have completed a draft of a piece of academic writing, you will have presented a thesis: a clear and definite statement of what your main point is. But before you've completed that draft — when you're in that no-man's-land between thinking about your topic and writing what you think — you will have a working thesis, which is a thesis that is subject to change, just as a working title is a title that is subject to change, and working documents are documents that are subject to change.

THE WORKING THESIS

A working thesis is essentially a pre-thesis. It's the thesis that you start out with, an initial main point that gives you a sense of the central emphasis of the essay you're about to write. It's what you think, or suspect, the main point of your essay will be.

It's important to have a working thesis, but it's also important to acknowledge that it's a *working* thesis — that is, you need to understand that in all likelihood your thesis will change as you go about the process of drafting your essay.

Here is the distinction one more time, just to be clear:

▶ **A thesis** is the carved-in-stone central point of a completed essay.
▶ **A working thesis** is an initial, tentative, temporary central point on which a writer focuses when setting out to begin drafting an essay.

And why is the working thesis tentative and temporary? Because it's your first attempt at staking out the territory of your essay, your first time saying, *Hey, this is what I have to say in this essay.* And the chances are pretty good that, having not yet written your essay, you don't really know for sure what your point is. And that's okay. The writing process is a process of discovery — the more we write about a given topic, the better we understand our own thoughts about it. Increased understanding leads to changed opinions — and thus to a modified working thesis.

In our experience, many college students — especially those who were recently in high school — come to their academic writing assignments laboring under the misconception that they are expected or even required to have a firm thesis in mind before they begin a writing project. In fact, we have talked with students who believe they need to know for certain what their thesis will be before they even begin the prewriting process.

This notion, in our humble opinion, is nonsense.

A *thesis* ought to be a confident articulation of what you, the writer, understand to be the truth about a meaningful topic. A *working thesis* guides you as you move from your initial sense of what you believe your essay will be about toward greater understanding of the topic or issue you're exploring. To put it another way, a working thesis is a hypothesis.

> **Fun fact!** *Hypothesis* is a Greek word that means "lesser thesis." So a hypothesis can be viewed as a thesis in training, or a probationary thesis that's just waiting to be confirmed.

As you work on building that greater understanding, your hunch about your topic will change. Your original idea about what your point might be — your working thesis, or hypothesis — will change. As a writer is confronted with new ideas, or even with new ways of thinking about old ideas, that writer modifies his or her point of view. Opinions grow and develop as additional information takes root in the writer's mind and becomes knowledge.

So if you were ever under the impression that you need to know exactly what your opinion is before you begin a writing project, we would like you to wrestle your way out from under that idea right now. There's a term for people who cling to their original ideas no matter how much evidence suggests that they're wrong. Actually, there are several terms: stubborn, obstinate, pigheaded. Foolish, even. (Yeah, we know: harsh. And yet accurate.)

On the flip side, there are also terms for people who change their minds when they're confronted with evidence that suggests their initial opinions need adjustment: smart, thoughtful, reflective — these terms describe people who are curious and flexible in their approach to new ideas.

Ultimately, the reason to articulate a working thesis is to give yourself the opportunity to measure your thinking against what you *think* you're thinking — and to change your thinking accordingly. Or as E. M. Forster once put it, "How do I know what I think until I see what I say?"

We need to see what we've said in order to know whether what we've said is right or wrong. And that, dear reader, is the purpose of the working thesis.

CRAFTING THE WORKING THESIS

By now you have no doubt accepted wholeheartedly the importance of the working thesis. Good for you! *But,* you're thinking, *how do I actually, y'know, create one?*

As always, we're gratified that you asked — and we have an answer for you.

On your journey from prewriting activities to working thesis, it's important that you remember the recursive, tail-swallowing nature of our old friend the Ouroboros from Chapter 3 (page 24). Specifically, you need to realize that just as reading is best done recursively — that is, through revisiting and reconsidering ideas — so is writing.

To help you understand writing as a recursive process, it can be useful to think of the prewriting process as occurring in three stages that are similar to the three levels of recursively reading a complex text:

▶ **The first level of prewriting** is all about your own initial thoughts about — or responses and reactions to — the topic at hand. This level is very subjective: What do you think? What do you feel? This level of prewriting is covered in fairly significant detail in Chapter 5.

▶ **The second level of prewriting** is all about gaining access to more objective ideas by considering external information — through talking and listening, for example, but especially through reading. This level of prewriting is largely about understanding and analyzing texts, which is discussed in Chapter 4.

▶ **The third level of prewriting,** like the third level of reading, seeks to combine the subjective with the objective in a kind of synthesis — a melding of ideas into a single sophisticated and inclusive new idea that will serve as the focal point for your first draft.

The final level of prewriting manifests itself in the working thesis, which synthesizes your prewriting and takes the form of the best hunch you've got as you move from the prewriting process into the writing process.

To articulate that hunch, and thus write down your working thesis, we suggest you ask yourself a few specific questions, making sure to write down your answer to each one:

Reality Check! **The Working Thesis**

▶ What made you decide to write about this topic in the first place?

▶ What was your very first thought (or feeling or belief) about this topic?

▶ What's the most important thing you've learned about this topic since that first thought?

Once you've answered these three simple questions, see if you can combine your answers into a single sentence. This sentence will be your working thesis, and you will use it as a controlling idea when you begin the drafting process.

Your working thesis will help you track your discoveries as a thinker and writer while providing a crucial focus for the first draft of your text. Don't worry too much about whether you have a thesis worth carving in stone at this point. In fact, you probably shouldn't have one, since drafting is ideally a process of discovery — and working with something "carved in stone" doesn't typically lead to discovery. As long as your prewriting activities result in some thoughts that will help you keep yourself on task within the guidelines of your assignment, you'll be in great shape when it comes time to move on to the next stage of the writing process.

▶ *Let Us Show You:* **The Working Thesis**

Armed with the results of the prewriting activities in Chapters 5 and 6, Casey is now ready to create a working thesis. By combining his answers to the three questions in the *Reality Check!* box above, he can articulate a working thesis for his writing assignment. First, the questions, and Casey's answers:

The Working Thesis

▶ **What made you decide to write about this topic in the first place?** That's easy. Plagiarism was the one part of the academic dishonesty policy that I wasn't really sure about. It was intriguing, and I wanted to know more about it.

▶ **What was your very first thought (or feeling or belief) about this topic?** Also easy. I thought that only losers and cheaters would ever plagiarize a paper.

▶ **What's the most important thing you've learned about this topic since that first thought?** Hmm. Well, I guess I've learned that it's probably more complicated than I thought at first. It's really not the no-brainer that I originally assumed it was.

Now, here's Casey's first attempt at a working thesis for this Freshman Year Experience paper.

Working Thesis for Casey's FYE Paper #1

Although it's easy to think that plagiarism is something that happens only when a person decides to cheat on purpose, it's really a much more complicated subject with many different sides to explore.

▶ *Talk Amongst Yourselves . . .*

Break into groups and discuss Casey's thesis. In what ways might it lead to an interesting essay? In what ways might it be tough for Casey to produce a good essay from it?

The thing to remember about the working thesis is that it's a tool whose purpose is to give you a touchstone — a reminder of what it is that you think you're writing about.

Casey can refer back to his working thesis throughout the drafting process that comes next, which will help him keep his draft at least somewhat on track. Later, as the draft develops, the working thesis will change in order to accommodate the new and better ideas that pop up as a result of the discovery that happens in writing. This transformation will happen for Casey . . . and it will happen for you, too.

▶ *Now You Try:* **The Working Thesis**

Okay, remember the assignment on page 80?

Sure you do! You've already done the prewriting — or most of the prewriting — for this assignment. That occurred back in Chapter 6 when you worked to understand the assignment and then did some brainstorming and freewriting and reality checking. And that reality checking almost certainly led you to do more reading, which brought you to a closer and more reliable understanding of the primary text and perhaps of some additional texts as well.

You're *almost* done with the prewriting process. All that's left is the creation of your working thesis — your very own hypothesis. Simply answer the key questions from the *Reality Check!* box on page 85, just as Casey did:

1. What made you decide to write about this topic in the first place? (*Note:* If your assignment has specific guidelines and thus has left you with no wiggle room, then this question is less important.)

2. What was your very first thought (or feeling or belief) about this topic?

3. What's the most important thing you've learned about this topic since that first thought?

Then turn your answers into a single sentence. When you've done that, voilà! You'll have your working thesis.

Above all, don't panic. Nothing's carved in stone for now. But in Part 3, which focuses on drafting, things will get a little more concrete!

Reality Check! Are You Ready to Draft?

You'll know it's time to move to the drafting stage when

▶ you've created *Yes, No,* and *Maybe* piles that prioritize all of the ideas you've generated;

▶ you've evaluated which ideas fit together and brought some order to the chaos;

▶ you've identified a subtopic for each group of related ideas;

▶ you've carefully considered what all of your subtopics add up to;

▶ you've identified a controlling idea that covers all of your subtopics; and

▶ you've taken that controlling idea and crafted a reasonable working thesis.

PART 3
Drafting

Chapter 8

Draft and Draft Again:
Give Your Ideas Room to Breathe

I have never written anything in one draft, not even a grocery list, although I have heard from friends that this is actually possible.
— Connie Willis

We know, we know — not everyone thinks in terms of "first drafts," or "rough drafts," or even "drafts." Some writers are fully capable of blasting their way through a really rough draft — one that has a shaky beginning, a messy middle, and a frantic end — while others need to tinker as they go, adding, deleting, sharpening, and moving bits and pieces along the way, so that their first draft is really more like a second or third draft.

And you know what? It doesn't matter. Whether you're a blaster or a tinkerer, how you draft isn't any more important, really, than whether you draft at a computer or with a No. 2 pencil on a legal pad. What matters is that you actually write something that you recognize as a draft. Drafting is an important part of the writing process.

At this point you may be wondering, *Why a draft? Why not just leap to the end and create the finished product? You know, cut out the middleman?* We hear you. We recognize the desire to just knock out that essay in one sitting and have it be met with admiration and a big, shiny A from your professor for its sheer brilliance. We've even felt that desire ourselves on more than one occasion.

But here's the problem: it doesn't work that way. The notion that anybody — and we mean *anybody* — can sit down and create a solid essay without going through the process of drafting and revising is just magical thinking. It's a myth. And not the good kind, with gods and goddesses, but the kind where you stomp your feet and hold your breath and you still don't get a pony. If you're going to write an essay, you'll first need to engage in the drafting process.

Reality Check! Are You Ready to Write?

▶ You understand the assignment and know exactly what you are supposed to be doing.
▶ You have brainstormed a suitable and interesting topic.

(continued)

- ▶ You've done all of the thinking and information gathering necessary for the assignment.
- ▶ You've explored your thoughts through a discovery process such as freewriting.
- ▶ You've compared the work you've done to the original assignment and are on task.
- ▶ You've sorted through your prewriting materials in order to make some preliminary judgments about your *Yes, No,* and *Maybe* ideas.
- ▶ You have a central idea in mind — a working thesis — that you can focus on.

How to Begin a Draft

That checklist is all very well and good, you're thinking. *But it still doesn't tell me how to get there, does it?* You're right: it doesn't.

But you're in luck, because we happen to have a model process you can follow — a recipe of sorts that's designed specifically to get you from the end of your prewriting stage to the beginning of your drafting stage. And like all functional recipes, it begins with a list of ingredients.

Reality Check! Ingredients for the Draft

Before you start drafting, make sure you have the following:

- ▶ the text of the original assignment for reference;
- ▶ your initial brainstorming notes, diagrams, or doodles that helped you focus on a topic;
- ▶ all of your freewrites, including both those done before and those done after your reality checks and information-gathering expeditions (ideally you have already sorted these and your other prewriting materials into *Yes, No,* and *Maybe* piles);
- ▶ your working thesis;
- ▶ a computer or a pen and paper;
- ▶ a reasonably quiet space in which to work.

FIVE STEPS TOWARD A SUCCESSFUL FIRST DRAFT

Step 1. Reacquaint Yourself with Your Ideas: To begin the drafting process, we strongly suggest you read through everything: the assignment, your notes, your freewrites — all of the words you have on hand that might be relevant to the creation of the assignment. Let your ideas wash over you for a dedicated period of time — say, ten to fifteen minutes. Have someone time you, as in a freewriting exercise, so that you can just focus on your reading.

Step 2. Find the Significance: Next, write down three interesting truths that come to mind as a result of having read through your prewriting materials. Don't copy anything from those materials, however; instead, rely on what you remember from your reading. Let the significant ideas, or truths, bubble up in your mind. When they do, write them down.

Step 3. Identify Examples: After you've written down three truths, consider each of them in turn. Don't try to think about all three at once, but rather devote some time to each one individually. As you're thinking about each truth, try to articulate clear, specific details — that is, vivid, concrete examples of that truth. Write them down as precisely as you can.

> Don't rush the process of finding clear, specific ideas that articulate each truth. It might take a half hour or longer, but that's okay. You're starting to build the all-important middle of your essay.

Once you've developed your three truths in some detail, return to your prewriting materials to see whether you've missed any major ideas that didn't make the three-truths cut: there's nothing magical about the number three, after all, and if your notes suggest one or two more truths that you don't want to lose sight of, now would be a good time to articulate and develop any additional sections that might make their way into your essay.

Step 4. Look at the Big Picture: Once you're convinced that you have identified several important truths and that you have articulated them clearly and made them vivid for yourself through specific detail, then it's time to realize what you have in front of you: the raw material for several paragraphs that will make up the body of your draft essay. At this point you may have only the beginnings of paragraphs — just ideas with some detail, rather than complete paragraphs. But that's okay: you're still just leading up to your draft. (When you get to Chapters 9 and 10, you will learn all about the qualities, structure, and content elements of paragraphs.)

Step 5. Revisit Your Working Thesis: There's one more thing you need to do before you dive into the draft itself: read through your several paragraph beginnings, think about what you've just read, and ask yourself, "So what?" In other words, ask yourself what all of these ideas add up to. The answer to that question will be your new working thesis — a revised and sharpened idea of the point that you want to make, the central claim you want to support and defend in your draft. And by now you should have a pretty good idea of how to support that claim.

▶ *Let Us Show You:* **Beginning a Draft**

Casey has done a reality check regarding his readiness to write (following the *Reality Check!* boxes on pages 91–92) and is now ready to go through the five steps toward writing a successful first draft of his essay about the plagiarism policy.

Beginning a Draft

After reading through his notes (step 1) and identifying his three truths (step 2), Casey digs deeper to come up with vivid details and examples to illustrate those truths.

Truth #1 — Plagiarism is tricky: Even before the Internet existed, the notion of "original ideas" or "original information" was shaky. How many of our thoughts are actually original? Can we even know the answer to that question? Probably not. Information sharing is a huge part of what it means to be human. That is why people who live in the same region typically share a common language — so they can communicate and share ideas, even ideas as simple as "Hey, run away from that bear!" So as soon as language comes onto the stage (and none of us really remember a time before it existed), keeping track of whose ideas are whose becomes murky and problematic.

Truth #2 — Availability of information: Nowadays, everything that has ever been written is available at the click of a mouse, which is both a blessing and a curse. It's a blessing because we can look up anything we want anytime we want to. If I get curious about Jane Austen's life or squid fishing or whatever, I can research the topic endlessly online. All human knowledge is available to me, as long as I have a way to access the Internet. On the other hand, it's a curse because our culture, especially academic culture, hasn't changed to account for this information. The college's plagiarism policy is an example of this.

(continued)

Truth #3 — Plagiarism and dishonesty: Some of what gets called "plagiarism" in a college classroom today is totally acceptable in the real world. I'm not talking about going to one of those "Free Essays 4U" Web sites, downloading an entire essay, and passing it off as my own work. I'm talking about using other people's ideas in my writing. It's not fair to assume I'm cheating or being dishonest if I do that.

Next, Casey looks at the big picture (step 4) and revisits his working thesis by asking "So what?" (step 5). His new working thesis looks like this.

New Working Thesis for Casey's FYE Paper #1

In the age of the Internet, when everything that's ever been written is available to everyone on the planet at the click of a mouse, it doesn't make sense to accuse honest college students of plagiarism just because they don't cite the source of every word or idea that isn't original.

► *Talk Amongst Yourselves . . .*

Find a partner in the class and discuss Casey's ideas. Which of his three truths seems the strongest to you? Why? To what extent does the new working thesis seem to reflect the content of those three ideas? What might your answer to the "So what?" question have been after reading the product of Casey's three-truths exercise?

► *Now You Try:* **Beginning a Draft**

Go back to the assignment we gave you in Chapters 6 and 7: to write a summary and response essay. Gather all of your prewriting materials and, using our Five Steps Toward a Successful First Draft on pages 92–93, work through how you might develop those ideas into an entire essay.

Remember to use both of the checklists provided earlier in this chapter. The *Are You Ready to Write?* checklist in the *Reality Check!* box on pages 91–92 is designed to ensure that you've done enough prewriting. The Ingredients for the Draft checklist in the *Reality Check!* box on page 92 reminds you of what you'll need to have handy in order to write that first draft.

Of course, we *do* acknowledge the existence of a particularly nasty condition that afflicts some writers as they set out to draft: writer's block. This condition can keep even the best-intentioned writers from getting their work done when they allow themselves to be bullied by it. Fortunately for you, we're here to help. Read on!

Overcome Writer's Block

If you've ever tried to sit down and write a draft but found yourself paralyzed, we understand. Those palpitations you were having were the result of a particular strain of panic known as blank-page syndrome, more commonly called **writer's block**. Its symptoms include staring at the computer monitor until droplets of blood pop out of your forehead. Writer's block is the scary monster that keeps good, conscientious writers like you from buckling down and getting that draft done.

In our vast experience, writer's block happens as a direct result of one of four things: you haven't done enough prewriting, you're not quite sure what a draft is, you're trying to start at the beginning of the essay, or you're actually *afraid* to write.

Luckily for you, we have a few words of advice that we hope you will find useful and even comforting.

Anti–Writer's Block Strategy #1: Get Ready

The symptoms are unmistakable: you've sat down to write but honestly don't know what to say. You're unclear about the task, you're muddled about your ideas, and you're less than confident that your information will stand up to even rudimentary questioning.

The solution to this problem is simple enough: **do more prewriting** — more thinking, reading, talking, venting, plotting, and stewing — before you try to draft. Don't force it. Step away from the blank computer screen and no one will get hurt. Review the prewriting strategies in Part 2 (see Chapter 5), and come back when your ideas begin to have words attached to them. In other words, don't skip any of the items on the Are You Ready to Write? checklist (pages 91–92).

The first reason for writer's block? You haven't done enough prewriting!

Checking off everything on that list ensures that you're ready to move forward with achieving the first important function of the draft: moving from disjointed thoughts to coherent ideas by getting those thoughts out of your head and onto paper.

Anti–Writer's Block Strategy #2: Know What a Draft Is — and What It Isn't

Okay, when you know that you've done enough prewriting, it's time to move on to drafting. But what does that mean? We've been talking about drafting as a verb — a process — but what's up with the noun? What exactly *is* a draft?

A **draft** is a preliminary version of your essay, subject to revision. When you acknowledge that what you're writing is a complete but imperfect first attempt at your essay, you're doing two important things: you're committing yourself to getting the draft done, and you're admitting to yourself that what you're writing will get better. And what is a "complete" version of your essay, exactly? Well, it's a collection of paragraphs (more on paragraphs in Chapters 9 and 10) that has a beginning, a middle, and an end but that is still very much a work in progress.

> The second reason for writer's block? You're not quite sure what a draft is.

So you've completed your prewriting, engaging in some strategies to get you from random notes to focused composition. You've even learned about the value of drafting — that drafting gives you something to work with and improve on. Surely that means you're ready to draft, right? Wait — what's that you say? There's another reason for blank-page syndrome that we need to address?

Anti–Writer's Block Strategy #3: Start Anywhere!

By now you've done so much prewriting that you're afraid your head's going to explode. Beyond that, you've gone through the Five Steps Toward a Successful First Draft (pages 92–93), and you're pretty clear about what a draft is. But you say you're still having trouble getting started? Ah, we think we see the problem.

By trying to write your essay from the beginning, you're giving yourself a daunting challenge: to start writing in the same place your reader will start reading (the introduction).

Think about it: not only is there no rule that says you have to start at the beginning, but it doesn't even make sense to start writing with the introduction. After all, the purpose of the introduction is to let the reader know what the rest of the essay says, and you haven't written the rest of the essay yet. It is a paradox,

> The third reason for writer's block is that you're trying to start at the beginning. That seems like the most logical place to start. But actually . . .

like our friend the Ouroboros from Chapter 3. And frankly, when we try to start writing a draft at its beginning, we sometimes feel like we are trying to swallow our own tail.

The solution? **Start writing anywhere** — just pick a point or a subtopic that you have an idea about and start writing. It doesn't matter which point or which subtopic — our preference is to start with the one that's closest to the surface of our brain, the one that's trying to get itself onto paper. And when you've finished with that idea, start a new paragraph with the next idea that calls attention to itself. Later you'll organize and develop those paragraphs in a more reader-friendly way — and you'll go back and write your introduction — but for now the idea is to get the big ideas down in concrete form so that you can see what you've got. (You'll learn much more about introductions and other elements of essay structure in Chapter 14. Good things come to those who wait.)

Most first drafts are fairly messy. They include things that will probably not make it to the final draft, they're often missing at least a few small pieces that you'll need to add later, they present their ideas in an order that's not necessarily very logical or reader-friendly, and the paragraphs tend to be out of control. Don't believe us? You should see the first (or second, or third) draft of this chapter. What a mess!

Anyway, all of that disorganization is okay. Once you've got that big, messy, disorganized chunk of text in front of you, you can much more easily see what needs to stay, what needs to go, what needs to move where — in short, you have something with which to achieve yet another important function of the draft: providing a framework within which you can evaluate and organize your ideas effectively.

We hope that by this point you can see the benefits of the prewriting-to-draft steps above: they give you everything you need to take the drafting plunge. Go ahead. You're ready. You have ideas, details, a working thesis, plenty of notes, the broad outline of a structure . . .

Hey, what are you waiting for? Oh, of course — the final strategy for overcoming writer's block.

Anti–Writer's Block Strategy #4: Write Without Fear

It's important to recognize that drafting is **writing without fear**. This is why you need to put plenty of time into prewriting, by the way: there's not much that's scarier than trying to present your ideas to an audience when you have zero ideas. Once you have the ideas, then at least that part is no longer frightening. But you also need to be prepared to communicate honestly. You have to be prepared to tell the truth about whatever it is that you're writing about. And that can be a little scary, too.

The fourth reason for writer's block? You're a little . . . well, let's just say you're a bit *apprehensive* about writing.

But I'm not scared, you're thinking. *A little frustrated, maybe. Annoyed. Angry, even. But scared? Nah.*

But here's the thing: those emotions (frustration, annoyance, anger) are very often simply reactions to the underlying emotion of fear. And it makes sense that the writing process sparks at least a little fear in us: perhaps we're not sure that what we write will be good enough, or that we can handle someone reading it and giving us a response. In short, we're not sure we're comfortable with the risks that come along with preparing a text that will be made "public" in one way or another. In fact, research consistently shows that in general, people place public speaking higher than death on their list of fears. Seriously.

But as someone's dear old grandmother used to say, "No risk, no reward," and also, "You cannot win if you do not play." It's important to realize that the draft of an essay represents your opportunity to *take a shot at it*, to *give it a whirl*. (Remember when we told you that *essayer* means "to try" in French? Hint: Chapter 1!) What's the worst that can happen? If your draft stinks, at the very least you'll get a clearer sense of the difference between what you've accomplished so far and what still needs to be done. That's it. No one dies. No one even fails a course, or an assignment. And in fact, by confronting your fears and laughing at them, you've already won. So now is the time to look yourself in the eye and say, *Hey, you. Yeah, you — the smart one with all the ideas. It's time to take those ideas out for a spin.*

Writing without fear also means that when you're drafting, you **don't censor yourself**. Don't judge your ideas too harshly; avoid the little voice that's telling you, *Oh no, that idea's too weird*. If it eventually turns out that, yeah, that idea actually *was* too weird, you can always get rid of it when you revise.

For now, when you're drafting, all ideas that are relevant to the assigned task — or that even just seem relevant — are good. Keep them. In a very real sense, drafting is for you, the writer. It's your opportunity to put down in words everything that you think might be important in relation to your assignment. It's your chance to figure out what you think is true or significant.

The very best reason to just hunker down and get a draft done is that you won't really know what you think until you've seen what you've said. Remember what we said in Chapter 6 about writing being a process of discovery? The best way to make discoveries is to create a draft without censoring yourself. Remember that the paper you ultimately hand in may not be the same paper you started writing. In fact, it almost certainly won't be — as long as you're engaging in the process effectively.

When we finally read our drafts, we often discover something interesting: what we thought our essay was going to be about turns out not to be what we've actually written about. The controlling idea that we started with (the original working thesis) somehow got buried or shoved aside to make room for a new, more interesting idea that bubbled up while we were drafting; in other words, we revised the working thesis. And that's okay. It's not a sign of failure. Rather, it's a sign of success — a sign that your writing process is one of discovery and learning. This is good, as long as you use that discovery as a means of getting from your working thesis to your real thesis. And that discovery can happen only if you refuse to censor yourself while drafting.

▶ *Let Us Show You:* **Actual Drafting**

Casey feels confident about drafting his plagiarism essay. He's not afraid; he's promised not to censor himself or worry about what comes out in this round. Below is the result of his first effort.

Draft Plagiarism Essay (I still need a title)

The Grays Harbor College Code of Conduct posted on the college's Web site states that disciplinary action may be taken regarding *All forms of student academic dishonesty, including cheating; falsification; plagiarism; facilitating, aiding or abetting dishonesty or engaging in any conduct specifically prohibited by a faculty member in the course syllabus or class discussion.* There are consequences for all of the behaviors listed, including plagiarism. It makes sense that the consequences for cheating should be severe, but plagiarism is a bit more complicated. Merriam-webster.com defines plagiarize as "to steal and pass off (the ideas or words of another) as your own: use (another's production) without crediting the source" or "to commit literary theft: present as new and original an idea or product derived from an existing source." But are any ideas really "original" in this day and age? With an Internet with everything that's ever been written available at a mouse click, it's ridiculous to expect college students to have the source of every word or idea that isn't original.

Even aside from the Internet, how many of our thoughts are actually original? Not very many, probably. We share information and ideas without even knowing it. That is why people who live in the same area share a common

---

(continued)

language — so they can communicate and share ideas, even ideas as simple as, "Hey, run away from that bear!" So as soon as using language comes onto the stage (and none of us really remember a time before it existed), whose ideas are whose becomes confusing. Nowadays, everything that has ever been written is available at the click of a mouse, which is both a blessing and a curse.

It's a blessing because we can look up anything we want anytime we want to. If I get curious about Jane Austen's life or squid fishing or whatever, I can research it as much as I want on the Internet. All knowledge is available to me, as long as I have a way to access the Internet. On the other hand, it's a curse because our culture, especially academic culture, hasn't changed to meet the new availability of information. Grays Harbor College's plagiarism policy is an example of this lack of progress.

Academia has been slow to change, which makes sense because it is built upon this idea of "intellectual property." Professors at universities are hired partly because they will do research and create original ideas. But when you think about it, their ideas aren't original, because they learned from their professors. But that is actually kind of beside the point: college students aren't college professors, and that is not how people in the real world treat information these days.

Things get called "plagiarism" in a college classroom that don't in the real world. I don't mean going to one of those "Free Essays 4U" Web sites (also known as cheating). I'm talking about random facts or bits of information used as a way to back up an opinion or interesting interpretations of a poem — things like that. If I'm having a conversation with someone about a movie we both saw, and I also read an interesting interpretation of that movie somewhere, I might present that idea to my friend without including the source. I'm not being dishonest and trying to trick my friend into thinking I'm of above average intelligence; I'm just sharing an interesting piece of information from a source I probably don't even remember. The information itself is more important than where it came from. If it makes my friend see things in a new way, who really cares if it's my idea or someone else's? It should be the same in a college essay. As long as I'm using information effectively to make a strong point, it shouldn't matter whether I cite every single source for every single idea that isn't my own. Not only is that unreasonable, it's basically impossible.

And there you have it: Casey's first draft, complete with a beginning, a middle, and an end. Does this mean it's perfect? Of course not. But it does mean that the draft is ready for some review — that is, it's ready for someone else to take a look at it and give Casey some feedback. We'll talk more about review and revision in Part 4 (Chapters 12–15).

▶ *Talk Amongst Yourselves . . .*

Break into groups and discuss Casey's draft. How developed and organized are the paragraphs? How distinct and fleshed out are the beginning, middle, and end? How well does the draft incorporate the relevant ideas Casey generated through prewriting? How clearly stated is the thesis? If it were your job to help Casey move on to the revision process in order to create a stronger, better essay, what advice would you give him?

▶ *Now You Try:* **Actual Drafting**

And now, the moment you've been waiting for: it's your turn to achieve that preliminary version of an essay — that chunk of writing that has a semblance of an introduction, a recognizable body, and, at least theoretically, a conclusion as well. And the really good news? Now that you've slain the four-headed writer's-block beast, you have all the tools you'll need at your disposal.

Reality Check! **Slaying Writer's Block**

▶ Have you done enough prewriting? Do you have enough ideas to get started on your draft?

▶ Are you clear about what a draft is and what it isn't?

▶ Are you willing to start writing anywhere, rather than forcing yourself to start with the introduction?

▶ Have you set aside your fear and decided to just go for it?

Gather all of the prewriting materials you've created in response to your Practice Essay Assignment #1. In case you've forgotten the original instructions, they look like this:

PRACTICE ESSAY ASSIGNMENT #1

Write a brief essay (around three pages) that summarizes and responds to one of the two essays listed below. Both essays are available in Appendix C at the back of this book. Your summary should demonstrate your understanding of the key points of the text; your response should present

---

(continued)

your reasoned view of what is most significant about the text. In other words, your essay will explain for your reader what you think your chosen text *says* and what it *means*, as well as what *you think* about it. Due in two weeks.

- "Bad Feminist" by Roxane Gay (see page 492)
- "Serving Life for Surviving Abuse" by Jessica Pishko (see page 501)

Next, create a first draft of a multiparagraph essay, making use of the techniques that we've described and modeled throughout this chapter:

▶ ensuring that you've completed your prewriting

▶ gathering and reviewing your notes

▶ identifying the various truths that bubble up as you read your notes while thinking of your main idea

▶ choosing at least one specific detail to illustrate each of your identified truths

▶ asking yourself "So what?" (revising your working thesis)

▶ answering your own question without fear, without censoring yourself, and without worrying too much about whether everything's in the right order

Keep in mind that your goal is to write a complete draft (with a beginning, a middle, an end — and a thesis!) that makes sense to *you*. If at any point along the way you start to feel lost or overwhelmed by your task, just remember that you can keep yourself on track by referring back to the various *Reality Check!* boxes you've encountered in this chapter.

When you think you're finished with your draft, measure it against this checklist to see if it's really complete and ready for revision:

Reality Check! **Is It Really a Draft?**

- ▶ It's organized in several developed paragraphs.
- ▶ It has a fairly well-developed beginning, middle, and end.
- ▶ It incorporates most or all of the relevant ideas and information that you've gathered.
- ▶ It has a thesis statement to control its focus.

Don't sweat too much over the organization, beauty, and elegance you'll need in order to appeal to your reader ... *yet*.

Chapter 9

Successful Paragraphs: Don't Leave Home Without Them

> A sentence should contain no unnecessary
> words, a paragraph no unnecessary sentences,
> for the same reason that a drawing should
> have no unnecessary lines and a machine no
> unnecessary parts.
> —William Strunk Jr.

So what is academic writing made of? (Hey, now. We heard that, you in the back row, and that's not where we were headed. Ahem.)

First and foremost, academic writing is made of words, which are arranged into phrases and clauses and sentences.

If the mere mention of phrases and clauses made you break out in a cold sweat, remember that you can always head over to Appendix A for some help. Knowing where to look up reasonable explanations of unfamiliar concepts can keep those panicky feelings at bay.

But there's an important structural unit in an academic text that's bigger than a sentence and smaller than an entire report, paper, or essay. You guessed it: it's the **paragraph**. In an essay (the type of writing we're focusing on in this book), paragraphs serve a few purposes: they introduce the essay and present the thesis statement, they support the thesis statement, and they conclude the essay.

We all recognize a paragraph when we see one, right? It's a group of sentences that demonstrates its existence as a paragraph by being indented on the page or by being separated from the group of sentences above or below it by an extra line break. Right now, for example, you're reading a paragraph that is distinct from the paragraph before it and the one after it, and it's easy to recognize where one paragraph ends and another begins. In other words, paragraphs are pretty simple for readers. They're a little trickier for writers, however.

As writers, we may get stuck on the very first part of the definition of a paragraph: it's a *group of sentences.* Wait a minute. A group of sentences? What kind of group? How many sentences? Some people will tell you that a paragraph has to have at least three sentences, while others will insist that a paragraph must have four or even six sentences at minimum. Someone once told us that a paragraph has to have at least nine sentences, but we think that person was perhaps trying to bamboozle us. *So, you might be thinking, how many sentences must a paragraph really have?* The answer to that question depends on what the paragraph needs to achieve.

Bamboozle is a great word. It comes from an old Scottish word, *bombaze*, which means "to perplex" or "to fool."

We've seen good paragraphs that were one sentence long, and we've seen good paragraphs that contained twenty or more sentences. Most paragraphs have somewhere between, say, three sentences and . . . uh . . . nine sentences? The point here is that there is no firm rule about how many sentences to put in a paragraph. Instead, *form needs to follow function*: in other words, a paragraph should have precisely as many sentences as it needs to accomplish its goals.

The Structure of Successful Paragraphs

And what are the goals of a paragraph? Well, every paragraph has two goals. One is to give structure to a small idea (i.e., a subtopic) within a larger idea (e.g., an essay or a report). The other is to make good on whatever the writer has promised in the topic sentence.

TOPIC SENTENCES AND MAIN POINTS

What's a topic sentence, you ask? A **topic sentence** stakes out the territory of the paragraph. It introduces the paragraph's content and suggests what the writer's point of view will be about that content. It may or may not introduce the main point, as we'll explain in a second.

The topic sentence accomplishes for a paragraph what an introductory paragraph does for an entire essay — that is, the topic sentence prepares the reader for both the style and the substance of the rest of the paragraph. And just as an essay's introductory paragraph often (though not always) includes the essay's thesis statement, a paragraph's topic sentence often — but not always — expresses the **main point** that the writer wishes to make in the paragraph.

As we'll explain in more detail in Chapter 10, the main point of a paragraph in an academic essay is generally a **claim**. A claim is an arguable statement, which means that it requires support. So, for instance, "Many Americans have dogs as pets" is *not* a claim because it's not arguable. It's simply a fact that many Americans have dogs as pets. But "Dogs make better pets than cats" is a claim because reasonable people can reasonably disagree with it. It's arguable, see? (We'll talk more — a lot more — about the relationship between arguable claims and their need for support in Chapters 16 and 17.)

The terms we're using here — topic sentence, main point, claim — overlap a bit. Just remember that the topic sentence of a paragraph introduces the content of the paragraph. Sometimes, but not always, the topic sentence presents the main point. And in an academic essay, the main point of a paragraph is always a claim.

INDUCTION VS. DEDUCTION

The placement of the main point within your paragraph — just like the placement of the thesis within an entire essay (more on this in Chapter 14) — depends on whether your reasoning in the paragraph is inductive or deductive.

Inductive Reasoning

Induction uses particular knowledge to arrive at general knowledge. In the context of argumentation, the *scientific method* — observation, hypothesis, experimentation, interpretation, conclusion — is known as **inductive reasoning**. To *induce* is to reason from the particular to the general, to draw conclusions from specific knowledge of examples.

It's like this: think of all the sandwiches you have eaten in your lifetime (that number is in the thousands, in the case of your authors), and consider that each sandwich is a particular example of the general category we refer to as "sandwich." If, through your careful attention to every sandwich you have ever eaten, you conclude that sandwiches have two pieces of bread and something in between, then you have drawn a general conclusion from particular examples — in other words, you have engaged in inductive reasoning.

Having formulated a hypothesis based on observation, you have unwittingly begun to use the scientific (or inductive) method. Congratulations! You are a sandwich scientist.

"Having formulated a hypothesis based on observation" is a good example of starting a sentence with a modifying phrase. Students often have trouble doing this correctly. Read more about modifiers in Chapter 25.

The major problem with inductive reasoning (you knew there'd be a problem, right?) is the infamous $n + 1$ rule. The meaning of this rule for your sandwich hypothesis is that, no matter how many traditional sandwiches you've eaten, it takes only one double-decker club sandwich to force you to change that hypothesis. You'll learn more about problems with inductive reasoning in Chapter 18.

Deductive Reasoning

You may not be surprised to learn that **deductive reasoning**, as a process, is essentially the opposite of inductive reasoning. That is, it uses general knowledge (a principle, let's say, or an axiom) to arrive at particular knowledge (a conclusion about what a specific example will turn out to be). In other words, it begins with a general statement of what is known to be true about a certain class or category and then predicts that the same truth will apply to a particular member of that class or category. For this reason, it is also sometimes referred to as *philosophical reasoning*.

Imagine that instead of drawing general conclusions about particular sandwiches, you were to begin with your axiomatic knowledge that sandwiches have two pieces of bread and something in between. You take this general knowledge and use it to predict what would appear on your plate if you asked your mom to make you a sandwich. In this case, you would have reasoned from the general to the particular. This deductive process is most often represented in something called a **syllogism**, which lays out the relationships among the known truth, the specific case to be considered, and the conclusion.

> If you didn't quite get their meanings from the context, remember that you can look up words like *axiomatic* and *syllogism* in the dictionary. Knowing things is cool.

Reality Check! The Sandwich Syllogism for Deductive Reasoners

▶ **Major premise:** All sandwiches have two pieces of bread and something in between.

▶ **Minor premise:** My mom will bring me a sandwich.

▶ **Conclusion:** My mom will bring me two pieces of bread with something in between.

Drawing on your general knowledge about the characteristics of things that belong in the category known as "sandwiches," you make a specific and logical food prediction. Believe it or not, when you make that assumption about what your mom will make for you, you are using deductive reasoning. Congratulations! You are now a sandwich philosopher.

Of course, even the most carefully constructed deductive reasoning has some problems, the first of which is remarkably similar to the $n + 1$ problem. It's entirely possible that your dad has recently discovered the joys of the chicken-and-veggie wrap and therefore brings you one when you ask for a sandwich.

As you may have guessed, the most common problem with deductive reasoning is the tendency to treat a general truth as if it were absolute — as if the word *all* had been silently inserted into the statement (for example, "all sandwiches have two pieces of bread and something in between"). You will no doubt be overjoyed to know that other problems with deduction are presented in Chapter 18.

Structuring with Induction and Deduction

Again, both essays and paragraphs will sometimes make their main point up front, and at other times they will save the main point for later, depending on whether they are structured inductively or deductively. An *inductive structure* begins with a stated or implied question and then presents details that lead up to the main point. A *deductive structure* begins with the main point, either stated or implied, and then presents the details to validate that point.

> Now you know that paragraphs can be structured inductively or deductively — Guess what? So can entire essays. We'll talk about this in Chapter 14.

Whether it appears in an inductive or a deductive paragraph, a good topic sentence will adhere to a few guidelines:

▶ It will be of sufficient *scope* (it will be neither so broad that it can't be explored in a single paragraph nor so narrow that there's really no point in exploring it in a paragraph).

▶ It will be *precise* rather than vague or general.

▶ It will come *early* in the paragraph — ideally as the first sentence, unless your paragraph requires a transitional sentence to set up the point of the topic sentence.

▶ *Let Us Show You:* Topic Sentences and Structure

Take a look at this paragraph from earlier in the chapter:

> As writers, we may get stuck on the very first part of the definition of a paragraph: it's a *group of sentences*. Wait a minute. A group of sentences? What

kind of group? How many sentences? Some people will tell you that a paragraph has to have at least three sentences, while others will insist that a paragraph must have four or even six sentences at minimum. Someone once told us that a paragraph has to have at least nine sentences, but we think that person was perhaps trying to bamboozle us. *So*, you might be thinking, *how many sentences must a paragraph really have?* The answer to that question depends on what the paragraph needs to achieve. We've seen good paragraphs that were one sentence long, and we've seen good paragraphs that contained twenty or more sentences. Most paragraphs have somewhere between, say, three sentences and ... uh ... nine sentences? The point here is that there is no firm rule about how many sentences to put in a paragraph. Instead, *form needs to follow function*: in other words, a paragraph should have precisely as many sentences as it needs to accomplish its goals.

In this inductively structured paragraph, the topic sentence (the first sentence) stakes out the territory of the paragraph, while the main point (the second-to-last sentence) is saved for later.

▶ *Talk Amongst Yourselves . . .*

Take a few minutes to write down your responses to the questions below. Then break into groups of three and discuss your responses with each other.

What do you think of the structure of the paragraph from earlier in the chapter? Do you agree that it's inductively structured? How would it look different if it were deductively structured? Do you think that the paragraph works well with its main point deferred to late in the paragraph, or would it be better if the claim were presented first?

▶ *Now You Try:* Topic Sentences and Structure

Take a look at each of the sentences below and try to determine whether or not it would make a good topic sentence, based on its **scope** and **precision**. Think about whether it's likely that each topic sentence would also be the main point of its paragraph. In other words, consider which topic sentences would probably introduce a deductively structured paragraph and which would introduce an inductively structured paragraph. If you get stuck, refer to our discussion of induction and deduction on pages 107–9.

1. What is sacrifice, really, and how can we recognize it when we see it?

2. Most people assume that the American Civil Liberties Union (ACLU) consistently opposes the ideas of the National Rifle Association (NRA), but the two groups have some surprising commonalities.

3. In my experience, there are three kinds of movies: important works of art, pleasant diversions, and complete wastes of time and money.

4. Many novice barbecuers ruin their first attempt at a London broil, but here's an easy way to do it right.

5. The first time I took Chemistry 101, I failed it miserably — mostly because I foolishly thought the course would be easy and thus didn't take studying seriously.

6. If you want to understand how planetary orbits work, it helps to take a look at how a few planets in our own solar system make their circuits around the sun.

7. The recent willingness of Americans to become foster pet owners has resulted in many fewer abused and mistreated animals.

8. On the surface, Macs and PCs look quite different, but once you get going, you'll notice some very significant similarities between the two types of computers.

9. The first time I visited the temple at Karnak, I was struck by three things: the massive size of the columns, the intricate carvings on the walls, and the intensity of the colors that remain after all these millennia.

10. I will never forget the day that I learned for the first time that my father, like any other human, is capable of making a mistake.

THE BODY OF THE PARAGRAPH

If the goal of a paragraph is to fulfill the promise of its topic sentence, how do you go about crafting a paragraph that actually accomplishes that goal?

This is where the biggest part of the paragraph — the **body** — comes in. The body of a paragraph is the middle section, the part between the beginning and the end, and its job is to provide specific details that will make the reader nod his or her head while thinking, *Ah, yes, I see where you were going with that topic sentence! It all makes sense to me now!*

How do you write a body that makes the reader respond in this way? You do it by recognizing that readers expect to be shown and not simply to be told.

Think of it this way: a paragraph's topic sentence suggests to the reader what you, the writer, believe is true. But readers, like all humans, are skeptical; they won't believe you just because you say so. They want you to *show them what you mean in that topic sentence.* The body of your paragraph does that — it responds to the reader's need for specific details, examples, and illustrations that will help to fulfill the promise of your topic sentence and validate the believability of the main point (which may or may not be stated in the topic sentence).

▶ *Let Us Show You:* **The Body**

Here's another look at that inductively structured paragraph from earlier in the chapter:

> As writers, we may get stuck on the very first part of the definition of a paragraph: it's a *group of sentences.* Wait a minute. A group of sentences? What kind of group? How many sentences? Some people will tell you that a paragraph has to have at least three sentences, while others will insist that a paragraph must have four or even six sentences at minimum. Someone once told us that a paragraph has to have at least nine sentences, but we think that person was perhaps trying to bamboozle us. So, you might be thinking, *how many sentences must a paragraph really have?* The answer to that question depends on what the paragraph needs to achieve. We've seen good paragraphs that were one sentence long, and we've seen good paragraphs that contained twenty or more sentences. Most paragraphs have somewhere between, say, three sentences and ... uh ... nine sentences? The point here is that there is no firm rule about how many sentences to put in a paragraph. Instead, *form needs to follow function:* in other words, a paragraph should have precisely as many sentences as it needs to accomplish its goals.

See how the sentences between the topic sentence and the main point provide specific details about the numbers of sentences in a paragraph? These sentences comprise the body of the paragraph, and as such they help the reader to understand the relationship between sentences and paragraphs (topic sentence) as well as to agree with the writer that there's no firm rule about how many sentences belong in a paragraph (main point).

THE CLINCHER OR CLOSING STATEMENT

So we've talked about the beginning of the paragraph (the topic sentence) and the middle of the paragraph (the body). What's left? Oh, yes: *the end.*

Each paragraph must have a conclusion that ties up the paragraph's content in such a way that the path to the next paragraph is logically paved (assuming there is a next paragraph). Most body paragraphs — that is, most paragraphs that are neither the introductory nor the concluding paragraph of an essay (more on this in Chapter 14) — end with a **clincher**.

As important as what a clincher *should* do is what it should *not* do: it shouldn't introduce a new idea, go off-topic, ask a question (necessarily), or mindlessly repeat content already in the topic sentence or in the body of the paragraph.

▶ *Let Us Show You:* **The Clincher**

A clincher is typically a single sentence that not only brings its own paragraph to completion but also clearly points to the topic of the following paragraph, as in the example we've been examining throughout this section:

As writers, we may get stuck on the very first part of the definition of a paragraph: it's a *group of sentences*. Wait a minute. A group of sentences? What kind of group? How many sentences? Some people will tell you that a paragraph has to have at least three sentences, while others will insist that a paragraph must have four or even six sentences at minimum. Someone once told us that a paragraph has to have at least nine sentences, but we think that person was perhaps trying to bamboozle us. So, you might be thinking, *how many sentences must a paragraph really have?* The answer to that question depends on what the paragraph needs to achieve. We've seen good paragraphs that were one sentence long, and we've seen good paragraphs that contained twenty or more sentences. Most paragraphs have somewhere between, say, three sentences and ... uh ... nine sentences? The point here is that there is no firm rule about how many sentences to put in a paragraph. Instead, *form needs to follow function*: in other words, a paragraph should have precisely as many sentences as it needs to accomplish its goals.

See how the beginning of the clincher ties up the content of its own paragraph, while the end of the clincher prepares the reader for the following paragraph about goals? This is precisely what a good clincher in a body paragraph does.

Understanding basic paragraph structure is an important first step in crafting good paragraphs, but beyond this, it's important to recognize that good paragraphs consistently demonstrate some key characteristics that are essential to clear academic writing.

Paragraph Quality: Unity, Development, Organization, Coherence

While paragraphs need to have a relatively predictable *structure*, with a beginning, a middle, and an end (also known as topic sentence, body, and clincher), they also need to exhibit some essential *qualities*, or characteristics, to be successful. Structure is necessary — meaning you'll need to have structure in order to have a paragraph — but not sufficient to guarantee a paragraph's effectiveness. A truly effective paragraph exhibits the four essential qualities described below.

ACHIEVE UNITY

When a paragraph has **unity**, it is sharply focused on a single topic — it is, quite simply, unified. The words *unity* and *unified* come from the Latin *unus*, which means *one*. A good paragraph has one topic. And that topic is dictated by your topic sentence. One way to ensure that your paragraph has unity is to think of your topic sentence as an umbrella: it covers what it covers, and anything it doesn't cover is out of its territory. If all of the sentences in your paragraph are covered by your umbrella — that is, if they all fit within the territory staked out by the topic sentence — then they'll all be cozy and dry instead of sticking out and getting wet.

That may be a weird analogy, but you get the point, right? When you're checking your paragraph for unity, just look for any soggy sentences — sentences that don't directly relate to the topic sentence and therefore aren't covered by its umbrella — and remove them (or move them to a more appropriate paragraph) so they don't catch a sniffle. And yes, we're done with that analogy now. Thank you for your patience.

DEVELOP YOUR PARAGRAPH

We say that a paragraph is *developed* when it provides sufficient specific detail — examples, explanations, descriptions, and so on — to make completely clear what is meant by its topic sentence (and by the main point, if that's in a different sentence — for instance, if a paragraph is structured inductively and the main point comes at the end, as we discussed above).

Development is the main job of the paragraph's body sentences. Take the paragraph on unity on page 113 as an example. The topic sentence offers a definition of unity. But we realized that a simple definition probably isn't enough to help beginning writers achieve the goal of unity for themselves. So we followed the definition with some explanation involving the root meaning of the word *unity*.

But then we thought, *The Latin thing might not be enough.* So we proceeded to share with you a descriptive example (the umbrella analogy) in the hope that perhaps a familiar visual image might help to clarify the concept. In the end, we felt fairly confident that the idea of unity had been presented with sufficient development to allow you, dear reader, to understand what was meant by our topic sentence.

ORGANIZE YOUR PARAGRAPH

The lucky paragraph that is well organized is one written by an author who has a plan and sticks to it.

The plan for a paragraph has to do with its **organization**, or order. If, for example, your paragraph analyzes a **process**, then it should present its points in chronological or sequential order — moving through time, or through steps, from beginning to end. A paragraph outlining a process that begins in the middle and then jumps backward before leaping ahead to the end would likely be confusing — it would be disorganized. A paragraph that starts at the beginning of the process and moves through a series of steps before concluding appropriately at the end is much more likely to be clear and meaningful.

Paragraphs with other purposes (telling a story, defining a term, making a comparison, etc.) will make use of other orders. The important thing for achieving an organized paragraph is that a plan exists and that the writer follows it: from beginning to end, from left to right, from top to bottom, from simple to complex, from least important to most important, from general to specific, and so on. There are many ways to organize a paragraph (see the discussion of different modes of rhetoric in Chapter 11); the important point here is that you must have an identifiable system for ordering your ideas.

ACHIEVE COHERENCE

The fourth and final characteristic of a good paragraph is **coherence**, which comes from the Latin *cohaerere*, meaning "to hold together."

The quality of coherence makes a paragraph hold together logically and reasonably. It's not enough that all of the sentences in a paragraph are about the same topic (this is *unity*) or that the paragraph provides plenty of specific details (this is *development*) or that the sentences appear in a planned order (this is *organization*) — these three qualities are necessary but not sufficient to make the paragraph successful.

For the paragraph to succeed, all of the sentences also need to fit together so that they represent a smooth progression of ideas. Each sentence needs to lead to the next one in a way that makes sense. We think one of the best ways to understand paragraph coherence is to look at an example of some paragraphs that don't have it. Perhaps you will remember this chunk of text from Chapter 6:

> We'd like to introduce you to a sassy little technique called **focused freewriting**. It's a level of idea generation, a step up from brainstorming. It's much more focused than brainstorming. Instead of generating individual words and phrases, freewriting will provide you with longer, more developed ideas. Brainstorming is *jotting*. Freewriting is *writing*.
>
> The basic idea behind freewriting is that you start with a single focused question from your brainstorming activities, set a timer for, say, five minutes, and start writing everything that comes into your head. Don't stop writing until the timer goes off. Take a moment to clear your head, get out a fresh sheet of paper (or scroll down to a new page), and set the timer to five minutes again. Move on to the next question.
>
> You will have recorded a wealth of raw material that you can potentially use as a starting point for the first draft of your written product. We're not saying that your freewriting is your first draft. It's not. It's likely to contain some nuggets of good, interesting writing that you can build on.

Please keep in mind that these sample paragraphs *lack coherence*. In other words, they are not very good paragraphs. In fact, they are BAD paragraphs. There. We said it.

Do you see what we did in that passage from earlier in the book? We tricked you.

The excerpt isn't *exactly* the same as what you read in Chapter 6; we removed some important words and phrases from it. This version has *unity* (it's all about the process of freewriting); it is *developed* (it provides several specific examples, explanations, and descriptions); and it's *organized* (it uses a chronological presentation of the steps involved in the process). But it lacks coherence. It doesn't progress smoothly. The sentences don't make logical sense because we have removed the **transitional words and phrases** that clearly show the relationships between ideas. As a result, these paragraphs are not as successful as they could be.

One of the best ways to improve the coherence of *an otherwise reasonable paragraph* (that is, a paragraph that is otherwise unified, developed, and organized) is to link its ideas together using clear transitional words and phrases. See if you think the following version of the Chapter 6 excerpt is better. (Note that this is the *actual* text from Chapter 6, with the transitional words and phrases highlighted in blue.)

At this point, we'd like to introduce you to a sassy little technique called **focused freewriting**. It's another level of idea generation — one that's a step up from brainstorming, for two reasons: first, it's much more focused than brainstorming; and second, instead of generating individual words and phrases, freewriting will provide you with longer, more developed ideas. In other words, brainstorming is *jotting*, but freewriting is *writing*.

The basic idea behind freewriting is that you start with a single focused question from your brainstorming activities. With that question in mind, set a timer for, say, five minutes, and start writing everything that comes into your head. Don't stop writing until the timer goes off. Once it does, take a moment to clear your head, get out a fresh sheet of paper (or scroll down to a new page), set the timer to five minutes again, and move on to the next question.

What you'll find is that after just a half hour, you will have recorded a wealth of raw material that you can potentially use as a starting point for the first draft of your written product. Note that we're *not* saying that your freewriting is your first draft. It's not. But it's likely to contain some nuggets of good, interesting writing that you can build on.

We hope you'll agree that the added transitional words and phrases give the reader important information about how the ideas fit together and about why those ideas are included in the first place.

▶ *Let Us Show You:* **Paragraph Structure and Quality**

Casey has decided to practice paragraph writing by pulling a chunk of content from the second plagiarism-project freewrite that you saw in Chapter 6. Below is his raw material.

> What do I know now that I didn't know when I did my first freewrite? Well, I know quite a bit more about what plagiarism actually is. Turns out it's not just deciding you're not going to write your own paper and that you're going to buy or steal one instead. Based on reading the definition of plagiarism in the student handbook, I'd have to say that plagiarism can be as minor as reading an idea, liking it, and saying pretty much the same thing in your own paper without mentioning that it was somebody else's idea. This makes me think that plagiarism is a lot trickier than it seemed when they explained it to us in high school.

Step 1: Identify a topic sentence. Casey's main point, which comes last in the chunk of freewriting, also makes a good topic sentence. So his paragraph will be deductively structured. He moves the main point to the top of the paragraph and makes it his topic sentence (highlighted in blue).

Plagiarism is a lot trickier than it seemed when they explained it to us in high school. What do I know now that I didn't know when I did my first freewrite? Well, I know quite a bit more about what plagiarism actually is. Turns out it's not just deciding that you aren't going to write your own paper and that you're going to buy or steal one instead. Based on reading the definition of plagiarism in the student handbook, I'd have to say that plagiarism can be as minor as reading an idea, liking it, and saying pretty much the same thing in your own paper without mentioning that it was somebody else's idea.

Step 2: Provide unity, development, and organization. Casey now needs to develop, unify, and organize his paragraph. For unity, he cuts the sentence that doesn't belong. For development, he adds a sentence about cheating and also a clincher (underlined). Finally, he moves two sentences around for the sake of organization (highlighted).

Plagiarism is a lot trickier than it seemed when they explained it to us in high school. ~~What do I know now that I didn't know when I did my first freewrite?~~ Turns out it's not just deciding that you aren't going to write your own paper and that you're going to buy or steal one instead. I thought it was simply about cheating. ~~Well,~~ I know quite a bit more about what plagiarism actually is now. Based on reading the definition of plagiarism in the student handbook, I'd have to say that plagiarism can be as minor as reading an idea, liking it, and saying pretty much the same thing in your own paper without mentioning that it was somebody else's idea. Plagiarism can be a problem for honest writers as well as for cheaters.

Step 3: Provide transitions. Transitions help paragraphs to achieve coherence, so Casey inserts phrases between ideas that more clearly show how they're related to each other (highlighted in blue). They make his paragraph much more coherent — in his humble opinion.

Plagiarism is a lot trickier than it seemed when they explained it to us in high school. Back then, I thought plagiarism was just deciding that you weren't going to write your own paper and that you were going to buy or steal one instead. In other words, I thought it was simply about cheating. But now that

I'm in college, I know quite a bit more about what plagiarism actually is. Based on reading the definition of plagiarism in the student handbook, I'd have to say that plagiarism can be as minor as reading an idea, liking it, and saying pretty much the same thing in your own paper without mentioning that it was somebody else's idea. Finally I get it: plagiarism can be a problem for honest writers as well as for cheaters.

► **Talk Amongst Yourselves . . .**

Find a partner in class and discuss Casey's work. To what extent does each step in the process add to the paragraph's effectiveness, and why is that the case? Compare the last paragraph to the original chunk of text from the freewrite. Which is stronger? Why? And how?

► **Now You Try: Paragraph Structure and Quality**

Take a chunk of content from one of your freewrites you did in preparation for Practice Essay Assignment # 1 — ideally, one of the *Yes* or *Maybe* ideas that you identified in Chapter 7 — and, following the same steps that Casey employed above, create a single paragraph that meets the following criteria:

1. It has all necessary components (topic sentence, body, clincher) and is clearly either inductively or deductively structured.
2. It achieves unity, development, and organization.
3. It achieves coherence through the use of meaningful transitions.

   Don't forget to show your paragraph to your instructor, or at least to a classmate, so that you can get some feedback on its effectiveness.

Reality Check! **Paragraph Structure and Quality**

Is your paragraph structured well?

- ► Does it have a clear topic sentence?
- ► Is it organized either inductively or deductively according to its needs?
- ► Does it have an effective body that supports the main point?
- ► Does it end with an effective clincher?

Is your paragraph of high quality?

- ► Is it unified around a single topic as presented in your topic sentence?
- ► Is it fully developed?
- ► Is it organized meaningfully?
- ► Are its ideas connected to each other coherently?

Chapter 10

Analytical Paragraphs:
A College Student's Best Friend

> The ultimate authority must always rest
> with the individual's own reason and critical
> analysis.
> —The 14th Dalai Lama

Now that you know how to recognize the components of a good, solid paragraph, it's time to learn how to write the type of paragraph you most likely will be writing throughout your college career: the **analytical paragraph**.

We can't overstate the importance of learning to write a good analytical paragraph. The analytical paragraph is the cornerstone of the academic essay — in fact, *every* paragraph in a scholarly paper (with the possible exception of the introduction and the conclusion) needs to be analytical.

> The word *analysis* comes from ancient Greek
> (and is the root word of *analytical*). Aristotle, the famous
> philosopher, used to talk about analysis all the time. It means
> breaking something that is complex into simple elements so that
> we can understand it better.

Most paragraphs in academic writing should be analytical in both purpose and structure. What does that mean? It means that every analytical paragraph — that is, every body paragraph in an essay that requires analysis — needs to use a *cycle of development*: a five-part process that includes a claim, context, evidence, analysis, and synthesis. A bare-bones outline of an analytical paragraph for any academic purpose would look like this in comparison to what you already know about paragraph structure:

Claim	Topic sentence
Context Evidence Analysis	Support & development
Synthesis	Clincher

When all of these elements are presented in a reasonable order, with enough specific detail, the result is a unified, developed, organized, and coherent paragraph.

Sounds simple enough, doesn't it? Actually, it *is* fairly simple. Elegant, even. And not really all that difficult, assuming you've spent sufficient time prewriting before trying to draft your paragraphs. If you *haven't* been doing your prewriting as we suggested throughout Part 2 of this book, then first of all, *tsk tsk*. And second, go back to Chapters 5, 6, and 7 to generate some good ideas before we move on. Go ahead. We'll wait.

Are you ready with your ideas now? Perfect.

We think the outline of the analytical paragraph that we've provided above is a good start. But we probably shouldn't leave it at a bare-bones outline. Explaining what we mean in a bit more detail might be useful.

The Claim

The **claim** is your main point, your arguable statement. As we discussed in Chapter 9, the claim might be the topic sentence of your paragraph, or it might come later if you're structuring the paragraph inductively. Remember that your claim should be fairly narrow (as opposed to the breadth of your thesis) because it is designed to carry the weight of only a single paragraph. It is, in a very real sense, the thesis of this one paragraph.

For example, let's say that we have decided to write an analytical paragraph in response to a cartoon by Roz Chast (see p. 122), whose work often appears in the *New Yorker* magazine. The first thing we'll need to do is read the cartoon recursively. You remember recursive reading, right? When you return to a text and read it again and again? We talked about it in Chapter 4? Well, what you learned about giving a complex text three readings is also true of "reading" other forms of communication, like cartoons. So we'll read Chast's cartoon three times: to allow ourselves an initial, subjective response, to examine the cartoon objectively in order to see how content is shaped by form (for a refresher on this idea, see pp. 41–42 in Chapter 4), and to combine our subjective and objective ideas into a reasonable interpretation of the meaning of the cartoon.

After much careful consideration of the cartoon's meaning, we have decided that we want to *analyze* and *comment on* the way Chast approaches her audience (people who have smartphones). With a light touch, she gets the audience to see a reflection of their dependency on their phones through the ridiculous apps in the cartoon. Our overall response to the cartoon is something like this:

> At first glance, Roz Chast's "myPhone" cartoon appears to be poking fun at people who are too dependent on their smartphones. However, upon closer inspection,

it's actually about *all* of us who use smartphones, and the extent to which we consider our phones to be almost an extension of ourselves.

Notice, by the way, that this claim is two sentences long. It doesn't have to be: many claims are a single sentence, while some are longer. In this case, we went for two sentences because our main idea is about the difference between what the cartoon seems to be at first and what our later interpretation turns out to be. (You can read more about crafting a good, supportable claim in Chapter 16.)

► *Let Us Show You:* **The Claim**

Mara has decided to practice these new skills by writing a fully developed analytical paragraph in response to Jonathan Swift's "A Modest Proposal." You may recall that Mara and Casey read Swift's famous essay three times (recursively!) back in Chapter 4. On the off chance that you didn't read it along with them six chapters ago, remember that the essay is presented in the reader at the back of this book. (You *could* read it now.)

At the end of Chapter 4, Mara wrote a brief summary and review of Swift's essay. She also developed an interpretation of the essay's meaning. Since interpretations of meaning are always arguable, this interpretation might make a good main claim for an analytical paragraph.

Step 1: The Claim	In Jonathan Swift's "A Modest Proposal," there's a difference between the author and the narrator he created.

▶ *Talk Amongst Yourselves . . .*

With a partner or in a small group, discuss Mara's claim. Is it truly an arguable statement? How could it be stronger? How could it be clearer? Do you think her claim is rich enough in ideas that an entire paragraph could be developed in support of it? Why or why not?

▶ *Now You Try:* **The Claim**

Guess what? You are *also* in a position to write an analytical paragraph in response to a text. As Mara was reading "A Modest Proposal" recursively, *you* were recursively reading Michael Byrne's "The Deep Sadness of Elk That Don't Run." In this chapter, Mara will go through each step in the development of an analytical paragraph — and so will you! So grab the notes you took on Byrne's essay at the end of Chapter 4, and let's get started.

The last thing you wrote back at the end of Chapter 4 was a statement summing up *what* you think Byrne's essay means and *how* you know that's what it means. Working from that statement, craft a single sentence that could serve as the claim for an analytical paragraph about the essay.

The Context

At this point, you probably will not be surprised to learn that the **context** is the setting for your paragraph — it clarifies the relationship between the territory of your claim, the territory of the evidence to come, and the territory of your entire essay. This is where you provide your reader with your GPS coordinates within your topic: when and where and under what circumstances will you be able to support this claim? The context is also the place for any necessary definitions or clarification of terms.

For example, let's say that we have just stated the claim on pages 121–22 about Chast's cartoon. We realize that we need to get the reader on the same page as us before we'll be in a position to present the evidence that validates the claim — in other words, we need to put our claim in a helpful context. Since our claim is about smartphones and how so many of us see them as extensions of ourselves, we might write something like this next:

> The apps on the "myPhone" externalize the kinds of thoughts we all have by handing them over to a smartphone to deal with.

See how the context explains our claim a bit more fully and provides a definition of what we mean when we talk about smartphones? The reader is now ready to see our evidence — the specific examples taken from the cartoon itself that will demonstrate that our claim is reasonable.

▶ *Let Us Show You:* **The Context**

Now Mara needs to put her claim about Swift's essay into a context that will help the reader understand the territory that the paragraph will cover in relation to that claim. Often, it's a good idea in the *context* section of the paragraph to define any terms that might be unfamiliar to the reader.

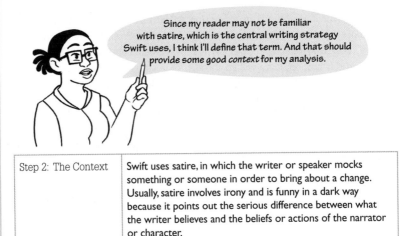

Since my reader may not be familiar with satire, which is the central writing strategy Swift uses, I think I'll define that term. And that should provide some good *context* for my analysis.

Step 2: The Context	Swift uses satire, in which the writer or speaker mocks something or someone in order to bring about a change. Usually, satire involves irony and is funny in a dark way because it points out the serious difference between what the writer believes and the beliefs or actions of the narrator or character.

▶ *Talk Amongst Yourselves . . .*

Within your small group, discuss Mara's definition of satire. How could it be improved? Why is it necessary in the paper? How useful is it to Mara in furthering her argument?

▶ *Now You Try:* **The Context**

Take a good, long look at the claim you developed about the meaning of Michael Byrne's essay. What are its components? What terms are you using that might need to be put into context for the reader? What reasons do you have for your interpretation of Byrne's essay? In a sentence or two, provide some context for your reader, so that he or she will be able to move smoothly from your claim to your evidence — which *we* will do in 3 ... 2 ... 1 ...

The Evidence

The **evidence** in an analytical paragraph comprises the specific details you choose to employ as direct support of your claim(s). When you're using a quote from a source as textual evidence, the quote should be brief (generally less than a complete sentence), and it must be integrated into your own sentence by way of a phrase that indicates what the quote is doing in your paragraph. It's best if this signal phrase makes use of an active and meaningful verb. (You can read more about evidence in Chapter 17, and more about integrating source material in Chapter 21.)

For example, after stating our claim about Chast's "myPhone" cartoon and then providing some context for that claim, we would next examine the cartoon's content and form in specific detail to determine which elements seem to best support (or validate) our interpretation. At first, we might just list those pieces of evidence, which could consist of any of the apps in the cartoon, such as these two:

"FatSpec: Am I fat?"

"Personfeel: How does (name) really feel about me?"

However, realizing that we cannot simply insert a bullet list into the middle of a paragraph as if that would take care of our obligation to support our claim, we instead focus on **integrating** the most interesting details into our own sentences using active and meaningful verbs:

Each app is devoted to a different example of the types of issues we all secretly worry about from time to time. For instance, "AgeMeter" covers the question "How old do I look?" while "LifeQues" deals with the question "What is the meaning of life?"

▶ *Let Us Show You:* The Evidence

Now that Mara has set the contextual stage for the heart of her interpretive argument, it's time to pull out the big guns: the evidence. For this part of the paragraph, she will "mine" Swift's essay to find specific examples that will help to support (or validate) her claim.

> To locate evidence, I had to look at the very end of the essay. That's where Swift lets his *real* opinion show through the mask of his horrible persona.

Step 3: The Evidence	For example, Swift writes that "a young healthy child … is a most delicious, nourishing, and wholesome food," but he later says, "let no man talk to me of other expedients" such as "taxing our absentees" or "using neither clothes nor household furniture except what is of our own growth and manufacture."

▶ *Talk Amongst Yourselves . . .*

Within your small group, discuss Mara's evidence. Are the quotes well suited to proving the paragraph's claim? To what extent are they reasonable, well-chosen examples of what Mara's claim is talking about? How effective is the context as a lead-in to the specific pieces of evidence cited?

▶ *Now You Try:* **The Evidence**

Go back to your notes about Byrne's essay, and review the entire text of the essay again, this time looking for the specific words and phrases that you believe are particularly good examples of what you're referring to in your claim. Then write a sentence — or two or three sentences, depending on how many interesting pieces of evidence you found — in which you present those examples as direct support of your claim. Be sure to actually *write your own sentences* containing Byrne's words and phrases — and put the author's words in quotation marks, as Mara has carefully done with Swift's words. (In Chapter 21 you will learn a lot more about integrating other people's writing into your own sentences ethically.)

The Analysis

The **analysis** is the part that most beginning student writers skip because they don't know about it, so listen up.

See, many students think that evidence speaks for itself — but it really doesn't. Why? Because academic writing is all about interpretation, and therefore it's about how you perhaps understand your topic differently from how others understand it. To analyze something, you take it apart in order to understand it. Your task in the analysis portion of the paragraph is to "unpack" your evidence by discussing both *how* and *why* it supports your claim.

It is always a mistake to believe that the reader will find an interpretation convincing based simply on your throwing a piece of evidence at a claim — even a claim that has been placed in a clear and reasonable context. Unexplained evidence will always mean exactly what the reader is predisposed to believe it means. That's why you have to explain what *you* mean.

For example, after identifying our claim about Chast's cartoon, putting it in context, and backing it up with evidence from our observations, we realize that we're not finished yet. We need to let the reader in on our thought process so that our reasoning will be clear and satisfying. In an attempt to create that clear, satisfying discussion, we might write something like this:

> The cartoon is funny for two reasons: the "myPhone" apps claim to help us answer questions that often don't have a simple answer (or perhaps any answer at all), but they are also examples of "navel gazing" at its worst. How narcissistic would it be to have a phone full of apps that allow us to deal only with the minutiae of our own lives? When we step back and actually look at the apps on our smartphones, most of us realize that many of our apps already fit that description.

Note that the analysis is often the longest section of a paragraph in an academic essay. This is because explanations need to be logical and complete for the argument ultimately to be compelling. It's important to share at least some of your thought process with your readers so that they can follow along without getting lost. (We'll talk more about logic in Chapter 16. And in Chapters 17 and 18. Logic is important.)

Another reason that the analysis is longer than other elements in the paragraph is that the process of analyzing — that is, the process of breaking down one's thought process and sharing it with a reader — almost always involves including additional evidence or examples to further develop the analysis. The different ways a person can "navel gaze," for example, were added to the analysis because they help to explain our interpretation of Chast's cartoon as well as her audience. This practice — explaining how different pieces of evidence are related to each other — is the cornerstone of logical academic analysis.

▶ *Let Us Show You:* **The Analysis**

The analysis may seem like the hardest part of writing a paragraph, but it is also the most interesting. After all, it's where you get to explain to the reader *why* you think what you think, or *why* you believe the evidence does a good job of backing up your claim. This is the part of the paragraph where you really get to discuss your topic. Here is Mara's analysis of the Jonathan Swift essay:

Step 4: The Analysis	Swift pretends to be a heartless rich guy who wants to solve the problem of poverty in Ireland by treating Irish babies as food and their mothers as breeding livestock. This is why he talks about "delicious" baby meat. But we know that the narrator is a character, and not Swift himself, when Swift ends his essay by providing a whole list of reasonable solutions to Irish poverty, like raising taxes on the rich and buying locally made products.

► **Talk Amongst Yourselves . . .**

Get together with your group and discuss Mara's analysis of the evidence. How effective is it? To what extent do the explanations Mara has provided help you to understand how the evidence is intended to support the claim that she began with? How clear is her reasoning to you? What questions are still left unanswered for you? Do you find yourself convinced by Mara's analysis? Why or why not?

► **Now You Try: The Analysis**

Now's your chance to really show your reader what you've got. You've presented your claim about "The Deep Sadness of Elk That Don't Run," so the reader knows what you think the meaning of the essay is. You've put that claim into context, so the reader knows the territory you think you're covering in this paragraph. You've even provided specific examples (evidence) of what you're talking about in your claim. But what if the reader doesn't think the way you do? Just in case, you should probably do as Mara has done, and *explain yourself.*

Take as long as you want — two sentences, three, five, whatever it takes — and explain how the specific evidence you've selected from Byrne's essay proves the point you're making in your claim. Remember that the analysis is usually the longest part of the paragraph for a reason: it's where you convince the reader that you're right about what you're saying.

The Synthesis

The **synthesis** is your paragraph's conclusion — its clincher. But in an academic essay, it's important that the clincher complete the logic of the analysis. To synthesize something, we put its parts back together and comment on the significance of the whole. Your task in the synthesis portion of the paragraph is to create unity out of the disparate elements of the paragraph (claim, context, evidence, analysis). The purpose of the synthesis is to reestablish the elegance and validity of the claim with which you began the paragraph while at the same time paving the way for the paragraph to follow.

For example, after presenting our analysis of the evidence from our observations of Chast's cartoon, we realize that we still need to wrap up our paragraph with a statement that unifies all of the paragraph's content in a satisfying way, so we might write something like this:

> So the cartoon is poking fun at us for relying too much on our phones, but also for being self-absorbed.

Note that this sentence of synthesis behaves just like any other paragraph clincher: it ties up the content of the paragraph by reaching a conclusion that reinforces or strengthens the claim from the beginning of the paragraph.

▶ *Let Us Show You:* **The Synthesis**

Now all Mara needs to do is to look at all the bits and pieces she created in the first four steps of the process (claim, context, evidence, and analysis) and ask: What does it all mean?

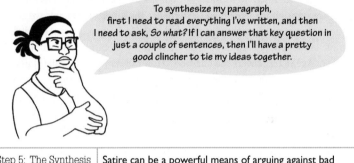

To synthesize my paragraph, first I need to read everything I've written, and then I need to ask, *So what?* If I can answer that key question in just a couple of sentences, then I'll have a pretty good clincher to tie my ideas together.

Step 5: The Synthesis	Satire can be a powerful means of arguing against bad ideas when those ideas are held by people who have all the power. In 1729, Swift used it to shame the wealthy landowners into recognizing the humanity of the Irish poor.

▶ *Talk Amongst Yourselves . . .*

Discuss Mara's synthesis with a small group of classmates. A good clincher should provide a satisfying sense of closure while leaving the reader willing (even eager) to think some more about the topic. To what extent does Mara's synthesis accomplish all of this? How could it be improved?

▶ *Now You Try:* **The Synthesis**

Okay, take a deep breath, and read through your claim, your context, your evidence, and your analysis of that evidence. Next, close your eyes, think about what you've just read, and write down a sentence or two that will provide your reader with the shining diamond of an *idea* at the heart of your paragraph. Make your final statement that says to the reader, *I've presented my idea, I've shown you my reasons, and now I offer you my conclusion.*

The Complete Analytical Paragraph

You don't stop after going through the five steps of analytical paragraph building, of course. Now you'll put all five elements of the analytical paragraph together — the claim, the context, the evidence, the analysis, and the synthesis — to create a fairly solid and reasonable draft paragraph. Here's our draft paragraph explaining what we think Chast's cartoon has to say about how humans relate to their smartphones:

> At first glance, Roz Chast's "myPhone" cartoon appears to be poking fun at those annoying people who are too dependent on their smartphones. However, upon closer inspection, it's quite different. It's actually about *all* of us who use smartphones, and the extent to which we consider our phones to be almost an extension of ourselves. The apps on the "myPhone" externalize the kinds of thoughts we all have and hand them over to a smartphone to deal with. Each app is devoted to a different example of the types of issues we all secretly worry about from time to time. For instance, "AgeMeter" covers the question "How old do I look?" while "LifeQues" deals with the question "What is the meaning of life?" So the cartoon is funny for two reasons: the "myPhone" apps claim to help us answer questions that often don't have a simple answer (or perhaps any answer at all), but they are also examples of "navel gazing" at its worst. How narcissistic would it be to have a phone full of apps that allow us to deal only with the minutiae of our own lives? And when we step back and actually look at the apps on our smartphones, most of us realize that many of our apps already meet that description. So the cartoon is poking fun at us for relying too much on our phones, but also for being self-absorbed.

Note the use of transitional words and phrases (remember them from Chapter 9?) that introduce and link the separate ideas throughout the paragraph: *however, while, but, when,* and *so.*

> Those transitional words and phrases in the paragraph above? Most of them are *conjunctions* — words that join other words and ideas together. See Appendix A for more information.

These are the words that help the reader see the relationships among the different ideas presented in the paragraph. Paying attention to how you choose and use transitional words and phrases will help you to *understand* your own ideas more fully and thus enable you to *communicate* those ideas more clearly to your reader.

▶ *Let Us Show You:* **The Complete Analytical Paragraph**

With just a bit of revision based on the principles of paragraph structure (topic sentence, body, clincher) and on the qualities of the effective paragraph (unity, development, organization, coherence), Mara can now craft a pretty good analytical paragraph about Swift and satire.

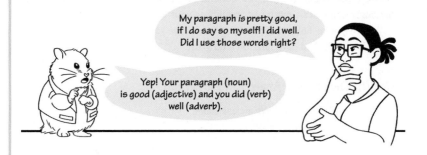

My paragraph *is* pretty good, if I *do* say so myself! I *did* well. Did I use those words right?

Yep! Your paragraph (noun) is good (adjective) and you did (verb) well (adverb).

In Jonathan Swift's "A Modest Proposal," there's a difference between the author and the narrator he created. Swift uses satire, in which the writer or speaker argues the *opposite* of what he truly believes in order to make a point. Usually, satire is funny in a dark way because it points out the serious difference between what the writer believes and the beliefs or actions of the narrator or character. For example, Swift writes that "a young healthy child . . . is a most delicious, nourishing, and wholesome food," but he later says, "let no man talk to me of other expedients" such as "taxing our absentees" or "using neither clothes nor household furniture except what is of our own growth and manufacture." Swift pretends to be a heartless rich guy who wants to solve the problem of poverty in Ireland by treating Irish babies as food and their mothers as breeding livestock. This is why he talks about "delicious" baby meat. But we know that the narrator is a character, and not Swift himself, when Swift ends his essay by providing a whole list of reasonable solutions to Irish poverty, like raising taxes on the rich and buying locally made products. Satire can be a powerful means of arguing against bad ideas when those ideas are held by people who have all the power. In 1729, Swift used it to shame the wealthy landowners into recognizing the humanity of the Irish poor.

▶ *Talk Amongst Yourselves . . .*

Break into groups and discuss Mara's complete paragraph. What are its greatest strengths? What could be improved? To what extent is Mara using the cycle of development, and how well is she using it to make a point that is clear, understandable, and rational?

▶ *Now You Try:* **The Complete Analytical Paragraph**

Now compile all of the raw material you've created in the last several pages, and create a paragraph as Mara has done above. You've done the hard part (the *thinking*) — now it's a matter of assembling your thoughts in order.

When you're finished, don't forget to show your paragraph to a peer for some feedback. And have fun! You'll do great.

Reality Check! **The Analytical Paragraph**

▶ Does your paragraph have a clear claim?

▶ Have you placed your claim into a clear context for the reader?

▶ Have you presented specific evidence to support your claim?

▶ Does your analysis of the evidence provide a clear explanation of its meaning?

▶ Have you synthesized all of the above into a clear clincher?

Chapter 11

Modes of Rhetoric:
Different Ways of Thinking

> Language shapes the way we think and
> determines what we can think about.
> — Benjamin Lee Whorf

If you have read Chapters 9 and 10 (and we sincerely hope you have), you now have a pretty good understanding of paragraphs: how they're structured, what qualities they should demonstrate, and why they tend to be analytical in academic writing.

You would be forgiven, dear reader, for believing at this point that you have a full and complete understanding of the paragraph's crucial function in academic writing. Alas, we're not done yet: there is one more layer of knowledge you need to grasp to ensure that your paragraphs consistently achieve their greatest possible effect in your essays.

Form Follows Function

Have you heard the phrase *form follows function* before? (Hint: Yes, you have—we talked about form following function in Chapter 9, on page 106.) Essentially it means that for any constructed or manufactured thing — such as a symphony or a film or a painting or a piece of furniture or a car or a building or a computer or, yes, even an essay — the form (or shape) of the thing should be determined by the thing's intended function (or purpose).

> The phrase *form follows function* comes from the great American architect Louis Sullivan, who created the first skyscraper. He used it as his guiding principle in designing buildings.

For example, if you're creating a piece of furniture whose function is to provide casual seating for a single person who wants to be close to the floor and who wants to toss his chosen piece of furniture around the room at will, then your design might very well take on the shape of a beanbag chair. And if you're designing a new computer whose intended purpose is to be a highly portable, multitasking resource with great process-

ing speed and a high-resolution screen for watching video files, you would do well to design it in the form of a tablet.

This principle of *form follows function* — the notion that the shape of a thing should be based on what that thing is expected to accomplish — is equally true of written texts like poems, stories, plays, and essays. If you're creating an essay whose purpose is to make readers feel outrage at an injustice while at the same time laughing darkly at the perfidy (you can look that word up!) of those committing the injustice, you might well decide that your essay should use the elements of the form known as satire, as our friend Jonathan Swift did in "A Modest Proposal."

On the other hand, if you're preparing a speech that you're hoping will tap into your audience's sense of patient optimism and their faith that justice will eventually prevail, you will perhaps borrow some of the shape and technique of the church sermon, as the President Barack Obama did in his eulogy for Clementa Pinckney.

The Modes of Rhetoric

Discussing form and function (or shape and purpose) is our way of introducing the **modes of rhetoric**, the strategies and tactics that will help you clarify for the reader what the intent of your writing is.

You may recall from your careful reading of Chapter 2 that the word *rhetoric* comes from the Greek *rhetor*, meaning "orator," "lecturer," or "teacher." The word *mode* comes from the Latin *modus*, meaning "manner," "method," or "kind." So the *modes of rhetoric* are the different manners of speaking, the various methods of lecturing, or the several kinds of teaching. In other words, when we talk about the modes of rhetoric, we are talking about distinct ways of presenting ideas for the general purpose of informing, convincing, or persuading an audience. These modes of rhetoric can be viewed and employed in either a general or a specific sense.

GENERAL VS. SPECIFIC MODES

In general terms, the modes of rhetoric tend to refer to the overall purpose of an entire piece of writing, such as an essay. An essay's **general rhetorical mode** depends on its desired overall effect on the reader — because form follows function, right? Or strategy follows purpose.

So if, for example, you want to write an essay whose general purpose is to expose the reader to new information, you will likely select the *expository* mode of rhetoric as an overall approach to your essay. On the other hand, if you wish to write an essay whose overall goal is to convince the reader that your point of view is correct, or perhaps even persuade the reader to take a particular course of action, then you will almost certainly select the *argumentative* mode of rhetoric as the guiding principle for the form of your essay.

Reality Check! The General Modes of Rhetoric

If your purpose is to ...	Then your essay will be ...
▶ understand	
▶ inform	informative
▶ explain	(exposition)
▶ enlighten	
▶ reveal	
▶ judge	
▶ convince	argumentative
▶ inspire	(evaluation)
▶ seek agreement	
▶ motivate	argumentative
▶ persuade	(proposal)
▶ call to action	

You can read about these general rhetorical approaches in more detail in Chapter 16, on pages 232–35.

But the general rhetorical mode is only the overall structure of an essay — the skeleton of the creature that is the text. A skeleton is certainly necessary if you want your creature to be able to stand or sit or move. But if you want a whole creature, you need a bunch of specific muscles and organs, and surface features like skin and hair, and . . . well, you get the idea, right? The general purpose of an essay might be to explain, which means that the general rhetorical mode (the skeleton) will be expository. But the specific tactics used along the way will have focused purposes — such as comparing or describing or defining — and those tactics are like the muscles and organs that hold a skeleton together and make it function properly.

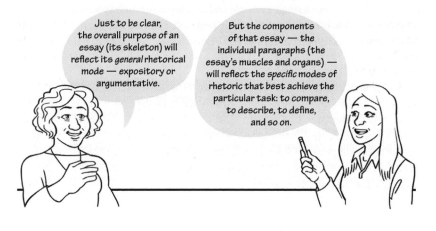

Just to be clear, the overall purpose of an essay (its skeleton) will reflect its *general* rhetorical mode — expository or argumentative.

But the components of that essay — the individual paragraphs (the essay's muscles and organs) — will reflect the *specific* modes of rhetoric that best achieve the particular task: to compare, to describe, to define, and so on.

In other words, form follows function, both generally and specifically!

You learned in Chapter 10 that the essential function of a paragraph in an academic essay is to support a claim through the presentation and analysis of specific examples (or evidence). However, not all claims require the same sorts of examples to be used as evidence, and not all evidence can be analyzed in the same way. For this reason, writers have at their disposal a wealth of specific modes of rhetoric that they can employ on a paragraph-by-paragraph basis in order to best achieve the goal established by each paragraph's main point. Because form always follows function, writers will choose a paragraph's mode of rhetoric (form) by understanding the essential purpose of that paragraph (function). It is our hope that you too will make use of this wealth of specific rhetorical modes — and to help you, we offer our handy Modes of Rhetoric Toolkit.

The Modes of Rhetoric Toolkit

To choose the best mode of rhetoric for a specific paragraph, you will need to understand what you're trying to accomplish in the paragraph. Do you want to tell a story that will help the reader see and feel what a particular event was like? What if you're supremely uninterested in evoking emotion and instead want to make clear for readers that there's a very logical and rational way to sort a group of people or things into categories? We would suggest that you use a different mode for each situation. What modes do you have to choose from? Check these out!

Exemplification (also known as *examples and illustrations*) is the most popular rhetorical mode. It does precisely what its name implies: it provides useful examples that illustrate the point being made in a paragraph. Some writers include multiple examples in a single paragraph, but often the most effective way to use this rhetorical mode is to choose a single example and develop it through specifically detailed illustration. The good **exemplification** paragraph answers the question *Such as?* Check out this excerpt from Daniel W. Drezner's essay "The Uses of Being Wrong":

> Even in the realm of theory, there are only a few cases of scholars' acknowledging that the paradigms they've constructed do not hold. In 1958, Ernst Haas, a political scientist at the University of California at Berkeley, developed a theory of political integration, positing that as countries cooperated on noncontroversial issues, like postal regulations, that spirit of cooperation would spill over into contentious areas, like migration. Haas used this theory — he called it "neofunctionalism" — to explain European integration a half-century ago. By the 1970s, however, Europe's march toward integration seemed to be going into reverse, and Haas acknowledged

that his theory had become "obsolete." This did not stop later generations of scholars, however, from resurrecting his idea once European integration was moving forward again. . . .

The persistence of so-called "zombie ideas" is something of a problem in the social sciences. Even if a theory or argument has been discredited by others in the moment, a stout defense can ensure a long intellectual life. When Samuel P. Huntington published his "clash of civilizations" argument, in the 1990s, the overwhelming scholarly consensus was that he was wrong. This did not stop the "clash" theory from permeating policy circles, particularly after 9/11.

Narration is the rhetorical mode you'll use when you want to tell a meaningful story. It is best achieved through the presentation of a detailed series of events in chronological order. Note that its focus is on showing what particular things happened (*and then what? and then what?*) as opposed to showing what the general situation was like. After reading a narration paragraph, the reader should have a very clear and vivid answer to the question *What happened?*

A particularly good example of narration comes from George Orwell's essay "Shooting an Elephant," written in 1936. You might already be familiar with Orwell since he wrote *Animal Farm* and *1984*, two excellent books that are often assigned in high school and college.

One day something happened which in a roundabout way was enlightening. It was a tiny incident in itself, but it gave me a better glimpse than I had had before of the real nature of imperialism — the real motives for which despotic governments act. Early one morning the sub-inspector at a police station the other end of the town rang me up on the phone and said that an elephant was ravaging the bazaar. Would I please come and do something about it? I did not know what I could do, but I wanted to see what was happening and I got on to a pony and started out. I took my rifle, an old .44 Winchester and much too small to kill an elephant, but I thought the noise might be useful *in terrorem*. Various Burmans stopped me on the way and told me about the elephant's doings. It was not, of course, a wild elephant, but a tame one which had gone "must." It had been chained up, as tame elephants always are when their attack of "must" is due, but on the previous night it had broken its chain and escaped. Its *mahout*, the only person who could manage it when it was in that state, had set out in pursuit, but had taken the wrong direction and was now twelve hours' journey away, and in the morning the elephant had suddenly reappeared in the town. The Burmese population had no weapons and were quite helpless against it. It had already destroyed somebody's bamboo hut, killed a cow and raided some fruit-stalls and devoured the stock; also it had met the municipal rubbish van and, when the driver jumped out and took to his heels, had turned the van over and inflicted violences upon it.

Description is closely related to narration, in that the two of them together make up everyone's favorite type of prose writing: fiction (i.e., novels and short stories). But whereas the focus of narration is to tell a story, the focus of **description** is to explore the physical, sensory reality of a person, place, or thing: *What does it look like? Sound like? Smell like? Taste like? Feel like?*

Descriptive paragraphs are typically organized in a spatial order, describing a tree from top to bottom, a song from beginning to end, a room from left to right, a meal from salad to dessert, and so on. The following description from Arthur Miller's 1998 essay "Before Air-Conditioning" is especially vivid. And yes, that's the same Arthur Miller who wrote all those great American plays like *Death of a Salesman* and *The Crucible*. Note how description blends into narration near the end of the paragraph.

> Given the heat, people smelled, of course, but some smelled a lot worse than others. One cutter in my father's shop was a horse in this respect, and my father, who normally had no sense of smell — no one understood why — claimed that he could smell this man and would address him only from a distance. In order to make as much money as possible, this fellow would start work at half past five in the morning and continue until midnight. He owned Bronx apartment houses and land in Florida and Jersey, and seemed half mad with greed. He had a powerful physique, a very straight spine, a tangle of hair, and a black shadow on his cheeks. He snorted like a horse as he pushed the cutting machine, following his patterns through some eighteen layers of winter-coat material. One late afternoon, he blinked his eyes hard against the burning sweat as he held down the material with his left hand and pressed the vertical, razor-sharp reciprocating blade with his right. The blade sliced through his index finger at the second joint. Angrily refusing to go to the hospital, he ran tap water over the stump, wrapped his hand in a towel, and went right on cutting, snorting, and stinking. When the blood began to show through the towel's bunched layers, my father pulled the plug on the machine and ordered him to the hospital. But he was back at work the next morning, and worked right through the day and into the evening, as usual, piling up his apartment houses.

Definition as a rhetorical mode focuses its attention on asserting the essential truth of a word or phrase — or, most often, an idea. Typically, this is done through a combination of restatement (using other words to explain the meaning) and examples (to show the reader what you mean) — although **definition** can be achieved in other ways, such as through *negation* (defining what something is by explaining what it isn't, through *contrast*), classification (defining by type), or *comparison* (defining something by explaining what's similar to it). Note that definition as a rhetorical mode is generally used to define abstract terms — that is, terms whose meanings are arguable or interpretable — rather than concrete terms, whose agreed-upon definitions can simply be looked up in a dictionary. Ultimately, the definition paragraph answers the question *What is it?*

Take a look at this selection from "A Jerk Can't See Himself as Others Do" by Sydney J. Harris. It was written in 1960, but jerks haven't really changed that much over the decades, have they?

> Thinking it over, I decided that a jerk is basically a person without insight. He is not necessarily a fool or a dope, because some extremely clever persons can be jerks. In fact, it has little to do with intelligence as we commonly think of it; it is, rather, a kind of subtle but pervasive aroma emanating from the inner part of the personality. I know a college president who can be described only as a jerk. He is not an unintelligent man, nor unlearned, nor even unschooled in the social amenities. Yet he is a jerk *cum laude*, because of a fatal flaw in his nature — he is totally incapable of looking into the mirror of his soul and shuddering at what he sees there.

Comparison and contrast is probably familiar to you as a writing strategy. Typically, when these terms are combined, they are being used to describe a general rhetorical mode that governs an entire essay rather than a specific mode that applies to a single paragraph. **Comparison** is used when a single paragraph seeks to highlight the significant similarities between two people, places, things, or ideas that most people would assume are different from each other. In other words, a comparison should be used only when it's worthwhile — and it's not worthwhile to point out the similarities between two things that everyone already knows are very much the same. The comparison answers the question *How are these two different things actually alike?*

Check out the following excerpt from *The Victorian Internet* by Tom Standage. It was written in 1998 — when the Internet was just a baby.

> Like the telegraph network, the Internet allows people to communicate across great distances using interconnected networks. (Indeed, the generic term *internet* simply means a group of interconnected networks.) Common rules and protocols enable any sort of computer to exchange messages with any other — just as messages could easily be passed from one kind of telegraph apparatus (a Morse printer, say) to another (a pneumatic tube). The journey of an e-mail message, as it hops from mail server to mail server toward its destination, mirrors the passage of a telegram from one telegraph office to the next. . . .
>
> More striking still are the parallels between the social impact of the telegraph and that of the Internet. Public reaction to the new technologies was, in both cases, a confused mixture of hype and skepticism. Just as many Victorians believed the telegraph would eliminate misunderstanding between nations and usher in a new

era of world peace, an avalanche of media coverage has lauded the Internet as a powerful new medium that will transform and improve our lives.

The flip side of the comparison paragraph is the **contrast** paragraph, which is employed when the writer wishes to point out the significant differences between two people, places, things, or ideas that at first appear to be similar to each other. Note that the same "worthwhile" principle applies for contrast — there's no point in trying to demonstrate how different two things are if the reader's likely response is, *Well, duh.*

The following contrast paragraph comes from "The Case for Reparations," an exceptionally detailed analytical essay by Ta-Nehisi Coates that was published in the May 2014 issue of the *Atlantic Monthly*. (The essay is well worth reading if you're interested in learning about the effects of slavery in the United States.)

> The lives of black Americans are better than they were half a century ago. The humiliation of WHITES ONLY signs is gone. Rates of black poverty have decreased. Black teen-pregnancy rates are at record lows — and the gap between black and white teen-pregnancy rates has shrunk significantly. But such progress rests on a shaky foundation, and fault lines are everywhere. The income gap between black and white households is roughly the same today as it was in 1970. Patrick Sharkey, a sociologist at New York University, studied children born from 1955 through 1970 and found that 4 percent of whites and 62 percent of blacks across America had been raised in poor neighborhoods. A generation later, the same study showed, virtually nothing had changed. And whereas whites born into affluent neighborhoods tended to remain in affluent neighborhoods, blacks tended to fall out of them.

Both comparison paragraphs and contrast paragraphs are typically organized in either a point-by-point structure (presenting each specific point of similarity or difference in turn, one after the other) or a block structure (presenting all points regarding Topic A and then all points about Topic B).

If I wanted to write a paragraph pointing out the differences between dogs and cats being left alone for a weekend, I could organize my contrast paragraph in one of two ways: point-by-point structure or block structure.

Paragraph Structures for Comparison and Contrast

Point-by-Point Structure	Block Structure
• Cats can ration their food for a day or two. • Dogs will eat everything immediately. • Cats have a "bathroom" and know how to use it. • Dogs need to be taken outside for their "bathroom" needs. • Cats can entertain themselves. • Dogs get lonely when you're gone. • Cats just look at you when you come home. • Dogs are giddy with joy when you come home.	• Cats can ration their food for a couple of days, they can take care of their "bathroom" needs without any help, they know how to entertain themselves without human intervention, and they barely notice when you've been gone for two days. • Dogs will eat all available food at their first opportunity, they require humans to help them with their "bathroom" needs, they get lonely without their humans, and they go nuts with happiness when their humans return.

As with all other decisions regarding modes of rhetoric, the structure of the comparison or contrast paragraph should be based on the principle of form following function: which organization strategy will best serve your purpose?

Next up is the causal analysis.

A causal analysis is a paragraph that examines the reasons that a particular reality exists or existed. That is, a **causal analysis** can look back and explain why something happened, or it can look at a present situation and explain why it is happening. Like a narration, a causal analysis is typically organized chronologically (first this happens, which causes this other thing to happen, etc.) — but unlike a narration, whose purpose is to answer the question *What happened?* the causal analysis answers the question *Why did/does that happen?*

No, not casual — causal, meaning "of or related to a cause."

Here's an example of a causal analysis from "Why We Crave Horror Movies," written by Stephen King. Yes, *that* Stephen King. The guy who brought you *Carrie* and *The Shining* and a whole lot of other books that keep you awake all night listening for weird noises.

When we pay our four or five bucks and seat ourselves at tenth-row center in a theater showing a horror movie, we are daring the nightmare.

Why? Some of the reasons are simple and obvious. To show that we can, that we are not afraid, that we can ride this roller coaster. Which is not to say that a really good horror movie may not surprise a scream out of us at some point, the way we may scream when the roller coaster twists through a complete 360 or plows through a lake at the bottom of the drop. And horror movies, like roller coasters, have always been the special province of the young; by the time one turns 40 or 50, one's appetite for double twists or 360-degree loops may be considerably depleted.

We also go to reestablish our feelings of essential normality; the horror movie is innately conservative, even reactionary. Freda Jackson as the horrible melting woman in *Die, Monster, Die!* confirms for us that no matter how far we may be removed from the beauty of a Robert Redford or a Diana Ross, we are still light-years from true ugliness.

And we go to have fun.

Effect analysis is a fairly close relative to the causal analysis. But whereas the causal analysis looks at a reality and wonders *why*, the **effect analysis** looks at a reality and asks, *What did/does/will happen as a result?* An effect analysis can explore the effects of a past event (*because that happened, this other thing happened*), or it can predict the effects of a current or future event (*because this is happening, this other thing will happen* — or *if this thing happens, then this other thing will happen*). The line between the causal analysis and the effect analysis is sometimes a fine one. Which mode you choose really comes down to the event (or situation or reality) you're analyzing and what you want to know about it: if you're interested in *why it happened*, then you want causal analysis, but if you're exploring *what happened as a result*, effect analysis is the tool to use.

James Surowiecki's essay "Later: What Does Procrastination Tell Us About Ourselves?" explores the effects of putting things off.

. . . [T]he percentage of people who admitted to difficulties with procrastination quadrupled between 1978 and 2002. In that light, it's possible to see procrastination as the quintessential modern problem.

It's also a surprisingly costly one. Each year, Americans waste hundreds of millions of dollars because they don't file their taxes on time. The Harvard economist David Laibson has shown that American workers have forgone huge amounts of money in matching 401(k) contributions because they never got around to signing up for a retirement plan. Seventy per cent of patients suffering from glaucoma risk blindness because they don't use their eyedrops regularly.

> Hmmm, procrastinating . . . does that sound familiar?

Procrastination also inflicts major costs on businesses and governments. The recent crisis of the euro was exacerbated by the German government's dithering, and the decline of the American auto industry, exemplified by the bankruptcy of G.M., was due in part to executives' penchant for delaying tough decisions. (In Alex Taylor's recent history of G.M., "Sixty to Zero," one of the key conclusions is "Procrastination doesn't pay.")

Process is exactly what it sounds like: it explores a multistep operation by breaking the operation down into its individual steps and presenting them in clear chronological order. **Process** paragraphs can be either instructive (telling the reader how to perform a particular action) or informative (showing the reader how a particular natural or mechanical occurrence works). Therefore, process paragraphs can be employed for topics ranging from how to tie shoes to how abiogenesis works. Ultimately, the process analysis answers the question *How is it done?* or *How does it work?*

I'm thinking that Michael Silverberg's advice will likely come in handy sometime in your near future.

Below is a process analysis by Michael Silverberg titled "How to Write a Cover Letter, According to Great Artists."

The trouble with most cover letters is that they sound canned. Using boilerplate formalities won't make you sound serious; it will just make it harder to tell one cover letter from another. Use your personality, even if it means channeling your anxieties about the job you hope to get. For instance, Eudora Welty opened with a bit of disarming humor when she applied for a job at *The New Yorker* in 1933 as an unknown 23-year-old writer with no experience:

> I suppose you'd be more interested in even a sleight-o'-hand trick than you'd be in an application for a position with your magazine, but as usual you can't have the thing you want most.

And she closes with a self-deprecating joke and an amazing pun:

> There is no telling where I may apply, if you turn me down; I realize this will not phase you, but consider my other alternative: the U of N.C. offers for $12.00 to let me dance in Vachel Lindsay's Congo. I congo on.

Both you and the person reading your application know that you're engaged in a dull little ritual. Anything to break up that monotony is likely to get you noticed.

Classification is the mode of rhetoric employed by a writer who wishes to demonstrate that multiple people, places, objects, or ideas can be sorted into categories based on clearly identified criteria and sound reasoning. The **classification** answers the question *What kinds are they?* or *Where do they fit?* It's important to note that a classification always sorts its subjects into three or more categories. If you are tempted to write a classification with only two categories, we urge you to consider instead writing either a comparison or a contrast paragraph, depending on whether it would be more interesting to highlight similarities or differences between the two groups. And of course, there's no such thing as sorting subjects into one category — but you knew that already, right?

The following paragraph classifying types of mustard is taken from an essay by Malcolm Gladwell called "The Ketchup Conundrum."

> Many years ago, one mustard dominated the supermarket shelves: French's. It came in a plastic bottle. People used it on hot dogs and bologna. It was a yellow mustard, made from ground white mustard seed with turmeric and vinegar, which gave it a mild, slightly metallic taste. If you looked hard in the grocery store, you might find something in the specialty-foods section called Grey Poupon, which was Dijon mustard, made from the more pungent brown mustard seed. In the early seventies, Grey Poupon was no more than a hundred-thousand-dollar-a-year business. Few people knew what it was or how it tasted, or had any particular desire for an alternative to French's or the runner-up, Gulden's. Then one day the Heublein Company, which owned Grey Poupon, discovered something remarkable: if you gave people a mustard taste test, a significant number had only to try Grey Poupon once to switch from yellow mustard. In the food world that almost never happens; even among the most successful food brands, only about one in a hundred have that kind of conversion rate. Grey Poupon was magic.

Division is sort of the flip side of classification — but whereas the classification analysis takes multiple subjects and organizes them into groups, the **division analysis** takes a single subject and breaks it down into its component parts. The division paragraph answers the question *What is it made of?* Note that the rhetorical strategy of division might seem at first to be useful only for scientific or engineering-related topics ("here's what the combustion engine is made of"), but division can be employed to great effect as part of a definition, explaining what some abstract concept is by showing what its parts are. Mary Beard uses division in this excerpt from her essay "The Public Voice of Women":

> There are only two main exceptions in the classical world to this abomination of women's public speaking. First, women are allowed to speak out as victims and as

martyrs — usually to preface their own death. Early Christian women were represented loudly upholding their faith as they went to the lions; and, in a well-known story from the early history of Rome, the virtuous Lucretia, raped by a brutal prince of the ruling monarchy, was given a speaking part solely to denounce the rapist and announce her own suicide (or so Roman writers presented it: what really happened, we haven't a clue). But even this rather bitter opportunity to speak could itself be removed. One story in the *Metamorphoses* tells of the rape of the young princess Philomela. In order to prevent any Lucretia-style denunciation, the rapist quite simply cuts her tongue out. It's a notion that's picked up in *Titus Andronicus*, where the tongue of the raped Lavinia is also ripped out.

The second exception is more familiar. Occasionally women could legitimately rise up to speak — to defend their homes, their children, their husbands or the interests of other women. So in the third of the three examples of female oratory discussed by that Roman anthologist, the woman — Hortensia by name — gets away with it because she is acting explicitly as the spokesperson for the women of Rome, after they have been subject to a special wealth tax to fund a dubious war effort. Women, in other words, may in extreme circumstances publicly defend their own sectional interests, but not speak for men or the community as a whole. In general, as one second-century AD guru put it, "a woman should as modestly guard against exposing her voice to outsiders as she would guard against stripping off her clothes."

And there you have it! The modes of rhetoric, all in one place. Just as a reminder, when it comes to patterns of paragraph organization, you have eleven basic options, as outlined in the *Reality Check!* box below.

Reality Check! The Specific Modes of Rhetoric

- ▶ Examplification
- ▶ Narration
- ▶ Description
- ▶ Definition
- ▶ Comparison
- ▶ Contrast
- ▶ Causal analysis
- ▶ Effect analysis
- ▶ Process
- ▶ Classification
- ▶ Division

Practice! The Modes of Rhetoric

Hey, remember these topic sentences from Chapter 9? Sure you do! These are the sentences that you evaluated for their usefulness in paragraphs that are either inductively or deductively structured. We'd like you to take another look at them, and this time we want you to see if you can identify what type of paragraph (or what *rhetorical mode*) each topic sentence would most logically introduce. Write your answers on the lines provided. Be sure to use the list of rhetorical modes in the *Reality Check!* box on page 145 as a guide.

1. What is sacrifice, really, and how can we recognize it when we see it?

   _____

2. Most people assume that the American Civil Liberties Union (ACLU) consistently opposes the ideas of the National Rifle Association (NRA), but the two groups have some surprising commonalities. _____

3. In my experience, there are three kinds of movies: important works of art, pleasant diversions, and complete wastes of time and money.

   _____

4. Many novice barbecuers ruin their first attempt at a London broil, but here's an easy way to do it right. _____

5. The first time I took Chemistry 101, I failed it miserably — mostly because I foolishly thought the course would be easy and thus didn't take studying seriously. _____

6. If you want to understand how planetary orbits work, it helps to take a look at how a few planets in our own solar system make their circuits around the sun. _____

7. The recent willingness of Americans to become foster pet owners has resulted in many fewer abused and mistreated animals.

   _____

8. On the surface, Macs and PCs look quite different, but once you get going, you'll notice some very significant similarities between the two types of computers. _____

9. The first time I visited the temple at Karnak, I was struck by three things: the massive size of the columns, the intricate carvings on the walls, and the intensity of the colors that remain after all these millennia.

   _____

10. I will never forget the day that I learned for the first time that my father, like any other human, is capable of making a mistake.

    _____

▶ *Let Us Show You:* **The Modes of Rhetoric**

Casey and Mara's history class has been assigned to write a brief informative paper that explains a specific governmental or political process in the United States. Casey has decided to write about the electoral college.

> If you don't know about the electoral college, we suggest you take a quick trip to the National Archives Web site, where you can familiarize yourself with the basics.

You remember the National Archives, right? We talked about it back in Chapter 3 when Casey and Mara were researching the context of the Gettysburg Address. The National Archives Web site is a treasure trove of information about the US government, and you can learn a lot about the electoral college by checking it out. Go ahead. We'll wait.

... Okay, now that you know a little something about the topic, let's take a look at how Casey is using recently gained knowledge about the modes of rhetoric to make some decisions about which specific tools to use for particular tasks within the essay — with an assist from Mara, who helps by keeping an eye on the principle that *form follows function.*

> I've been assigned to inform the reader by explaining it. So I know that the skeleton of my essay will be expository.

> And to fill out your skeleton you'll need muscles, organs, skin, and hair (and can I just say, Ew!) — otherwise known as specific ideas.

Casey's Notes on His Paragraphs	Mara's Feedback
For my introduction, I think I'll show the personal side of how the electoral college can affect the individual voter by telling the story of my Aunt Jane, who thinks her West Coast vote is wasted every four years.	Telling a story . . . Sounds like you're going to start with a narrative paragraph.
In my first body paragraph, I'd better explain what the electoral college is by showing what it *isn't* — for example, I've learned that it's not really direct democracy.	This sounds like a contrast paragraph or definition through negation.
I don't think most people know how the electoral college works. I should probably explain that to avoid any confusion as I move forward.	This sounds like a process paragraph followed by a causal analysis paragraph.
Another paragraph should get into the background a little bit by exploring why the framers of the Constitution thought the electoral college would be a good idea. What happened to make them create this system?	
For my conclusion I'll start with what the framers expected the electoral college to accomplish and then explore what its actual result has been for people like my Aunt Jane, who have actually stopped voting at all. I think I should try to show how apathy is a direct consequence of the electoral college.	Your conclusion will analyze the effect, so it will be an effect analysis paragraph.

▶ *Talk Amongst Yourselves . . .*

Take a few minutes to write down your responses to the questions below. Then break into groups of three and discuss your responses with each other.

What do you think about the decisions Casey has made about how to pursue several different rhetorical modes in several paragraphs in this essay? To what extent do these specific modes — narration, definition, process analysis, causal analysis, contrast analysis, and effect analysis — seem to be the appropriate means to achieve the goals he has expressed interest in? Which modes of rhetoric would you have chosen to achieve those same goals, and why would you have chosen them? Would you have included more or fewer modes?

And beyond this, how well do you think Casey's specific modes of rhetoric will work together to create an essay that achieves the general rhetorical strategy of informing the reader?

In other words, is *form* consistently following *function* in Casey's work on the electoral college paper?

▶ *Now You Try:* **The Modes of Rhetoric**

We're thinking that the strategies and tactics of Jonathan Swift's "A Modest Proposal" are becoming strangely familiar to you by now. So how about testing that familiarity? Number the paragraphs in Swift's essay (there are thirty-three of them, by the way). Then read through the essay and try to identify the mode of rhetoric used in each paragraph, referring back to the list of modes in the *Reality Check!* box on page 145.

Some paragraphs' organizing principles will be easier to spot than others. You might, for example, determine that a single paragraph uses more than one mode of rhetoric, or that several short paragraphs together constitute a particular mode of rhetoric. That's okay. Good writers learn to improvise variations on established patterns of development.

After you've completed your assessment of Swift's rhetorical modes, be sure to discuss your answers with your professor and/or classmates. If there's disagreement, does that necessarily mean that someone's right and someone's wrong? Or is it possible that the modes of rhetoric can sometimes be subject to interpretation?

▶ *Bonus Task!*

Way back at the end of Chapter 2, we asked you to look at any current writing assignment you were working on and analyze its rhetorical situation. You remember, right? It's the exercise that looks almost exactly like the *Reality Check!* box below.

Reality Check! **The Rhetorical Situation**

1. What is the exigence? In other words, what compels you to write? (To review *exigence*, go back to page 16 in Chapter 2.)
2. Who is involved in the exigence? What are their roles?
3. What are the relationships/power dynamics between you and others involved?
4. Where and when are you creating your writing?
5. Who are you in relation to the context of your writing?

(continued)

6. Who is your intended audience? Is it the same as your actual audience?

7. What decisions will you make regarding methods of communication?

8. What can you say about the institutions governing all of the above?

If you still have your notes from this task — and you should! — get them out and review them. What do your answers to the questions about context tell you about the overall goal you might want to achieve in your writing assignment? Based on that goal, do the following:

1. Make a list of specific goals that individual paragraphs in your essay might achieve — in other words, identify specific functions that you would like your paragraphs to fulfill.

2. Determine which of the specific modes of rhetoric would be most likely to achieve each of those goals — in other words, make a paragraph-writing plan in which form follows function.

PART 4

Revising and Editing

Chapter 12

Levels of Revision:
One Step at a Time

In writing, you must kill all your darlings.
—William Faulkner

Sooner or later, every writer who has handed a text over to a reader hears the frustrating comment, "I'm not sure what your point is." Whether it comes from a classmate, a friend, a professor, or some other well-meaning person, it's maddening: after all, you've just spent all that time thinking, exploring, organizing, focusing, developing your ideas — and several other *-ings* to boot. *You* know what your point is, so how could your reader be so obtuse? We've been there.

Revision Is for the Reader

Here's the problem: you're not yet communicating. And that's okay. Remember in Chapter 8 when we said that drafting is for the writer? Well, we really meant it. All the hard work you've engaged in so far has helped you figure out what you think, which is great. But now you need to recognize that it's not enough for you to make sense to yourself; you need to make sense to others. At this point you need to accept a crucial truth: while drafting is for you, revising is for others — specifically, revision is for your reader.

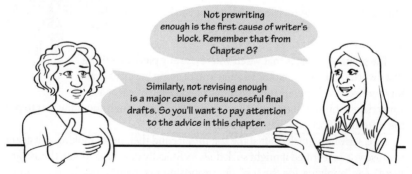

Writing is both an internal, self-directed activity and an external, other-directed activity. That is, writing is a *process* that helps the writer to understand his or her own thoughts — and it's also a *product* that communicates the writer's thoughts to the reader. The dual nature of writing's purpose is, in part, why we have both drafting and revision.

Drafting is useful for you, the writer, because it lets you see what you have to work with, but it's not terribly useful for the reader because it hasn't yet taken your reader into consideration. Revision happens when you go back and look at your draft with the reader in mind and do whatever it takes to make your writing (and therefore your ideas) easy for your reader.

That's right, we said *easy for your reader.* Although it might seem counterintuitive, it takes more work and skill to create a piece of writing that is easy to understand and delightful to read than it does to create a piece of writing that is confusing and difficult to read.

For example, something like this makes sense to its author:

> Through after-school and mentoring programs, working to create a sense of belonging in school and early intervention, we can begin to create a successful solution in potentially decreasing the problem.

But it might not make sense to its *reader.* The reader may quite reasonably say, *Um . . . what?* Because that's what people say when things don't make sense.

The author needs to revise this sentence to make its meaning clearer to the reader. Something like this would work:

> Schools should implement early interventions such as after-school mentoring programs to create a sense of belonging among students, potentially decreasing the dropout rate.

Whew.
That's better.
That was scary
for a second.

LEARN TO CARE AND NOT TO CARE

The key to effective revision is that you must care and also, when appropriate, not care. *Sure,* you're thinking, *but what does that mean?*

The point of caring is that when you revise any piece of writing that's worth revising — either because you're going to earn a grade for it or because someone is going to make you a job offer (or accept a marriage proposal) based on it — you need to care enough about the text to put the time and effort into making it better.

Sure, writing a quick draft at the last minute and then never looking at it again because you're terrified it might suck does technically qualify as "doing the assignment" (or "applying for the job" or "proposing marriage"), but if you want to actually produce a piece of writing that you're proud of (or that at the very least might impress your professor or prospective employer or spouse), you'll need to revise.

The process of revision — and by this we mean really reworking your draft, not just fixing a few comma splices — takes time and attention to detail. You're going to have to read what you've written many times and think of ways to make it better, in terms of both structure and content. In other words, to revise a piece of writing, you must *care enough*.

The point of *not* caring, on the other hand, is that while you are oh-so-seriously revising, you need to distance yourself enough from your draft that you can cut words, sentences, and (gasp!) entire paragraphs that don't belong or are not improving your text.

Our students sometimes say that we're really asking them to rewrite, not revise — but *potato, potahto.*

Just as a healthy relationship involves caring deeply about your significant other while at the same time avoiding an unhealthy, codependent attachment, revising a draft requires you to commit yourself passionately to your work while at the same time not getting so attached to what you've written that you cannot imagine it differently. You need to be able to take an honest look at what you've written and decide what goes and what stays. One of the best ways to get that "honest look" is to open yourself up for feedback from a reader.

Preparing to Revise: Get Feedback

Students in English and composition classes typically get two types of feedback about their written work: peer review and instructor critique. There are two major differences between peer review and instructor critique, one obvious and one less so. First of all, your instructor is an expert and your fellow students — well, they *aren't* experts. So your instructor knows exactly what kinds of advice to give you to help you revise, whereas your peers may be unsure of their advice or (*oh no!*) even wrong.

PEER REVIEW: WHAT TO EXPECT

But that's okay, because — and this is the second major difference between peer review and instructor critique — peer review is often as helpful to the reviewer as it is to the person whose work is being reviewed.

When you examine someone else's work with the intention of giving that person advice about how to improve it, during the process you often learn things about what to do and what not to do in your own writing. You think through the assignment and what it requires of you in a way that maybe you didn't when you wrote your own draft. You notice that your peer's thesis statement is vague and unclear and make a mental note to revisit your own. You covet your peer's witty, conversational tone and resolve to work on developing your own writing voice.

Useful Critiques

So what should you be doing when you review a draft for a peer? Well, first, we think you should be nice — but not too nice.

What we mean by that is that your peer might be nervous about submitting a draft for review by a fellow student, and it would be a shame to humiliate him or her. After all, he or she has tried so hard. But at the same time, your peer has gone to the trouble of having a draft done before the final deadline, so you might as well provide some useful feedback.

In other words, the only thing worse than hearing "Your paper is horrible and you should never write anything ever again" is to be told "Your paper is perfect exactly the way it is and you shouldn't change anything." While the former is cruel, the latter is totally useless — and also cruel, if your peer doesn't change a word and then earns a bad grade based on your advice.

What to Comment On

When we have students do peer reviews in our classes, we typically ask them to describe what they see going on in their peer's essay and to refrain from offering suggestions for actual revision. This is another way peer review differs from instructor critique. As a fellow student, you aren't as qualified as the professor to advise specific changes, but as a fellow human, you are certainly qualified to provide your peer with another set of eyes and another brain to consider his or her draft thoughtfully, and to share honestly what you see.

In other words, a good peer review is generally *descriptive* rather than *prescriptive.*

What, then, should you observe when reviewing a peer's essay? Your professor will probably give you instructions for peer review, but we've also drawn up a peer review checklist that gives you some specific advice, just in case. For each area of observation described in the checklist on pages 157–58, you will do the most good for your peer not by correcting but by making notes of strengths and weaknesses from your own perspective.

Peer Review Checklist

The Big Stuff (Content and Structure)	The Little Stuff (Coherence and Precision)
Review the essay's **title** as well as its **introduction** and **conclusion**. (See Chapter 14.) Think about the relationships among these three components. Do the title, introduction, and conclusion match, or do they disagree? This question addresses the essay's unity.	Identify the writer's **transitions**: words, phrases, and sentences that link together the ideas in the essay. Are the transitions consistently effective in creating a coherent argument? (See Chapters 9 and 15.)
Find the essay's **thesis**, or main point. Is it clear? Is it well positioned? Does it meet all facets of the assignment? Review the original assignment to ensure that your peer's thesis is on target. (See Chapter 14.) Then identify each paragraph's **topic sentence**: do the topic sentences all relate to the thesis in a meaningful way? (See Chapter 9.)	Are **sentence structures** correct and effective, or are there fragments, comma splices, fused sentences, and awkward shifts in construction? (See Chapter 25.)
Identify the specific **factual evidence** used to support each claim. Is the evidence well chosen? Is it well integrated? Is it interpreted and analyzed? These questions address the essay's logic. (See Chapter 17.)	Is **grammar** used effectively, or are there errors in subject/verb agreement, pronoun case, pronoun reference, etc.? (See Chapter 24.)
Identify specific appeals to the reader's **needs and values**. Are these appeals appropriate to the argument? Do they evoke rather than manipulate the reader's emotions? These questions address the essay's **engagement**. (See Chapter 19.)	Examine the essay's **diction**: are words used correctly and effectively, or are there examples of words that have been misused or are not thoroughly understood? (See Chapters 15 and 24.)
Identify specific uses of **expert opinion**. Are these uses appropriate to the argument? Are they well chosen? Are they interpreted and commented on? These questions address the essay's **credibility**. (See Chapters 20–22.)	Examine the **citation** of quoted or paraphrased textual evidence. Are the sources ethically and accurately cited according to the assigned citation style? (See Appendix B.)
Think carefully about the **assumptions** your peer may be making about how evidence relates to claim, about what readers need or value, or about the qualifications/authority of expert sources. Do any of these assumptions create a problem in the communication triangle (the relationship among writer, reader, and text)? These questions address the essay's **reasoning**. (See Chapters 17 and 18.)	Is the **punctuation** in the essay clear and effective? Does the writer appear to understand the different uses of commas, semicolons, and colons, for example? Are quotation marks, hyphens, and apostrophes used effectively? (See Chapter 26 and Appendix A.)

(continued)

Observe the **order and organization** of the essay's paragraphs: Is the organization logical? Does each paragraph belong? Do ideas appear in a reasonable order, or would they benefit from reorganization? These questions address the essay's **structure**. (See Chapter 14.)

Has the essay been proofread carefully for **surface-level errors**? Are there careless errors of spelling or typography that should be corrected? Does the essay follow the assigned format completely and accurately? (See Chapters 15 and 23.)

▶ *Let Us Show You:* Peer Review

You may recall that at the end of Chapter 8, Casey completed a draft essay about plagiarism. Now it's about time in the writing process for a peer review. So, just like any good student, Casey has decided to submit his draft for a thoughtful, constructive peer review. And like any thoughtful classmate, Mara has agreed to provide the peer review.

Draft Plagiarism Essay (I still need a title)

The Grays Harbor College Code of Conduct posted on the college's Web site states that disciplinary action may be taken regarding *All forms of student academic dishonesty, including cheating; falsification; plagiarism; facilitating, aiding or abetting dishonesty or engaging in any conduct specifically prohibited by a faculty member in the course syllabus or class discussion.* There are consequences for all of the behaviors listed, including plagiarism. It makes sense that the consequences for cheating should be severe, but plagiarism is a bit more complicated. Merriam-webster.com defines plagiarize as "to steal and pass off (the ideas or words of another) as your own: use (another's production) without crediting the source" or "to commit literary theft: present as new and original an idea or product derived from an existing source." But are any ideas really "original" in this day and age? With an Internet with everything that's ever been written available at a mouse click, it's ridiculous to expect college students to have the source of every word or idea that isn't original.

> Including a definition is a good idea — but are these your words? If not, you need to put them in quotes.

> Your thesis is clear, but it might be overstated — does your essay show that plagiarism rules really are "ridiculous"?

Even aside from the Internet, how many of our thoughts are actually original? Not very many, probably. We share information and ideas without even knowing it. That is why people who live in the same area share a common language — so they can communicate and share ideas, even ideas as simple as, "Hey, run away from that bear!" So as soon as using language comes onto the stage (and none of us really remember a time before it existed), whose ideas are whose becomes confusing. Nowadays, everything that has ever been written is available at the click of a mouse, which is both a blessing and a curse.

> This is an interesting point. But does the last sentence really fit with the rest of the paragraph?

It's a blessing because we can look up anything we want anytime we want to. If I get curious about Jane Austen's life or squid fishing or whatever, I can research it as much as I want on the Internet. All knowledge is available to me, as long as I have a way to access the Internet. On the other hand, it's a curse because our culture, especially academic culture, hasn't changed to meet the new availability of information. Grays Harbor College's plagiarism policy is an example of this lack of progress.

> This is another interesting point. Can you support it with examples?

Academia has been slow to change, which makes sense because school is built upon this idea of "intellectual property." Professors at universities are hired partly because they will do research and create original ideas. But when you think about it, their ideas aren't original, because they learned from their professors. But that is actually kind of beside the point: college students aren't college professors, and that is not how people in the real world treat information these days.

> Can you talk about what "original ideas" are?

Things get called "plagiarism" in a college classroom that don't in the real world. I don't mean going to one of those "Free Essays 4U" Web sites (also known as cheating). I'm talking about random facts or bits of information as a way to back up an opinion or interesting

(continued)

interpretations of a poem — things like that. If I'm having a conversation with someone about a movie we both saw, and I also read an interesting interpretation of that movie somewhere, I might present that idea to my friend without including the source. I'm not being dishonest and trying to trick my friend into thinking I'm of above average intelligence; I'm just sharing an interesting piece of information from a source I probably don't even remember. The information itself is more important than where it came from. If it makes my friend see things in a new way, who really cares if it's my idea or someone else's? It should be the same in a college essay. As long as I'm using information effectively to make a strong point, it shouldn't matter whether I cite every single source for every single idea that isn't my own. Not only is that unreasonable, it's basically impossible.

> Good example — but I'd like to know more. Can you discuss how a conversation with a friend is similar to writing an assignment for a college class?

▶ *Talk Amongst Yourselves . . .*

Now that you've read Casey's draft essay, take a few minutes to write down your responses to the questions below. Then break into groups of three and discuss your responses with each other.

What are your first reactions to Casey's essay? In other words, what is your subjective response? How would you sum up the main point of the essay in your own words? How well do you think it makes and supports that point? What advice would you give Casey to improve his essay? Perhaps equally important, what are your reactions to Mara's peer review? Are her questions helpful? Has she missed things that you would comment on if you were the peer reviewer?

▶ *Now You Try:* Peer Review

At the end of Chapter 8 you completed a first draft of Practice Essay Assignment #1, and chances are that some of your classmates did the same. Now it's time to offer your peer-reviewer services to a colleague who's in the market for some feedback. (If you don't remember how to read recursively, head over to Chapter 4 for a refresher before moving on.)

Making use of your recursive reading skills, read your peer's draft, referring to the peer review checklist on pages 157–58. As you go through the draft a second time, be more analytical.

Annotate the draft: make notes that answer the questions on the checklist as appropriate — yes, right there on the page if you'd like.

Are you expected to be an expert on writing? No! Remember that your central task in peer review is to give the writer your perspective on the draft. What's working well, from your point of view? What could be improved?

Reality Check! Peer Review

We have three pieces of advice for you as you engage in peer review:

▶ Be as specific as you can be.
▶ Be constructive by providing positive suggestions.
▶ If you have to choose between generosity and honesty, choose honesty.

INSTRUCTOR CRITIQUE: WHAT TO EXPECT

As we mentioned earlier, the biggest difference between peer review and instructor critique is *expertise*. You can't fairly expect your peers (classmates) to be qualified experts on writing. After all, they're enrolled in the same class you're in, right? But you can — and *should* — expect your instructor in a writing class to be an expert on writing. This means that you can — and *should* — place a higher degree of confidence in the accuracy of your instructor's comments than you do in your peer's comments. In other words, if your peer review and your instructor critique disagree about the effectiveness of your thesis or the correctness of your grammar or pretty much anything in your draft, you should probably place more weight on your instructor's assessment.

What Will Your Professor Say?

Generally speaking, your instructor's critique will provide feedback on the same issues that your peer will address during peer review — the elements cited in the peer review checklist on pages 157–58. In this respect, feedback from your peer and feedback from your instructor are equal. But there will be differences between them as well.

For one thing, your instructor's comments will be more definitive and confident than your peer's. Whereas a peer might write something like, "It might just be me, but I can't find your thesis," your instructor is much more likely to write something like, "You will need to make a clear thesis statement," or even "Where is your thesis? It seems to be missing." The difference between their comments is natural and can be attributed to the degree of confidence each reader has in his or her ability to provide useful feedback.

A second crucial difference between peer review and instructor critique is that your instructor is most likely in *permanent teaching mode*, which means that he or she will often ask questions rather than make statements. So instead of saying "You need to cite a source here," your instructor is likely to say, "Do you need to cite a source here? This information seems to be borrowed from somewhere." Do not be fooled by the question; it does not mean that the instructor doesn't know the answer. It means that your instructor would like *you* to answer the question for yourself, since learning is more effective when students solve puzzles instead of being given the answers.

> Did you notice that the phrase
> "learning is more effective when students
> solve puzzles instead of being given the answers"
> is written partially in the passive voice? It works here,
> but in most cases you'll want to use the active voice.
> Chapter 24 explains why.

When you review your instructor's critique of your writing, you should review it actively (i.e., be the student solving puzzles) rather than passively (i.e., be the student who is given the answers). To be that active student, you will need to put some effort not only into reading your professor's critique but also into understanding the feedback that he or she has presented.

What Will Your Professor Mean?

There's a certain amount of interpretation that goes into understanding the comments your instructor makes on your draft. This means that you, as the writer of the draft, need to commit to interpreting the feedback if you want to improve your writing.

The first step in making that commitment is to actually read your instructor's comments. This might sound like silly or unnecessary advice, but a surprisingly high percentage of students ignore instructor feedback — either because they're uncomfortable with criticism or because they mistakenly believe that critique is just something *extra* that they can take or leave. Does this mean that you need to make every change suggested by your instructor? Well, no, not necessarily. It is, after all, *your* essay. But you would be foolish not to seriously *consider* each comment — and you can't consider something that you don't read or fully understand.

To ensure that you understand your professor's feedback, look at each comment individually. Make sure you know which passage in your draft the professor's note refers to, and think about how you might address the specific concern of the comment. We strongly suggest that you **take notes** in the margins right next to your instructor's comments so that later, when you are ready to revise, you will have a record of how you interpreted the critique.

It's possible that some of your instructor's comments will be difficult for you to interpret. Your professor might use a term that you're not familiar with or ask a question whose answer you really don't know. What do you do then? Fortunately, this problem has a one-word solution: *Ask.*

If your professor allows in-class time for questions about critique and review prior to revision, take advantage of the opportunity. Bring your critiqued draft to class with you, along with your own interpretive notes. This will put you in an excellent position to ask specific, meaningful questions when you are given the chance.

If no class time is dedicated to critique/review follow-up, we encourage you to remember that your instructor almost certainly holds daily or weekly office hours — a time when the instructor is at his or her desk, just *waiting* for an interested and engaged student to stop by for some one-on-one help. Be that student.

Professors love it when interested, engaged students drop by during office hours with specific, meaningful questions. Seriously.

A final note about getting feedback from qualified professionals: most colleges and universities have a **writing center** — a help desk staffed by trained writing consultants whose jobs entail working one-on-one with students seeking to improve their writing skills. When your available hours don't mesh with your instructor's office hours, or when you simply feel the need to get some qualified feedback from an alternate source, the writing center is a terrific resource. We urge you to take advantage of this assistance and expertise, which is often available both in person and online.

So how do you proceed with revision after you've received feedback from your peers, your instructor, and maybe even a writing center professional? What do you do first?

That's right. First you spend precisely three minutes throwing yourself a pity party because someone dared to find fault with your beautiful writing. And then — you revise.

Four Levels of Revision: Content, Structure, Coherence, and Precision

It might be tempting to start with something that feels manageable, like reviewing the punctuation problems outlined in Chapter 26 of this book and fixing them all. But we beg you to reconsider. Our advice is that you start with the big stuff and work your way down to the little stuff.

Specifically, we think you should make every effort to build a revision plan that answers each of the questions in the *Reality Check!* box below. We strongly encourage you to follow the checklist's steps in order. This will allow you to first tackle a few major concerns before moving on to smaller or less substantive issues.

And why would you want to tackle the big stuff before moving on to the little stuff? To save yourself time and effort! If you focus on content and structure first, then some of your big changes will likely eliminate some of your smaller problems.

Reality Check! The Four Levels of Revision

Step 1: Content Revision (covered in detail in Chapter 13)

▶ How well does your essay meet the requirements of the original assignment?

▶ How clear and appropriate is your thesis?

▶ How well have you supported your thesis with relevant and specific details?

▶ How unified is your essay? Are there any irrelevant parts?

Step 2: Structural Revision (covered in detail in Chapter 14)

▶ How effective is your introduction?

▶ How well does the overall order of the essay reflect your inductive or deductive structure?

▶ How balanced are the subtopics covered in the body of the essay?

▶ How effective is the conclusion?

Step 3: Editing for Coherence (covered in detail in Chapter 15)

▶ How effective are the transitions between ideas in your essay?

▶ How appropriate is your tone in relation to the topic and audience?

Step 4: Proofreading for Precision (covered in detail in Chapter 23, with reference materials outlined in Chapters 24–26 and Appendix A)

▶ How effective are your sentences in terms of structure, word usage, and grammar?

▶ How correct is your writing in terms of spelling, punctuation, and mechanics?

So there you have it: our patented four-level approach to revision. We hope the reasoning behind global-to-local (or big-to-small) revision has become clear and that you understand why we strongly recommend dealing with content before tackling structure and resolving structural problems before adjusting for coherence and precision.

But in case our reasoning isn't as clear as we'd hoped, we offer an analogy: it doesn't make sense to put time and effort into trimming, buffing, and polishing the toenails on a foot that's just going to be amputated. (Our imagery is a little gross — but hey, we'll do whatever it takes to make you the confident writer you were born to be!)

▶ *Let Us Show You:* **Preparing to Revise**

Now that Casey has received some feedback on his draft essay (remember the review Mara provided back on pages 158–60?), it's time for him to develop a revision plan. Being very conscious of our advice to tackle the big stuff first, Casey is trying to focus only on those issues that should be addressed in the first stage, which is content revision.

> Wow, it's really hard to resist the urge to just move some commas around.

> Yeah! But the big stuff here means finding ways to support your thesis better. Luckily, you have the content-level revision checklist to follow.

Casey's Content-Level Revision Plan

1. Revise my thesis so that its tone matches the rest of the essay.
2. Develop the "original ideas" paragraph so that my reasons are clear.
3. Explain why information and knowledge are the same thing.
4. Come up with a good example of "intellectual property."
5. Explain why I think academic culture hasn't changed over time.
6. Figure out a way to more clearly link the movie conversation example to my main point.

► *Talk Amongst Yourselves . . .*

Find a partner in the class and discuss the way Casey has prioritized revision tasks based on Step 1 of our four-level approach. What would you have placed as the highest priority? How might your own list based on Mara's feedback differ from Casey's?

► *Now You Try:* **Preparing to Revise**

Okay, now it's your turn. Ready?

1. Print out a copy of the draft of Practice Essay Assignment #1 that you completed at the end of Chapter 8. (Alternatively, if you've recently written a draft of an assignment for another class you're currently taking, you might print that out instead.)

2. Show your draft to someone. Your professor, a classmate, or a consultant in your campus writing center would be best — it doesn't really matter who reads and reviews your draft *as long as the person is familiar with the original assignment you were given.* We can't stress this enough: feedback from someone who has no idea what you were assigned to write is not very useful, and it can in fact lead to disastrous results if the person advises you that it would be "really cool" to do something that isn't appropriate to the assignment.

3. Ask your reviewer to write notes on your draft: comments, observations, questions — anything is okay, really, as long as the notes are responsive to what you've written in a way that is honest and constructive.

4. Read through your reviewer's notes very carefully and make a list of issues that you think you'll need to address to improve your essay.

Hang on to that list. You'll be needing it . . . soon!

Chapter 13

Content Revision: Say What You Mean, and Mean What You Say

> Whenever there's something wrong with your writing, suspect that there's something wrong with your thinking.
> — Patricia T. O'Conner

We have, on occasion, overheard students talking about revising their papers before turning them in for a grade. It warms our hearts, because every time someone revises a draft, an angel gets its wings.

But we have also overheard many a conversation that goes something like Mara and Casey's above. At this point, we usually stop listening because we are depressed. If you are tempted to file away the word *revise* in the same mental folder where you keep the word *proofread*, then settle in with a cup of coffee (or tea — we don't judge) because this chapter is for you. And honestly? This chapter is for everyone who needs to rethink his or her first-draft ideas — which is pretty much all of us.

Revision Means Re-vision

When your writing teacher asks you to revise, he's not suggesting that you forgot to use the spell-checker — even though it's possible that you did indeed forget to use the spell-checker. No, your writing teacher understands that the word *revise* comes from the Latin *revisere*, which means "to look at again; to visit again; to look back upon." If this definition of **revision** seems somewhat familiar to you, that might be because it's analogous to the definition of *recursive* that we discussed back in Chapter 4. Remember? Revisiting, reconsidering, reencountering, reexperiencing? Recursion is good for both reading and writing.

Revision is a much more meaningful activity than mere spell-checking and proofreading. Don't get us wrong: both spell-checking and proofreading are important parts of getting your final draft ready to go public, but they need to occur *after* you've put honest effort into re-vision — into *seeing* your essay *again*.

One reason that we seek peer review and instructor critique of drafts (see Chapter 12) is to help us see our own writing from another perspective — the perspective of the reader. If we spend too much time viewing our drafts as *writers* and not as *readers*, we run the risk of losing sight of the big picture. We might, in other words, be unable to see the forest for the trees.

When we say, "see the forest for the trees," the forest, represents your ideas, while the trees represent the specific elements — such as words and sentences — that make up the forest. You need to keep your eye on the forest of *what* you are saying before you focus on the twigs and leaves of *how* you are saying it.

It's important to recognize that when you commit to revising your writing, you're committing to revisiting it fully. That means that you have to come at it fresh, as if you've never read it before, and you have to devote yourself to making it better in ways both large and small. Don't be afraid to address the big stuff — and address it sooner rather than later.

Sometimes students are reluctant to revise at the content level because they're afraid they'll have to reconsider whether they're really saying what they mean to say. When this happens to you, rejoice! Far from being a sign of failure, reconsidering your own ideas and the way you're presenting them is a sign of success.

Think about it: Would you rather skip the heavy lifting, run the spell-checker, and turn in something that you *know* could and should be better? Or do you want to put in the necessary effort to write an essay you can be proud of?

If you're ready for content revision, then you're ready to take a deep breath and dive into the first stage of the four-step revision plan we gave you in Chapter 12 (see the *Reality Check!* box on page 164).

Reality Check! Content Revision

▶ How well does your essay meet the requirements of the original assignment?

▶ How clear and appropriate is your thesis?

▶ How well have you supported your thesis with relevant and specific details?

▶ How unified is your essay? Are there any irrelevant parts?

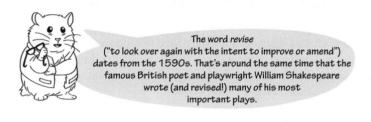

The word *revise*
("to look over again with the intent to improve or amend")
dates from the 1590s. That's around the same time that the
famous British poet and playwright William Shakespeare
wrote (and revised!) many of his most
important plays.

DOES YOUR DRAFT ADDRESS THE ASSIGNMENT?

The first thing to consider is whether your essay meets the basic assignment criteria. Get out the assignment sheet you were given, or pull it up on your Web browser, and refresh your memory as to what you were asked to do in the first place. If you need a reminder of all of the ways to understand an assignment, you might want to review the checklist on page 50 in Chapter 5. No, really. You should review it. It will take about five minutes — but it's worth it to make sure you're still on-task, right?

If everything checks out, then move on — but if not, then you'll have to do some refocusing before you can move on to the other steps in content-level revision. If your draft is off task, you will need to evaluate whether you will be able to get back on track by yourself. For instance, if you were assigned to use three sources and you've used only two, then you can probably find the third source on your own.

If, however, you discover that your draft fails to meet its assignment in a more significant way, don't be shy about asking for help from your professor, from a classmate, from the writing center — really, from anyone who is in a position to know and *understand* what you've been assigned to do. Informed feedback can be invaluable in refocusing your approach to the task.

Once you are back on track, it's time to take a long, hard look at your main idea: what is it, and how is it presented?

DOES YOUR THESIS HAVE ISSUES?

Once you're sure that your essay meets the basic assignment criteria, it's time to take a step back and assess your main point, or **thesis**. (If you're having trouble remembering what a thesis is, revisit Chapter 7.)

▶ How is your thesis working for you? Does it accurately reflect your main point?

▶ Did you get any feedback from peer reviewers or from your professor that indicates you might want to rethink the point you are making?

▶ Are there any logical, ethical, moral, or practical problems with your thesis?

If your main idea has issues, then you'll need to consider whether the problems are things you can explain away as you write, or whether these problems are so overwhelming that it would make sense to adjust the point you want to make. Notice we say *adjust*, not *completely change*.

When students get feedback suggesting a need for change, they sometimes freak out and want to change topics completely. Please, whatever you do, don't do that. It puts you back at square one.

We've said this before in different ways, but we think it's worth repeating: Good writing doesn't become good by magic or luck. It gets better through work and revision. So don't cut and run when you come across a problem in your writing — just make what you've written *better*.

Sometimes the best way to make your draft better is to rethink your main point. Remember back in Chapter 7 when we talked about the working thesis? Sure you do! It's called a *working* thesis because it's temporary — it's what you *think* your main point will be when you're just starting to write your draft.

By the time you've actually written your draft, it's entirely possible that your focus will have shifted. Writing is a process of discovery, and it's likely that drafting will have caused you to discover that you want to make a somewhat different main point. Again, this isn't bad news — it's good news, because it's evidence that you are in fact improving your essay.

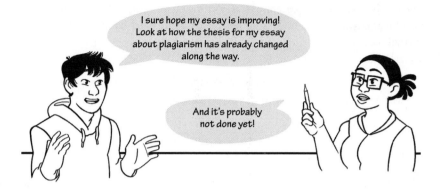

Here's Casey's very first attempt at a working thesis, from page 86 in Chapter 7.

> Although it's easy to think that plagiarism is something that happens only when a person decides to cheat on purpose, it's really a much more complicated subject with many different sides to explore.

Next, as part of preparing to write a first draft of the essay, Casey asked himself what his point really was, and he came up with this refocused version of his working thesis (see page 96 in Chapter 8).

> In the age of the Internet, when everything that's ever been written is available to everyone on the planet at the click of a mouse, it doesn't make sense to accuse honest college students of plagiarism just because they don't cite the source of every word or idea that isn't original.

Different, huh? And by the time he wrote the first draft of his essay, he had made the thesis shorter and a little stronger (page 101 in Chapter 8).

> With everything that's ever been written available at a mouse click thanks to the Internet, it's ridiculous to expect college students to have the source of every word or idea that isn't original.

And that brings us to the present, as Casey's revising for content. He's *still* tinkering with his thesis, trying to make sure he's really saying what he means. Here's his current thesis:

> With the entire Internet available at a mouse click, it's impossible to expect college students to have the source of every word or idea that isn't original.

DOES YOUR ARGUMENT WORK?

Once you're sure that the point you're making is the point you really want to make — and that you've stated it clearly — take a look at the thoroughness and solidity of the argument you've written. And yes, even if your essay is essentially informative, it is still an argument (more on this topic in Chapter 16).

Does the body of your paper **support** your thesis in a clear way? You will probably recall from Chapters 9 and 10 that the central job of each paragraph in the body of your essay is to provide the details necessary to show the reader the validity of your thesis and your topic sentences. Go through your essay paragraph by paragraph with this idea in mind. Be sure to note any paragraphs that make a point but then fail to fully develop the point through examples or other rhetorical modes (see Chapter 11).

If the claims presented in your paragraphs aren't clearly articulated, or if certain sections of the essay wander off-topic and don't work to directly support the thesis, try recrafting those sections. If your support falls short in some places — perhaps you've left a point ambiguous, or you've left the evidence to speak for itself rather than analyzing it and explaining clearly how it supports your point — then you'll need to work on those as well. Again, if you need guidance with these tasks, you will probably want to review our advice in Chapter 10 on analytical paragraphs.

Content-level revision often involves a fair amount of rigorous thinking to ensure that you are presenting the best and clearest possible case for your reader, thus encouraging the reader to agree that you are making a very good point.

IS YOUR ESSAY UNIFIED?

A final consideration during content revision is whether any chunks of your draft are soggy because they have been left out in the rain and aren't covered by the umbrella of your thesis. You remember our discussion on pages 113–14 back in Chapter 9 of how a topic sentence serves as an umbrella for the other sentences in a paragraph, right? There was even a picture of an umbrella, very much like the one on the facing page. Ringing any bells? Anyway, our point is that an essay, like a paragraph, needs to achieve **unity**. That is, the reader needs to feel that the entire essay is about one topic — and, at the same time, that the entire essay is working to develop and support the essay's main point. **Thus, the** *thesis* **is to the** *essay* **what the** *topic sentence* **is to the** *paragraph*: **a central idea that unifies the content related to it.**

Just as you might find and eliminate a sentence that clearly doesn't fit within a paragraph, you may also find sentences or even paragraphs that don't fit within your essay. Cutting a chunk of your writing isn't always pleasant, especially if you've worked hard on it, or if you like the way you've written it. But if its presence is weakening your essay, then you will need to let it go.

Note that we've saved the *cutting* part of content revision for the end. This is because a paragraph that seems not to fit at first might actually be quite appropriate once you've revised your thesis — or once you've developed the paragraphs around it.

In other words, don't decide to eliminate anything from your draft until you are certain that your thesis works and that your essay develops well enough to support that thesis. It's better to *over*write (at first!) and then have to omit a few passages than to cut something that you later will wish with all your heart that you hadn't.

▶ *Let Us Show You:* Content-Level Revision

Having indulged in a three-minute pity party over Mara's review of his draft essay (see pages 158–60 in Chapter 12), Casey has returned his focus to more practical matters and is preparing to move forward with his content-level revision. The first step in this process is creating a revision plan — remember Casey's plan from the end of Chapter 12?

Revision Tasks for Plagiarism Essay (Draft)

1. Revise my thesis so that its tone matches the rest of the essay.
2. Develop the "original ideas" paragraph so that my reasons are clear.
3. Explain why information and knowledge are the same thing.
4. Come up with a good example of "intellectual property."
5. Explain why I think academic culture hasn't changed over time.
6. Figure out a way to more clearly link the movie conversation example to my main point.

Now Casey needs to go through the plan step by step and make the necessary revisions to improve the overall content of his draft.

Casey has marked all of his changes so that Mara — who's doing another peer review for him — can compare them to the unrevised version. He has also included a working essay title.

Who Cares About Plagiarism? (Content-Level Revision)

The Grays Harbor College Code of Conduct posted on the college's Web site states that disciplinary action may be taken regarding "All forms of student academic dishonesty, including cheating; falsification; plagiarism; facilitating, aiding or abetting dishonesty or engaging in any conduct specifically prohibited by a faculty member in the course syllabus or class discussion." There are consequences for all of the behaviors listed, including plagiarism. It makes sense that the consequences for cheating should be severe, but plagiarism is a bit more complicated. Merriam-webster.com defines plagiarize as "to steal and pass off (the ideas or words of another) as your own: use (another's production) without crediting the source" or "to commit literary theft: present as new and original an idea or product derived from an existing source." But are any ideas really "original" in this day and age? With the entire Internet ~~with everything that's ever been written~~ available at a mouse click, it's ~~ridiculous~~ impossible to expect college students to have the source of every word or idea that isn't original.

Even aside from the Internet, how many of our thoughts are actually origi-nal? ~~Not very many, probably.~~ We share information and ideas without even knowing it. That is why people who live in the same area share a common language — so they can communicate and share ideas, even ideas as simple as, "Hey, run away from that bear!" ~~So as soon as using language comes onto the stage (and none of us really remembers a time before it existed),~~ With the Internet, the question of whose ideas are whose becomes even more confus-ing. Nowadays, everything that has ever been written is available at the click of a mouse, which is both a blessing and a curse.

It's a blessing because we can look up anything we want anytime we want to in order to access information and gain knowledge. If I get curious about Jane Austen's life or squid fishing or whatever, I can research it as much as I want on the Internet. All ~~knowledge~~ information is available to me, as long as I have a way to access the Internet. On the other hand, it's a curse because our culture, especially academic culture, hasn't changed to meet the new availability of information. Grays Harbor College's plagiarism policy is an example of this lack of progress.

Academia ~~has been slow to change~~ still focuses on plagiarism as a kind of intellectual theft, which makes sense because ~~it~~ school is built upon this idea of "intellectual property." Professors at universities are hired partly because they will do research and create original ideas. But when you think about it, their ideas aren't original, because they learned from their professors. ~~But that is actually kind of beside the point.~~ And even besides that, those rules are about professors; college students aren't college professors, and ~~that is not how~~ people in the real world don't treat information as property these days.

Things get called "plagiarism" in a college classroom that don't in the real world. I don't mean going to one of those "Free Essays 4U" Web sites (also known as cheating). I'm talking about random facts or bits of informa-tion used as a way to back up an opinion or interesting interpretation of a poem — things like that. If I'm having a conversation with someone about a movie we both saw, and I also read an interesting interpretation of that movie somewhere, I might present that idea to my friend without including the source. I'm not being dishonest and trying to trick my friend into thinking I'm of above average intelligence; I'm just sharing an interesting piece of

(continued)

information from a source I probably don't even remember. The information itself is more important than where it came from. If it makes my friend see things in a new way, who really cares if it's my idea or theirs? It should be the same in a college essay. As long as I'm using information effectively to make a strong point, it shouldn't matter whether I cite every single source for every single idea that isn't my own. Not only is that unreasonable, it's basically impossible.

* Maybe that whole idea should be the introduction?

▶ *Talk Amongst Yourselves ...*

Break into groups and discuss Casey's response to peer review. To what extent has Casey responded to each of the significant content-level problems that Mara pointed out in her review? Which issues, if any, have been left unresolved? If this were your draft, how might you approach content-level revision differently?

▶ *Now You Try:* **Content-Level Revision**

Remember the task we gave you at the end of Chapter 12? We asked you to show your draft essay to someone — your professor, a classmate, a consultant in your campus writing center — for feedback and, after receiving that feedback, to compile a list of the revision tasks you think you'll need to complete.

Remember that we also told you to hang on to that list because you would need it soon? Well, consider it "soon." Here's what comes next:

Now that you have a list of revision tasks based on your reviewer's response to your draft, you have exactly three minutes with which to throw yourself a pity party (why should you get any more or less time than Casey got?), and then it's time to (drumroll please!) ... develop a content-level revision plan by considering that feedback in relation to the content revision checklist we provided earlier in this chapter (see page 169).

If you organize the steps in your plan according to the priorities established in the checklist, then you will have a solid to-do list for revising your essay — one that is similar to the list of tasks Casey presented on page 174.

We think you'll find that considering content problems one at a time — in relation to a reasonable checklist of "big picture" issues — makes the first major step in the revision process a manageable one. Because many, if not most, of the tasks in your content-level revision plan will begin with the word *think*, you probably will not dive into rewriting quite yet. Instead, it's good to remember during the early stages of revision that thinking is never a waste of effort. Take your time and do it right. When you've done enough thinking about the content areas that need revision, you'll know it — because you will feel that it's time to do some more writing. Which brings us to the next step: revise your first draft to improve the content.

In this chapter we have focused primarily on the first stage of revision, which emphasizes strengthening and clarifying the content of your essay. Subsequent chapters in this section will focus on revising for structure (Chapter 14) and for coherence and precision (Chapter 15).

But to be fully prepared for the structural revision that comes next, there's one more thing you'll want to do.

Reverse Engineer Your Draft

Back in the day, we were taught that prewriting involves drawing up a detailed, formal outline with obscure roman-numeral headings and endless sections and subsections. Scary stuff, especially when you're still in the predrafting stage of the writing process.

Don't get us wrong. We *do* believe in making a plan that orders the potential elements of an essay, but the formal outline seems like a particularly torturous exercise at the very beginning of the process, when your ideas haven't yet taken shape in a draft.

However, we find the formal outline very useful as a way to review the structure of your draft later on. Once you have completed a draft and received some feedback from an instructor or a peer, and after you have initially revised for content in response to that feedback, you can reverse engineer your draft by outlining its components. In this way, you can check the organization of your draft to see if it's as thoroughly and effectively presented as it could be — and the formal outline is a great tool for just such a reality check.

THE FORMAL OUTLINE: OH, RELAX! THIS WON'T HURT A BIT!

So what is a formal outline anyway? How is it different from those organizational notes you scribbled all over the place during the prewriting phase?

A formal outline is different because it's a single, complete accounting of the ideas already contained in your draft, in the order in which they already appear. The **formal outline** is a focused summary of your essay that you can review, revise, and use as a guide to the structural changes you want to make in your essay.

In our view, the formal outline serves three important purposes:

▶ It allows you to **compare the content** you *actually* have in your draft with the content that you know you *should* have in your draft.

▶ It **reveals the holes in your essay** where any missing content rightly belongs (as well as any empty content that's filling space but not serving any identifiable purpose).

▶ It lets you **see the overall organization** of a multipage essay without flipping back and forth between pages.

That formal outline sounds pretty sweet. Where can I get one?

The good news is — you've already got one! It's right there in your draft.

It's true. If you've written a complete draft, you actually already have a formal outline — it's just a matter of identifying the components and plugging them into the appropriate slots in your formal-outline format.

THE FORMAT OF A FORMAL OUTLINE

Now about that format: there are a few different accepted schemes for labeling the elements in a formal outline, but we'll just show you the standard outline format. The general idea is to break your essay down into its largest chunks and label each chunk with a number (or letter) to indicate that those chunks are equal to each other in category. Then you break down each of those chunks into its component pieces and label those smaller pieces with numbers or letters of a different category.

The length and complexity of the essay will determine how many levels of detail your outline will require. By "levels of detail," we simply mean points, subpoints, descriptive details, and evidence that supports the points. Each progressive level of detail is indented farther than the preceding (higher) level.

Standard outline format uses capital roman numerals for the first level of detail, capital letters for the second level, Arabic numerals for the third level, lowercase letters for the fourth level, and lowercase Roman numerals for the fifth level (most outlines don't go beyond a fifth level of detail). The following is a formal outline of Chapter 1 of this book, presented in standard format. You might notice that the levels of detail here don't necessarily correspond to the headings in the chapter, just as the outline levels for an essay won't necessarily correspond to any section headings that appear in the essay. This is because a thorough outline attempts to dig deeper into the levels of content than section headings do.

Outline of Chapter 1

   I. Good writing takes courage.

      A. Writing feels risky.

      B. Organizing your thoughts into a text can be scary.

  II. Most college writing takes the form of an essay.

      A. In college, *paper* often means the same thing as *essay*.

      B. The word *essay* means "to try."

         1. By this definition, writing an essay is really just making an attempt at creating a text.

      C. College is all about keeping an open mind.

         1. When you think you can improve and learn, you are less frustrated and are more likely to succeed.

         2. Carol Dweck has identified some of the characteristics of successful students.

         3. A group exercise asks you to consider what type of learner you are.

 III. Writing is more than a product — it's a process.

      A. There are steps involved.

      B. In this book, we'll give you those steps.

      C. The process is just as important as the final product.

 IV. Not all writers use the same process.

      A. Some writers like to start writing right away, while others like to think about or discuss their ideas for a while.

      B. Some writers like to write by hand, while others like to type.

      C. Some writers like to outline first, but others prefer a more relaxed approach to organizing their writing.

  V. The writing process has stages.

      A. A *Reality Check!* box lists the stages involved in writing a college paper.

         1. These *Reality Check!* boxes are a regular feature of this book, so expect to see more of them.

         2. The book itself is organized around the stages of the writing process.

         3. A *Reality Check!* box offers tips on how to use this book.

      B. Try not to rush through or skip any steps.

      C. As you continue to write, you'll develop a process that works for you.

      D. For now, use our process until you become more confident.

The act of creating the outline allows us (one might even say *forces* us) to see what we have actually written and compare it to what we know we *meant* to write. It also shows us how well the various topics and subtopics have been balanced within the overall text: Are some topics covered in insufficient detail? Are others covered in *too much* detail? Have we spent more or less time on any topic than we intended to?

Finally, the outline provides us with a neat and tidy summary of the entire text (in this case, Chapter 1). With our reverse-engineered outline, we can easily see whether our essay is organized in a meaningful and sensible way without reading the entire thing each time we consider making a change to the order of its contents.

The Sentence Outline

By the way, if you've been reading very carefully, you may have noticed that the example on page 179 is what's known as a **sentence outline** — an outline in which each entry is a complete sentence rather than a word or phrase. These outlines are a little harder to write, but we believe they're worth it. When you make yourself summarize the major points of your essay in complete sentences, you ensure that your essay is actually *saying something* about each topic and subtopic you've chosen to include. Sentence outlines also force you to *understand* everything you've said in your essay. And if you understand what you're saying, there's a good chance your reader will, too.

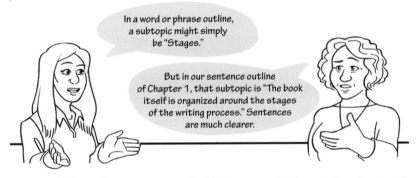

We can almost hear you saying, *Duh! It's my essay! Of course I understand it.* But oh, dear reader, please trust us when we tell you that the meaning of a college essay — especially a college essay that includes words and ideas borrowed from research sources — can sometimes manage to escape its author. When this happens, it makes us very sad. So we strongly encourage you to use sentence outlines when you're reality checking your draft to prepare for structural revision: aside from all its other benefits, the sentence outline may actually cause you to understand your own thoughts better.

► *Let Us Show You:* Reverse Engineer Your Draft

Casey is ready to make a formal outline of his draft to help him see how effective his content-level revision has been. Mara is on board to review the outline when Casey is done.

Formal Outline:

Who Cares About Plagiarism?

by Casey N. Pointe

   I. Introduction: We don't have to cite information when we talk, so why do we need to cite it when we write?

     A. In a conversation with a friend, I repeated information that I read online about a film.

     B. I didn't name the source because it wasn't necessary.

     C. Why do college professors require us to cite sources, then?

     D. Thesis: This story makes me question the plagiarism rules at colleges and universities today.

  II. Plagiarism is against the rules of the college.

     A. Plagiarism is defined as a form of cheating.

     B. There are consequences for plagiarizing.

     C. It's problematic to define plagiarism as cheating because there are no original ideas.

       1. We have access to all kinds of ideas that aren't our own because of the Internet.

     D. It's unreasonable to expect us to cite everything.

 III. With the Internet, the question of whose ideas are whose has become even more confusing.

     A. There's no such thing as an original idea.

     B. The Internet has made this more confusing than it was already.

       1. We have access to everything ever written on the Internet.

Marginal notes:

Now that you've changed your introduction, this looks pretty balanced and reasonable.

Here's your main point.

This looks like two different topics — plagiarism and original ideas.

Maybe this "original idea" stuff belongs with the ideas above.

(continued)

IV. The Internet is both a blessing and a curse.

    A. It's a blessing because I can look up anything anytime I want.

        1. If I get curious about Jane Austen's life or squid fishing or whatever, I can research it as much as I want on the Internet.

    B. It's a curse because our culture, especially academic culture, hasn't changed to meet the new availability of information.

        1. Grays Harbor College's plagiarism policy is an example of this lack of progress.

V. Academia has outdated views of "plagiarism."

    A. Academia views plagiarism as theft because academia is built on the idea of intellectual property.

        1. Professors get hired and keep their jobs by coming up with original ideas.

    B. People in the "real world" don't view intellectual property in the same way.

    C. College students aren't professors.

VI. Things get called "plagiarism" in a college classroom that don't in the real world.

    A. We don't cite everything we read in everyday life, but we do use the information.

    B. Intentional cheating is different.

        1. Cheating Web sites are an example.

    C. It's unreasonable and impossible to expect us to cite every idea that's not our own when we write.

Margin notes:

It seems like maybe "blessing" and "curse" are two different topics.

Is this too many ideas for one paragraph? Maybe separate academia from "real world"?

The cheating point doesn't seem to fit in the middle of this conclusion.

And you have another new thesis!

▶ *Talk Amongst Yourselves . . .*

Take a few minutes to write down your responses to the following questions. Then break into groups of three and discuss your responses with each other.

How useful do you think Casey's formal outline will be for the structural revision? To answer this, you might want to compare the outline to the peer-reviewed draft (with Mara's marginal critique notes) on page 158 in

Chapter 12 as well as to the content-level revision earlier in this chapter. Does this outline, and Mara's notes on it, suggest structural changes that Casey needs to make to strengthen his draft? If so, what are they?

► *Now You Try:* **Reverse Engineer Your Draft**

Now that you have revised your draft essay for initial content-level issues, review your new draft carefully. Prepare an accurate formal outline of its content. When you're finished, ask a peer to annotate the outline as Mara has done for Casey — or annotate it yourself. Either way, the annotations will remind you of sections that need to be separated, combined, moved, removed, expanded, or even created.

Happy outlining! We'll see you in Chapter 14, where we'll get into more detail about structural revision.

Chapter 14

Structural Revision: Does It Have to Be a Five-Paragraph Essay?

> Style and structure are the essence of a book; great ideas are hogwash.
> —Vladimir Nabokov

Remember when you learned to ride a bicycle? The training wheels helped for a while — as you learned balance, as you got comfortable on the seat. But once you got the hang of riding, you began to notice that those extra little wheels that once gave you so much freedom now held you back. They got in the way more than they helped you — not to mention how much they embarrassed you around your friends who no longer used them.

The **five-paragraph essay** is kind of like those training wheels. When you have never written an essay or are not used to thinking about the structure of an argument, the five-paragraph essay model is one way to get used to the idea of thesis and support. It teaches some important lessons when you're starting out — for example, an essay should have an introduction, a body, and a conclusion. In addition, the purpose of the essay should be stated at the end of the introduction. And finally, the support in the body should be linked directly to the thesis, which should conveniently break down into three important subtopics.

Here's an example of a thesis statement for a five-paragraph essay: *Cats are better pets than dogs for three reasons: they are independent, they are clean, and they are quiet.* After you've written an introduction that leads up to this thesis, all you need to do to complete the essay is to write three body paragraphs — with each paragraph supporting one of the claims about cats — and then write a conclusion.

However, as you may have begun to suspect, some topics cannot be adequately handled using a three-part thesis and three neatly corresponding body paragraphs. The training wheels are now in your way, so to speak. Okay, so maybe your friends won't make fun of you for relying too heavily on the five-paragraph essay. But clinging to that structure will hold you back when you want to write about something that doesn't easily break into three parts.

So *does* your academic paper have to be a five-paragraph essay? In short, no — unless, of course, your professor has said it must. We recommend learning what you can from the five-paragraph essay model and then moving on from it when you're ready.

The question remains: what should an essay be? It will most likely have an introduction, a thesis statement, some supporting paragraphs, and a conclusion — beyond that, *form* should follow *function* (remember that phrase from Chapter 11?). In other words, the structure of your writing should support your subject. What you write depends on what you're trying to achieve; it depends on your essay's **purpose**, which includes the context you're writing in, the topic you're writing about, your approach to that topic, and the audience you're writing for. So what you end up writing might be shorter or longer. It might be a standard five-paragraph essay, or it might be something else.

In this chapter we'll try to give you everything you need to know so that you can give that amorphous thing you've been working on (sometimes known as a *draft*) some real structure.

Structure Your Draft

Your first draft probably already has some structure. Ideally it begins to make and support a point. When you revise, you begin to fine-tune that structure by really thinking about the most effective way to support your main point, or **thesis**. In other words, you reshape (or *re-form*) your essay in response to what the desired *function* of your essay is. Every piece of expository or argumentative writing requires a specific **structure** so that it may succeed logically, ethically, and emotionally.

Note that we're talking about the *order* in which things appear on the page in your essay — not the order in which you *actually* write things.

In other words, the fact that your essay should have an introduction does not mean that you should write the introduction first. In fact, you probably shouldn't, for reasons we discussed in Chapter 8.

You may be familiar with the advice, "Tell them what you're going to tell them, tell them, and then tell them what you told them." It gives you everything you need to know about structuring your writing. Well, okay, maybe not everything. But it contains an element of truth: academic writing always needs a beginning (let's call it an "introduction"), something in the middle (we'll call it the "body," morbid as that may sound), and some way of concluding (heck, let's call it a "conclusion").

You may have noticed that we've now talked about two different "bodies": the body of an essay and the body of a paragraph. They're basically the same thing, but on different scales. The body of an essay is what supports that essay's thesis statement, and it's composed of a series of body paragraphs. The body of a paragraph supports and develops that paragraph's topic sentence, and it is composed of a series of sentences. In fact, a paragraph is a microcosm of an essay, structurally speaking.

Beginning college students generally do best when they first construct their essays according to a strict formula and then experiment with that formula as they gain experience and confidence. In other words, every writer needs to master the rules before they can break the rules. In general, the more experienced and confident the writer, the more subtle and innovative the essay's structural elements.

In Chapter 9, we talked about paragraph structure as either deductive or inductive based on whether its topic sentence comes at the beginning or the end of the paragraph. An essay too can be organized deductively or inductively, depending on whether its thesis is presented as a premise (at the beginning) or as a conclusion (at the end).

Inductive Organization

An **inductively structured** essay begins with a question or topic to be explored, presents information from which a conclusion is to be drawn, evaluates that information, and finally formulates a conclusion. In other words, an inductive essay answers a question posed at the beginning by providing facts that lead up to the thesis, which appears at the end of the essay.

The word *inductive* comes from the Latin verb *inducere*, meaning "to lead toward." The word *deductive*, on the other hand, comes from the Latin verb *deducere*, meaning "to lead away."

Deductive Organization

A **deductively structured** essay begins with a statement to be proven, provides support for this statement, evaluates the support, and concludes by demonstrating that the thesis has been proven valid. In other words, a deductive essay uses the thesis as both a point of departure and a destination; the reader is led away from the thesis but then returns to it in the end.

Inductive vs. Deductive Essay Structure

	Inductive Essay Structure	Deductive Essay Structure
The Introduction...	... presents the **question** to be answered by the thesis.	... presents the **thesis**.
The Body...	... presents and analyzes the **evidence**.	... presents and develops the **support** for the thesis.
The Conclusion...	... synthesizes the evidence and answers the question by presenting the **thesis**.	... reasserts the validity of the **thesis**.

Our general advice is to structure *inductively* — that is, pose a question in your introduction that will be answered at the end of the essay — if you think your thesis is likely to be met with resistance. (You might encounter resistance if your essay discusses a controversial or unfamiliar topic, for example.)

Conversely, we advise structuring *deductively* — presenting your thesis as the culmination of your introduction — if you think your reader will be tempted to agree with you from the outset but will nevertheless appreciate the details you provide. This approach is more common with more familiar topics.

Reality Check! Inductive vs. Deductive Structure

▶ Is your topic likely to be familiar to your reader?
▶ Are you confident about your main point (thesis)?
▶ Is your main point (thesis) relatively uncontroversial?

A *Yes* response to all of the above questions indicates that a deductive structure will probably serve you well. A *No* response to any of these questions suggests that you should consider structuring your essay inductively.

▶ Let Us Show You: The Overall Structure

Now that Casey has written the first draft of his plagiarism essay (Chapter 8), received feedback on his draft and developed a revision plan (Chapter 12), and made some initial content-level revisions and reverse engineered his draft through outlining (Chapter 13), it's time that he looked at the overall structure of his essay. His first question, of course, is whether he should structure his essay inductively or deductively.

Structuring Your Essay Inductively or Deductively

▶ Talk Amongst Yourselves ...

Find a partner and discuss Casey's decision to follow an inductive structure for the revised plagiarism essay. Why did those *No* answers suggest induction rather than deduction? Find a partner and discuss Casey's decision to follow an inductive structure for his revised plagiarism essay. Why do his *No* answers suggest induction rather than deduction? How will starting the essay with a question rather than a thesis in the introduction change the way the rest of the essay develops?

▶ Now You Try: The Overall Structure

You know what's coming next, don't you? You guessed it: after rereading your draft essay — which you've already revised for content-level issues, right? — use the Inductive vs. Deductive Essay Structure checklist to evaluate the structure of your draft. Determine whether your revised essay should be structured around a question to be answered (inductive) or around a thesis to be supported (deductive).

Effective Body Paragraphs

You'll remember (we hope) that in Chapters 9 and 10 we talked about paragraph structure. Earlier in this chapter we described a paragraph as a microcosm of an essay, and it is. The thesis statement of an essay is like the topic sentence of a paragraph — both state a main point, and both require support and development. The conclusion of an essay is like the clincher in a paragraph — both provide the reader with a satisfying sense of closure.

And just as a paragraph has a body, an essay has a **body**. Much like a paragraph's body, an essay's body has a threefold purpose:

▶ **to develop the content** of the essay
▶ **to provide evidence** in support of the essay's ideas
▶ **to fulfill the promise** of the essay's introduction

Don't know whether you're ready for the kind of commitment that "fulfilling the promise" implies? Relax! All we mean is that as you revise, you might notice that the point you set out to make when you began writing isn't the point you've ended up making after all. There are two ways to deal with this situation: revise your thesis statement, or revise your support. Your thesis statement is like a promise to the reader, and if at the end of your essay you haven't finished arguing that thesis or your paper veers in a different direction and doesn't return, your reader will be annoyed.

The annoyance your reader feels when you don't deliver on your thesis is kind of like the way you feel when your roommate doesn't follow through on a promise to wash the dishes. ARGH!

In general, the body of your essay — that is, the **support** or **development** — explains and demonstrates why the things you've said in your introduction are both true and important. Generally speaking, it's best to envision your body paragraphs as *subsections* of your thesis in a deductively structured essay, or as *steps* leading up to your thesis in an inductively structured essay. These subsections, or steps, are organized around *minor claims*, highlighting their function as components of the paper's thesis.

Revising your essay's body involves addressing the purpose, ordering, and internal organization of individual paragraphs.

The first thing to consider is whether any of the minor points you make in your essay — that is, any of the main ideas of your paragraphs — are problematic. They are problematic if they don't serve the overall **purpose** of your essay well. Do any of them need to be rethought? Are they off task? Do they begin with one idea but then veer off in another direction? If so, there are three ways to deal with that: change the point of the paragraph, take the paragraph out, or make the argument of the paragraph stronger.

If the purpose of each paragraph is clear and effective, then the next thing to consider is the **ordering** of paragraphs in your essay. Beginning with your weakest point and ending with your strongest one is generally a good idea; you might find it useful to apply this logic when trying to decide the order your paragraphs should go in if no specific ordering system (chronological, spatial, climactic, etc.) is required.

Once you have ensured that your paragraphs are presented in the best possible order, it's time to work on the **internal organization** of each paragraph. As a reminder, each of your body paragraphs should demonstrate not only the *structure* you learned about in Chapter 9 (topic sentence, body, clincher or closing statement) but also the *qualities* you learned about in that same chapter (unity, development, organization, and coherence).

Does each paragraph have a distinct focus (topic sentence) that works to support the thesis? Is each paragraph fully developed with sufficient detail? Are your paragraphs making good use of the analytical paragraph structure (Chapter 10) that is so important in academic writing? Does each paragraph employ an appropriate organizational pattern, or mode of rhetoric (Chapter 11)? Are any of your paragraphs too long or too short? Do any of them lack a useful beginning, middle, or end? Do any of your paragraphs seem to be torn between two different topics and therefore lack unity?

The *Reality Check!* box below should help you make meaningful revisions to the body of your essay.

Reality Check! Effective Body Paragraphs

Does each paragraph in the body of the essay

- ► have a clear **topic sentence?**
- ► have a clear **main point?**
- ► achieve **unity** by sticking to the established topic?
- ► demonstrate sufficient **development?**
- ► provide sufficient **analysis** of its details?
- ► follow a clear **organizational pattern** or mode of rhetoric?
- ► achieve **coherence?**
- ► have a clear **clincher?**
- ► appear in the best possible **order** for the essay's purpose?

▶ *Let Us Show You:* Effective Body Paragraphs

The time has come for Casey to revise the body of his essay. Is he thrilled about it? Well, not exactly.

Reviewing Your Essay

Who Cares About Plagiarism? (Body Paragraphs)

The Grays Harbor College Code of Conduct posted on the college's Web site states that disciplinary action may be taken regarding "All forms of student academic dishonesty, including cheating; falsification; plagiarism; facilitating, aiding or abetting dishonesty or engaging in any conduct specifically prohibited by a faculty member in the course syllabus or class discussion." There are consequences for all of the listed behaviors, including plagiarism.

> The first body paragraph covers the subtopic of what the actual rules about academic dishonesty are.

It makes sense that the consequences for cheating should be severe, but plagiarism is a bit more complicated. Merriam-webster.com defines plagiarize as "to steal and pass off (the ideas or words of another) as your own: use (another's production) without crediting the source" or "to commit literary theft: present as new and original an idea or product derived from an existing source."

> The second body paragraph has been split from the first one because it presents a new, narrower subtopic: plagiarism.

But are any ideas really "original" in this day and age? With the entire Internet available at a mouse click, it's impossible to expect college students to have the source of every word or idea that isn't original. It's hard enough to remember who said what just in daily life. But when the average hour at the computer takes you to a hundred different Web sites, there's just no way. With the Internet, the question of whose ideas are whose becomes even more confusing. Nowadays, everything that has ever been written is available at the click of a mouse, which is both a blessing and a curse.

> The "original" idea had been in paragraph 2, but is now in body paragraph 3 about the Internet.
>
> This new example (an hour at the computer) replaces the "run away from that bear!" example, which was vivid but irrelevant.

It's a blessing because we can look up anything we want anytime we want to in order to access information and gain knowledge. If I get curious about Jane Austen's life or squid fishing or whatever, I can research the topic

> This paragraph about "a blessing" needed to be split from the paragraph about "a curse."

(continued)

as much as I want on the Internet. All information is available to me, as long as I have a way to access the Internet.

On the other hand, it's a curse because our culture, especially academic culture, hasn't changed to meet the new availability of information. Grays Harbor College's plagiarism policy is an example of this lack of progress.

> Now that it's in its own paragraph, the "curse" section needs development.

Academia still focuses on plagiarism as a kind of intellectual theft, which makes sense because school is built upon this idea of "intellectual property." Professors at universities are hired partly because they will do research and create original ideas. But when you think about it, their ideas aren't original, because they learned from their professors.

> This addresses intellectual property, so the part comparing profs to students seemed like a new idea.

And even besides that, those rules are about professors; college students aren't college professors, and people in the real world don't treat information as property these days.

> New paragraph: students vs. profs and the "real world." Definitely its own idea, but not developed.

▶ *Talk Amongst Yourselves . . .*

Find a partner and discuss Casey's revised body paragraphs. To what extent does the body of the essay now come closer to achieving its goals of fully developing and supporting the essay's subtopics? To what extent do the paragraphs in the body fulfill their purpose, as detailed in Chapters 8, 9, and 10? What further revision appears still to be needed, based on Casey's decisions about paragraph unity and development, and why?

▶ *Now You Try:* **Effective Body Paragraphs**

Using Casey's work as a model, revise the body paragraphs in your draft essay. Be sure to refer to the Effective Body Paragraphs checklist on page 191 as you consider and then make changes to the structure of your essay's body.

When you're finished, annotate your revised paragraphs (just as Casey's revised paragraphs are annotated on pages 193–94) to reflect your observations about the revision.

Specialty Paragraphs: The Introduction (and the Main Point)

The **introduction** is the first part of the essay — but as we discussed in Chapter 8, it's not necessarily the part you write first. The introduction should be at least one paragraph long but may run to several paragraphs, particularly in a longer essay. The introduction to an essay should not announce itself ("This essay will be about . . .") because such an introduction is intensely, eye-poppingly boring. You should try to accomplish a few things when you write an introduction:

▶ engage the reader's interest
▶ set the tone of the essay
▶ introduce the essay's main point

V-SHAPED INTRODUCTIONS

As a general rule — and we say *general* because every essay is different, and sometimes it's better to break a rule than to force things — the introductory paragraph should be "V shaped": it should begin broadly and slowly taper until it reaches the main point. We caution you, however, against beginning *too* broadly.

For instance, it would be okay to begin an analysis of Shakespearean sonnets by making broad statements about Shakespeare's views of love, or perhaps even about Renaissance views of love, but beginning with something like *Since the beginning of time, all human beings have thought about love* — tempting as it might be to do so — would be weak in two ways. First of all, such a statement doesn't really say anything: it's not a lie, but it's what logicians might call "vacuously true," meaning that it's true without having any significance whatsoever. Second, it's much too broad. If you begin your introduction at the level of mankind in general, good luck reaching your main point by the end of the paragraph.

> Think of the scope of your introduction as being like the beam of a flashlight rather than that of a floodlight — you want to illuminate relevant subject matter, not an entire zip code.

THE MAIN POINT

Typically, at the tip of the V-shaped introduction lies the essay's main point, which can be either a thesis statement or a central question, depending on the overall structure of your essay.

The V-Shaped Introduction

OPENING: Broad but not too broad
– a flashlight, not a floodlight.

BODY: Specific,
engaging detail to
narrow the scope
of the opening.

The Essay's
Main
Point

If your essay's structure is **deductive**, then your thesis should be explicitly stated at the end of the introductory paragraph. The **thesis statement** is the main claim of the essay: while an essay might have several or even many claims, only one claim represents the essay's true, overarching purpose. The thesis is therefore the central point of the argument. It's what you, the writer, are planning to prove in your paper (for example, *Circus clowns are frightening because they're so aggressively cheerful*).

If your essay's structure is **inductive**, then the introduction should end with the central question that your essay will seek to answer. This question can be presented explicitly (for example, *Why are circus clowns so frightening?*), or it can be implied through the presentation of an indirect question (for example, *This leads us to wonder why circus clowns are so frightening*).

▶ *Let Us Show You:* **The Introduction (and the Main Point)**

Just as it's often a good idea when drafting to set aside any work on the introduction until the body is fleshed out, you might also choose to delay addressing the introduction when *revising*. We suggest drafting the introduction last because it's hard to know what you're introducing until you've written it — and you'll understand even better what you're introducing after you've wrestled with revising your body paragraphs.

Casey understands that his introduction will serve as a road map for the direction (and tone!) of the rest of his essay. Beyond this, he now knows specifically what the V-shaped introduction needs to accomplish. Armed with this knowledge as well as his content-level revision and formal outline from Chapter 13, Casey tackles the introduction:

Planning the Introduction

Casey's Revised Introduction

A while ago I had a conversation with a friend about a movie we both saw. Because I had also read an interesting interpretation of the movie somewhere, I presented that idea to my friend to see what she thought of it. It never occurred to me that I had a duty to tell her the source of the idea. I don't think I was being dishonest and trying to trick my friend into thinking I'm of above average intelligence; I was just sharing an interesting piece of information from a source I honestly didn't even remember. At that moment at least, the idea itself was more important than where it came from. This idea made my friend see the movie in a whole new way, so who really cares if it was my idea or not? Nobody, really. So why do college professors care so much about acknowledging sources of information? This story makes me question the plagiarism rules at colleges and universities today.

The opening sentence is a flashlight rather than a floodlight, covering a reasonable scope.

The reader can relate to this story — who hasn't talked with a friend about a movie? — so it engages the reader's interest.

The tone is commonsensical, so the reader expects the whole essay to feel this way.

The main idea is clearly inductive: it directly asks a question and then implicitly asks the central question about plagiarism

▶ *Talk Amongst Yourselves ...*

Break into groups and discuss the questions below.

What's your reaction to Casey's revised introduction to the plagiarism essay? How good is the story about the friend as an introductory technique? To what extent does it help to accomplish one or more of the introduction's expected tasks? Which do you think is stronger — this new introduction or the definitions that began Casey's earlier draft? (See page 101 in Chapter 8 for the original version of the introduction.) And how about the inductively presented main idea: is Casey's implied question as effective as the original deductive thesis statement?

▶ *Now You Try:* The Introduction (and the Main Point)

Now that you've determined whether your essay should be inductively or deductively structured and you've revised your body paragraphs, you know a few things about how to revise your introduction. Following Casey's lead, create a revised introduction, using the three essential tasks of a good introduction and the idea of the V-shaped introduction as your guide.

Specialty Paragraphs: The Conclusion (and the Main Point)

The conclusion is the final element in the essay. It comprises at least one full paragraph and may consist of several paragraphs, particularly in a longer essay.

There are three things a conclusion *should* do:

- ▶ **resolve** the essay's content without leaving loose ends
- ▶ make a truly **re-vised** statement about the essay's main point
- ▶ **invite** the reader to think further

The first two tasks are closely related: the essay will feel resolved, or completed, when you've clearly articulated your final thesis. The statement of the thesis in a conclusion is a true *re-vision* of the main point, regardless of whether your essay is structured inductively or deductively. In an inductively structured essay, your conclusion will present your thesis statement for the first time. In a deductively structured essay, you will return to your thesis in a fresh (not redundant) way that addresses any unanswered questions that still remain in your essay.

The conclusion is a great time for you to SEE your main point again. You remember the whole "re-vision" thing from Chapter 13, right?

The third task (inviting the reader to think more) requires you to walk a fine line. On the one hand, you shouldn't introduce any new information in the conclusion because your audience will want you to explore and develop it, and you don't have time for that in the last paragraph. On the other hand, however, you don't want to just repeat a bunch of things you've already said — that would be boring and unnecessary. Try to think of your conclusion as your last chance to reach your audience — to make them remember your argument and want to think more about it.

In other words, the conclusion sums up your argument, provides a sense of resolution, and reconfirms the validity of your thesis.

With that said, there are three things a conclusion should *not* do: it should *not* announce itself ("In conclusion, . . ."), it should *not* bring up any new information, and it should *not* be a simple regurgitation of the thesis statement. Why? Well, new information with no discussion is frustrating, and both announcements and regurgitation are boring. Frustrated and bored are *not* how you want your reader to feel.

Reality Check! The Conclusion

A good conclusion should:

► resolve the content of the essay
► make a revised statement of the main point
► invite the reader to think further

A good conclusion should *not*:

► announce itself ("In conclusion, . . .")
► bring up any new information
► be a simple reiteration of a previously stated thesis

Finally, be wary of simply inverting the "V" from your introduction and calling it a conclusion. While this strategy does work to conclude an essay, frankly it just isn't very interesting. It's not a gutsy way to end your essay, and most likely no one will remember it. Your conclusion is the last impression you will leave with your audience, so make it a good one. Leave them thinking, not yawning.

► *Let Us Show You:* The Conclusion (and the Main Point)

So far Casey has revised the body and the introduction of his draft essay. Now it's time to work on the conclusion.

I guess I'll use what's left of the conclusion from my first draft. But is that all I'll need to write a strong ending?

Why not go through the whole Conclusion *Reality Check!* box, too? It can only help.

Casey's Revised Conclusion

When all is said and done, things that are called "plagiarism" in a college classroom aren't viewed that way in the real world. I don't mean going to one of those "Free Essays 4U" Web sites (also known as cheating). I'm talking about using random facts or bits of information as a way to back up an opinion or an interesting interpretation of a poem — things like that. As long as students are using information effectively to make a strong point, it shouldn't matter whether they cite every single source for every single idea that isn't their own, and they shouldn't be punished for it when they don't. Not only is that kind of rule unreasonable, but it's also basically impossible to follow.

As long as ideas like "cheating" Web sites and the effective use of random facts, etc. are developed in the essay body, this conclusion does not bring up new information.

This idea seems to resolve the essay's content.

This idea seems to be the thesis, at the end of an inductively structured essay. So it is not "regurgitated."

▶ Talk Amongst Yourselves ...

Take a few minutes to write down your responses to the questions below. Then break into groups of three and discuss your responses with each other.

What do you think of Casey's revised conclusion? Do you agree with the margin notes? Does each note identify a strength or a weakness in Casey's conclusion? Are there any elements of the Conclusion *Reality Check!* that haven't been addressed in the notes?

▶ Now You Try: The Conclusion (and the Main Point)

Using your revised introduction and the Conclusion *Reality Check!* on page 200, revise the conclusion of your essay. Be sure to ask for help — from your professor, from a classmate, from a consultant in the writing center — if you run into difficulty with this task or if you just need some feedback.

When you've finished, structure your entire draft by integrating your revised introduction, your revised body paragraphs, and your revised conclusion, as Casey has done below.

Who Cares About Plagiarism? (Complete Structural Revision)

A while ago I had a conversation with a friend about a movie we both saw. Because I had also read an interesting interpretation of the movie somewhere, I presented that idea to my friend to see what she thought of it. It never occurred to me that I had a duty to tell her the source of the idea. I don't think I was being dishonest and trying to trick my friend into thinking I'm of above average intelligence; I was just sharing an interesting piece of information from a source I honestly didn't even remember. At that moment at least, the idea itself was more important than where it came from. This idea made my friend see the movie in a whole new way, so who really cares if it was my idea or not? Nobody, really. So why do college professors care so much about acknowledging sources of information? This story makes me question the plagiarism rules at colleges and universities today.

The Grays Harbor College Code of Conduct posted on the college's Web site states that disciplinary action may be taken regarding "All forms of student academic dishonesty, including cheating; falsification; plagiarism; facilitating, aiding or abetting dishonesty or engaging in any conduct specifically prohibited by a faculty member in the course syllabus or class discussion." There are consequences for all of the listed behaviors, including plagiarism.

It makes sense that the consequences for cheating should be severe, but plagiarism is a bit more complicated. Merriam-webster.com defines plagiarize as "to steal and pass off (the ideas or words of another) as your own: use (another's production) without crediting the source" or "to commit literary theft: present as new and original an idea or product derived from an existing source."

But are any ideas really "original" in this day and age? With the entire Internet available at a mouse click, it's impossible to expect college students to have the source of every word or idea that isn't original. It's hard enough to remember who said what just in daily life. But when the average hour at the computer takes you to a hundred different Web sites, there's just no way. With the Internet, the question of whose ideas are whose becomes even more confusing. Nowadays, everything that has ever been written is available at the click of a mouse, which is both a blessing and a curse.

It's a blessing because we can look up anything we want anytime we want to in order to access information and gain knowledge. If I get curious about Jane Austen's life or squid fishing or whatever, I can research the topic as much as I want on the Internet. All information is available to me, as long as I have a way to access the Internet.

On the other hand, it's a curse because our culture, especially academic culture, hasn't changed to meet the new availability of information. Grays Harbor College's plagiarism policy is an example of this lack of progress.

Academia still focuses on plagiarism as a kind of intellectual theft, which makes sense because school is built upon this idea of "intellectual property." Professors at universities are hired partly because they will do research and create original ideas. But when you think about it, their ideas aren't original, because they learned from their professors.

And even besides that, those rules are about professors; college students aren't college professors, and people in the real world don't treat information as property these days.

When all is said and done, things that are called "plagiarism" in a college classroom aren't viewed that way in the real world. I don't mean going to one of those "Free Essays 4U" Web sites (also known as cheating). I'm talking about using random facts or bits of information as a way to back up an opinion or an interesting interpretation of a poem — things like that. As long as students are using information effectively to make a strong point, it shouldn't matter whether they cite every single source for every single idea that isn't their own, and they shouldn't be punished for it when they don't. Not only is that kind of rule unreasonable, but it's also basically impossible to follow.

Using the Revising for Structure *Reality Check!* box on page 204 as you engage in the four tasks presented in this chapter will put you in an excellent position to carry out a thorough revision of your draft based on the global issues of content and structure. And don't worry yet about editing and proofreading — we'll be talking about those local revision tasks in Chapter 15.

Reality Check! **Revising for Structure**

Before moving on to revising for coherence and precision, ask yourself these questions:

▶ Does the essay clearly present either an inductive or a deductive thesis placement?

▶ Does the organization of the body support the inductive or deductive thesis structure?

▶ Is each body paragraph fully developed with sufficient detail?

▶ Does the introduction effectively fulfill all of its functions?

▶ Does each body paragraph present useful evidence that fulfills the promise of the introduction?

▶ Does the conclusion effectively fulfill all of its functions while avoiding common pitfalls?

Chapter 15

Editing for Coherence and Precision: Words Mean Things

> One of the reasons that art is important is sometimes it actually feels more coherent than life. It orders the chaos.
> — Jeffrey Eugenides

Once you've addressed the global levels of revision — content and structure — it's time to devote your attention to local revision issues such as coherence.

The coherence level of revision is really about effective editing. Although we often use the terms *editing* and *proofreading* interchangeably, they actually denote very different things. Proofreading involves checking your draft for correctness in grammar, spelling, punctuation, and typography — it is revising for *precision*. We will cover the proofreading level of revision in Chapters 23–26.

Editing, on the other hand, involves looking out for the finer points that aren't really about the content or structure of your essay but are more involved than correcting technical errors. The "finer points" that we revise when editing for coherence include transitions and tone.

> You might recall from Chapter 9 that COHERENCE is about sticking together.

In an essay, **coherence**, or "sticking together," means that the various pieces — paragraphs, sentences, phrases, and words — not only feel like they belong in the same essay but also represent a rational, satisfying, smooth progression of clear ideas within a stable structure.

Use Transitions to Create Coherence

One of the most important ways that you can achieve coherence in your essay structure is to use transitional words and phrases. **Transitions** help the reader perceive your essay as a coherent whole, rather than as a series of loosely strung together ideas.

As a general rule, the size of a transition is commensurate with the elements being joined. This means that phrases and clauses are typically joined by individual transitional words, entire sentences are joined by phrases and clauses, and whole paragraphs are joined by entire sentences.

TRANSITIONS WITHIN SENTENCES AND PARAGRAPHS

The most common transitions are individual words called **conjunctions**. The grammatical job of conjunctions is to join together words, phrases, and clauses — and ideas — within sentences. (See Appendix A, pages 449 and 455, for definitions of clauses and phrases; see Chapter 25 for a look at common problems with clauses and phrases.)

Conjunctions are extremely important because they connect ideas to each other in a way that provides not only grammatical coherence but also interpretive coherence. In other words, conjunctions join ideas together in a way that tells the reader *how* those ideas are related to each other. Think about the difference between the following sentences:

> The sky lit up, **so** I went outside.

> The sky lit up, **but** I went outside.

Each of these sentences contains the same two clauses. Each clause represents an idea: the first clause is about the sky lighting up, and the second clause is about going outside. The only difference between the two sentences is the conjunction joining the clauses: *so* is a word that suggests *causality* (the second thing happens *because of* the first thing), while *but* is a word that expresses *contrast* (the second thing happens *in spite of* the first thing).

As a result of those two tiny but very significant transitional words, the sentences have two entirely different meanings. The first sentence suggests that fireworks or a sunrise or some other pleasant thing motivated the writer of the sentence to go outside and observe the lit sky. The second sentence, on the other hand, suggests that lightning or a fire or some other unpleasant thing lit up the sky and that the writer thought it actually was not advisable to go outside.

Coordinating conjunctions (such as *so* and *but* in the examples above) and their cousins the **subordinating conjunctions** (such as *while* or *although*, both of which have been used in this chapter already) are the most common single-word transitions used to connect ideas together. These and other joining words can be used to communicate a wide variety of meanings.

Reality Check! Useful Transitions

► **Addition:** *also, and, besides, furthermore, indeed, moreover*
► **Causation:** *as, because, consequently, for, hence, since, so, therefore, thus*
► **Choice:** *nor, or, whether*

> ► **Chronology:** *after, before, finally, first, meanwhile, next, then, until, when, while*
> ► **Comparison:** *as, as if, likewise, similarly*
> ► **Condition:** *if, unless*
> ► **Contrast:** *although, but, however, instead, nevertheless, otherwise, still, yet*
> ► **Illustration:** *for example, for instance, in fact, specifically*

Practice! Using Transitions in Sentences

Use transitional words (conjunctions) to combine each pair of sentences below into a single, meaningful sentence. Try using several different words for each pair of sentences, and try using them to *begin* the new sentence as well as *between* the two ideas. See how transitions can change the way we interpret a sentence?

1. Elliot was slipping out of consciousness. He had a sudden realization.
2. The morning was entirely normal. A helicopter landed on the back lawn.
3. Regina's cats are adorable. They're really hungry.
4. Uncle Hal's knee is acting up. The summer rains are coming.

These conjunctions and transitional phrases that are used to join ideas together in sentences are also used to link sentences within a paragraph. For a reminder about the role of transitions in improving the coherence of paragraphs, refer to page 116 in Chapter 9.

TRANSITIONS BETWEEN PARAGRAPHS

Transitions between paragraphs, on the other hand, connect much bigger units of thought. Therefore, they typically require bigger transitions, such as entire clauses or sentences.

Transitions between the paragraphs in an essay help to achieve continuity throughout the entire essay. If the individual paragraphs in your essay each have a distinct focus or idea — and they should — then you will need to smooth out the edges of all of those distinct ideas to show how they work together toward the single goal of supporting your essay's thesis.

The key to writing good paragraph transitions is to use the sentences that appear at the beginning and end of each paragraph. In other words, use a paragraph's **topic sentence** and **clincher** (see pages 106 and 112 in Chapter 9) to provide an overview of that paragraph while simultaneously linking it to the adjacent paragraphs by providing an echo of the preceding paragraph (in the case of the topic sentence) or a hint of the next paragraph (in the case of the clincher).

> Imagine paragraph transitions as a needle and thread. At the beginning of each new paragraph, you take your needle back to the previous paragraph and pierce the edge of its cloth and then return to the paragraph that you're working on.

> Right! In this way, you sew the two paragraphs together by connecting shared content or repeating key words or phrases to create a smooth transition between ideas.

Remember that good paragraph transitions don't happen naturally, even for the best and most experienced writers. First drafts rarely contain good transitions between the major ideas of the essay. This is why we consider checking for paragraph transitions to be such an important part of revising for coherence.

Reality Check! Coherent Transitions

▶ Are conjunctions used meaningfully within sentences?
▶ Are transitional words and phrases used effectively between sentences?
▶ Are paragraphs linked effectively through the use of transitional phrases, clauses, and sentences?
▶ Are you using your paragraphs' topic sentences and clinchers to aid in transitional coherence?

▶ *Let Us Show You:* Coherent Transitions

After Casey finished his structural revision, he revised a few paragraphs that still seemed to need more development. Then he refined his essay title and added the relevant information about his class in the top left corner of the first page of his paper. Now he's ready to revise with an eye toward his transitions — both between ideas and between paragraphs. As usual, Mara is on board to provide feedback.

Casey N. Pointe
FYE 101
Professor McGonagall
College Policy Essay Assignment

Who Cares About Plagiarism? (Transitions)

A while ago I had a conversation with a friend about a movie we both saw. Because I had also read an interesting interpretation of that movie somewhere, I presented that idea to my friend to see what she thought of it. It never occurred to me that I had a duty to tell her the source of the idea. I don't think I was being dishonest and trying to trick my friend into thinking I'm of above average intelligence; I was just sharing an interesting piece of information from a source I honestly didn't even remember. At that moment at least, the idea itself was more important than where it came from. This idea made my friend see the movie in a whole new way, so who really cares if it was my idea or not? Nobody, really. So why do college professors care so much about acknowledging sources of information? This story makes me question the plagiarism rules at colleges and universities today.

> "So" isn't enough to get from movies to professors.
>
> Add a phrase to link "colleges and universities" to the more specific rules at this college?

The Grays Harbor College Code of Conduct posted on the college's Web site states that disciplinary action may be taken regarding "All forms of student academic dishonesty, including cheating; falsification; plagiarism; facilitating, aiding or abetting dishonesty or engaging in any conduct specifically prohibited by a faculty member in the course syllabus or class discussion." There are consequences for all of the listed behaviors, including plagiarism.

It makes sense that the consequences for cheating should be severe, but plagiarism is a bit more

> You jump from "consequences" to "severe" without including what the consequences are.

(continued)

complicated. Merriam-webster.com defines plagiarize as "to steal and pass off (the ideas or words of another) as your own: use (another's production) without crediting the source" or "to commit literary theft: present as new and original an idea or product derived from an existing source."

But are any ideas really "original" in this day and age? With the entire Internet available at a mouse click, it's impossible to expect college students to have the source of every word or idea that isn't original. It's hard enough to remember who said what just in daily life. But when the average hour at the computer takes you to a hundred different Web sites, there's just no way. With the Internet, the question of whose ideas are whose becomes even more confusing. Nowadays, everything that has ever been written is available at the click of a mouse, which is both a blessing and a curse.

This transition seems okay — "but" shows that this paragraph will argue against the paragraph before it.

It's a blessing because we can look up anything we want anytime we want to in order to access information and gain knowledge. If I get curious about Jane Austen's life or squid fishing or whatever, I can research the topic as much as I want on the Internet. All information is available to me, as long as I have a way to access the Internet. The Internet allows me to learn anything I want from anyone I want. It could be said that the Internet is a blessing because it creates knowledge.

Maybe don't start with "it's" — the reader might have to think too much about what "it" is.

On the other hand, it's a curse because our culture, especially academic culture, hasn't changed to meet the new availability of information. Grays Harbor College's plagiarism policy is an example of this lack of progress. The rules seem like they were written by people who still go to libraries and write everything by hand. They just haven't caught up with those

This transition makes it seem like it's culture that is a curse. Can you make it clearer that you're still talking about the Internet?

of us who have had computers and the Internet our whole lives.

Academia still focuses on plagiarism as a kind of intellectual theft, which makes sense because school is built upon this idea of "intellectual property." Professors at universities are hired partly because they will do research and create original ideas. But when you think about it, their ideas aren't original, because they learned from their professors. Sometimes I think it's very hard to tell where the line is between learning from someone and plagiarizing someone's idea, and honestly I think professors are probably more likely to cross that line than students because professors don't usually credit their sources when they're teaching.

This paragraph could use a good transitional phrase or even a whole sentence. It starts out very bluntly.

And even besides that, those rules are about professors; college students aren't college professors, and people in the real world don't treat information as property these days. Normal people just don't worry about whether they're giving credit to people for their ideas on a regular basis. There are more important things to worry about.

"And even besides that" sounds funny. It's almost like you're making an excuse.

When all is said and done, things that are called "plagiarism" in a college classroom aren't viewed that way in the real world. I don't mean going to one of those "Free Essays 4U" Web sites (also known as cheating). I'm talking about using random facts or bits of information as a way to back up an opinion or an interesting interpretation of a poem — things like that. As long as students are using information effectively to make a strong point, it shouldn't matter whether they cite every single source for every single idea that isn't their own, and they shouldn't be punished for it when they don't. Not only is that kind of rule unreasonable, but it's also basically impossible to follow.

I wonder if "when all is said and done" is too much like "in conclusion." Change?

▶ *Talk Amongst Yourselves . . .*

Break into groups and discuss the notes Mara has made about the coherence of Casey's latest draft. To what extent do you agree with her suggestions for improvement? Where else in the draft do you think transitions would help?

▶ *Now You Try:* **Coherent Transitions**

If we've kept an accurate accounting of your progress (and we think we have), you should have a draft of your essay that has been revised for structure, annotated, and revised again based on that annotation. Remember? You did all of that back in Chapter 14.

Now we'd like you to read through your latest draft carefully and annotate it, just as Mara has done for Casey, to identify places both within and between paragraphs where a well-placed and precisely chosen transition will improve the overall coherence of your essay.

When you're finished, show both your draft and your notes to your professor, or to a classmate (or heck, to your favorite barista) — show them to anyone who will give you some feedback about your analysis of your draft's coherence.

Achieve a Coherent Tone

Coherence is about more than just transitions — it's about connecting with your audience by using language that is appropriate for the situation. And that's where tone comes in. **Tone** is created by the way a writer arranges words in sentences (this is called *syntax*) as well as by the words he or she chooses to use (also known as *diction*).

DICTION

The word **diction** refers to the words a writer uses — which explains why a book full of words is called a *dictionary*. Problems with diction generally fall into one of two categories: errors in usage, and misjudgments of situation.

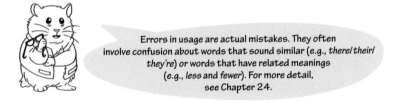

Errors in usage are actual mistakes. They often involve confusion about words that sound similar (e.g., *there/their/they're*) or words that have related meanings (e.g., *less* and *fewer*). For more detail, see Chapter 24.

In this chapter, we're focusing on the second problem: misjudgments of the writing situation that result in diction choices that damage your tone.

MISJUDGING THE RHETORICAL SITUATION

A mistaken judgment about the relationships among yourself, your topic, and your reader might cause you to choose words that are inappropriate to your writing context. This can lead to the sort of diction problem that damages your tone as a writer.

Dangers of Overwriting

Choosing the right words is a vital component of effective writing. Student writers are sometimes vague and unclear and, at the same time, pretentious because they are insecure — they are terrified that they don't really know what they want to say while also trying hard to impress their audience with their expansive vocabularies. So they end up making the mistake Joey makes in that episode of *Friends* in which he's trying to write an impressive letter of recommendation for his friends Chandler and Monica, who want desperately to adopt a baby. In the letter, he gushes, "They're warm, nice people with big hearts." Then, worried that he doesn't sound impressive enough, he goes to his thesaurus and writes a new and improved sentence: "They're humid, prepossessing *Homo sapiens* with full-sized aortic pumps." Hilarious, right? Well, if you're Joey, perhaps not so much.

The best way to avoid **overwriting** is to remember that you are trying to communicate with your audience, not trick them into thinking you are smart. You *are* smart, and you have *great* ideas. Believe it or not, it takes more skill and confidence to write with clarity and precision than it does to find a bunch of confusing words to beat your audience into submission.

You know how some people try to "enhance" their natural beauty with tons of makeup, fancy clothes, an artificial tan, and even plastic surgery, yet in the end they seem to mask their beauty instead?

The same thing can happen with writing. When you find yourself overwriting, back up and ask yourself, "What am I really trying to say here?" and then say it — as *simply*, *clearly*, and *directly* as possible.

Dangers of Underwriting

Overwriting and underwriting are two sides of the same coin — two versions of the same ultimate problem. Overwriting produces flowery, pretentious language, and underwriting produces vagueness or lack of context. But both produce incoherence, and they can arise from similar causes.

While overwriting often results from caring too much, **underwriting** — being vague, unclear, or sloppy with your word choice — can result from caring too little. (If you don't remember our discussion of caring and not caring, see page 154 in Chapter 12.) Not all underwriting is a result of carelessness, of course. Although sloppiness often correlates with a certain lack of care, underwriting that is unclear is often the result of genuine confusion about grammar — especially the use of verbs, pronouns, and modifiers (see Chapter 24). And underwriting that is vague is typically a pretty good hint that you're not really sure about what you mean. At that point, you need to think some more and try again.

We can't tell you how many times we've received e-mails from students that read like this: "Hey, when is the thing due? Thanks, Jayden." We are left wondering, *Jayden who? What class are you in? What "thing" are you talking about?*

We know that some students write vague e-mails because they are used to speaking a lot and writing very little. Writing requires more precision and specificity than speaking does because a face-to-face conversation comes with a whole bunch of context. If we can *see* and *hear* Jayden because he came up to us after class to ask, "When is the thing due?" then we will likely recognize both his face and the class he's in — and with any luck, we will have recently talked about a "thing" that's due.

The good news is that both overwriting and underwriting can be fixed. Picture yourself explaining your ideas to your audience. Is the audience your professor, your classmates, or some combination of the two? Whichever it is, imagine that person or those people as you revise. Ask yourself what you are really trying to say and how you can convey your ideas as clearly, directly, and coherently as possible. In the following pages, we'll be asking you to think more specifically about your diction and the ways in which it affects the coherence and tone of your writing.

Practice! Diction Problems

See if you can identify and correct any examples of misused or poorly chosen words in the following sentences.

1. I sympathize, but there problems don't really effect me.
2. This argument is over, so please stop flagellating the deceased equine.
3. Roberto left town because there were some circumstances.
4. Tillie couldn't hear the sermon because the church has such awful agnostics.

Appropriate Language Use

Most words, like most actions, may be appropriate in one situation but not in another. Words themselves are neutral. This means they have no inherent moral value. Thus, when we refer to appropriate or inappropriate language, we are not talking about "good words" and "bad words." The very concept of *good* and *bad* words is a problematic argument based largely on a history of class snobbery. It's a great story that starts in 1066, but we don't have time to go into it right now.

Of course, there's not much we can say that George Orwell didn't already say in his essay "Politics and the English Language." You've read it, right? It's easy to find online — and well worth the read. You don't even have to thank us.

So words themselves are neither good nor bad; however, every choice in diction has a consequence. Good, thoughtful writers will be mindful of the communication triangle (look back at page 13) when they're choosing words and will make every attempt to select the words that are most fitting for the situation (or writing task). Using words that fit the writing situation and being consistent about word choice will go a long way toward ensuring your essay's coherence.

AVOID INAPPROPRIATE LANGUAGE

Inappropriate language — word choice that doesn't fit the writing situation very well — generally falls into one of five categories: jargon, pretension, euphemism, slang, and offensive language. Keep in mind that the examples that follow are not examples of *bad* or *wrong* words. Rather, they are examples of types of usage that are likely to be inappropriate in many academic or professional writing situations.

Avoid Jargon

A writer using **jargon** employs specialized terminology that is familiar to people within a certain profession, hobby, or trade but unfamiliar to people outside that group. Jargon might be perfectly appropriate if an auto mechanic is publishing an article in *Auto Mechanics' Weekly*, because the magazine's readers can be expected to understand specialized terms. But if the auto mechanic were to publish that same article in *Better Homes and Gardens*, then the jargon would likely be a problem.

Jargon can be a problem for writers with specialized skill and vocabulary in almost any field: the law, professional sports, computer programming — or our favorite jargon-filled field of expertise, medicine. Consider the sentence "The patient presented with elevated systolic and diastolic as well as lacerations and contusions," which in nonjargon reads more simply as "The patient had high blood pressure as well as cuts and bruises."

If you are at risk of inappropriately burdening your reader with jargon in your writing, we suggest you ask someone who is *not* a member of your group to read your draft and provide feedback about any terms he or she doesn't understand.

Avoid Pretentious Language

Writers who use **pretentious language** are *pretending* to have more sophisticated, flowery, intellectual diction than what's natural to their normal writing voices. Frequently, but not always, pretentious language takes the form of using big words when smaller ones would do just as well — and oftentimes would do *better*.

As Mark Twain once said, "Don't use a five-dollar word when a fifty-cent word will do." For example, don't say "masticate my provisions" when you can say "chew my food."

That doesn't mean you should completely avoid big words. But don't use a big word just for the sake of using it; use it only if there isn't a more common synonym.

Pretension is a common problem among college students, who sometimes think they have to "sound smarter" than they are (whatever that means). If you find yourself tempted to say something like "Indubitably the oft-mollycoddled progeny of our more affluent citizenry awaken with stunned reluctance to the vicissitudes of maturity," please, we urge you to reconsider. Take a deep breath and write something else instead, such as "Often the spoiled children of wealthy parents are shocked by adult responsibilities."

Avoid Euphemism

The perfectly lovely term *euphemism* derives from a Greek word meaning "pleasant sounding." Thus, a **euphemism** is a word or phrase that is used to make something that isn't necessarily pleasant (or something that people aren't comfortable talking about) sound more pleasing or more acceptable. In our culture, we generally use euphemisms to discuss certain subjects such as sex ("we made love"), death ("she passed away"), and bodily functions ("I used the restroom"). In these instances, euphemism is typically appropriate because it maintains a level of decorum without obscuring a truth that should be revealed.

Sometimes, however, writers use euphemism inappropriately — for example, when they need to communicate an unpleasant reality and wish to make it sound less bad in order to avoid taking responsibility. In this way, euphemism sometimes functions in the same way as the passive voice (a subject that we cover in Chapter 24). An example would be "We plan to right-size our operations through the reallocation of financial resources away from human resources," which is a euphemistic way of saying "We plan to lay off/fire some of our employees."

Any time you run across a euphemistic phrase (*economically disadvantaged*, *collateral damage*, *vertically challenged*), ask yourself whether it's being used ethically or whether it's meant to obscure an important truth for less than ethical purposes.

Avoid Slang

Slang isn't what you think it is. Really. When most people hear the word *slang*, they think of profanity, those colorful words, most of them a mere four letters long, that we use when we hit our thumbs with hammers. Slang, they think, is the same as "words your mom yells at you for saying." Alas, while many slang terms do fall under the heading of "words you get in trouble for saying in third grade," most slang falls outside of that category.

Slang is a bit like jargon: it is vocabulary used and understood by people who share a common experience. But rather than coming from shared expertise, slang comes from a shared time and place — it is often regional and almost always generational.

My slang and my mom's slang? Totally different. Trust me.

Slang words are words that take on definitions other than their original denotative meanings. Some slang words have been around so long that their original meaning is all but lost or ignored. *Cool*, for example, is almost never used to mean "not quite cold" but rather is used in most cases to express approval of something: "It's cool if you use my computer," or "Hey, cool shoes."

Some words become so grounded in their slang definitions that we would be shocked to hear them used in their original sense. When did you last hear someone say, "Yes, our outing to the beach was very happy and gay"? We're going to take a wild guess here and say never. As with other types of diction in this section, slang isn't inherently bad or wrong — but with a few exceptions (like *gay*), slang is vague and imprecise, and that is why it's not appropriate in most academic writing.

> Most slang revolves around the use of adjectives — words that describe nouns or pronouns. Each generation comes up with its own way of describing things. For example, these slang terms used to describe excellence: *tip-top, smashing, groovy, gnarly, wicked.* For more on adjectives, see Appendix A.

Think about it: if you were to write, "The movie was so twisted it just blew me away," how would your reader know what you mean? When you're tempted to use slang in formal writing, simply ask yourself, *What do I really mean by that?* By answering this question about each slang term, you'll create stronger, more precise sentences, such as, "The movie had such a shocking reversal at the end that I was completely taken by surprise."

Avoid Offensive Language

What makes language offensive? And how can you possibly avoid offending anyone? After all, you can't be held responsible for what might bother someone else, right?

Well, yes and no. On the one hand, you can't be expected to know that a particular reader has an unfortunately violent reaction to the word *window*. In such a case, it's truly the reader's problem. Nor are you expected to adopt a vocabulary that is so politically correct that you must use euphemisms to avoid any possible hurt feelings.

However, a good general rule to follow in academic and professional writing is to avoid using words that exclude or label people or groups in a way that those people or groups would likely find offensive. This rule is easy to follow if you remember to think in terms of in-group and out-group people: if you are a member of the group you are describing, you have more leeway in your diction choices than you would if you were not a member of the group (you can get away with using a word like *redneck* if you identify yourself as one, but not if you don't).

It also helps to remember that much of the language that offends people is offensive because it is imprecise or inaccurate. For example, if you insist on saying "An effective salesman should develop expertise in the product he's selling," you're likely to offend the significant percentage of salespeople who aren't male. And if you write that "Spanish is widely spoken in the western United States because of all the Mexican immigrants there"? Well, you're likely to offend the many Spanish-speaking people in the western United States who are not actually from Mexico.

And of course, do keep in mind those colorful little four-letter words we discussed earlier. While they're perfectly fine words in and of themselves, they are generally not appropriate in academic or professional writing — so save them for your e-mail messages to friends or for the lyrics to that great song you've been meaning to write. Or perhaps you might slip one or two of them into that college English textbook you're writing — just to see if your students are paying attention.

Reality Check! Coherence and Tone

▶ Are all words in your draft, including homophones and near homophones, used correctly?

▶ Have you eliminated any passages that were *overwritten* and were therefore too focused on impressing rather than expressing?

▶ Have you eliminated any passages that were *underwritten* and were therefore vague and unclear?

▶ Have you avoided using any inappropriate *jargon*?

▶ Have you avoided using any *pretentious language*?

▶ Have you avoided using any inappropriate *euphemisms*?

▶ Have you avoided using any inappropriate *slang*?

▶ Have you avoided using any *offensive language*?

▶ *Let Us Show You:* Editing for Coherence and Tone

When last we visited Casey's essay "Who Cares About Plagiarism?" Casey had taken notes on his draft with an eye toward improving its coherence through the use of transitions. Now that he's made those changes, Casey needs to annotate his draft for overwriting, underwriting, and inappropriate word choice, among other things. In other words, it's time for him to make note of his *tone*.

Casey N. Pointe

FYE 101

Professor McGonagall

College Policy Essay Assignment

Who Cares About Plagiarism?
(Draft — Edited for Coherence)

A while ago I had a conversation with a friend about a movie we both saw. Because I had also read an interesting interpretation of the movie somewhere, I presented that idea to my friend to see what she thought of it. It never occurred to me that I had a duty to tell her the source of the idea. I don't think I was being dishonest and trying to trick my friend into thinking I'm ~~of above average intelligence~~ smart; I was just sharing an interesting piece of information from a source I honestly didn't even remember. At that moment at least, the idea itself was more important than where it came from. This idea made my friend see the movie in a whole new way, so ~~who really cares if it didn't matter whether~~ it was my idea or not. This makes me wonder why college professors care so much about acknowledging sources of information. This story makes me question the plagiarism rules at colleges and universities today.

Like most colleges and universities, Grays Harbor College has a Code of Conduct posted on the college's

Pretentious language

Offensive tone

Web site that states disciplinary action may be taken regarding "All forms of student academic dishonesty, including cheating; falsification; plagiarism; facilitating, aiding or abetting dishonesty or engaging in any conduct specifically prohibited by a faculty member in the course syllabus or class discussion." There are consequences for all of the listed behaviors, including plagiarism, which can result in punishment up to and including expulsion.

It makes sense that the consequences for cheating should be severe, but plagiarism is a bit more complicated than cheating. Merriam-webster.com defines plagiarize as "to steal and pass off (the ideas or words of another) as your own: use (another's production) without crediting the source" or "to commit literary theft: present as new and original an idea or product derived from an existing source."

But are any ideas really "original" ~~in this day and age~~ anymore? With the entire Internet available at a mouse click, it's impossible to expect college students to ~~have~~ know the source of every word or idea that isn't original. It's hard enough to remember who said what just in daily life. But when the average hour at the computer takes you to a hundred different Web sites, there's just no way to remember them all. With the Internet, the question of whose ideas are whose becomes even more confusing. ~~Nowadays~~ Today, everything that has ever been written is available at the click of a mouse, which is both a blessing and a curse.

The Internet is a blessing because we can look up anything we want anytime we want to in order to access information and gain knowledge. If I get curious about Jane Austen's life or squid fishing ~~or whatever~~, I can research the topic as much as I want on the Internet. All information is available to me, as long as I have a

Vague

Wrong word

Imprecise

Vague

Vague

(continued)

way to access the Internet. The Internet allows me to learn anything I want from anyone I want. It could be said that the Internet is a blessing because it creates knowledge.

On the other hand, that blessing is a curse because our culture, especially academic culture, hasn't changed to meet the new availability of information. Grays Harbor College's plagiarism policy is an example of this lack of progress. The rules seem like they were written by people who ~~still go to~~ sit behind dusty stacks of old books in libraries and write everything by hand using a feather dipped in ink. They just haven't caught up with those of us who have had computers and the Internet our whole lives.

Don't want to offend regular people who go to libraries and write by hand!

As a result, the college still focuses on plagiarism as ~~a kind of~~ intellectual theft, which makes sense because school is built upon this idea of "intellectual property." Professors at universities are hired partly because they will do research and create original ideas. But when you think about it, their ideas aren't original, because they learned from their professors. Sometimes I think it's very hard to tell where the line is between learning from someone and plagiarizing someone's idea, and honestly I think professors are probably more likely to cross that line than students because professors don't usually credit their sources when they're teaching.

Vague

So maybe the plagiarism rules should be about professors. College students aren't in academia like professors are; they're in the real world. And people in the real world don't treat information as property these days. Normal people just don't worry about whether they're giving credit to people for their ideas on a regular basis. There are more important things to worry about.

In the real world, people don't care about so-called "plagiarism." I don't mean they approve of going to one of those "Free Essays 4U" Web sites (also known as cheating). But people are fine with picking up random facts or bits of information from the Internet and using them to back up an opinion ~~or an interesting interpretation of a poem — things like that~~. As long as students are using information effectively to make a strong point, it shouldn't matter whether they cite every single source for every single idea that isn't their own, and they shouldn't be punished for it when they don't. Not only is ~~that kind of rule~~ the plagiarism policy unreasonable, but it's also basically impossible to follow.

> Vague — and new content (missed this in Chapter 14)

> Vague

▶ *Talk Amongst Yourselves ...*

Break into groups and discuss the most recent changes to "Who Cares About Plagiarism?" How good a job has Casey done of improving the transitions between ideas based on the annotated draft on pages 209–11? How about the changes made in this draft to eliminate problems with overwriting, underwriting, and tone? How much have these edits improved the essay? Have they created any problems? What other problems with coherence do you think need to be addressed, and why?

▶ *Now You Try:* **Editing for Coherence and Tone**

Okay, you know the drill by now: print out a copy of the revision you prepared in response to the assignment on page 212 — the draft of your essay, edited for transitional coherence. Or you can work on another essay, if that's what you have decided to do.

Next, using the Coherent Transitions and Coherence and Tone checklists (*Reality Checks!* on pages 208 and 219) as guides to what you learned about transitions and language use in this chapter, mark up your draft for any changes that will improve the coherence and tone of your essay. Then make the changes. As always, it's a good idea to get feedback from a professor or peer once you've edited.

When you've completed this step, you'll have finished your global revision (content and structure) as well as your editing for coherence and tone. There's just one more step in the revision process: editing for clarity and precision (also known as proofreading). This final step is covered in detail in Chapter 23, "Writing with Style."

PART 5

Writing Effective Arguments

Chapter 16

Making an Argument: It's Rational — and Fun!

> Logic takes care of itself. All we have to do is
> look and see how it does it.
> — Ludwig Wittgenstein

In his treatise *Rhetoric*, the Greek philosopher Aristotle lays out a set of rules or guidelines that writers should follow when making arguments.

So what? you may be thinking. *I don't really argue all that often. What do I need with rules?*

You might not be aware of this, but it's hard to get through five minutes without encountering or making an argument. Don't believe us? The following are all arguments:

Aristotle's rules of rhetoric are interesting.

I have too much homework.

Let's go to the movies.

It's true. Each of the statements above is an argument, or at least the beginning of an argument, because, believe it or not — everything is an argument!

Everything's an Argument! *No, It Isn't!* Yes, Actually, It Is!

Well, okay, not *everything* is an argument — the front lawn isn't an argument, for example, and neither is a salmon or a bowl of noodles — but pretty much anything one might say or write or sing or even paint can be seen as an **argument**. Or, to put it another way, every bit of communication is, in one way or another, an argument.

You may recall that, back in Chapter 11, we mentioned that specific examples of academic writing can typically be classified either as expository or as argumentative, depending on whether the central purpose of the text is to inform or to convince or persuade. While this is true, it is also true that if we use the purest definition of argument — Aristotle's definition of argument, actually — then all academic writing, even expository writing, is argumentative. At least in its structure, if not necessarily in its tone. In an informative essay, the writer is simply arguing that what he or she says is true.

So what exactly is an argument, anyway? Here is a definition:

> An *argument* is a conversation that begins with a premise — which is an arguable statement (or claim) — and develops through the presentation of supporting details that guarantee the validity of the claim.

This definition uses terms such as *claim* and *support,* which you may recall reading about in Part 3. These terms come from the Toulmin method, a popular way of understanding how arguments work. It's named for Stephen Toulmin, a British mathematician and physicist who created his argumentation method as an attempt to build a bridge between the formal logic of mathematics and Aristotle's rhetorical principles for spoken or written argument. We'll use elements of the Toulmin method to talk about argument later in this chapter, but first we'd like to introduce you to a component of classical Greek argument that also underpins the Toulmin method: *logos.*

The Need for *Logos*: Evidence and Reasoning

Here's what *logos* looks like in Greek: λόγος. Because I knew you'd be curious.

According to Aristotle — whose ideas we still follow today — a crucial component of any argument is *logos,* which refers to the systematic use of reasoning in discourse.

Is that definition too much? We'll break it down for you.

Discourse is conversation, whether written or spoken. And as you might guess from looking at the word, **reasoning** basically means giving reasons. Reasons for what? Well, reasons

for believing that something is true or for having an opinion about something. So for our purposes, *logos* means giving reasons for what you think in your writing. (Later in this chapter you'll learn that we call this *supporting your claims.*)

Today we can honor Aristotle's memory and simultaneously prove ourselves intellectually superior to the vast majority of the world's advertisers, politicians, and cable news personalities by using *logos* in our own writing. At its heart, the quality of *logos* in an argument is rational support for a claim.

ESTABLISHING *LOGOS* BY PROVIDING EXAMPLES

We think *logos* is important. Really, really important. Why? Well, you may have noticed that the word itself bears a striking resemblance to a word that refers to the quality of reasonableness: *logic.* Readers will find arguments compelling only if the writer's explanations are logical — meaning that they include evidence and reasoning.

Consider the following paragraph:

> Recent legislation banning smoking in all public places is a bad idea. I like smoking. It feels good, and I think I look hot when I'm holding a lit cigarette. Besides, I don't like smoking at home or in my car, and who likes to smoke outdoors, especially if it's rainy or windy or too sunny? Smoking indoors in public places is a really good thing.

How well does this sample argument work?

You might be thinking, *This I-like-smoking thing is an almost perfect example of a horrible argument!* And what can we say? When you're right, you're right.

If you're reading with a critical eye, you are looking for the validity of a text's arguments. The preceding sample argument, for example, wouldn't convince anyone that the ban on smoking in public places is a bad idea. In fact, it might go so far as to convince those who were leaning toward that point of view that they are wrong, and that all smoking everywhere should be banned immediately.

Why might the "I like smoking" argument drive its own supporters away? Because it lacks *logos*. In other words, it does not offer

▶ **a way for us to evaluate it** (what would make the proposal "bad" or "good"?);
▶ **any observable evidence** (factual information offered to prove the validity of the claim); or
▶ **a link** between the topic (public legislation against smoking) and the supporting detail (what the arguer personally likes — smoking).

Does this mean that the entire premise of the argument is fatally flawed? Not at all. The argument as it is presented does not have sufficient proof and reasoning to establish its *logos*. However, its premise *could* be supported. In other words, the writer could *provide more details* that would back up the claims being made.

To establish *logos*, an argument must include specific, concrete details (people, places, things) that serve as reliable evidence. These details allow the reader to evaluate the reasonableness of the premise. This is the most basic way to establish *logos*.

In the case of the sample argument on page 229, the writer could begin to build a logical argument in favor of public smoking by first explaining that the legislation banning smoking in public places infringes on personal freedoms and is therefore potentially unconstitutional. Then the writer could provide case studies and other pieces of specific evidence that would show why his or her opinion about public smoking has merit. For example, the writer could point to the continuing popularity in some cities, even among nonsmokers, of smoking establishments such as bowling alleys and cocktail lounges. (This doesn't mean you'd find the argument convincing. It just means that it would be a real argument.)

CLAIMS VS. STATEMENTS OF FACT

Claims are what distinguish arguments from nonarguments. They are also what distinguish essays from reports. Whether they are beginning college students or students returning to college after some time away from the classroom, students who are unaccustomed to academic writing can find it tricky to make the transition from writing reports to writing essays. The difference between an essay and a report is that a report is generally a presentation of *facts*, whereas an essay is an argument that makes and supports *claims*.

A **claim** is a statement that has enough room in it to be argued — a statement that requires support. It is a statement with which a reasonable person could reasonably disagree. When a writer makes a claim, he or she takes a position.

A **fact** is a statement that can be proven true through observation. It is a statement about which reasonable people cannot reasonably disagree. When a writer offers facts in support of a claim, he or she is presenting reasons for the reader to find the claim convincing or at least valid.

Just a reminder: the main claim in an essay is called its thesis. We devoted big chunks of Chapters 7, 8, 13, and 14 to thesis statements. You've read those chapters, right? We wrote them just for you.

At times when you're writing an essay, you'll be tempted to state claims and then let them sit there as if you have somehow made a point. But until you've backed your claims up with facts, you haven't really made an argument. On the flip side, you'll sometimes be tempted to simply state facts instead of making claims because facts are easier to manage. But facts don't actually make a point unless they are offered in support of a specific claim.

Claims and facts live in symbiosis —
that is, they are in an interdependent relationship.
If you're missing one or the other, you don't have
an argument.

Practice! Claims vs. Facts

Identify each of the following statements as either a claim or a fact based on your judgment as to whether the statement is one about which reasonable people could reasonably disagree. Note that this exercise will be easier if you do it with a partner or partners who qualify as reasonable people.

1. Today's "upside-down" technical degrees allow students to earn bachelor's degrees in increasingly specialized fields of study.
2. Changes in technology have led to an increase in long-distance romantic relationships in America.
3. *Ulysses* is so full of local in-jokes and particularities that the reader practically needs to be from Dublin to understand it.
4. Stephen Jay Gould's writing about science is clearer and easier to understand than Stephen Hawking's.
5. The lettering in illuminated versions of the Qur'an at one time constituted the totality of visual art in the Islamic world.
6. More people should take the bus to work to reduce the environmental impact of commuting.
7. Contrary to hundreds of years' worth of popular opinion, King Richard III almost certainly did not murder his two young nephews.
8. Some economists claim that cutting government spending improves the economy, but in a recession, the opposite is true.
9. Nitrogen concentrated on the soil surface can form an "acid roof" that negatively affects root growth.
10. Dogs possess levels of empathy that make them highly suitable as companion animals.

Different Claims for Different Purposes

Now you know that a claim is an arguable statement, which is why it's the thing that begins an argument. But not all claims are precisely the same. In fact, there are three types of claims, and each launches a different type of argument.

EXPOSITIONS AND CLAIMS OF FACT

An **exposition** is a type of argument that reveals to the reader a surprising or little-known truth. It sets out to demonstrate what is true, and to prove that a particular situation exists, has existed, or will exist.

When you are assigned to explain the root causes of the American Civil War, or to discuss the essential qualities of Baroque music, or to hypothesize the environmental effects of switching from petroleum to biodiesel, you are being asked to write an exposition. The goal of the exposition is to explain, to understand, to inform, and to enlighten, and it achieves these goals by making and supporting a *claim of fact*.

A **claim of fact** argues that a situation exists, has existed, or will exist. In other words, it argues that something is, was, or will be true. A claim of fact is not the same as a regular old fact, because a claim of fact is arguable. That means there is room for debate.

Take a look at this claim:

Artificial intelligence is not a possibility for the future but a reality today.

This is a claim of fact because we cannot completely prove or disprove it. We can certainly argue whether it is true or false. We can also give examples of why we are taking this position. However, at the end of the day the claim is debatable because — for starters — the definition of "artificial intelligence" is arguable.

The following excerpt comes from "The Uses of Being Wrong," an **expository essay** (one that rests on a central claim of fact) written by Daniel W. Drezner and published in July 2014. You may recall reading this passage back in Chapter 11 as an example of the rhetorical mode of **exemplification** (examples and illustrations).

Even in the realm of theory, there are only a few cases of scholars' acknowledging that the paradigms they've constructed do not hold. In 1958, Ernst Haas, a political scientist at the University of California at Berkeley, developed a theory of political integration, positing that as countries cooperated on noncontroversial issues, like postal regulations, that spirit of cooperation would spill over into contentious areas, like migration. Haas used this theory — he called it "neofunctionalism" — to explain European integration a half-century ago. By the 1970s, however, Europe's march toward integration seemed to be going into reverse, and Haas acknowledged that his theory had become "obsolete." This did not stop later generations of scholars, however, from resurrecting his idea once European integration was moving forward again. . . .

The persistence of so-called "zombie ideas" is something of a problem in the social sciences. Even if a theory or argument has been discredited by others in the moment, a stout defense can ensure a long intellectual life. When Samuel P. Huntington published his "clash of civilizations" argument, in the 1990s, the overwhelming scholarly consensus was that he was wrong. This did not stop the "clash" theory from permeating policy circles, particularly after 9/11.

EVALUATIONS AND CLAIMS OF VALUE

An **evaluation** makes and defends a judgment for the reader. It draws a conclusion about the relative moral, ethical, or aesthetic worth of a particular object, event, person, or idea. Evaluative arguments are also sometimes called *opinion* papers.

When you are assigned to determine whether Ronald Reagan or Bill Clinton engaged in more egregious scandals while in office, or to judge whether the death penalty is good or bad for society, or to show that Steven Spielberg (or J. J. Abrams, or Kathryn Bigelow, or whoever) is the most artful film director of all time, then you are being asked to write an evaluation. The goal of the evaluation is to justify, approve, condemn, or compare, and it does so by making and supporting a *claim of value*.

A **claim of value** argues that something — a person, a place, a thing, an event, an idea — is good or bad, right or wrong, beautiful or ugly, and so on. In other words, it makes a judgment about the value of a topic in broadly positive or negative terms and based on moral, ethical, or aesthetic criteria. The claim of value is always built upon a claim of fact; that is, it takes something that exists, has existed, or will exist — something that is true — and makes a judgment about it. This claim of fact may be stated directly or implied.

Consider this statement:

> Setting aside time for prayer in public schools is good for society's mental health.

This is a claim of value because it argues that a particular thing is good. You can see that it rests on two implied claims of fact: that prayer has been held in public schools and that mental health is a societal issue.

The next excerpt comes from "Shooting an Elephant" (1936), an **evaluative essay** (one that rests on a central claim of value) by George Orwell. You may recall reading a different selection from this essay back in Chapter 11 as an example of the rhetorical mode of **narration**.

All this was perplexing and upsetting. For at that time I had already made up my mind that imperialism was an evil thing and the sooner I chucked up my job and got out of it the better. Theoretically — and secretly, of course — I was all for the Burmese and all against their oppressors, the British. As for the job I was doing, I hated it more bitterly than I can perhaps make clear. In a job like that you see the dirty work of Empire at close quarters. The wretched prisoners huddling in the stinking cages of the lock-ups, the grey, cowed faces of the long-term convicts, the scarred buttocks of the men who had been flogged with bamboos — all these oppressed me with an intolerable sense of guilt. But I could get nothing into perspective. I was young and ill-educated and I had had to think out my problems in the utter silence that is imposed on every Englishman in the East. I did not even know that the British Empire is dying, still less did I know that it is a great deal better than the younger empires that are going to supplant it. All I knew was that I was stuck between my hatred of the empire I served and my rage against the evil-spirited little beasts who tried to make my job impossible. With one part of my mind I thought of the British Raj as an unbreakable tyranny, as something clamped down, in *saecula saeculorum*, upon the will of prostrate peoples; with another part I thought that the greatest joy in the world would be to drive a bayonet into a Buddhist priest's guts. Feelings like these are the normal by-products of imperialism; ask any Anglo-Indian official, if you can catch him off duty.

PROPOSALS AND CLAIMS OF POLICY

A proposal presents a feasible plan for addressing a negative situation. It sets out to solve a specific problem. Proposal arguments are also sometimes called *policy* or *solution* papers.

When you are assigned to come up with a plan for resolving your city's land-use zoning controversy, or to offer a way of dealing with corruption caused by the unlimited use of money in political campaigns, or to present a design for a rain-powered automobile to combat global climate change, you are being asked to write a proposal. The goal of the proposal is to convince, persuade, and call to action, and it does so by making and supporting a *claim of policy*.

A claim of policy goes a step further than judging or evaluating a situation: it proposes that a particular course of action be taken to solve a problem. Policy claims are always built on both a claim of fact (a problem exists) and a claim of value (the problem is bad). Depending on the degree of controversy surrounding the problem to be solved — is its existence widely accepted, and is it commonly considered a serious problem? — the claims of fact and value may be implied rather than directly stated.

Here's another claim:

To improve the state's economy, we need to convince the legislature to raise the minimum wage.

This is a claim of policy because it argues that we should do something; it proposes that we take a course of action in response to a problem. You can also identify the claims of fact and value that this claim of policy rests on: the state economy is suffering (a claim of fact), and a suffering economy is a bad thing (a claim of value).

The following excerpt comes from a **proposal essay** (one that rests on a central claim of policy). The essay, "Drugs," was written by American essayist Gore Vidal. This essay wasn't included in Chapter 11, but for those of you keeping score at home (or in the classroom), this excerpt makes use of the rhetorical mode of *effect analysis*.

> It is possible to stop most drug addiction in the United States within a very short time. Simply make all drugs available and sell them at cost. Label each drug with a precise description of what effect — good and bad — the drug will have on whoever takes it. This will require heroic honesty. Don't say that marijuana is addictive or dangerous when it is neither, as millions of people know — unlike "speed," which kills most unpleasantly, or heroin, which is addictive and difficult to kick.
>
> For the record, I have tried — once — almost every drug and liked none, disproving the popular Fu Manchu theory that a single whiff of opium will enslave the mind. Nevertheless many drugs are bad for certain people to take and they should be told about them in a sensible way.
>
> Along with exhortation and warning, it might be good for our citizens to recall (or learn for the first time) that the United States was the creation of men who believed that each man has the right to do what he wants with his own life as long as he does not interfere with his neighbor's pursuit of happiness (that his neighbor's idea of happiness is persecuting others does confuse matters a bit).

▶ *Let Us Show You:* Identifying Claims

Mara and Casey have developed a pretty good sense of what claims are, as well as an understanding of the different types of claims — at least in theory — so they've decided to do an experiment with Jonathan Swift's "A Modest Proposal." But as is often the case with pretty much any complex subject, having an understanding of the *theory* of claims is not the same as putting that understanding into practice.

Discussing Claims in "A Modest Proposal"

▶ **Talk Amongst Yourselves ...**

Find a partner and discuss the claims in either Barack Obama's "Amazing Grace" Clementa Pinckney eulogy or David Foster Wallace's "This Is Water" commencement address. (You remember these speeches, right? You watched one of them way back in Chapter 2 — long enough ago that you may need to watch it again.) Does one type of claim appear to dominate the argument? Or is there a fairly even distribution of claim types? What is the argument's main claim, or thesis? What type of claim is it?

► *Now You Try:* **Identifying Claims**

Determine whether each of the following statements is a claim of fact, a claim of value, a claim of policy, or not a claim at all. If it *is* a claim, discuss whether it would likely be the thesis of an exposition, an evaluation, or a proposal argument.

1. People ought to use less fertilizer in their yards because it causes nitrogen to accumulate in ecosystems.

2. T. S. Eliot is a more accessible modernist writer than James Joyce.

3. Indoor cats typically live longer than outdoor cats.

4. More people should take the bus to work to reduce the environmental impact of commuting.

5. A liberal college education was much broader a hundred years ago than it is today.

6. Calligraphy is the most beautiful form of art.

Qualifiers and Reservations

We should caution you about one common mistake in college writing: *making very broad claims.* Very broad claims are difficult, if not impossible, to support. If you find yourself attempting to write an essay based on a very broad claim — for example, "People these days have no manners," or "Movies are better than TV shows" — try to narrow your scope: whittle your claim down to a more manageable size and make it much more specific. You can do this by attaching *qualifiers* to your claim or by presenting a *reservation* to it.

Qualifiers are words or phrases that put a claim in context and narrow its scope. They are best presented with the claim itself, but they can appear anywhere in an argument. When you find yourself beginning an argument with an overly broad claim, try asking yourself, *What do I really mean?* or *Why am I saying that?* These questions will help you to narrow your claim through qualification.

For example, if we begin with the claim "Movies are better than TV shows," we can make the claim more interesting and supportable (i.e., narrower) by asking *how* and *why* and *to what extent* it's true. If we are thoughtful in answering those questions, then before we know it we will have qualified the claim by including more detail: "*Most* movies *out of Hollywood* have better *production values* than programs on *broadcast television*." That narrows the claim in four ways.

Now we can support it much more reasonably.

Aside from qualifiers, claims also sometimes have **reservations** attached. A reservation is a specific exception to a claim rather than a general limitation on it. Whereas qualifiers are needed for claims that are too broad, reservations are required when a claim has one clearly identifiable problem to overcome. Such a problem is sometimes referred to as an *exception* because it represents a situation in which the claim doesn't apply. In other words, the claim is true *except* within that particular situation or condition.

For example, the claim we made earlier about prayer in public schools has a fairly significant problem: the possibility that instituting prayer in public schools could result in discrimination based on religion. So we might want to attach a reservation to our claim — something like, "*Unless doing so results in discrimination based on religion*, setting aside time for prayer in public schools is good for society's mental health."

Practice! Narrowing Claims

Read the following overly broad claims and then attach qualifiers and reservations to each one to make it more manageable as the thesis statement of an essay. For added fun, see how many different specific claims you can make that fit reasonably within the huge territory of each broad claim. If you can come up with ten good claims for each, you'll win a prize! (Just ask your professor about the prize — we're sure he or she has one for you.)

1. Modern psychology has helped people a lot.
2. *The Catcher in the Rye* is the best book ever written.
3. Humanity should stop having wars.

▶ *Let Us Show You:* Understanding Claims

Casey's college algebra instructor, Professor Moriarty, has assigned the class to read and analyze a math proof (a math proof is an argument that justifies a mathematical statement). It looks like this:

> **Definition 1:** $N = \{1, 2, 3, \ldots\}$
> **Definition 2:** $U = \{n \in N \mid n \text{ is uninteresting}\}$
>
> **Theorem:** $U = \emptyset$
> **Proof:** Assume $U \neq \emptyset$. Then $\exists \ u \in U$ s.t. $u \leq v \forall v \in U$
> u is the *first* element of U, $\therefore \ u \in N/U$. $\Rightarrow\Leftarrow$ $\boxed{\text{Done}}$

Fortunately for Casey, Professor Moriarty has explained that in math, a proof is simply a logical argument — an argument presented through numbers and symbols in addition to words. Because many students are more comfortable with words than with mathematical symbols, the professor decided that a written explanation of the mathematical argument — that is, an essay — might make the proof easier to understand.

Analyzing an Essay on Math

"All of the Counting Numbers Are Interesting: A Theorem with a Proof" is an essay by Mick Bourbaki, who, according to Professor Moriarty, is the younger and somewhat *lesser* brother of Nicolas Bourbaki, the famous mathematician. Because the proof itself is beyond Casey's immediate grasp, and because Bourbaki's essay is an explanation of that proof, Casey has decided to rely on what he knows about essays to help him figure out the proof.

In other words, Casey plans to draw on what he knows about written arguments to work his way through the meaning of Bourbaki's essay. Casey understands that an argument contains a central claim and a series of minor claims, all of which will be supported. Therefore, his first step in understanding the argument of the proof is to understand the claims that it makes. That's not so hard. All he needs to do is annotate.

All of the Counting Numbers Are Interesting: A Theorem with a Proof
by Mick Bourbaki

In Mathematics clear definitions are essential. A *theorem* in math is a proven statement. It is not proved just beyond a reasonable doubt. It is not proved to the point where it is only 99.999% true and no one can offer evidence against it. In Math, such statements would be called *conjectures* or *hypotheses* — statements that are generally suspected for good reasons to be true, but for which there is no known proof.

> This is a claim of value — or is it a claim of fact? I'm going with claim of fact because in math, I think "essential" means "necessary."

A *theorem* in mathematics must have a valid *proof.* And the theorem is *true* relative to the *axioms* (*axioms* are statements *assumed* to be true without proof) and *definitions* from the area of mathematics where the theorem applies. The *proof* is usually a bunch of connected logical statements with varying amounts of exposition in between. The Pythagorean Theorem, the one about right triangles that everybody who has made it through enough algebra has heard of, was proved by Pythagoras over two thousand years ago. It is true relative to the axioms and definitions of Euclidian geometry, the geometry of the Cartesian coordinate plane. So it's *really* true. It's not going to be overturned by some new discovery.

> Assumed without proof? Why? What are axioms, and why are they assumed to be true?

On to the theorem and proof.

Theorem: *All of the Counting Numbers Are Interesting.*
Before we prove this, we need to be clear about the
definition of the Counting Numbers. For us, they are the
numbers we all learn to count with when we're children:
1, 2, 3, 4, 5, 6, ... The ". . ." is important. It means there is
no end to the Counting Numbers — they go on forever.
Also, there is a natural order to the numbers; that is,
everyone who understands counting knows 3 < 7. If you
don't know that, don't play poker unless you like losing.

> I'm calling this a claim of value because "interesting" is definitely a judgment. I think it's the essay's thesis — but it's pretty broad and maybe hard to support.

Now, the *no end* and *natural order* things seem
intuitively obvious to us — it's hard to see how they
couldn't be true — so maybe we should be able to prove
that they are true. But we can't prove them true without
making other, less intuitive assumptions. So for us, it's
safe to assume that those two properties are true. Axioms
are often things that seem intuitively true but turn out
not to be provable, or to be provable only after we make
other, less intuitive assumptions. Every theorem proved
true in math is dependent on one or more axioms and
definitions. So there's lots of truth in math, but it's all
assumed truth or relative truth, not absolute truth.

> Oh, here's a claim of policy! But it's not really a part of the proof. Maybe that's why he drops it.

> These sound like statements of fact, but they might be *claims* of fact. Are they arguable? Or are they more like "axioms," claims that are assumed to be true?

Proof:
Well, **1** is the first counting number. And the first of
anything is interesting by the fact of it being first — first
airplane flight, first person to climb Mount Everest,
first heart transplant, first person to cross the finish line,
etc. So 1 is interesting.

> "Proof." That's helpful! That tells me the support is coming.

(continued)

2 is the second counting number, but it's the first prime number (meaning it's divisible only by 1 and by itself), so 2 is interesting.

3 is the first odd prime number, so 3 is interesting.

4 is the first square, meaning 4 = 2 x 2, so 4 is interesting.

5 is the first prime number that is a sum of two prime numbers (5 = 2 + 3), so 5 is interesting.

6 is the first perfect number, meaning it is the sum of its proper divisors — that is, 6 = 1 + 2 + 3 (the next perfect number is 28) — so 6 is interesting.

Hm. These statements are the proof, but I think they're all claims because "interesting" is arguable. Can claims be supported with claims?

We're making great progress here! Or are we? The ". . ." is going to make this proof impossible to complete with our current approach because we'll never run out of counting numbers that we must show are interesting.

We need to be sneaky rather than straightforward.

We're going to do a *Proof by Contradiction*. The basic idea of proof by contradiction is to assume that what we're trying to prove is actually false and then seek a logical contradiction to that assumption. If we can find the contradiction, then the assumption must be false. And if the assumption is false, then the original theorem must be true. Obvious, right? It's sneaky logic, but it's valid.

So assume our theorem is False. That is, assume that Not *All of the Counting Numbers Are Interesting.* Note that this does not mean there are no interesting Counting Numbers — just that there is at least one Counting Number that is uninteresting. So we don't

Here's a new claim — I think the word "great" makes it a claim of value.

And here's a claim of policy — it argues what we need to do to prove the main claim.

This seems like a claim of fact, arguing what counts as valid logic in math.

know how many Counting Numbers are uninteresting and we don't know which ones are uninteresting, but at least one is uninteresting. We'll list these Uninteresting Counting Numbers in their natural order as $u_1, u_2, u_3, \ldots$ Natural order, remember, means that $u_1 < u_2 < u_3 < \ldots$

Maybe they go on forever, maybe not, but we know we have at least that first one. But wait a minute: we already know the first of anything is interesting, and u_1 is the first uninteresting counting number, so it must be interesting. This is a logical contradiction. If we assume *Not All of the Counting Numbers Are Interesting*, we have proved the existence of a number that is both interesting and uninteresting at the same time. Impossible. Therefore, the assumption *Not All of the Counting Numbers Are Interesting* is False, and so our original theorem, *All of the Counting Numbers Are Interesting*, is a True statement. And our theorem is proved.

Unless you're a big fan of logic, a proof by contradiction can feel a little underhanded. But it's logically just fine.

I don't think there are any claims in this section.

Wait. This says we've proved something and then says that what we've proved is impossible. Are these claims?

And here he returns to his thesis.

But here's a restatement of the claim from a few paragraphs ago. Its placement at the end makes it feel more important than the thesis.

It's okay if you don't understand the essay yet. This was just your first reading.

Oh, yeah. Recursive reading: if you want to understand something, you need to read it three times.

Casey identified a lot of claims and asked good questions. But he's still not sure he understands the essay's argument.

As Casey recalls, you generally need to read a text three times (at least) before you begin to understand it. So far, he's only looked at the *beginning* of the argument (its claims). Next he'll look at how Bourbaki supports his claims. That's the heart of the argument.

► *Talk Amongst Yourselves . . .*

With a small group of your classmates, discuss Casey's annotations of Bourbaki's essay. What claims has Casey missed in the essay? Are there any passages marked as claims that you don't think actually are claims? Explain. Do you share Casey's concerns about the logic of the assumptions required in axioms?

And what do you make of Casey's questions about the "Proof" section? Are the highlighted passages statements of fact, or are they claims? How can you tell? Finally, what do you make of Casey's concern about understanding Bourbaki's essay? Does it seem likely that a second and third reading might help Casey? Would recursive reading help *you* to understand the essay better?

► *Now You Try:* **Understanding Claims**

In the reader at the back of this book, you'll find an essay by Neil deGrasse Tyson titled "The Cosmic Perspective" (page 506). Give it a good, close reading, and then do the following:

1. Identify the claims presented in the essay.

2. Identify the type of each claim (claim of fact, claim of value, or claim of policy).

3. Evaluate each claim for its scope: Is it too broad? Too narrow? Just right?

4. Identify any qualifiers that limit the claims.

5. Examine the claims in context to see whether any reservations are attached.

6. Identify the main claim (thesis) of the essay. What kind of claim is it? Based on your answer, what kind of essay is this: an exposition, an evaluation, or a proposal?

Chapter 17

Supporting an Argument: Just *Saying* It Doesn't Make It So

> Everyone is entitled to his own opinion, but not to his own facts.
> — Daniel Patrick Moynihan

As you know by now, a claim by itself is not an argument — although we have met plenty of people who think it is. We recognize these people as having been raised in the "Because I said so!" school of argumentation, and while we may find other things about them adorable, we are not impressed with their ability to argue meaningfully.

If you want to argue in a rational, ethical, good-faith way — and of course you do! — then you will remember that the first thing you should do after presenting a claim is to support it.

When writers **support** a claim, they provide clearly articulated reasons to help the reader accept the validity of the claim. Broadly speaking, there are two ways to support a claim: by presenting factual evidence and by making an appeal to the reader's needs and values. (We discussed appealing to the reader back on page 21 in Chapter 2, and we'll discuss needs and values in much greater detail in Chapter 19, on pages 286–88.)

Expert opinion may be considered a third type of support. It generally (though not always) consists of either evidence or an appeal from a recognized authority on the subject at hand.

Factual Evidence

The first type of support, **evidence**, is necessary to show the reader that your argument is valid and that you, as the writer, are rational. Evidence is *factual* information: a statement or statements that can be proven true or false through observation.

People often mistakenly assume that factual evidence must necessarily be numbers (statistics). While it's true that numbers are a highly valued type of factual evidence, other statements of fact are, or at least can be, equally valid. Anything that can be proven true or false is a fact, and any fact can be presented as evidence.

All of the following are examples of factual statements:

More than half of all homes in the United States have three or more TVs.

My uncle Sven was born in Wisconsin in 1956.

High school football teams, on average, win more home games than away games.

While these statements are facts, they aren't yet *evidence* that supports an argument. Why? Because they aren't being used to support a claim yet. However, you can easily imagine what sort of claim each fact might support. Perhaps the first one would support a claim about overreliance on entertainment or technology. The second fact could be used to support a claim about conditions in the Midwest in the mid-twentieth century. And the third might support a claim about playing conditions that give athletes confidence. See how that works?

Back in Chapter 16, we presented a claim of policy about raising the minimum wage. Remember?

To improve the state's economy, we need to convince the legislature to raise the minimum wage.

Unless they already wholeheartedly agreed with this claim, most readers would think, *Oh, yeah? Why do you say that?* If we want to build a valid argument, we would likely respond with a piece of factual evidence such as this one:

For every percentage point that personal income increases, investment in local industry increases by 2 percent.

The preceding example is a statement of fact, meaning that it's a statement that can be proven true or false according to accepted standards by examining economic data. And yes, it falls into the category of numerical, statistical evidence. But we could also support the minimum-wage claim with factual evidence that is *not* statistical. For example, we might present as support a statement like the following:

Shortly after the legislature last raised the minimum wage, words like *recession* stopped appearing in newspapers around the state.

This piece of evidence is no less factual than the statistic about the correlation between income and investment: either statement can be proven true or false.

Awesome! you may be thinking. *Claim plus evidence equals argument!*
Well, not quite.

EVIDENCE DOESN'T SPEAK FOR ITSELF

Imagine for a moment that we presented the claim on page 246 with a piece of factual evidence and then said *Ta-da! End of argument.* Would that argument be convincing?

> To improve the state's economy, we need to convince the legislature to raise the minimum wage. For every percentage point that personal income increases, investment in local industry increases by 2 percent.

If we were you, we wouldn't be convinced yet. Something more than *just evidence* is needed to support a claim convincingly, because evidence truly doesn't speak for itself. The *writer* has to speak for it. In other words, the writer needs to provide some *discussion* of the evidence in order to build a rational argument.

Remember back in Chapter 10 when you learned about analytical paragraphs? Sure you do! That was the chapter in which we outlined the structure of the typical college-essay paragraph:

Elements of the Analytical Paragraph

- Claim
- Context
- Evidence
- Analysis
- Synthesis

When we pair a piece of evidence with a claim, we do so because we *assume* the evidence actually supports the claim. That is, we have some ideas about why this particular piece of information (percentage increases in personal income and local investment, for example) does a good job of validating the opinion we've just expressed in the claim (the legislature should raise the minimum wage).

Acknowledging Your Assumptions

In the Toulmin method (which we referred to briefly in Chapter 16 — it's where the terms *claim* and *support* come from), this assumption about how the evidence supports the claim is called a warrant. To make things easier here, we'll just refer to warrants as assumptions — and to be clear, there's nothing inherently wrong with assumptions. We'd hardly be able to get through the day if we didn't rely on hundreds of assumptions — for example, we assume that the chair we recently occupied is still there when we sit down again without looking.

And yet, as we know from quirky old Grandpa Eugene, who used to repeat "You should never assume because it makes an *ass* of '*u*' and *me*" over and over again at Thanksgiving, not all assumptions are created equal. It might be reasonable to assume that people prefer to eat food on a regular basis, but it is probably less reasonable to assume that people prefer to eat meat on a regular basis. The kinds of things you can take for granted when writing depend on who your reader is and what his or her situation is. (This concept is discussed in much greater detail in Chapter 19.)

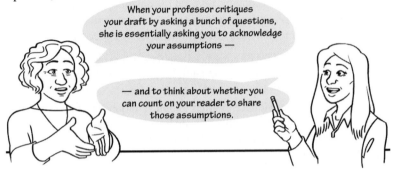

For an argument to succeed, its audience must find the argument's assumptions reasonable. When assumptions are controversial or questionable, they require backing; that is, they must be directly stated and then supported. A writer's assumptions about how evidence should be understood and interpreted can be a problem if his or her reader doesn't share those assumptions. The reason that writers need to explain their evidence (using context, analysis, and synthesis) is that readers don't live inside writers' heads. A reader cannot be expected to *guess* what a writer means.

▶ *Let Us Show You:* Supporting Claims with Factual Evidence

Casey and Mara have decided to develop an argument around the minimum-wage claim, and they want to gain a clearer sense of how they should explain the evidence so that the argument is logically satisfying for the reader. They're looking for feedback to help them grow their claim/evidence combo into an analytical paragraph. They've asked us for responses. As ya'll see, we mostly ask them questions. Here's the claim again:

> To improve the state's economy, we need to convince the legislature to raise the minimum wage. For every percentage point that personal income increases, investment in local industry increases by 2 percent.

And here is our list of questions for Casey and Mara:

▶   What does "investment in local industry" mean?

▶   And how is that related to the state's economy?

► For that matter, how are *personal, local,* and *state* actually connected?

► Why does investment in local industry improve the economy?

► Do you need a mini-lesson on what the economy actually is and on how its components affect each other?

Answering these questions will help them understand how and why they need to develop their argument.

Assumptions about evidence used in an argument usually rest on the truth, relevance, or soundness of that evidence — as you can see in the questions we asked Mara and Casey. They can resolve our questions and concerns by providing some context and analysis and a synthesis of the evidence used in their argument, which Mara has written in the following paragraph:

To improve the state's economy, we need to convince the legislature to raise the minimum wage. One of the ways the minimum wage affects the economy is through the relationship between income and spending. For every percentage point that personal income increases, investment in local industry increases by 2 percent. This means that when people have even a little more money to spend, they tend to spend proportionally *more* of that money supporting their local economy — for example, by shopping at local stores and patronizing small local businesses. When the local economy grows through increased personal spending, the state's overall economy improves for two reasons: more money is in circulation, and more revenue is raised on the money spent (through sales and service taxes). Those additional pennies per hour resulting from an increased minimum wage truly do spread out to the local and state economies.	Claim Context Evidence Analysis Synthesis

► *Talk Amongst Yourselves . . .*

Break into groups and discuss the preceding annotated paragraph. How well has Mara explained the argument? After reading the context, analysis, and synthesis, what questions or objections do you still have about whether the evidence truly supports the claim? In other words, what other assumptions might Mara need to acknowledge for her argument to be valid? Finally, which part of the argument is the longest? Why is that the case? Is that appropriate?

▶ *Now You Try:* Supporting Claims with Factual Evidence

For each of the following mini-arguments (claim *plus* evidence), see if you can identify the assumptions the arguer is making about how the evidence supports the claim. In other words, after reading each pair of statements, write down a list of questions you have about the meaning or validity of that argument, as we did for the previous minimum-wage argument.

Mini-argument #1

Claim: The federal government should take back the military weapons and vehicles that were given to local police department SWAT teams in the United States after 9/11 to help them deal with terrorism and hostage situations.

Evidence: Some 80 percent of all local police SWAT operations in the United States that involve military weapons and equipment are raids to carry out searches of private homes, usually for drugs; only 7 percent are related to terror or hostage situations.

Mini-argument #2

Claim: The phrase *Internet privacy* is an oxymoron — privacy on the Internet just doesn't exist in the real world.

Evidence: Every "cookie" stored on a computer can be used for tracking a user's actions.

Appeals

Appeals, the second type of support, are actually appeals to the reader's *needs and values*, which we will discuss in detail in Chapter 19. For now, it's enough that you understand that when writers appeal to readers' needs and values, they make the effort to support their claims with statements designed to engage their readers *emotionally*. Such support is different from factual evidence, which engages readers *logically*. This balance between logic and emotion (or between *logos* and *pathos*) will be addressed thoroughly in Chapter 19.

> Just as *logos* is related to logic,
> *pathos* is related to a bunch of "feeling" words: sympathy,
> empathy, apathy. Why? Because *pathos* is the Greek word for
> "feeling" or "emotion."

These appeals can be factual statements, but more often they are claims based either on facts or on principles that the writer believes the reader will agree with. Ultimately, an appeal to the reader's needs and values is a statement that encourages the reader to consider what is good, bad, necessary, dangerous, and so forth. The statements below are all examples of appeals to needs and values:

> A society that values life must value the lives of all of its citizens, regardless of their actions.

> People who are struggling to pay the rent aren't interested in donating to charities.

> Higher education provides a greater possibility of job satisfaction.

Again, these statements aren't yet *support* or *evidence* because they haven't been offered as a way of validating a claim. But we can imagine what sort of claim each appeal might support, right?

▶ The **first appeal** might support a claim against capital punishment.

▶ The **second appeal** could support a claim about how to raise money for charities.

▶ The **third appeal** could support a claim about the value of going to college.

Note that the third appeal could also support a claim about which employees are most satisfied in their jobs. So imagining what support backs up which claim takes some careful consideration.

Let's look at some more examples. Back in Chapter 16, we presented the following claim of fact:

> Artificial intelligence is not a possibility for the future but a reality today.

As always, we assume that the reader's response to this claim will be, *Oh, yeah? What makes you think that?* Because we cannot rely on the reader to automatically agree with our claim, we need to offer some support — for example:

> In general, we're afraid to acknowledge that machines might possess the capacity for conscious thought that humans have.

See how this statement appeals to the reader's need to feel that, as a human, he or she is not the same as a machine? It also appeals to the reader's understanding that sentience — the ability to think, reason, or be self-aware — is a uniquely human value.

APPEALS DON'T SPEAK FOR THEMSELVES, EITHER

When writers support their claims with appeals to needs and values, they are assuming certain things about their readers' needs and values — just as a writer using factual evidence assumes certain things about the truth, relevance, and soundness of the evidence. As with any assumption in any argument, the writer should *identify and acknowledge assumptions about needs and values.*

▶ *Let Us Show You:* **Supporting Claims with Appeals**

Casey and Mara have decided to get to the bottom of the assumption(s) about needs and values in the artificial intelligence claim. Allison opens by posing the claim.

Uncovering Assumptions about Needs and Values

Based on Casey and Mara's questions, we can develop an analytical paragraph — one with an *appeal* instead of factual evidence.

Artificial intelligence is not a possibility for the future but a reality today. Even though there are examples of human inventions that can be called "intelligent," we still tend to think of artificial intelligence as something out of a futuristic novel. Why? Well, in general, we're afraid to acknowledge that machines might possess the capacity for the very human practice of conscious thought. Most people are willing to consider that humans aren't alone in being able to think, in part because they have had enough contact with animals to recognize that at least some nonhuman creatures demonstrate that they're thinking on some level. But it's harder to accept the idea of machines having that same capability — and it's especially hard when the thinking done by machines these days appears to involve rational reasoning. Whether we like it or not, we are now living in a world that has developed artificial intelligence.	Claim Context Appeal Analysis Synthesis

Casey has one additional question: *What do you mean when you say that there are examples of human inventions that can be called "intelligent"?* He brings up another important point: because appeals to needs and values are often claims rather than facts, they sometimes need to be developed using factual evidence as support. It's entirely reasonable for a reader to want to understand what we assume about the truth, relevance, or soundness of the factual evidence that machines with intelligence exist. In other words, reasonable readers will want us to explain our assumptions as well.

For that reason, if we were writing an entire essay about artificial intelligence, we would likely follow the preceding paragraph with one that presents and analyzes the fact that *there are examples of human inventions that can be called "intelligent."*

▶ *Talk Amongst Yourselves . . .*

Take a few minutes to write down your responses to the following questions. Then break into groups of three and discuss your responses with each other.

What do you think of our annotated paragraph on page 253? Do the context, analysis, and synthesis we've provided help to resolve any questions or objections about whether the appeal truly supports the claim? Are there other assumptions about needs and values that need to be acknowledged for our argument to be valid? And how about Casey's follow-up question? Do you see how an argument can develop fully and logically when the writer answers questions about his or her assumptions?

▶ *Now You Try:* **Supporting Claims with Appeals**

Below is another mini-argument, this one made up of a claim plus an appeal. Read the statements and see if you can identify the assumptions the arguer is making about how the appeal supports the claim. To accomplish this, write down a list of questions that you have about the meaning or validity of the argument, following Casey and Mara's example on page 252 for the artificial intelligence argument.

Mini-argument

Claim: Every kid should be given a dog.

Appeal: Dogs teach kids to have responsibility.

Expert Opinion

As we stated earlier, **expert opinion** is considered a third type of support, but much of the time it's simply a twist on one of the other two types of support. At its heart, most expert opinion is either evidence or an appeal from an *authoritative source.* However, some expert opinion is what we might call "pure" expert opinion — it's neither factual evidence nor an appeal to needs and values. Instead, it is an *interpretation of factual evidence* by someone who is qualified to offer such an interpretation. The following statements are all examples of expert opinion:

Appeal to needs and values offered by an authoritative source: Thomas Paine claimed, "That government is best which governs least."

Factual evidence presented by an authoritative source: The sleeping medication Ambien was responsible for seventy-eight impaired-driving arrests in 2005, according to the Washington State Patrol.

Interpretation of factual evidence from the point of view of a "qualified" source: The writings of L. Ron Hubbard reveal that all criminality is caused by a lack of self-respect.

If you do a Google search of L. Ron Hubbard, you will understand our use of quotation marks around "qualified." (It means that we're not sure he is a qualified source at all.) You'll find more about what qualifies as an authoritative source in Chapters 20 and 21.

Even expert opinions must be offered in support of a claim. Back in Chapter 16, we presented the following *claim of value*:

> Setting aside time for prayer in public schools is good for society's mental health.

We obviously need to provide some support for this claim, so here you go:

> According to Sheffield Hallam University, people who pray frequently have significantly higher self-esteem and lower incidence of clinical depression.

It may occur to you, as you look at this combination of claim and expert opinion, that even experts need to be questioned on occasion.

NOT EVEN EXPERT OPINION SPEAKS FOR ITSELF

When writers support their claims with expert opinion, they are assuming that the reader will accept the authority or qualifications of the expert. Compare this to how a writer using factual evidence assumes certain things about the truth, relevance, or soundness of the evidence. Or you might compare it to how a writer using appeals assumes certain things about shared needs and values. As with any assumption in any argument, the writer should identify and acknowledge *assumptions about authority*.

> ► *Let Us Show You:* **Supporting Claims with Expert Opinion**
> Mara and Casey take up the challenge of examining the authoritative assumptions in this latest mini-argument. Most of all, they want to make sure this information is not just coming from some random person or organization. Here's the mini-argument again:
>
> > Setting aside time for prayer in public schools is good for society's mental health. According to Sheffield Hallam University, people who pray frequently have significantly higher self-esteem and lower incidence of clinical depression.
>
>
> *Who at Sheffield Hallam University says that prayer is good for mental health? Is it a person? A committee? Is he or she a qualified authority on psychology?*
>
> The assumptions that need to be acknowledged could be framed as: Who is the source of this claim? What are his/her/their credentials? From here, we can

develop an analytical paragraph in which expert opinion replaces factual evidence or an appeal to needs and values:

Setting aside time for prayer in public schools is good for society's mental health.	Claim
Children find it difficult to study and learn when they are occupied with other problems, including psychological problems.	Context
According to psychologists at Sheffield Hallam University, people who pray frequently have significantly higher self-esteem and lower incidence of clinical depression.	Expert Opinion
If prayer provides people with a better chance at having high self-esteem, that can only improve the atmosphere in public schools generally and the performance of students individually since self-esteem improves the learning process. Depression has also been shown to be a barrier to effective learning.	Analysis
If prayer can be a positive force that helps children to learn better, then there's every reason to be in favor of allowing prayer in public schools.	Synthesis

▶ *Talk Amongst Yourselves . . .*

Find a partner and discuss Mara's examination of the assumptions in our argument. How valid are her questions and concerns? Beyond the assumption about authority that Mara brings up, what other assumptions — about the factual evidence itself or about the appeal to the reader's needs and values — do you think need to be acknowledged? What other means of support might this argument need to be convincing?

▶ *Now You Try:* **Supporting Claims with Expert Opinion**

One more time! Below is a mini-argument made up of a claim *plus* an expert opinion. Read the statements and see if you can identify the assumptions the arguer is making about how the expert opinion supports the claim. To accomplish this, write down a list of questions that you have about the meaning or validity of the argument, following Mara's example on page 255 for the school-prayer argument.

Mini-argument

Claim: A chimpanzee should be granted legal personhood.

Expert Opinion: Steven Wise says that chimpanzees are cognitively complex and should be treated as such.

Before we move on to the last section of this chapter, let's quickly review the relationships among the claims, support, and assumptions that lie at the heart of the Toulmin method of argument:

Reality Check! **The Elements of Argument**

▶ All **claims** — whether claims of fact, value, or policy — need to be supported.

▶ All **support** — whether evidence, appeals, or expert opinion — needs to be explained in analytical paragraphs (see Chapter 10) because support does not speak for itself.

▶ All three types of support are or can be valid, as long as you consider your **assumptions**:

   • When you use factual evidence, you strengthen your *logos* — as long as you consider your assumptions about the *substance* of the evidence. (There's more on *logos* throughout Chapters 16–18.)

   • When you use appeals to needs and values, you strengthen your *pathos* — as long as you consider your assumptions about which needs and values *motivate* the reader. (Chapter 19 has more on *pathos*.)

   • When you use expert opinion, you strengthen your *ethos* — as long as you consider your assumptions about the *authority* of your expert. (You'll find more on *ethos* in Chapters 20–22.)

Arguments and Counterarguments

Sometimes an argument has a valid counterargument — an opposing viewpoint that is not easily dismissed by modifying claims with qualifiers or reservations (which we told you about in Chapter 16, remember?), or even by explaining assumptions, as discussed throughout this chapter.

For example, suppose that Mara read our analytical paragraph about school prayer and came back with a very good question that we could not easily dismiss. Here's her question: If Sheffield Hallam University is in England, are English laws on freedom of religion the same as American laws? In other words, is this source relevant?

When confronted by an opposing viewpoint, writers can strengthen the overall reasonableness of their arguments by providing a rebuttal. Most rebuttals are simply a section of an argument, as we'll discuss below. But sometimes an entire argument can be a rebuttal: see, for example, "The Radical Practicality of Reparations" by Ta-Nehisi Coates, or "Race and Mental Traits: Nicholas Wade's Third Error" by Sam Wang. Both of these essays can be found online by searching both title and author.

A **rebuttal** briefly presents the opposing viewpoint and then sets out to — well, to defeat it, actually. A good rebuttal is always fair in its presentation of the opposing viewpoint. *Unfairness* results in an unfortunate mistake known as a straw man fallacy (you can read about it in Chapter 18). But once the writer has presented the opposing argument as accurately and objectively as possible, he or she has no obligation to argue in favor of it or even discuss it in a particularly favorable light.

In presenting a rebuttal, we do our best to show the reader why our own point of view is superior. *Unless* something very strange happens, such as the following:

> Some people might say that there can't be prayer in public schools because the First Amendment says that the government can't establish religion. Since public schools are a part of the government, they can't make rules that establish religion. But "prayer" doesn't have to be a religious thing. It can simply be spiritual, like meditation or even just quiet time. It doesn't even have to be prayer, for that matter.

Uh-oh. See what happened there at the end? We'll give you a hint: when we wrote out the counterargument that we were planning to rebut, we found ourselves agreeing with it.

When this happens, as it sometimes does, it's necessary to reframe the original argument. In our case, we realized that it was possible to eliminate the original problem of having prayer in schools. We needed to figure out whether the benefits of "prayer" *are* still benefits even when the "prayer" is simply meditation.

If something similar happens to you, don't despair! Embrace the reality that you have just learned something new and, as a result of your new knowledge, have changed your opinion. There are far, far worse things in life than modifying your position when that position is challenged by a new understanding.

▶ *Let Us Show You:* Arguments and Counterarguments

All of this new information about supporting an argument has Casey in the mood to revisit Mick Bourbaki's essay, this time with an eye toward identifying the relationship between claims and support.

Identifying the Relationship Between Claims and Support

All of the Counting Numbers Are Interesting:
A Theorem with a Proof
by Mick Bourbaki

In Mathematics clear definitions are essential. A *theorem* in math is a proven statement. It is not proved just beyond a reasonable doubt. It is not proved to the point where it is only 99.999% true and no one can offer evidence against it. In Math, such statements would be called *conjectures or hypotheses* — statements that are generally suspected for good reasons to be true, but for which there is no known proof.

A *theorem* in mathematics must have a valid *proof*. And the theorem is *true* relative to the *axioms* (*axioms* are statements *assumed* to be true without proof) and *definitions* from the area of mathematics where the theorem applies. The *proof* is usually a bunch of connected logical statements with varying amounts of exposition in between. The Pythagorean Theorem, the one about right triangles that everybody who has made it through enough algebra has heard of, was proved by Pythagoras over two thousand years ago. It is true relative to the axioms and definitions of Euclidian geometry, the geometry of the Cartesian coordinate plane. So it's *really* true. It's not going to be overturned by some new discovery.

On to the theorem and proof.

Theorem: *All of the Counting Numbers Are Interesting.*

Before we prove this, we need to be clear about the *definition* of the Counting Numbers. For us, they are the

The first claim is supported by factual definitions — and maybe an appeal to our need for certainty? It seems effective.

This is developed with facts and examples from experts. I'm pretty sure that Pythagoras and Euclid are authoritative enough.

numbers we all learn to count with when we're children: 1, 2, 3, 4, 5, 6, . . . The ". . ." is important. It means there is no end to the Counting Numbers — they go on forever. Also, there is a natural order to the numbers; that is, everyone who understands counting knows 3 < 7. If you don't know that, don't play poker unless you like losing.

This paragraph relies on "axioms," assumptions that are safe to use because they're accepted. But still, the examples are factual.

Now, the *no end* and *natural order* things seem intuitively obvious to us — it's hard to see how they couldn't be true — so maybe we should be able to prove that they are true. But we can't prove them true without making other, less intuitive assumptions. So for us, it's safe to assume that those two properties are true. Axioms are often things that seem intuitively true but turn out not to be provable, or to be provable only after we make other, less intuitive assumptions. Every theorem proved true in math is dependent on one or more axioms and definitions. So there's lots of truth in math, but it's all assumed truth or relative truth, not absolute truth.

Tricky. This explains why math relies on assumptions, and leads to qualifying the underlined claim (that truth in math is not "absolute"). But he's not supporting his thesis" yet.

Claim

Proof:

Well, **1** is the first counting number. And the first of anything is interesting by the fact of it being first — first airplane flight, first person to climb Mount Everest, first heart transplant, first person to cross the finish line, etc. So 1 is interesting.

Again, these "*n* is interesting" statements are all claims. But this section is all factual evidence, so I guess the claims are well supported.

(continued)

2 is the second counting number, but it's the first prime number (meaning it's divisible only by 1 and itself), so 2 is interesting.

3 is the first odd prime number, so 3 is interesting.

4 is the first square, meaning 4 = 2 x 2, so 4 is interesting.

5 is the first prime number that is a sum of two prime numbers (5 = 2 + 3), so 5 is interesting.

6 is the first perfect number, meaning it is the sum of its proper divisors — that is, 6 = 1 + 2 + 3 (the next perfect number is 28) — so 6 is interesting.

Still, is it *my* problem that I don't find the first prime number that is the sum of two prime numbers interesting? Or is that the argument's problem?

We're making great progress here! Or are we? The ". . ." is going to make this proof impossible to complete with our current approach because we'll never run out of counting numbers that we must show are interesting.

Another safe assumption: that numbers are infinite.

We need to be sneaky rather than straightforward.

We're going to do a *Proof by Contradiction*. The basic idea of proof by contradiction is to assume that what we're trying to prove is actually false and then seek a logical contradiction to that assumption. If we can find the contradiction, then the assumption must be false. And if the assumption is false, then the original theorem must be true. Obvious, right? It's sneaky logic, but it's valid.

Are all these assumptions normal in math? It seems like I'm being asked to *trust* too much.

So assume our theorem is False. That is, assume that <u>Not</u> *All of the Counting Numbers Are Interesting.*

Note that this does not mean there are <u>no</u> interesting Counting Numbers — just that there is at least one Counting Number that is uninteresting. So we don't know how many Counting Numbers are uninteresting and we don't know which ones are uninteresting, but at least one is uninteresting. We'll list these Uninteresting Counting Numbers in their natural order as $u_1, u_2, u_3, \ldots$. Natural order, remember, means that $u_1 < u_2 < u_3 < \ldots$

Maybe they go on forever, maybe not, but we know we have at least that first one. But wait a minute: we already know the first of anything is interesting, and u_1 is the first uninteresting counting number, so it must be interesting. This is a logical contradiction. If we assume *Not All of the Counting Numbers Are Interesting*, we have proved the existence of a number that is both interesting and uninteresting at the same time. Impossible. Therefore the assumption *Not All of the Counting Numbers Are Interesting* is False, and so our original theorem, *All of the Counting Numbers Are Interesting*, is a True statement. And our theorem is proved.

Unless you're a big fan of logic, a proof by contradiction can feel a little underhanded. But it's logically just fine.

> More factual statements here. But there's something about what "we" find interesting or uninteresting that's setting off alarms for me.

> Once you sort through the twists and turns, it's logical. But I feel almost like I'm being *bullied* into agreeing. I'm not satisfied.

> He's right. It *does* feel a little underhanded. I'm still not sure why.

Casey did a great job of marking up Bourbaki's support and assumptions. But he's not satisfied. He's still not sure that he has a solid handle on the essay's argument that all of the counting numbers are "interesting."

Thanks to Mara, Casey gets what's going on in the essay now, but somehow he's still not convinced by its argument.

▶ *Talk Amongst Yourselves . . .*

Break into groups and discuss Casey's annotations of Bourbaki's use of support. How sound are the comments pointing out the use of factual evidence, appeals, and expert opinion? What other assumptions (or *warrants*) can you find besides those Casey identified? What do you make of Casey's sense that there's a good counterargument to be made? What do you think leads Casey to believe that Bourbaki's argument might require a rebuttal in response to a good counterargument? Finally, do you have a sense of why Casey is ultimately unsatisfied by Bourbaki's argument?

▶ *Now You Try:* **Arguments and Counterarguments**

Time for a brand-new essay analysis! Aren't you excited? We knew you would be!

Turn to page 511 in the reader at the back of this book and read Brent Staples's essay "Black Men and Public Space," originally published in *Ms.* magazine in 1986. Once you've read the essay, go through it paragraph by paragraph, as Casey has done with Bourbaki's essay on pages 260–63, and annotate the text by answering the questions below.

1. What is the main claim (thesis) of the essay?

2. Generally, how does Staples support this main claim?

3. What are the essay's minor claims (claims within each paragraph)?

4. What support does Staples offer for each minor claim?

5. What type of support is it (evidence, appeal, or expert opinion)?

6. Is the support sufficient to validate the claim?

7. What assumptions connect each claim to its support?

8. Are the assumptions acknowledged and explained, or are any of them problematic?

9. Does Staples present any rebuttals of counterarguments?

10. Can you identify any possible counterarguments that could/should be addressed through rebuttal?

Chapter 18

Faulty Reasoning: Bouncing the Check Your Argument Wrote

> Contrariwise, if it was so, it might be; and if
> it were so, it would be; but as it isn't, it ain't.
> That's logic.
> — Lewis Carroll

Now that you have a solid understanding of the relationship between your claim and its support, and you also understand how important this relationship is in forming a reasonable argument, we need to consider the various ways that this key relationship can crash and burn.

When an otherwise reasonable argument goes haywire, the result is called a logical fallacy. Because such fallacies are about the relationship between claims and support — and about the reasoning that links the claims and support — they are essentially *bad assumptions* that the writer makes. As you know from reading Chapter 17, assumptions are not logical fallacies in and of themselves: they are neutral processes of reasoning and are only as good or bad as the arguments they're in. When these processes are abused, or used poorly — well, the results aren't pretty.

Faulty (or *fallacious*) reasoning is sometimes the deliberate act of a dishonest person, just like plagiarism — something that Casey wrote about in earlier sections of this book and which *we* will write about at length in Chapter 22. But often, just like plagiarism, faulty reasoning is the ignorant act of an honest person.

> By the way,
> *ignorant* doesn't mean "bad" or "unintelligent."
> It simply means "uninformed." When a writer
> *ignorantly* plagiarizes, that simply means the writer
> is uninformed about how to use other people's
> ideas in his or her own writing.

All of the fallacies we discuss in this chapter are at least occasionally used by people who are up to no good — people who are trying to win an argument by cheating. However, our assumption about *you*, dear reader, is that any occurrence of one of these fallacies in your writing would be the result of an unfortunate rookie mistake (i.e., ignorance). So our advice for you in this chapter is practical, not moral.

Reasoning: A Quick Review

As a quick reminder, *logos*, or logic, is all about evidence and reasoning. You may recall from Chapter 9 that reasoning can be **inductive** or **deductive** (see pages 107–9 for examples). Inductive reasoning, like the scientific method, looks at particular pieces of factual evidence in order to draw a general conclusion. Deductive reasoning, a more philosophical method of thinking, begins with a premise (a statement of general truth) and then applies it to a specific case built on that general premise. When your reasoning goes south on you, regardless of whether it's inductive or deductive, the results will torpedo your *logos* and generally mess up your argument.

In a nutshell, bad assumptions about evidence become fallacies that undermine *logos*. Generally, a fallacy occurs because the writer has misjudged the evidence required to support a claim. As a result, the evidence *needed* is different from the evidence the writer has *actually presented*. Bottom line? The amount and quality of evidence should come pretty close to what the argument requires. Otherwise your *logos* suffers.

Problems with Factual Evidence (or Inductive Fallacies)

The most common fallacy of induction is the **hasty generalization**, which happens when a writer draws a general conclusion from insufficient, unrepresentative, or biased evidence. Often this fallacy is the result of an insufficient use of statistics: the writer declares a broad "truth" after examining only a small sample.

For ages, hasty generalizations have been the source of racist and sexist stereotypes — inaccurate generalizations made about a group of people based on limited contact with that group. If we want to carry it to the extreme, we might say that almost any statement about people in the form *All _____s are _____* (*All women are talkative*, for example, or *All Asians are good at math*) is a stereotype, since it is rare to find a group of people who all match up with any truly meaningful predicate.

Of course, hasty generalizations don't have to be about people; they can just as easily be about places or things or events or ideas or — well, pretty much anything that can be placed into a group. Student writers are

Don't let the word *predicate* scare you. A *subject* is what you're talking about, and a *predicate* is what you're saying about the subject. Easy, right? See Appendix A for more help like this.

particularly susceptible to committing this error when carelessly using the rhetorical strategy of classification — for example:

> I had some brussels sprouts once and they tasted very bitter. Then I had some asparagus, and it too tasted bitter. As a result, I have come to the conclusion that all green vegetables are bitter.

Needless to say, by making this hasty generalization about green vegetables, this poor soul will now miss out on the joy of eating sugar snap peas.

On the flip side of the evidence-deficient hasty generalization is the **snow job** fallacy, also known as the *kitchen sink gambit* or *lying with factoids*. This fallacy occurs when a writer overwhelms the reader by throwing mountains of irrelevant or questionably relevant evidence into an argument rather than providing well-chosen facts that actually support the claim directly. For example:

> This "global warming" argument is nonsense. Last winter was actually colder in some parts of the country than the previous year's winter had been, and snowfall increased significantly. And as for summer, well, the most recent summer in my part of the country was hardly summer at all, with cooler temperatures than usual. That certainly doesn't sound like "warming" to me!

Committing this type of fallacy can be an innocent mistake — student writers sometimes do it when they are first learning to use research and don't know how to choose evidence — but it is still a mistake. So try not to do it, okay? (You'll learn all about choosing and using research sources in Part 6 of this book.)

Sometimes the problem isn't so much skimpy evidence (as in the hasty generalization) as it is a complete absence of evidence. This fallacy is known as an **appeal to ignorance**, and it occurs when a writer asserts that a claim is true not because he or she has evidence to *support* the claim but because no evidence has been provided to *refute* the claim. The reverse is also an appeal to ignorance — that is, asserting that a claim is false not because any evidence has been offered to refute it but because no evidence has been offered to support it. For example:

> *Here's a fun appeal to ignorance: Life cannot exist on other planets because you have not yet proven to me that it does. So there!*

> Elves exist! I know this is true because you have not proven that they don't exist.

A related violation of inductive reasoning is **argument from belief**, in which a writer asserts that a claim is true, even in the face of overwhelming evidence to refute it, simply because he or she can easily believe it's true. There's also a reverse version — let's call it an **argument from disbelief** — in which a writer rejects a claim supported by mountains of evidence simply because he or she can't believe the claim is true. Both are serious problems. See if you can determine which fallacy is which in the examples below:

> I know that this house sits on a floodplain and has evidence of past water damage, but I just feel in my heart that everything will be okay. I don't really think that I need flood insurance.

> Even though doctors pretty much unanimously say that multivitamins have no benefit and often cause health problems, I just really feel like I need to take them anyway.

Reality Check! Inductive Fallacies

▶ **Hasty generalization:** Have you drawn a conclusion too quickly based on skimpy evidence?

▶ **Snow job:** Have you randomly chosen facts to support a claim rather than choosing evidence wisely?

▶ **Appeal to ignorance:** Have you decided something is true just because you haven't seen proof that it's false, or decided something is false because you haven't seen proof that it's true?

▶ **Argument from belief/disbelief:** Have you adopted a position simply because it's believable or rejected one simply because it's not?

Practice! Inductive Fallacies

See if you can figure out which inductive fallacy is ruining the logic of each statement below:

1. There have been no reports of falsified records, which likely means that officials are very good at falsifying their records secretly.

2. When I arrived on campus, the first six students I saw were women in their midtwenties. I was surprised that the student population wasn't younger and more male.

3. I know that respected economists support Keynesian policies, but I just can't accept that the government's spending more money is a good thing.

4. Charter schools are better than public schools because charter school teachers and administrators often come from professions other than education, charter schools aren't bound to follow the public school curriculum, and charter schools allow parents a choice.

Problems with *Thinking About* Evidence (or Deductive Fallacies)

Now that we've covered bad assumptions about evidence that result in faulty inductive reasoning, we can examine the other way to violate *logos*, which is to make an error in your reasoning — that is, your thinking. This type of violation is known as a fallacy of deduction. Deductive fallacies are errors that writers make in understanding, analyzing, and interpreting their own reasons in support of the claims in their arguments. There are more types of deductive fallacies than inductive fallacies because there are more ways to mess up your thinking than there are ways to misapply evidence.

Generally, an error in reasoning involves bad judgment about the relationship between what a reason says and what it means. Bottom line? The reasons you *present* in an argument ought to say precisely what you *mean*. There are several subgroups of fallacies of deduction.

FAULTY SYLLOGISMS

Several of the most common deductive fallacies are syllogistic, meaning that they are flaws in the logical construction of a syllogism. Remember syllogisms? If not, you might want to review pages 108–9 in Chapter 9 before continuing with this section. But if all you need is a quick reminder, then here you go:

The Sandwich Syllogism for Deductive Reasoners

▶ **Major premise:** All sandwiches have two pieces of bread and something in between.

▶ **Minor premise:** My mom or dad will bring me a sandwich.

▶ **Conclusion:** My mom or dad will bring me two pieces of bread with something in between.

As you may recall from our discussion in Chapter 9, the logic of a syllogism can sometimes fall apart. When that happens, you have a faulty syllogism on your hands. A common syllogistic fallacy is the *non sequitur*, which is a Latin phrase meaning "it does not follow." When the conclusion of a syllogism does not logically follow the major and minor premises, the result is a non sequitur. Note that the conclusion is not necessarily false. But the argument is still faulty because the connection between the premise and the conclusion is broken. Check out this example:

The Ballerina Syllogism

Major premise: All ballerinas wear ballet slippers.
Minor premise: Crystal wears ballet slippers.
Conclusion: Crystal is a ballerina.

Please Note!

This is a non sequitur.
It isn't logical.
It's a bad syllogism.

See the problem? The major premise is about all *ballerinas*, not about all people named Crystal. There's a significant disconnect between the major premise, which is about what all ballerinas do, and the minor premise, which is about what someone who may or may not be a ballerina does. We don't know whether Crystal is a ballerina or not. She might be — but if she is, it's not because of the sheer awesomeness of this syllogism. For all we know, Crystal just thinks ballet slippers are comfortable.

Circular reasoning does exactly what it sounds like: it loops the logic of the syllogism around itself. It basically argues that the conclusion is equivalent to the major premise by using a claim (or a reworded claim) to support its own point. For example, we can remember countless frustrating summer evenings when the sun had not yet fully set but our parents would still tell us to get ready for bed. "But why?" we would say, quite sweetly and not at all with a whiny tone. "It's time for bed," our long-suffering parents would say. "But why?" we would persist. "Because," they would say with less patience, "it's bedtime."

Got it? *It's time for bed because it's bedtime.* This is classic circular reasoning — perhaps not too horrible when it comes to coaxing four-year-olds into their Bugs Bunny footie pajamas, but definitely a problem in academic writing. Students are most likely to commit this error when they're writing about topics they don't fully understand.

What can we say about **begging the question**? Well, first we should say what it *isn't*: to beg the question is not simply to *raise* an interesting question. Rather, it is to assume an unsupported claim is true and then use that claim as if it were evidence to build the rest of the argument.

Begging the question is a fallacy that uses information from its own conclusion to prove itself and then make another claim based on that "proof." In other words, it's the next illogical step in circular reasoning. Check out the actual, real-life examples of begging the question on the next page.

You can't give me an F on this paper because it's an A paper!

PE is pointless, so we should remove the PE requirement from the AA degree.

Learning standard grammar is unnecessary when we already write well.

Each of these statements is illogical because it assumes something that has not been proven yet and then uses that assumption as if it were evidence in order to draw a conclusion. In the first statement, the question of whether the paper is truly an A paper is *the matter that is being decided*, not *a fact that has already been proven*. To use "it's an A paper" to prove that the paper does not deserve an F begs the question. Written as a syllogism, the faulty logic becomes clearer.

The "A Paper" Syllogism

Major premise: An A paper does not deserve an F.
Minor premise: My paper is an A paper.
Conclusion: My paper does not deserve an F.

Please Note!

This begs the question.
It isn't logical.
It's a bad syllogism.

Remember our discussion of "vacuously true" statements back in Chapter 14? A statement that is vacuously true is true without having any significance whatsoever. Its truth is *empty like a vacuum*. The major premise above is vacuously true, while the minor premise rests on the very question that has not been decided yet: whether or not the paper is an A paper.

Related to begging the question is the fallacy of many questions, also known as **confusing the question**. It happens when a writer sneaks in two questions at once, with the main question depending on a specific answer to a question that's only *implied*. The classic example is a trick question asking whether someone has stopped doing something unsavory — for instance: *Have you stopped cheating on your taxes?*

You see the problem, right? By asking whether a person has *stopped* cheating on his taxes, the writer presumes that the person is guilty of having cheated on his taxes in the first place. This fallacy, like circular reasoning, can be a problem in academic writing even when it's innocently deployed. Can you spot the presumed but unsupported "fact" in the following question? *Why should we expect traffic circles to help with traffic congestion in our town when they haven't worked anywhere else in the country?*

Reality Check! Faulty Syllogisms

▶ **Non sequitur:** Have you established a nonsensical syllogism that violates its own logic?

▶ **Circular reasoning:** Have you tried to prove a claim by using that same claim as evidence?

▶ **Begging the question:** Have you assumed that a claim is true and then used that claim as if it were evidence to build an argument?

▶ **Confusing the question:** Have you embedded too many questions in a single question?

Practice! Faulty Syllogisms

See if you can figure out which syllogistic fallacy is ruining the logic of each statement below:

1. If the average person can't be trusted to pay attention to politics, why should everyone have an equal vote?
2. Because all professors are educated and Mr. Jones is educated, Mr. Jones is a professor.
3. Sex education classes are good because they educate students about sex.
4. Travel is unnecessary when everything worth seeing is right here at home.

THE DERAILED TRAIN OF THOUGHT

Sometimes an argument starts out okay and then takes an odd turn into illogic. The idea train makes it out of the station, but before long it switches to the wrong track and ends up making an unplanned stop in the State of Confusion.

Often, the derailed logic train is a victim not only of bad judgments but also of shoddy thinking about causes and effects. The most prevalent of these cause-and-effect fallacies is the *post hoc, ergo propter hoc* fallacy.

The *post hoc* fallacy assumes that because one event follows another, the first event caused the second event. In other words, it assumes that *chronology equals causation*. The logic is quite simple, really (which is what makes it fallacious): *A happened, and then B happened; therefore, A caused B. Case closed.* Except the case really isn't closed. Most superstitions are based on the classic *post hoc* construct: *A black cat walked in front of me this morning, and that's why I spilled coffee on my new skort.* While it's easy to recognize the illogic in a superstition, it's somewhat more challenging to recognize it in an argument about a more serious topic. See if you can articulate what's wrong with the logic in the following example:

In the past twenty years, the depiction of sexual activity on TV has increased. Last year, teen pregnancy rates were higher than they were twenty years ago. Therefore, sex on TV causes teenage pregnancy.

> *Post hoc, ergo propter hoc* is not only a cool thing to say but also a Latin phrase that translates literally to "after this, therefore because of this."

Even identifying a reasonable cause for an effect can cause trouble. The **fallacy of the single cause** assumes that there is only one simple explanation for an effect, even though multiple causes are likely or at least possible.

The single-cause fallacy is tricky — on the one hand, there's some valid reasoning behind Occam's razor, a principle that says that of multiple possible answers, the least complicated explanation is often correct. But the fallacy of the single cause is essentially Occam's razor run amok: it ignores complex explanations because a single, *simple* cause is available. This fallacy is common among writers who would prefer to *know* the answer rather than to *find* the answer. For example: *Childhood obesity is clearly the result of the explosion of junk food advertising.*

Another common fallacy of causation is the **slippery slope** fallacy, which assumes without sufficient reason that a single initial cause will set into motion an entire chain of events. This cause-and-effect fallacy rests on the assumption that if one false step is taken, not only will a particular effect occur, but so will another, and another, and another . . . until we slide all the way down the hill. This type of illogical thinking is also known as the *domino theory* because, well, what happens when you knock one domino over? That's right: they all fall down.

Try to count the effects on the way down this slippery slope:

> If a junior high school student tries a cup of coffee during her three-day trip to the Math Olympics, it's only a matter of time before she decides to try other drugs. Oh, sure, she'll be satisfied with caffeine for a while, but she'll soon grow tired of that and try alcohol. From there, it's a short step to marijuana and hard drugs. One day, coffee; the next day, heroin!

Another way to derail a train of thought is to divert it on purpose. When writers deliberately point their readers in the wrong direction to avoid the hard work of arguing the point at hand, they are using diversionary tactics. The **red herring fallacy** diverts attention from the actual argument by changing the subject and focusing on something new instead of the original issue. Similar to the red herring fallacy is the **straw man fallacy** — you may recall that we mentioned this fallacy in Chapter 17, during our discussion of counterarguments. A straw man argument involves misrepresenting or oversimplifying an opponent's argument, thus making the opponent's position appear easier to argue against in a sort of fake rebuttal. See if you can spot elements of both of these diversionary tactics in the following example:

> Feminists need to drop this argument about income equality between the genders. Why on earth should every female employee be paid exactly the same as every male employee? That's just ridiculous.

Reality Check! The Derailed Train of Thought

▶ **Post hoc, ergo propter hoc:** Have you assumed that correlation is the same as causation?

▶ **Fallacy of the single cause:** Have you made it seem as if something is attributable only to one simple cause when it's likely that more causes are involved?

▶ **Slippery slope:** Have you made assumptions about a series of possible effects?

▶ **Diversionary tactics (red herring and straw man fallacies):** Have you distracted the reader from the actual argument?

Practice! The Derailed Train of Thought

See if you can figure out which of the previous fallacies is ruining the logic of each statement below:

1. Young people today disrespect their elders because that's the behavior they see modeled on television.
2. I'm not going to wash my car today. Every time I do, it rains.
3. Those who want the United States to switch to the metric system are trying to turn America into Europe.
4. Missing even a single day of class can put you behind in your work, which just gets worse as the rest of the class moves forward and you fall further behind.

FAILURES OF PERSPECTIVE

The last set of deductive fallacies consists of errors that occur as a result of **faulty perspective**. Typically these fallacies happen when a writer fails to understand how comparisons actually work. In fact, there's one major perspective fallacy that's all about comparison (*false analogy*), and a second one that's all about contrast (*false dilemma*).

But before we explain these two fallacies, it's important to point out that there's nothing inherently illogical about comparisons and contrasts themselves. They can be very useful and logical. An **analogy**, for example, points out figurative similarities between two otherwise unlike things for the purpose of understanding. Analogies can be useful in arguments when they are used to make unfamiliar concepts understandable by comparing them to familiar, concrete things. So if we wanted to explain our fascination with psychology to someone who is completely unfamiliar with the field, we might come up with something like this:

Psychology is like having a key to a locked room, but the key is *in* the room.

This analogy actually works pretty well as an introduction to the paradox of psychology, which is that the brain is both the *locked room* to be entered and the *tool used* to enter that room. Cool, right?

If developed further and used in an argument, however, this analogy might soon become a **false analogy**. If you reasoned that, because the brain is like a key in the way described above, the brain can therefore be put on a key ring for safekeeping, some people might question your judgment — as well they should, given that you have just ruined a lovely analogy by trying to extend it and use it as the basis for an illogical argument. It would be equally fallacious to push the "locked room" comparison to the point of illogic: *Because psychology is in a locked room, we don't have the right to access it.*

The **false dilemma** is also known as the *either-or fallacy* or *black-and-white thinking*. Either it gives the reader only two choices even though more than two choices exist, or it grossly oversimplifies a complex situation by assuming that two things are opposites when they're really not. Has anyone ever asked you whether you are a Democrat or a Republican? If so, that person presented you with a false dilemma. Just look at your voters' pamphlet before the next big election. After reading about the Green Party, the Libertarian Party, the Socialist Workers Party, and the Constitution Party, you will probably start to realize that the Democratic Party is not really the opposite of the Republican Party — nor are those two parties the only two choices available.

When a student writer presents a false dilemma, it is often the result of lazy thinking. It's just easier to toss out a prefabricated construct like up/down, good/evil, or liberal/conservative than it is to discuss the reality that there's room between up and down, that there are things that are neither good nor evil, or that there are people and ideas that are somewhere between (or beyond!) liberal and conservative. For example:

What do you mean sometimes you feel at ease at parties but sometimes you don't? Look, you're either an introvert or an extrovert. Which is it?

Finally, in case you think that identifying a violation of *logos* in someone's argument is the ultimate "gotcha!" we need to tell you about one more fallacy. When you assume that a single fallacy destroys an entire argument, you're committing the **fallacy fallacy** (don't you just love it?). In other words, you find one error in an argument's reasoning and assume that naturally the argument's conclusion is false. Remember Crystal and the question of whether or not she's a ballerina?

The Ballerina Syllogism	*Please Note!*
Major premise: All ballerinas wear ballet slippers.	This is a non sequitur.
Minor premise: Crystal wears ballet slippers.	It isn't logical.
Conclusion: Crystal is a ballerina.	It's a bad syllogism.

This syllogism fails to prove that Crystal is a ballerina because it's illogically applied. Therefore, Crystal's not a ballerina, right? *Wrong!* She may very well be a ballerina, for all we know. The fatally flawed syllogism we offered doesn't prove that she *is* a ballerina, but it also doesn't prove that she *isn't*. Therefore, when going on a fallacy-hunting expedition, take care: fallacies in and of themselves do not disprove an argument — they just torpedo the reasoning in a specific *part* of the argument.

Reality Check! Failures of Perspective

▶ **False analogy:** Have you pushed a figurative comparison too far for logic?

▶ **False dilemma:** Have you failed to recognize that there are more than two sides to an issue?

▶ **The fallacy fallacy:** Have you assumed that one mistake in reasoning destroys an entire argument?

Practice! **Failures of Perspective**

See if you can figure out which fallacy of perspective is trying to ruin the logic of each statement below:

1. Because handing the car keys to a sixteen-year-old is like giving a toddler a loaded gun, we should make sure that all cars are locked safely away from teenagers.
2. One paragraph of your essay misstates my premise about honey badgers. As a result, your entire analysis of the evolution of the badger family is suspect.
3. At this point, we can either get money out of politics or say goodbye to democracy.

▶ *Let Us Show You:* **Effective Reasoning**

Having left themselves hanging on a few important questions after reading Mick Bourbaki's "All of the Counting Numbers Are Interesting" back in Chapters 16 and 17, both Mara and Casey are interested in determining whether there are any problems with inductive or deductive reasoning in the proof. Casey is still not feeling confident in his analysis, especially around the middle part of the proof.

All of the Counting Numbers Are Interesting:
A Theorem with a Proof
by Mick Bourbaki

In Mathematics clear definitions are essential. A *theorem* in math is a proven statement. It is not proved just beyond a reasonable doubt. It is not proved to the point where it is only 99.999% true and no one can offer evidence against it. In Math, such statements would be called *conjectures* or *hypotheses* — statements that are generally suspected for good reasons to be true, but for which there is no known proof.

A *theorem* in mathematics must have a valid *proof*. And the theorem is *true* relative to the *axioms* (*axioms* are statements *assumed* to be true without proof) and *definitions* from the area of mathematics where the theorem

These are just definitions. No logic problems so far.

applies. The *proof* is usually a bunch of connected logical statements with varying amounts of exposition in between. The Pythagorean Theorem, the one about right triangles that everybody who has made it through enough algebra has heard of, was proved by Pythagoras over two thousand years ago. It is true relative to the axioms and definitions of Euclidian geometry, the geometry of the Cartesian coordinate plane. So it's *really* true. It's not going to be overturned by some new discovery.

On to the theorem and proof.

We're still relying on authority here, but it doesn't seem to be a problem in terms of evidence or thinking.

Theorem: *All of the Counting Numbers Are Interesting.* Before we prove this, we need to be clear about the *definition* of the Counting Numbers. For us, they are the numbers we all learn to count with when we're children: 1, 2, 3, 4, 5, 6, ... The ". . ." is important. It means there is no end to the Counting Numbers — they go on forever. Also, there is a natural order to the numbers; that is, everyone who understands counting knows 3 < 7. If you don't know that, don't play poker unless you like losing.

Is it a hasty generalization here to talk about "we all" and "everyone"? No, I don't think so. We do all learn to count.

Now, the *no end* and *natural order* things seem intuitively obvious to us — it's hard to see how they couldn't be true — so maybe we should be able to prove that they are true. But we can't prove them true without making other, less intuitive assumptions. So for us, it's safe to assume that those two properties are true. Axioms are often things that seem intuitively true but turn

There's a little bit of a leap here. Should we assume they're true because we can't prove them? But still, both assumptions are explained and reasonable.

(continued)

out not to be provable, or to be provable only after we make other, less intuitive assumptions. Every theorem proved true in math is dependent on one or more axioms and definitions. So there's lots of truth in math, but it's all assumed truth or relative truth, not absolute truth.

Proof:

Well, **1** is the first counting number. And the first of anything is interesting by the fact of it being first — first airplane flight, first person to climb Mount Everest, first heart transplant, first person to cross the finish line, etc. So 1 is interesting.

2 is the second counting number, but it's the first prime number (meaning it's divisible only by 1 and itself), so 2 is interesting.

3 is the first odd prime number, so 3 is interesting.

4 is the first square, meaning 4 = 2 x 2, so 4 is interesting.

5 is the first prime number that is a sum of two prime numbers (5 = 2 + 3), so 5 is interesting.

6 is the first perfect number, meaning it is the sum of its proper divisors — that is, 6 = 1 + 2 + 3 (the next perfect number is 28) — so 6 is interesting.

We're making great progress here! Or are we? The "..." is going to make this proof impossible to complete with our current approach because we'll never run out of counting numbers that we must show are interesting.

> Here's the logical problem: The reason for the claim hasn't been established. The argument never proves that being first is interesting.

> And it isn't, necessarily! My first thought in the morning is usually "Coffee" or "I need to pee." Neither of which is interesting.

> So that makes this a classic case of begging the question! Using an unsupported claim as if it were support is a logical fallacy.

We need to be sneaky rather than straightforward.

We're going to do a *Proof by Contradiction*. The basic idea of proof by contradiction is to assume that what we're trying to prove is actually false and then seek a logical contradiction to that assumption. If we can find the contradiction, then the assumption must be false. And if the assumption is false, then the original theorem must be true. Obvious, right? It's sneaky logic, but it's valid.

All of this is reasonable enough.

So assume our theorem is False. That is, assume that *Not All of the Counting Numbers Are Interesting*. Note that this does not mean there are <u>no</u> interesting Counting Numbers — just that there is at least one Counting Number that is uninteresting. So we don't know how many Counting Numbers are uninteresting and we don't know which ones are uninteresting, but at least one is uninteresting. So we'll list these Uninteresting Counting Numbers in their natural order as $u_1, u_2, u_3, \ldots$. Natural order, remember, means that $u_1 < u_2 < u_3 < \ldots$

But this just builds on the illogically begged question.

We don't have a valid definition for either "interesting" or "uninteresting." So that begging the question thing just keeps going.

Maybe they go on forever, maybe not, but we know we have at least that first one. But wait a minute: we already know the first of anything is interesting, and u_1 is the first uninteresting counting number, so it must be interesting. This is a logical contradiction. If we assume *Not All of the Counting Numbers Are Interesting*, we have proved the existence of a number that is both interesting and uninteresting at the same time. Impossible. Therefore the assumption *Not All of the Counting Numbers Are*

This part is fun because the logic is really solid. It makes sense as an argument, but it doesn't really support the main claim about all counting numbers being interesting.

(continued)

Interesting is False, and so our original theorem, *All of the Counting Numbers Are Interesting*, is a True statement. And our theorem is proved.

But it isn't proved, really. It's just that it hasn't been *disproved*.

Unless you're a big fan of logic, a proof by contradiction can feel a little underhanded. But it's logically just fine.

Being able to identify logical fallacies is a great tool because it helps you figure out where the holes in your argument are.

Analyzing an Argument by Identifying Logical Fallacies

Now I have a name for the problem in Bourbaki's thesis: begging the question.

So does that fallacy kill the essay for you?

Not really. He didn't convince me that all of the counting numbers are interesting. But he did prove that proofs by contradiction are interesting!

I wonder if that was his point the whole time?

▶ *Talk Amongst Yourselves . . .*

Break into groups and see whether you can find any fallacies of *logos* in Bour-baki's essay that Casey missed. If you do, try to explain why they're examples of faulty reasoning. Then, looking at the fallacies that Casey identified as well as at any others you might have found, decide which of them are important problems in the essay and which aren't. Are there any fallacies that you think are fatal to the success of the argument? If so, why? Be careful! Make sure you're not indulg-ing in the fallacy fallacy! Finally, what do you think of Casey's assertion that Bourbaki's essay failed to support its thesis but succeeded in proving that proofs by contradiction are interesting? Do you agree? Why or why not?

▶ *Now You Try:* **Effective Reasoning**

In Chapter 16, you read Neil deGrasse Tyson's essay "The Cosmic Perspective" in order to identify its claims. Then, in Chapter 17, you examined both claims and support in Brent Staples's essay "Black Men and Public Space."

Now we'd like you to reread either Tyson or Staples, but this time annotate the essay for its logical soundness. Look very carefully not just at *whether* the author uses evidence but at *how* he uses it. Does he commit any fallacies of induction or deduction?

Be sure to use the Tune Up Your Reasoning checklist below as a guide to your analysis of the argument. And don't forget to share your analysis with your professor or a classmate to see how you did.

Reality Check! **Tune Up Your Reasoning**

▶ Make sure you have avoided inductive fallacies by **using evidence** reasonably and responsibly without resorting to any of the following:
  • hasty generalizations
  • snow jobs
  • appeals to ignorance
  • arguments from belief
▶ Make sure you have avoided deductive fallacies by **thinking clearly** about the logic of your argument without falling for any of the following:
  • non sequiturs
  • circular reasoning
  • begging the question
  • confusing the question
  • *post hoc, ergo propter hoc*
  • fallacies of the single cause

(continued)

- slippery slopes
- diversionary tactics (red herring and straw man fallacies)
- false analogies
- false dilemmas
- fallacy fallacies

Chapter 19

Engaging the Reader: Oh, *That's* What You Meant by "Conversation"!

> When I get ready to talk to people, I spend two-thirds of the time thinking what they want to hear and one-third thinking about what I want to say.
> —Abraham Lincoln

In *Rhetoric*, Aristotle tells us that a compelling argument has three qualities: *logos*, which we've already covered; *pathos*, which we'll cover in this chapter; and *ethos* (don't worry — it's covered in Chapters 20–22). As you know, *logos* (logic) is the quality of argument that satisfies the human need for proof, for evidence, for reasonableness. But humans need more than logical explanations. They also need to *care*. In this chapter, we'll look at the quality of argument that balances *logos* by encouraging us to care. That quality is called ***pathos***.

Pathos is a Greek word meaning "feeling" or "emotion." (We talked about *pathos* back in Chapter 17.) The English language has borrowed the root of the Greek word to create a number of words that have to do with feelings or emotions as the Grammster explains below.

Ultimately, *pathos* is all about the writer's efforts to make his or her argument resonate with the reader as a human being who has *needs and values* (remember those?) and therefore feelings. *Pathos* is crucial because a solid argument not only will be logically sound but also will be emotionally satisfying for the reader. *That's nice*, you may be thinking, *but how exactly am I supposed to know what my reader's needs and values are?* We think Maslow's hierarchy of human needs is a good place to start our explanation.

> The word *sympathize*, for example, means "to feel for," while *empathize* means "to feel with" — and of course *apathy* means "lack of feeling."

Needs and Values: Maslow's Hierarchy

As we mentioned in Chapter 17, a highly successful argument makes good use of *pathos*. This means that the writer appeals to a set of underlying needs and values that he or she shares with the reader. How, you ask? Through the use of specific and vivid detail (which we'll discuss later in this chapter). At this point, you might be thinking how helpful it would be if there were some well-organized, easily understandable way to articulate those needs and values. Well, you're in luck: we've brought along someone to help us explain how you figure out the underlying needs and values of your arguments.

And now, without further ado, we'd like to introduce today's guest expert on human needs and values, Abraham Maslow. Maslow (1908–1970) was an American psychologist and philosopher who is best known for developing a prioritized list, called **Maslow's hierarchy of human needs**, that shows what human beings need and/or want. It looks like this:

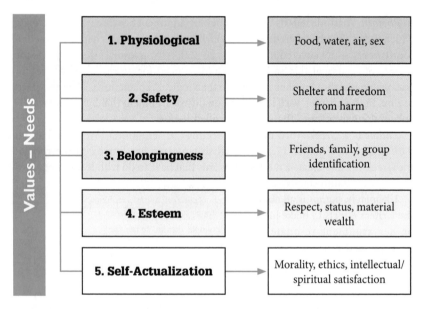

A useful way to think about this hierarchy when you're writing an essay is in terms of **needs** versus **values**. The top two items (representing food, water, air, safety, shelter) are clearly needs. The bottom two items (representing status, wealth, respect, intellectual and spiritual achievement) are clearly values. The middle tier (friends, family, tribal belonging) can go either way — while we all need love and companionship for life to be worth living, we don't die if deprived of either for stretches of time.

So what does all of this stuff about Maslow's hierarchy have to do with you and that essay about aquifers that you have to write for your environmental science class? This question brings us back to the communication triangle that we first looked at in Chapter 2. Here it is again, but you'll notice that for the purposes of this discussion we've added a little visual aid in the form of an arrow leading from writer to reader:

An essential part of the relationship between writer and reader is the writer's obligation to appeal to the reader's needs and values. To craft a successful argument, you'll need to think about what your own needs and values are and try to ensure that they match those of the reader. If both you and your reader share all the relevant needs and values, that's great — extremely rare, but great.

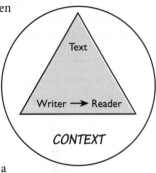

More likely, though, there will be competing needs and values, so it's in your best interest as a writer to figure out how you can ensure that you are appealing to needs and values that are important to your reader. In other words, if you're presenting a Level 4 (esteem) argument to an audience that's struggling to hang on to its Level 2 (safety and security) needs, then you will have a difficult time being persuasive.

Appealing to needs and values really is a question of audience. For example, it's probably a mistake to try to convince your reader of the urgency of replacing unattractive school uniforms (self-actualization) if she is desperately trying to avoid living in her car (basic safety and security).

Keeping in mind Maslow's hierarchy and the communication triangle, you can adjust your argument to promote your own needs and values while at the same time addressing the legitimate needs and values of your reader. By making a good-faith effort to *converse* with the reader, you are much more likely to craft an argument that is ultimately successful. How do you do this? By thinking about who will be reading, imagining the reader's level of knowledge about the topic, and making educated predictions about the reader's likely feelings about the topic. (See pages 21–22 in Chapter 2 if you need a refresher on audience awareness.)

▶ *Let Us Show You:* Connecting with the Reader

As an example of what we're talking about, let's take the concluding paragraph from the first draft of Casey's essay on plagiarism. Casey's not very confident that he had his audience in mind at all when he wrote it — and he certainly wasn't thinking of the professor who assigned him to write the essay.

Things get called "plagiarism" in a college classroom that don't in the real world. I don't mean going to one of those "Free Essays 4U" Web sites (also known as cheating). I'm talking about using random facts or bits of information as a way to back up an opinion or interesting interpretation of a poem — things like that. If I'm having a conversation with someone about a movie we both saw, and I also read an interesting interpretation of that movie somewhere, I might present that idea to my friend without including the source. I'm not being dishonest and trying to trick my friend into thinking I'm of above average intelligence; I'm just sharing an interesting piece of information from a source I probably don't even remember. The information itself is more important than where it came from. If it makes my friend see things in a new way, who really cares if it's my idea or someone else's? It should be the same in a college essay. As long as I'm using information effectively to make a strong point, it shouldn't matter whether I cite every single source for every single idea that isn't my own. Not only is that unreasonable; it's basically impossible.

▶ *Talk Amongst Yourselves . . .*

Read Casey's draft of his concluding paragraph twice, first from the point of view of a college student (one component of Casey's audience) and then from the (imagined) perspective of a college professor (the other component of Casey's audience). Then find a partner and discuss the *pathos* of the paragraph. How did your emotional reaction differ from your first reading to your second reading? Why? What different needs and values might a college student and a college professor have, and how might those differing needs and values affect the way Casey revises his paragraph? Where and how does he appeal to specific needs and values, as outlined in Maslow's hierarchy?

▶ *Now You Try:* Connecting with the Reader

Remember reading Brent Staples's essay "Black Men and Public Space" back in Chapter 17? Good! Now reread the first two paragraphs of that essay, presented below, and then try to articulate each of the following:

▶   Who is the essay's intended audience? How can you tell?

▶   In what ways does the author appear to empathize with his audience(s)?

▶   What specific appeals to needs and values does Staples make? Do those appeals seem appropriate for the audience you've identified?

▶   What specific strategies or techniques can you identify that are designed to evoke emotion in the reader?

My first victim was a woman — white, well dressed, probably in her early twenties. I came upon her late one evening on a deserted street in Hyde Park, a relatively affluent neighborhood in an otherwise mean, impoverished section of Chicago. As I swung onto the avenue behind her, there seemed to be a discreet, uninflammatory distance between us. Not so. She cast back a worried glance. To her, the youngish black man — a broad six feet two inches with a beard and billowing hair, both hands shoved into the pockets of a bulky military jacket — seemed menacingly close. After a few more quick glimpses, she picked up her pace and was soon running in earnest. Within seconds she disappeared into a cross street.

That was more than a decade ago. I was twenty-two years old, a graduate student newly arrived at the University of Chicago. It was in the echo of that terrified woman's footfalls that I first began to know the unwieldy inheritance I'd come into — the ability to alter public space in ugly ways. It was clear that she thought herself the quarry of a mugger, a rapist, or worse. Suffering a bout of insomnia, however, I was stalking sleep, not defenseless wayfarers. As a softy who is scarcely able to take a knife to a raw chicken — let alone hold it to a person's throat — I was surprised, embarrassed, and dismayed all at once. Her flight made me feel like an accomplice in tyranny. It also made it clear that I was indistinguishable from the muggers who occasionally seeped into the area from the surrounding ghetto. That first encounter, and those that followed, signified that a vast, unnerving gulf lay between

(continued)

nighttime pedestrians — particularly women — and me. And I soon gathered that being perceived as dangerous is a hazard in itself. I only needed to turn a corner into a dicey situation, or crowd some frightened, armed person in a foyer somewhere, or make an errant move after being pulled over by a policeman. Where fear and weapons meet — and they often do in urban America — there is always the possibility of death.

Components of *Pathos*: Empathy and Evocation

Connecting with your audience on the level of needs and values really comes down to the difference between evoking and emoting. Evoking will genuinely engage the reader — that is, it will encourage the reader to feel invested in your argument — while emoting generally will not.

Emoting is typically a bad idea in academic writing, because it involves a direct expression of emotion in a way that *tells* the reader about feelings rather than *showing* the reader the specific details that will allow the reader to feel on his or her own. Writers who emote run the very real risk of being perceived as having overplayed their *pathos*, and thus of being regarded as melodramatic. Imagine (or remember — we don't judge) the friend who calls at 3 a.m. to discuss his breakup, making you reluctant to answer any late-night calls.

Emoting is not a very good tactic, ultimately, because it defeats the purpose of *pathos*, which is to appeal to the *reader's* emotions. Evoking emotion is a much better strategy for achieving *pathos* in writing. When a writer evokes emotion, he or she creates emotion by calling it up or summoning it in someone else — the reader — rather than simply expressing it as it exists within his or her own consciousness.

EVOKING EMOTION: SHOW, DON'T TELL

A great way to engage your readers without going overboard is to **show** them what you think (and presumably what you'd like them to think!) rather than just **tell** them what to think. This excellent piece of advice can be traced back to many sources, including Ernest Hemingway, who was talking about writing fiction and poetry. But we think this advice is just as valid for writers of arguments. Nobody likes to be told what to think. In fact, most of us respond to being told what we should think by rebelling against it, even if we know it's true. No, instead we need to *see* what the writer means and find the powerful truth within it for ourselves.

By *showing* your readers what you think (in an attempt to persuade them to agree with you), we mean giving vivid, relatable examples to back up the claims that you are making.

Relatable to whom? you might be asking now.

To make your writing relatable to your reader, you first need to think about who your reader is, as we've discussed before, and then use Maslow's hierarchy to help you think about what your reader's needs and values are. Then you'll be able to think of examples that your reader can relate to.

> Nice use of *whom* there! Did you know that the word *whom* exists for the same reason the word *me* exists, or the word *him*? For more on pronoun case, see Chapter 24 and Appendix A.

This will help you connect with your reader by allowing him or her to draw his or her own conclusions rather than just taking your word for it.

▶ *Let Us Show You:* Empathy and Evocation

But don't just take *our* word for it — below we present three exhibits for your enjoyment.

Exhibit A

The mandatory minimum sentences for drug offenders introduced in the 1980s by Reagan administration drug czar William Bennett have resulted in a skewing of priorities in the American justice system. Under the mandatory minimums of recent decades, increasing numbers of defendants convicted of nonviolent controlled-substance offenses have been sentenced to lengthy prison terms. Although prison capacity has increased in most states during that time, cell space has not kept pace with drug convictions, and the resultant overcrowding has led to the early release of significant numbers of violent felons in order to provide space for those convicted of drug-related crimes.

We think you'll find that Exhibit A is a serviceable beginning to an argument aimed at convincing the reader that mandatory-minimum drug sentencing has had a negative effect on the American justice system. We'll go a step further and say that we think you'll find the combination of claims and support — or at least of claims and the *promise* of support, since we have not yet included any statistics to back up factual statements about numbers of prisoners and cells — to be reasonable, rational, and perhaps even convincing.

But do you really care about this argument? Does it mean anything to you personally? If the argument went on for several paragraphs, and you weren't assigned to read it for a class or otherwise compelled to read it for practical reasons, would you keep reading? Or would you nod briefly in acknowledgment of the argument's validity, yawn, and move on to something more interesting?

We're guessing that unless you already had an interest in the topic because of personal experience, you'd yawn — and we don't blame you. That's where *pathos* comes in. A little *pathos* can make your argument interesting by making it personal. It balances the objectivity of *logos* by providing vivid descriptions of subjective experience. This subjective experience is what makes us human; it's what keeps us from robotic devotion to pure logic — which is not a huge risk for most of us, but still.

If you found Exhibit A boring, that is because it fails to achieve *pathos* — it *tells* but doesn't *show*.

Now imagine what happens to our mandatory-minimum argument if we decide to make up for our dull, predictable, bone-dry Exhibit A by cranking our *pathos* controls up to 11 through the use of *way too much* emotion:

Exhibit B

Poor Seth James (names have been changed), the twenty-four-year-old father of an innocent baby girl, was sentenced to an extreme ten-year prison term in 1998 for growing marijuana in his basement with the intent to distribute, even though he wasn't a dealer. He just smoked some marijuana himself and gave the rest to his poor, suffering father, who needed it to endure intense pain from his cancer treatment. Seth should have been sentenced to a short term in county jail followed by a fine, probation, and community service; instead, he was thrown into the state's hellish maximum-security prison system, where he remains to this day, unable to be with his loving wife and growing daughter. And while Seth has been locked up, who has been let out? Sick, violent predators, that's who: at least three rapists and murderers (and those are just the cases we know about) have been freed from Seth's prison in order to make room for more minor drug offenders. While Seth wastes away behind bars, innocent victims are preyed upon by the twisted psychopaths let loose on society by a criminal-justice system that doesn't care about our safety.

After reading Exhibit B, the words that come to mind might be: *Whoa! Calm down!* That's because the paragraph *emotes* rather than *evokes* emotion and therefore fails to achieve *pathos*.

Even if your natural tendency is to agree with the writer's point of view on this issue, we think you'll be tempted to distance yourself from Exhibit B because the argument has gone into overkill. The writer tries to force the reader to feel a particular way, but a reader's instinctive reaction to emotional bullying is to resist it. For this reason, be very careful to avoid the overuse of *pathos* in your writing. As a general rule, your reader will resent you if you blast away at him or her with an emotional fire hose. You will be far safer if you simply lead your reader to a sparkling pond of specific and vivid details and allow him or her to sip a few handfuls at a time so as to reach his or her own genuine feelings about the situation you're addressing.

Ah, when to use *his or her* rather than *their* — good question. When the noun is singular, as in "the reader," the pronouns that refer to that noun must also be singular. So use *he or she* rather than *they*, and *him or her* rather than *them*. For more on pronoun agreement, see Chapter 24.

Having already tried writing this paragraph with no *pathos* and with too much *pathos*, let's see what happens when we aim for just the right amount of *pathos*:

Exhibit C

Consider, for example, the case of Seth James (not his real name), a twenty-four-year-old father and college student who was arrested in 1998 for growing marijuana in his basement with the intent to distribute. An investigation following his arrest showed that he had never sold any of the marijuana; rather, he kept a small amount for personal use and gave the rest to his father, who had trouble managing the pain and nausea of his cancer treatments and found that smoking marijuana helped. Seth had no prior convictions or arrests, and everyone involved in his case — including the arresting officer, the prosecutor, and the superior court judge who heard the case — agreed that justice would be best served by a short term in county jail followed by a fine, probation, and community service. However, the federal mandatory minimum sentence for his crime was ten years in prison. The judge, powerless to exercise his own judgment, expressed sorrow at being forced to impose the sentence. As of this writing in early 2006, Seth remains behind bars in Southern Michigan Prison in Jackson. His daughter, a toddler at the time of his arrest, is now eleven years old. In the eight years since Seth's incarceration, at least three of the scores of violent felons who were granted early release from Jackson in order to make room for drug offenders have re-offended: one committed rape, another committed murder in the course of an armed robbery, and a third hunted down his ex-wife and followed through on an earlier promise to kill her and then himself.

We think you'll agree that Exhibit C finally achieves *pathos* by *showing* rather than *telling*.

> I'll let you in on a secret: Exhibit C is more successful than Exhibit B largely because of good grammar choices. Sound crazy? Read on.

Note that the specific details provided in Exhibit C are presented in such a way that they *evoke* emotion rather than *announcing* or *forcing* emotion. As such, the paragraph encourages the reader to feel a variety of emotions — sadness, regret, indignation — rather than venting the emotions of the writer in a way that makes the reader uncomfortable, defensive, or dismissive. We hope you'll agree that the writer achieves a significantly better result in Exhibit C than in Exhibit A, where the writer avoids *pathos* altogether, or in Exhibit B, where the writer goes overboard on the *pathos*.

USE VIVID AND ACTIVE LANGUAGE

One very good way to make sure you're showing rather than telling — and to ensure that you're evoking rather than emoting — is to use vivid nouns and verbs. Nouns and verbs are more effective at conjuring concrete images in readers' minds than are lots of adjectives and adverbs (also called modifiers). In fact, using too many modifiers often makes the reader feel manipulated and resentful instead of more involved in a text.

Don't believe us? Okay, here's an exercise so you can test-drive our theories.

▶ *Talk Amongst Yourselves . . .*

Break into groups and discuss the differences in language between Exhibits B and C. Which exhibit uses more adjectives and adverbs? Which uses precise, specific nouns and verbs? What is the effect? (Do you need extra help with these questions? Review what nouns, verbs, adjectives, and adverbs are in Appendix A, and then review our advice about word choice and tone in Chapter 15.)

▶ *Now You Try:* **Empathy and Evocation**

Make a list of all of the societal problems that are addressed, directly or indirectly, within Exhibits A, B, and C that we presented a little earlier in this chapter. Using that list as a springboard, brainstorm a longer list of problems within society that you believe are significant enough to demand a solution. Then answer the following questions:

▶ Which of the problems on your list will you choose to address?

▶ How will you solve the problem?

▶ Who is your intended audience?

▶ What sort of approach will you need to take to achieve effective *pathos* with that audience?

Damaging Your *Pathos*: Making Bad Assumptions About Needs and Values

In a nutshell, bad assumptions about the reader's needs and values become fallacies that affect *pathos*. These fallacies are errors in the use of appeals to support claims in an argument. Underlying those errors is usually a misjudgment about the needs and values of the writer versus the needs and values of the reader. Bottom line? The *writer* has an obligation to consider the needs and values of the *reader*, and not the other way around. Otherwise *pathos* suffers.

The simplest of these bad assumptions involves mistakenly believing that certain values are universal. For example, a writer might assume that all readers share the value of *tradition*. Traditions are good, right? Who doesn't like a nice tradition? But another writer might assume that all readers share the value of *progress*. Progress? Why, that's moving forward! Who doesn't love that?

You see what we're getting at, right? At some point, a broadly defined value bumps into another broadly defined value — for example, tradition and progress may both become relevant to an argument — and the resulting conflict highlights the problem with assuming too much about which values are universal.

MISJUDGING APPEALS

An **appeal to tradition** assumes that the reader will value consistency above all else. Such an appeal argues that because something has been done a certain way for a long time, it should continue to be done that way: *The United States* *always holds presidential elections on the Tuesday after the first Monday in November. Why switch to weekend voting when the present system has been in place for so long?*

Appeals to tradition fail to recognize that people make mistakes, have bad ideas, or even hold prejudices for a really, really long time. When an appeal to tradition is offered instead of some other type of support, the argument will fail with anyone who doesn't share the writer's reverence for the old ways. Writers tend to make this mistake when their inexperience or ignorance limits their ability to acknowledge alternatives.

The flip side of the appeal to tradition is the **appeal to novelty**, which assumes that the reader will be just as excited as the writer is about things that are new. For example, *upgrading all of your software to the latest versions will vastly improve your system's function.*

The person who commits this fallacy — or falls for it — loves change for the sake of change. He or she is the sort of person who will buy a product just because its box says "*New and Improved!*" Like the appeal to tradition, the appeal to novelty presents the newness of a thing or an idea as if that newness were a valid substitute for *actual reasoning.*

Like appeals to tradition and novelty, a **bandwagon appeal** makes dubious assumptions about what the reader is likely to value or believe. The bandwagon appeal assumes that because a large number of people do or believe something, others will or should "jump on the bandwagon," as the saying goes. This fallacy is used most visibly in advertising, in taglines like *The Toyota Squid is the best-selling car in the world — buy one before they're all gone!* Or try this appeal on for size:

> A majority of Americans doubt the official story that Lee Harvey Oswald acted alone in assassinating President Kennedy. Therefore, the assassination must have been a conspiracy.

Bandwagon appeals are nonsensical because they assume that if many people like or believe something, then that something must be good or right. Sometimes, however, great numbers of people are idiots. A lot of people believe that humans are mortal, and they're right. On the other hand, a lot of people still believe that reality television is real and that professional wrestling is unscripted — and in the past, a lot of people believed that the earth stood still and everything else in space moved around it. Our point is this: the fact that everyone believes something tells us nothing except that everyone believes it, which is pointless.

The fallacy of *ad hominem* — Latin for "to the man" — argues against a *person* rather than the person's *ideas* by making personal attacks that are irrelevant to the matter at hand. For example, *we shouldn't take Mayor Gordon's ideas about public parks too seriously. I mean, everyone has seen the photos of her wild college days on the Internet.*

Although the name-calling and accusations are unpleasant and often unfair, the worst thing about *ad hominem* is that it moves the argument away from its merits, shutting down what might otherwise be an interesting exchange of actual ideas. In other words, the *tone* of *ad hominem* arguments is often uncivil and distressing, but even without the unhelpful tone, the underlying problem with this fallacy is that it injects *irrelevance* into the discussion.

The **noble effort appeal** asks the reader to approve a less-than-stellar argument simply because the writer has *tried* to come up with a good idea. This fallacy crops up when a writer has attempted to resolve a problem and has essentially given up: *I know this isn't the best solution, but it's truly the best I can do right now.*

It may not surprise you to know that as teachers we have run into this fallacy — also known as the *Hey, I tried, so give me credit!* fallacy — on many, many occasions. When a student commits this fallacy in an academic essay, it often appears in the conclusion. Why? Because that's where the student is most likely to notice that he hasn't really supported his thesis but decides that he *really* doesn't feel like revising the whole thing. Check this out:

> In conclusion, this essay was much harder to write than I thought it would be. I did a lot of research and put all sorts of time into sorting through the facts, but in the end, I still couldn't find a definitive answer to the question of whether the moon landing was faked. Opinions continue to differ on this question, but I did learn a lot, and that's what really counts.

Reality Check! Misjudging Appeals

▶ **Appeal to tradition:** Have you assumed your reader will value "the way it's always been done"?

▶ **Appeal to novelty:** Have you assumed your reader will value change for the sake of change?

▶ **Bandwagon appeal:** Have you assumed your reader will be swayed by peer pressure?

▶ *Ad hominem:* Have you attacked the person instead of the idea?

▶ **Noble effort appeal:** Have you appealed to your reader for credit just because you tried?

Practice! **Misjudging Appeals**

See if you can figure out which poorly judged appeal is ruining the logic of each statement below:

1. Adam Sandler's latest movie must be truly excellent—more people went to see it on its opening weekend than any other movie this summer.
2. You really have to love Bruce Springsteen and the E Street Band in concert. They work so hard to put on a show!
3. I know that the theater would be more functional if we removed the broken pipe organ from the orchestra pit, but it's always been there and people like to see it.
4. I used to think T. S. Eliot's poetry was amazing until I read that he had anti-Semitic views.
5. Smithers rewrote the company's organizational chart, which was absolutely necessary since it hadn't been revised in several months.

FALLACIES OF MANIPULATION

The general term for a wide variety of manipulative scare tactics is the **ad populum fallacy**. *Ad populum* is Latin for "to the people," which sounds innocent enough, but trust us, it isn't. *Ad populum* fallacies occur when reasoning is replaced with appeals that are calculated to encourage strong, gut-level reactions — for example, *Why should we push for increased student financial aid when we had to work our way through college without any help?*

The fallacies in this category collectively appeal to the strongest and least rational of the reader's emotions — and they generally do this in a manner so manipulative as to be abusive. *Ad populum* fallacies can prey on a whole range of emotions, but they most commonly appeal to fear, ridicule, spite, and greed. Less dark, but no less manipulative, are appeals to flattery, pity, loyalty, and wishful thinking.

The fallacy of **misleading vividness** involves describing a person, a place, or an event in such overwhelming detail that the reader can hardly escape the vivid images. Typically, this fallacy involves using words to evoke grotesque, graphic, or upsetting visions in the minds of readers in order to convince them that something is a serious problem — even if it isn't. For example, *standardized testing is a nightmare, with students suffering from cold sweats, uncontrollable shaking, and sudden bouts of nausea.*

Misleading vividness is the "show" version of manipulating through word choice. The "tell" version is called judgmental language or **loaded words**, insulting or pejorative terms that are deployed in an argument to force the reader to align himself or herself with the writer and against the target of the words: *A vote for Hemmings is a vote for terrorism* is an example of this fallacy.

Occasionally a writer will slip into a state of laziness so debilitating that he or she is rendered incapable of providing details to support a claim or even of finding the words to express an opinion. When this happens, the writer might attempt to clinch the argument by presenting a **thought-determining cliché**, which substitutes a tired old saying or a played-out metaphor for actual ideas. Sometimes this fallacy is used to misdirect the reader by changing the subject, but more often it is used to end the debate with a prepackaged notion rather than an actual point — for example, *I'm sure you have some fine ideas about campaign finance reform, and everyone's entitled to his or her own opinion, but you can't always get what you want.*

A variation on this fallacy involves inserting a **random quote** from a famous person that's tangentially related to the topic at hand without commenting on its relevance to the argument. For example, a writer might choose to finish an essay about the difficulties of enacting education reform by quoting Confucius: "The journey of a thousand miles begins with a single step." While the quote itself is true enough, and we can see a sort of vague connection between long journeys, single steps, and education reform, what has the quote actually added to the argument? (Hint: Not much.)

Reality Check! Fallacies of Manipulation

▶ **Ad populum fallacy:** Have you appealed to such strong emotions in your reader that logic fades?

▶ **Misleading vividness:** Have you manipulated the reader through exaggerated descriptions?

▶ **Loaded words:** Have you bullied the reader through intimidating labels?

▶ **Thought-determining cliché:** Have you withdrawn from your argument and let a cliché take over?

Practice! Fallacies of Manipulation

See if you can figure out which fallacy of manipulation is ruining the logic of each statement below:

1. The president's proposal to reform the health insurance industry's rules would be fine if it weren't pure, unabashed crony capitalism.

(continued)

2. Look, I'm as empathetic as the next person, but if we take pity on those who would seek to harm us, then they will rip us limb from limb and leave only bloody stumps.

3. Ultimately, the famine may have been caused by overpopulation, or by corrupt officials' diverting aid packages from the people, or even by global climate change — but all we really know is that God works in mysterious ways.

4. Everyone is free to agree with Mr. Bennett's ideas, just as everyone is free to be easily fooled by bogus arguments.

Reality Check! Engaging the Reader

▶ Have you thought carefully about your reader within the context of the communication triangle?

▶ Have you addressed the reader in a way that appeals to his or her needs and values?

▶ Does your writing consistently evoke emotion in the reader rather than emoting your own feelings?

▶ Does your essay successfully avoid the pitfalls of misjudging or manipulating *pathos?*

▶ *Let Us Show You:* Engaging the Reader

Professor Yoda has assigned the students in Mara's Freshman Year Experience class to find and read a short essay about any issue relevant to college education. They will then need to write a brief essay that demonstrates their understanding of the text as well as their opinion of the author's ideas. Mara has chosen to read and respond to "The Speech the Graduates Didn't Hear" by Jacob Neusner. (It can be found online if you'd like to read it.)

Mara needs to see whether her essay is as reader-friendly as she wants it to be. In other words, she needs to check her *pathos.* So with Casey's help, she reviews her work so far, using the Engaging the Reader *Reality Check!* box above.

Humbled by Reality	
"The Speech the Graduates Didn't Hear" by Jacob Neusner is a speech intended for a college commencement ceremony, but its unorthodox, brutally honest content is far from the conventional graduation day	This title sounds good, as long as you really mean it. Strong words — but they still sound objective.

speech. The speech begins by telling the graduates they have grown up in an unrealistic world, with no sense of consequences or failure. But they are told that they will quickly learn how harsh real life is, and that they will realize how little college actually taught them.

> Wow, sounds like a harsh essay. But as long as you're being accurate in your summary, it's okay.

In the speech, the graduates are portrayed as childish, spoiled, ungrateful, and ignorant. To this, the teachers responded with flexibility, feedback, and support. However, the speech claims that this is because the teachers "did not want to be bothered," as opposed to caring about the students' success. The speech concludes by saying there is nothing about graduation to take pride in, and that on that day they must begin to learn what real life is.

> These sound like loaded words. Maybe use an example or two so the reader knows you're not being unfair?

> I think "they" refers to the graduates, but it's a little confusing.

The speech was refreshing to read and effectively humbled me as a student myself. The idea that institutions baby their students resonated with many of my experiences. It made me feel guilty for all the sloppy assignments I have turned in, and for thinking that an A– is the worst thing in the world that could ever happen to me.

> "Resonated" is a cool word.

> Good tone — both students and teachers will appreciate it, I think.

However, the speech seemed to lump together all students into one big category of spoiled brats, to which I take offense. The speech disregards the different backgrounds and obstacles students must overcome outside of college; many of us have experienced "real life" far beyond the extent that this speech implies.

> Maybe this would be better if it weren't about you? It's like a reverse *ad hominem*.

> This sounds a little like a noble effort appeal.

If not taken too seriously, the speech is a good dose of reality. It offers a window into what teachers really think, although I do hope that not all teachers are as dishonest and unchallenging as they are portrayed in the speech. It is easy to get caught up in the college world, and this speech forces students to take a step back into reality.

> This might feel like a hasty generalization to a teacher.

> Do you really "hope" this? Or do you know it? It feels a little manipulative.

▶ *Talk Amongst Yourselves . . .*

Take a few minutes to write down your responses to the questions below. Then break into groups of three and discuss your responses with each other.

Checking a draft essay for its reader appeal is a very sophisticated task. How would you improve on Casey's annotations? As you know, Mara's essay has the same two audiences that most college papers have: her classmates and the professor. Which of these audiences does Casey seem to be thinking of in his annotations? Why might that be? Would making the changes Casey suggests alienate either audience? Why?

▶ *Now You Try:* **Engaging the Reader**

We'd like you to take a shot at analyzing the *pathos* of an essay. In the reader at the back of this book, you'll find an essay titled "The Deep Sadness of Elk That Don't Run" by Michael Byrne (see page 490). You read it in Chapter 4 and again in Chapter 10, remember?

Note that it will be easier to assess the author's use of *pathos* if you first ensure that you understand the argument's *logos* — that is, its system of claims and support. Once you feel confident that you understand both the main point of the essay and the author's use of minor claims and support to develop that point, read the essay recursively with an eye toward assessing its *pathos*.

Reality Check! **Assessing *Pathos***

▶ Who is the essay's intended audience? How can you tell?

▶ In what ways does the author appear to empathize with his audience?

▶ Identify places in the essay that appeal to the reader's specific needs and values. Are these appeals effective? Are they appropriate? Why or why not?

▶ What specific strategies or techniques can you identify that are designed to evoke emotion in the reader?

▶ Are there places where the author emotes instead of evoking? Explain.

▶ Does the essay make any misjudgments in its appeals (appeals to tradition or novelty, bandwagon or noble effort appeals, *ad hominem*)? Explain.

▶ Does the essay manipulate the reader through the use of scare tactics, misleading vividness, loaded words, or thought-determining clichés? Explain.

PART 6

Researching Effectively

Research and Sources:
The Intellectual Treasure Hunt

> It is a good morning exercise for a research scientist to discard a pet hypothesis every day before breakfast.
>
> — Konrad Lorenz

Okay, we know you might be thinking, *What exactly* is *research, anyway, and why should I bother doing it?* You might be vaguely aware that what passed for research in high school isn't going to cut it in college. But you're probably not sure why that is, or what college-level research is exactly. To put it simply, research for most college students means finding a bunch of information about a topic and reading it. Why should you bother? So that you can learn enough about the topic you're researching to be able to talk about it in an informed and intelligent way.

So far that sounds like what you did in high school, or maybe even in middle school, right? The difference is that in a college-level research paper, you'll need to use carefully chosen, authoritative sources and be meticulous about citing all of the information you borrow.

Don't get us wrong: high school students should do those things, too, and often they do — but in our experience at least, students who wrote research papers in middle school or high school often have ideas about research that are different from what their college professors expect them to do. So even if you've done research before, you should approach our advice about research with an open mind.

Strengthen Your Argument with Research

Sometimes — pretty much always, actually — we think we know more about a given subject than we really do. This may be true of you as well, and if so, then like us you frequently find yourself in a position to engage in some research prior to drafting and revising your assigned academic writing.

The word *research* can be used very broadly. In general, it means going beyond your own thoughts, feelings, memories, and knowledge base in order to gather information to use in your writing. **Informal research** includes conversations (with experts and laypersons alike), observations of the people and things around you, and generally living your life — surfing the Web, watching TV, reading books for fun, going to the movies. We all engage in informal research naturally, and for purely practical reasons that have nothing to do with college writing assignments that require academic research. You do informal research when you need to find a place to get some coffee in an unfamiliar town, or when you're trying to decide what classes to take — or even when you're just curious about something.

Doing Informal Research

When you're only *generally* interested in finding out about something you're unfamiliar with — dwarf stars, Middle English, the Harlem Renaissance, the historical record of the Chicago Cubs — you can fire up the Google or even go straight to (gasp!) *Wikipedia*. After all, you're just trying to find out some general things about a topic that is a blank to you. You're laying down a base coat of knowledge.

Informal research rocks. But in our discussion of research in these chapters, we are not concerned with informal research (that is, the research you do as a natural by-product of living and being generally curious).

Instead, our focus here is on **formal academic research**, which is what your professors mean when they say they want you to "do research." It's a less *natural* process than informal research and has everything to do with college writing assignments that require academic research. Generally, people do formal academic research only when they are required to do so for scholastic or professional reasons — unless they're really dorky, as your humble authors occasionally are. Formal academic research involves making use of credible, authoritative, expert sources of information that are relevant to your studies. (Don't worry. We'll talk later in this chapter about how sources can meet all of these expectations.)

As for us, we love research. But perhaps you're one of those people who go all cold and clammy at the thought of library catalogs and online databases, in which case we're here to offer you some advice. Academic research is a manageable process as long as you understand the tools required and the steps involved — and we're going to break down that process and walk you all the way through it in this chapter and the next two chapters. By the time we finish, we hope you will feel perfectly qualified to undertake any assignment your professors might toss in your direction.

Just in case it's not clear yet, formal academic research has a lot to do with sources. Keep that in mind!

But before we begin, it's important that you understand the crucial ingredient that makes research what it is: sources.

What *Are* Sources, Anyway?

We have discovered that sometimes when we introduce the word *source* in class, our students assume that we're talking about a person, perhaps because of the way the word is used in the popular media. We can't tell you how many times we've heard things like, "The source of the story was Mel Gibson's former publicist" — but that's not the kind of *source* we're talking about here.

A **source**, for the purpose of college research writing, is generally a piece of writing (an article, a report, a story, a study, and so on) or some other means of communicating information (a video, a chart or graph, or a photo, for example) that a writer uses to support a claim or claims in an essay. To be considered a *usable* source, it must be clearly identified so that any reader can find it and refer to it. It must be published or documented in print, online, on a DVD, or in some other way. There are two broad categories of sources: primary and secondary.

PRIMARY SOURCES

Primary sources are original creations, without any analysis, commentary, or interpretation. Primary sources include news articles, diaries, maps, historical documents, original experimental data, and artworks of all sorts (poems, novels, films, paintings, symphonies, etc.).

In general, research assignments in lower-division college classes (such as the college writing class you are almost certainly enrolled in right now) focus more on secondary sources — sources that provide commentary, analysis, or interpretation rather than being original creations. (We'll describe secondary sources in much more detail in the next section.) You will likely focus more on secondary sources than primary ones in your first year or two of college because your role is largely to learn from

Remember when I said in my plagiarism paper that truly original ideas don't exist anymore? Turns out those original ideas exist in primary sources. Oops!

the experts in a given field before you become an expert in that field yourself. Students in upper-division classes or higher are much more likely to use primary sources because they are moving closer to *being* experts in their fields and are practicing the necessary skills, such as analyzing original artifacts for themselves rather than relying on experts to help them.

However, first- and second-year college students are sometimes asked to use primary sources in a research writing assignment. Before you're finished with your general undergraduate requirements, you will probably work with primary sources in an assignment such as one of the following:

▶ an interpretation of the meaning of a poem
▶ a comparison of two news articles chronicling the same historical event
▶ an analysis of technique in a painting or film or piece of music

We won't say much more about primary sources, and there's a good reason for that. Because primary sources are specialized to the classes they're linked to (paintings in art classes, for example), and because understanding and evaluating primary sources should be taught by those with authority in the field (such as art professors teaching about paintings), you can safely assume that your professors in those classes will give you further guidance about primary sources.

SECONDARY SOURCES

As we stated a few paragraphs back, **secondary sources** provide commentary, analysis, or interpretation, and they're used more commonly than primary sources in introductory college-level research. Why? Well, because in their first couple of years, college students are busy gaining authority. And one of the best ways to gain authority is to consult and learn from experts. You do this informally when you attend class, listen to lectures, and join in class discussions.

You do it formally when you consult sources from those with authority outside the confines of the class. And what do those authoritative people do in the secondary sources they create? They analyze the subjects of their expertise. Or, in the words of our favorite online thesaurus (because we're weird that way), they consider their subject — or any of the other synonyms listed in the chart below:

Relevance ⬤ A-Z	Complexity
Synonyms for analyze	
resolve	scrutinize
consider	test
evaluate	interpret
study	rehash
inspect	assay
investigate	figure
spell out	confab

Yes, secondary sources are those created by people who do all of the above (see chart), because that's often the sort of thing experts — people with authority — do. Secondary sources are commentary: they expose and argue about their subjects. Secondary sources include nearly all types of nonfiction books (biography, history, analysis, criticism) as well as most articles in periodicals. Ultimately, secondary sources are materials created by people who are doing essentially what you're doing: researching a topic and presenting their findings. The essential difference between the authors of these sources and you is that they have already established the authority that you are now creating for yourself.

The Research Process: It's Not as Scary as You Think

It really isn't. And it's even less scary if you break it into small pieces, which is exactly what we're going to help you do with our seven manageable steps. All you need is an assignment or a topic, and we'll walk you through the rest, from formulating a research question to finding excellent sources to working those sources into your writing. And when we've finished explaining the process of researching, we'll talk about how to ensure that you're acknowledging (or *citing*) those sources ethically. Have no fear — and read on!

The way we see it, there are **seven essential steps in the research process**, and we'll be telling you all about them in this and the following chapter. Here are the steps:

1. posing a strong research question
2. finding sources
3. narrowing your research results
4. evaluating and choosing the most appropriate sources
5. understanding your sources
6. taking good notes
7. integrating sources into your essay

(Of course, once you've gone through all seven steps in the research process, you'll need to make sure that you've used those sources *honestly* — we'll discuss this in detail in Chapter 22.)

One of the biggest problems that students have with academic research is that they don't know what to look for. Oh, sure, they know that they're supposed to write about, say, werewolves. But they haven't really thought carefully about *what exactly* they want to write about werewolves.

A big part of this problem can be solved by following the guidelines we offered in "Understanding the Assignment" back in Chapter 5 (see pages 50–55). Once you've done that, you should have a pretty good sense of the intended scope and focus of your essay. You should know, for example, whether you're expected to write an expository essay about the real cases of lycanthropy in the nineteenth century, or an evaluative essay about whether Lon Chaney was a better werewolf in the movies than David Thewlis, or perhaps a proposal essay about how best to avoid being turned into a werewolf.

STEP 1   Formulate a Strong Research Question

Even armed with a specific purpose, you're still not quite ready to start your research until you have articulated a specific research question. The research question is crucial: it keeps your search for information focused, reasonable, and manageable. And why is this important? Because research can get out of control fast, which will frustrate you.

Here are a few things you should know about posing a good research question:

▶ First, it will be **open-ended**. It will *not* be a simple yes-or-no question. Research questions should challenge you to give complex, multifaceted, thorough answers rather than simplistic, binary responses. Yes-or-no questions tend to elicit answers that don't lead anywhere, and thus they just aren't very interesting. If you were to ask, "Have werewolf stories changed in the past fifty years?" the answer would almost certainly have to be *Yes*. That's not very interesting. But instead you could ask, "How do today's werewolf stories compare to those of fifty years ago?" and then you'd be getting somewhere. You'd need multiple sentences — paragraphs, even — to answer that.

▶ Second, it will be **broad enough** to cover the intended scope of your essay, yet **narrow enough** that your research will be sharply focused on that intended scope. In our experience, students have more trouble with the second requirement than with the first. It's tempting to think that writing a paper about a broad topic will be easier than writing one about a narrow topic. But in fact the opposite is true. Faced with answering a research question like "What is cool about werewolves?" you'll likely find yourself overwhelmed. You won't know where to begin because the question is just too broad and therefore vague.

▶ Third, it will be **open-minded**, meaning that your question won't contain a preconceived notion of what the answer will be. If you begin your research already sure of what you'll find, you won't really be doing research but instead will be looking for confirmation of your biases. This doesn't mean that your paper should be totally objective. Once you've begun to read up on your topic, you'll start to form opinions about what you're reading, and that's a good thing. Just don't let the opinions you have before you start researching color the research process you're about to begin.

Asking an Open-Minded Research Question

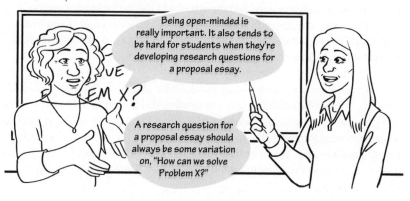

▶ Finally, a good research question will **ask something that is worth answering**, meaning that your question will be answerable only after you have carefully explored and thought about the available information. Although you should try to abandon preconceived ideas of what you'll find through your research, you should be able to imagine interesting answers to your research question. If you can't, revise the question.

Now that we're armed with some good advice about how to pose a research question, it might be helpful to take our newfound skills out for a test drive. Let's say we've chosen to write an evaluation of whether Lon Chaney or David Thewlis is a better movie werewolf. The first thing we'll need to do is spend a few minutes posing possible questions in order to settle on the one most likely to lead us to good research, and therefore to a good essay. Ready? Here goes:

How about this question?		And the survey says . . .
1. Is Lon Chaney a better movie werewolf than David Thewlis?	👎	If we want our essay to be one word long — either "yes" or "no" — then, sure. Otherwise, this question breaks the first rule of good research questions.
2. What kind of movie werewolf was Lon Chaney?	👎	Hey, weren't we assigned to write about both Chaney and Thewlis? This question seems to have misplaced half of its topic.
3. What kind of movie werewolf is David Thewlis?	👎	Chances are, after reading the response immediately above this one, you already know what's wrong with this question.
4. What are the characteristics of a good movie werewolf?	👎	This one is getting warmer. Still, it's very broad and it doesn't actually address the assignment directly.
5. Why is David Thewlis a better movie werewolf than Lon Chaney?	👎	Tricky! This one seems to go straight to the heart of the assignment, but it breaks the rule about open-mindedness: it assumes the answer without doing any research.
6. Which of the characteristics of a good movie werewolf are on display in Lon Chaney's performance compared to David Thewlis's performance?	👍	And we have a winner! This question combines good parts of the otherwise faulty questions above, and it responds to the assignment without breaking any rules.

See how answering question 6 in its entirety would lead us to have enough information to support an evaluative essay about whether Chaney or Thewlis is a better movie werewolf? And see how there are, inherent within that question, several hints as to what we should look for in potential research sources (characteristics of good movie werewolves, elements of the performances by Chaney and Thewlis)?

Reality Check! Strong Research Questions

▶ Is it open-ended (not a yes-or-no question)?
▶ Is it broad enough to justify an essay?
▶ Is it narrow enough to be covered well in just one essay?

(continued)

- ▶ Is it open-minded (meaning you haven't already answered the question in the question)?
- ▶ Is it worth answering (meaning you can imagine interesting answers to the question you've asked)?

▶ *Let Us Show You:* **The Research Question**

Casey and Mara have a new writing assignment. We're going to use their assignment to demonstrate the process of coming up with a good research question.

CASEY AND MARA'S ENGLISH 101 WRITING ASSIGNMENT

Research Paper Assignment: Choose an issue affecting education today that you suspect your reader would not know very much about. Research to discover the truth about an aspect of that issue that you think will surprise your reader. Make use of at least three valid, authoritative academic sources, and write a three- to five-page expository essay that is supported with sufficient references to those sources, cited in MLA format. Work with your peer partner to review and critique each other's progress throughout the research process.

Casey's first thought on receiving this assignment is relief. After all, he's already been thinking about an issue affecting education today: plagiarism. It should be okay, he thinks, to repurpose the topic — meaning he would use the same work to complete two different assignments. However, after asking his professor about it, he has discovered that double-dipping is also considered academic dishonesty. It defeats the purpose of research, which is to discover previously unknown ideas and information.

So Casey continues to search for a suitable topic. Meanwhile, Mara has decided she wants to write about issues of academic equality and inequality — maybe something about educational opportunity. Since she knows this is a huge topic, she did some initial research into what the issues might be, and she ran across the topic of academic doping, which is when a student takes performance-enhancing drugs in order to do better in school. Now she's formulating her research question.

Formulating the Research Question

▶ *Talk Amongst Yourselves . . .*

Find a partner in the class and discuss the following questions.

How helpful was Casey's advice to Mara? How would your advice to her have been different? To what extent did Casey's advice help Mara to formulate a good, strong research question? What other advice would you give Mara before she sets off to research the answer to her question?

▶ *Now You Try:* **The Research Question**

If you are fortunate enough to already have a research assignment from one of your classes, by all means take this opportunity to work on creating your research question for that assignment.

But in case you haven't been presented with a research assignment yet, try this one:

PRACTICE ESSAY ASSIGNMENT # 2

Go back to the longer of the two lists of societal problems you compiled in Chapter 19, on page 295. Choose the problem that interests you the most and write a three- to five-page expository research essay about a specific cause or effect of that problem. Be sure to use at least three valid research sources. Due in three weeks.

Remember to focus on the *process* of the assignment — the steps involved — so that you don't get overwhelmed. Don't think about the final *product* yet.

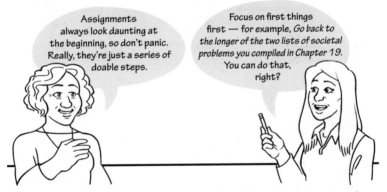

> Assignments always look daunting at the beginning, so don't panic. Really, they're just a series of doable steps.

> Focus on first things first — for example, *Go back to the longer of the two lists of societal problems you compiled in Chapter 19.* You can do that, right?

For now, your assigned task is to develop a suitable research question whose answer promises to be a surprising or little-known truth about a particular cause or effect of the problem you're researching. Remember to evaluate your question against the checklist on pages 313–14 and to seek feedback from a peer or professor as you refine your question.

STEP 2 Find Sources

Once you have settled on an appropriate research question, you will need to engage in a search of available sources. A good way to start is to think about the various resources available at your college and how those resources might fit with your particular research needs.

The vast majority of academic research undertaken by college students is done in one of two ways: using the college library or using the Internet. Sometimes students do both at the same time, which we'll discuss in a moment. Whether you're in the library or on the Internet, you will be able to find both primary and secondary sources. You will also find that sources can be valid or sketchy, useful or useless, regardless of whether you're searching the library shelves or the Web.

FIND RELIABLE SOURCES

Whether you're doing live or online library research, be very mindful of what it means for a source to be *reliable*. Ideally, it means the source is credible, authoritative, and expert. It's likely that you won't know whether a source meets all of those criteria until you've read the entire thing (more on this later). Short of reading the whole source, there's no surefire, 100 percent accurate way to know whether a potential source is one that will be suitable for academic research, but we do have a few words of advice to help you in making that determination.

> ### *Reality Check!* Reliable Sources
> ▶ Does the source list an author or authors?
> ▶ Has the source been published in an identifiable forum, such as in a journal or on a named Web site?
> ▶ Is the publication itself (the journal, the Web site) relevant to the topic (e.g., an article about taxes on a Web site devoted to discussing the economy)?
> ▶ Does the source use standard grammar and punctuation and avoid typos? (Sloppy writing is an indication that a source is unreliable.)

You can run into some *non*-authoritative, *non*-expert, *non*-scholarly sources even in a college library. Our campus library has *People* magazine, for example. But if the Reliable Sources *Reality Check!* box above isn't enough to tell you whether or not certain sources will be appropriate, your professor or a librarian can help you figure out which sources you probably shouldn't use.

Many college library Web sites have online chat functions that allow you to ask a librarian for help regardless of whether you're using the college's library for your search. But depending on when you're asking the question, you may need to wait a little while for an answer — which is frustrating for those of us who have come to think of ten seconds as being *far too long* to wait for anything on the Internet.

USING THE LIBRARY

The most reliable way to search for useful sources is through your college library, using either the actual, physical, bricks-and-mortar-and-shelves-full-of-books library or its virtual, bits-and-bytes, ones-and-zeros collection of **online databases**.

Wait — what? you're asking. *What is this online database thing?* Yes, it's true — your college library almost certainly subscribes to one or more large collections of research available through both general and specialized academic search engines. Examples of online databases include:

- ▶ Academic Search Complete
- ▶ ProQuest Research Library
- ▶ JSTOR (collection of academic journals, books, and primary sources)
- ▶ ERIC (for education-related issues)
- ▶ SIRS Issues Researcher (for social issues)

Note that most college libraries have many more specialized collections that are tailored to the needs of students in particular classes and programs — for example, *Poetry and Short Story Criticism*, *Nursing & Allied Health Source*, *Criminal Justice Periodicals*, and even *Auto Repair Reference Center*.

Each type of library (live or online) has its advantages when you are doing research. In our experience, in-person research is satisfying because we can consult with the librarian, who is usually a genius, and because we like the feel and smell of books. Online research, on the other hand, is convenient because we can do it in our jammies at three in the morning.

In other words, both physical library research and online library research are good ways to inform yourself; which of them you choose is largely a matter of personal preference and convenience.

USING THE BROADER INTERNET

For most of you, what will seem to be the easiest first step is to go directly to Google, type in your search term, and press "Enter." However, consider this: using the power of the entire Internet to locate information can be frustrating because *it's the whole Internet*. It's pretty much anything and everything ever written or recorded anywhere by anyone at any time. It's a whole lot of stuff, and that can be both good and bad.

Internet Research: A Giant Blessing

Sometimes a general search of the Web (say, a Google search) will not be a practical approach to your assignment. For example, your professor may stipulate that you must use only peer-reviewed professional journals. Some of these are hard to find on the Web; some professional journals don't allow access for free, and if you don't know the names or URLs of the publications you're trying to find, it's really difficult to locate them through a general search of the entire Internet. In such cases, we recommend that you do so by way of the college library's holdings or databases, as described in the "Using the Library" section on pages 318–19.

But if Google is truly your go-to resource for academic research, and you have not been instructed to limit the scope of your sources through a particular database, we strongly suggest that you use Google *wisely*. After all, Google's company motto is "Don't be evil," and we think that it's your responsibility as a Google *user* to do the same. In other words, help the search engine in its quest to be good to you.

You can meet that responsibility by using the Internet as a tool — a very big and powerful tool that does one thing really, really well: it stores and catalogs mountains and seas and planets of virtual information so that we can access all of it (or at least a lot of it). The Internet is a whole universe made up of ideas, and it fits into your phone. That's pretty awesome, right?

But you need to *respect* a tool so big and powerful. If you've ever used a power saw or a car or any other powerful machine, you know that you have to use it carefully in order not to get hurt. We think of the Internet in the same way, and therefore we offer you the following tips for "safe webbing."

Reality Check! Practice Safe Webbing

▶ Start your search using Google Scholar, which narrows your results to scholarly publications and thus helps to protect you from untrustworthy information.

▶ Refine your broader search by limiting it to specific domain types, if appropriate (see Chapter 3, page 29).

▶ Keep in mind the Reliable Sources *Reality Check!* on page 317 — it's even *more* important to check a source's reliability when you're searching the broader Web.

If you follow the advice above, you should be able to use the Web — that vast collection of *everything* — to conduct academic research in a responsible way.

Internet Research: A Bit of a Curse

You knew this was coming, right? The downside of the vast and awesome Internet is that you have to be careful about what you accept as good information. Consider this: the Internet is a democracy. That is, anyone can post stuff on the Web, and everyone's voice can be heard. But not everyone can publish work in a scholarly journal. You may come across a Web page that looks very slick and professional and trustworthy and uses all sorts of statistics and big words, but it may very well be the product of Bobby, who has way too much time to play with the server in his basement. Bottom line: you have to be vigilant about Web sites and other materials that pop up in a Google search.

> We had a student who once quoted and cited an article from the *Onion* as an actual source of reliable information.

Remember also that Google searches and even Google Scholar searches can result in thousands of listings that aren't relevant to what you were really looking for, even if they somehow correspond to the precise parameters of the search words you've used. For this reason, try to be patient: if your online search initially retrieves garbage, modify your search parameters. Try synonyms. Try variations on your keywords (for example, "censor" instead of "censorship") or related terms (for example, "free press" or "free speech"). This is good advice even when you're searching specific databases on your college library's Web site.

We have one other point to make about using the Web for research. The Internet isn't just a democracy — it's also a conglomeration of *commercial ventures*, which means that a lot of people are on the Web to make money. As a result, you may sometimes find potential sources that are unavailable in full text unless you pay a fee. ***Never* pay for academic research sources.** Instead, if you find a source that looks interesting based on the title, author, publication, and perhaps a brief abstract or summary of the source, but you can't read the whole thing, record all of the publication information and take it to your friendly, knowledgeable college librarian. The chances are pretty good that he or she will be able to help you access it for free.

▶ *Let Us Show You:* Finding Sources

Having identified a good research question, Mara is now ready to start looking for some useful research sources. For her first search, she used Google Scholar and entered the search term "study drugs." As you might already have guessed, she found a great many articles about drug studies but nothing about drugs that help students to study.

Narrowing Search Terms

Bingo! When Mara narrows down her search term to "academic doping," she finds good leads on Google Scholar — the first page of results from that search appears below. Next, she'll use the library's search engine.

Academic doping or Viagra for the brain?
JC Lucke, SK Bell, BJ Partridge, WD Hall - EMBO reports, 2011 - embor.embopress.org
Recent developments in neuroscience have raised the possibility that
neuropharmaceuticals and other interventions could be used to enhance brain processes in
'normal'people who are not impaired by mental illness or disorder. The terms 'cognitive ...
Cited by 15   Related articles   All 9 versions   Cite   Save

Smart drugs for cognitive enhancement: ethical and pragmatic considerations in the era of cosmetic neurology
V Cakic - Journal of medical ethics, 2009 - jme.bmj.com
... been presaged for some time. However, although several authors15 16 17 18 have
considered the issue of "**academic doping**", none have examined the main ethical
issues to any large extent. This is despite the widespread ...
Cited by 111   Related articles   All 7 versions   Cite   Save

Australian university students' attitudes towards the acceptability and regulation of pharmaceuticals to improve academic performance
S Bell, B Partridge, J Lucke, W Hall - Neuroethics, 2013 - Springer
... for what reasons [10]. If cognitive enhance- ment is considered by authorities to be
'**academic doping**' this could have a direct impact on policies toward enhancement
use of stimulants [4, 7, 18]. Proponents of cognitive enhancement ...
Cited by 20   Related articles   All 8 versions   Cite   Save

A comparison of attitudes toward cognitive enhancement and legalized doping in sport in a community sample of Australian adults
B Partridge, J Lucke, W Hall - AJOB Primary Research, 2012 - Taylor & Francis
... View all references; Lucke et al. 2011b12. Lucke, JC, Bell, SKPartridge, BJ 2011b. **Academic
doping** or Viagra for the brain?. EMBO Reports, 12: 197–201. [CrossRef], [Web of Science ®]
View all references; Partridge 201014. Partridge, B. 2010. Response. ...
Cited by 14   Related articles   All 2 versions   Cite   Save

Modafinil and memory: Effects of modafinil on Morris water maze learning and Pavlovian fear conditioning.
T Shuman, SC Wood, SG Anagnostaras - Behavioral neuroscience, 2009 - psycnet.apa.org
... The drug is also widely prescribed off-label to enhance alertness, attention, or memory for
dementia, attention deficit hyperactivity disorder, excessive daytime sleepiness, and depression
(O'Connor, 2004); an illicit market exists for **academic doping** as well (Garreau, 2006). ...
Cited by 36   Related articles   All 13 versions   Cite   Save

Substance use to enhance academic performance among Australian university students
J Mazanov, M Dunn, J Connor, ML Fielding - Performance Enhancement & ..., 2013 - Elsevier
Use of substances to enhance academic performance among university students has prompted
calls for evidence to inform education and public health policy. Little ...
Cited by 11   Related articles   Cite   Save

▶ *Talk Amongst Yourselves* ...

Break into groups and discuss the results of Mara's Google Scholar search. Based on what you know of her research question, which of the specific sources would you say warrant further exploration? Which do not? In other words, based only on what appears in the search results, see whether you can determine which sources Mara should click on in order to save them as possibilities for her paper. Explain your choice(s).

▶ *Now You Try:* Finding Sources

Mara isn't done with her search yet — in fact, we've showed you only the first six results of about 19,000. Yes, the Internet is *big*.

Armed with the research question you formulated in Step 1 (see pages 310–12), use one of your college library's search engines (ProQuest, Academic Search Complete, or JSTOR, for example) or Google Scholar — or even a broader Google search modified to include only the most appropriate domains (such as .edu and .gov) — to identify a list of potential sources for your essay. As a general rule, you should initially identify at least twice as many sources as you think you'll need. Why? Because you'll need to narrow them, naturally.

STEP 3   Narrow Your Research Results

Now that you've compiled a list of potential research sources — all of them reliable, as far as you can tell — you will need to evaluate your sources carefully in order to separate the sort-of-interesting from the truly appropriate. So how do you decide which sources are going to be the most useful?

Rather than read every source in its entirety, which would take too much time, you will make an initial evaluation of each source based on the following criteria. Check these evaluation criteria in order: the questions at the top of the list can be evaluated after a cursory look at the source, while those at the bottom can be evaluated only after a bit more investigation.

Type of Source: This is a two-part evaluation. First, does your specific writing assignment require you to use certain types of sources — for example, are some publications approved while others are not? Second, are you required — or do you prefer — to use primary sources over secondary sources? These questions can usually be answered by reviewing the written assignment or by asking your professor, and the type of a particular source is usually quite easily identified.

Currency: This one's simple: How *old* is the source? Was it written last month? Last year? In 1875? The question of currency is sometimes crucial, as it would be in an essay about technological advances in medicine, for example. At other times it's less relevant — for instance, in an essay about the American Civil War. And sometimes you may find that currency is undesirable: if you're researching what critics thought of John Keats's poetry during his lifetime, you probably want to consult sources written in the early nineteenth century.

Authority: This one takes a little more time and effort. The question here is whether the author of your source material is qualified and credible. Is he or she an expert in the field that your research question is concerned with, as opposed to simply an expert in *something*? Does this author have a reliable voice on the issue? Does he or she have qualifications and credentials that can be identified and verified? You'll find that some source materials, such as peer-reviewed journals in specific fields — the *Journal of the American Medical Association*, for example — provide brief descriptions outlining the qualifications and expertise of authors. Many source materials, however, do not provide such helpful information, so you may find that you need to engage in a second level of research to determine the authority of your source. Typically, if the author of your source is credible, a simple Google search will turn up evidence of the author's expertise (professional position, degrees earned, publications, etc.).

Relevance, Part 1: After you've weeded out as many search results as you can by looking at the title, date, publication information, and author of potential research sources, you can begin to further narrow your search results and head toward choosing sources by *skimming* the sources that remain. You don't need to read fifty books or articles thoroughly to know which might be relevant to your argument; it's enough just to glance at the abstract (if one is given), introductory paragraph, and conclusion of each source — or just start reading and stop when you know whether or not you want to use what you're reading. You'll eventually go back and thoroughly read all the sources you've chosen to determine their true relevance (this is Relevance, Part 2, part of Step 4, which we'll discuss in the next chapter). For right now, though, your main task is to get to the point where you are ready to choose. This should be enough to give you a sense of what might be useful to you and what you don't want to bother with.

Reality Check! Narrowing Your Research Results

A Yes answer to each of the following questions means you'll keep your source around . . . for now.

▶ Is the source **reliable** according to the Reliable Sources checklist on page 317?

▶ Is the source the right **type**?

▶ Is the source **current**? And does that matter to your assignment?

▶ Is the source **authoritative**? Is its author identifiably qualified to address the topic?

▶ Without having read it, do you think the source seems **relevant** to your research question?

▶ *Let Us Show You:* Narrowing Your Research Results

Mara used the Narrowing Your Research Results *Reality Check!* box to look through the first thirty or forty results of her Google Scholar search on "academic doping" and harvest the handful of sources that seemed most useful. She then did a similar search inside her library's ProQuest search engine, which resulted in several repeats but also a few new sources she hadn't seen before. She knows this narrowed list of sources is still tentative because research and writing are always full of surprises.

Keeping Track of Narrowed Research Results

Mara's Narrowed Research Results in MLA Format

Arria, Amelia, and Robert DuPont. "Nonmedical Prescription Stimulant Use among College Students: Why We Need to Do Something and What We Need to Do." *Journal of Addictive Diseases*, vol. 29, no. 4, Oct. 2010, pp. 417-26.

Berry, D., et al. "Detection of Feigned ADHD in College Students." *Psychological Assessment*, vol. 22, no. 2, June 2010, p. 325.

Centers for Disease Control and Prevention. "Facts about ADHD." *Centers for Disease Control and Prevention*, Centers for Disease Control and Prevention, 16 July 2013, www.cdc.gov/ncbddd/adhd/facts.html. Accessed 8 Aug. 2013.

Labbe, Allison K., and Stephen A. Maisto. "Development of the Stimulant Medication Outcome Expectancies Questionnaire for College Students." *Addictive Behaviors*, vol. 35, no. 7, July 2010, pp. 726-29.

Lucke, J. C., et al. "Academic Doping or Viagra for the Brain?" *EMBO Reports*, vol. 12, no. 3, Mar. 2011, pp. 197-201, www.nature.com/embor/journal/v12/n3/full/embor201115a.html. Accessed 12 July 2013.

McCabe, Sean Esteban, et al. "Non-medical Use of Prescription Stimulants among US College Students: Prevalence and Correlates from a National Survey." *Addiction*, vol. 100, no. 1, Jan. 2005, pp. 96-106.

U.S. Drug Enforcement Administration. "Drug Scheduling." *DEA/Drug Scheduling*, U.S. Department of Justice, www.justice.gov/dea/druginfo/ds.shtml. Accessed 11 July 2013.

▶ *Now You Try:* **Narrowing Your Research Results**

Just as Mara has done, go through the list of potential sources you found in Step 2 and narrow it down, using the handy Narrowing Your Research Results *Reality Check!* box on page 324. Keep in mind that you're not *choosing* your sources yet; you're not making a commitment to any particular source at this point. Rather, you're creating a *Yes-Maybe* pile and a *No* pile from among the many possible sources you've located. (Remember the selection process from Chapter 7?)

This process gets your search results down to a manageable list for more careful review. There will be time enough for choosing the specific sources that you will actually use in your paper. It will happen soon. *Very* soon, in fact.

Chapter 21

Choosing and Using Sources: Do It Wisely

> Borrowing knowledge of reality from all sources, taking the best from every study, . . . brings together the highest enlightenment of the ages.
> — Ernest Holmes

As you now know, hunting down good sources for research writing is a time-consuming process. Yes, we admit it: doing research takes time. But it doesn't take *too much* time — as long as you're researching effectively. We're quite confident that you have been researching effectively up to this point in the process because you have read Chapter 20. (You *have* read it, right? If not, now is a good time to do that.)

Just as writing is both a process and a product, so is research. Whereas Chapter 20 focused on the process of researching, this chapter will focus on creating the product of your research. The essential ingredients that go into your research product — that make a research paper different from other essays — are the actual words, ideas, and data of the sources that you will ultimately include.

So remember when we said there would be a time for choosing the most relevant sources for your paper? Sure you do! We just said it, right at the very end of Chapter 20! Well, now's that time.

Just in case we're being too subtle here, we're trying to make sure you've read Chapter 20.

On the next page, you'll see how the next section is titled "Step 4". That's because Steps 1 through 3 are in Chapter 20 — which you should read, by the way.

STEP 4 Evaluate and Choose Sources

After you've whittled your original list of sources down to a manageable number by engaging in Step 3 (Chapter 20, pages 323–24), it's time to evaluate what's left and choose the pieces you'll actually use. But first you should probably refer back to your specific assignment.

> ### *Reality Check!* The Research Assignment
>
> ▶ Have you been asked to use a particular number of sources?
> ▶ If you haven't been given a number of sources to use, what's the scope of the assignment? Is it your basic three- to five-page essay, or is it longer?
> ▶ Are there other requirements or guidelines regarding what types of sources you should use (or stay away from)?

In a short, three- to five-page essay, a handful of sources (three or four) should suffice. If it's a significantly longer essay — for example, a twelve- to fifteen-page term paper — you'll likely need at least twice as many sources. It's good to go into the evaluating-and-choosing-sources stage of research with a good idea of how many and what type of sources you are required to use.

WATCH FOR BIAS IN YOUR SOURCES

When it comes time to choose from among the several sources that have made it through your narrowing process, there are a few important qualities to consider, the first one being bias. Many people think that *bias* means "opinion." Although in general parlance the two words are used interchangeably, in evaluating research sources they mean distinctly different things. An opinion is a point of view or an interpretation of facts. In other words, it is a judgment based on reason. It is a claim — an arguable statement — that can be backed up with support.

For example, I have a *bias* toward international travel, that simply means I like it. If a source has a bias toward one side of an argument, that source is academically unreliable.

But in academic research, a **bias** is a prejudice — a point of view based on something other than facts, a judgment based on something other than reason. Biases are typically based on *entrenched beliefs* (such as religious beliefs or strong political philosophies) or *vested interests* (i.e., the source's author has something to gain by holding the opinion) rather than on a desire to discover the truth.

Or as the writer Upton Sinclair once said, "It's difficult to get a man to understand something when his salary depends upon his *not* understanding it."

There's nothing inherently wrong with using a source that expresses an opinion — as long as you're *aware* that the source expresses an opinion, and as long as you're ethical about the way you present that opinion in your essay — but there *is* something inherently wrong with using a source that is biased.

When evaluating a source for signs of bias, look for evidence that the author is ignoring alternative viewpoints for ideological reasons or for reasons of self-interest. One pretty safe indicator of bias is sponsorship: if you've found a scientific study that claims that watching TV cures cancer, and you see that the study was financed by one of the major television networks, then you might want to put that source right back where you found it and keep looking.

CHOOSE THE MOST RELEVANT SOURCES

Relevance, Part 2 — True Relevance: Once you've determined that the source is of the right type, that its publication date is reasonable for your purposes, that its author is credible and qualified, that it provides information on a topic that seems to be in your zip code, and that its opinions seem grounded in fairness and reason, you'll need to consider whether the ideas presented in the source are truly relevant to the topic you wish to explore in your essay.

In other words, you'll want to ask yourself: *Does this source actually provide at least a partial answer to my research question?* The only way to evaluate the true relevance of a source is to read it in its entirety, which is why we suggest you engage in the other five parts of evaluation before gauging true relevance. If you have determined that your source meets all six evaluation criteria (the four from Step 3 and the two we've just told you about), the source is a keeper. Hold on to it.

Reality Check! **Evaluating and Choosing Sources**

This one's quick. Once you have settled on your narrowed list of sources in Step 3, read each source completely. Then ask the following two questions of each one:

1. Is the source unbiased? In other words, are its opinions and conclusions based on logic and reason?
2. Is the source truly relevant to your task? In other words, will it help you to answer your research question?

If the answer to both questions is *Yes*, then congratulations! You have found a source to use in your essay!

▶ *Let Us Show You:* Evaluating and Choosing Sources

When last we saw Mara's list of sources, she had whittled it down to seven from among the more than twenty sources that looked like possibilities after her searches through Google Scholar and the college library's search engines. She has now read all seven sources carefully and has decided to keep six to use in her essay.

Source & Authority		And Mara says . . .
1. Arria & DuPont (*Journal of Addictive Diseases*)	👍	This one's great! Written by doctors who are researchers in exactly the field I'm researching. Full of interesting facts.
2. Berry, Ranseesn & Sollman (*Psychological Assessment*)	👍	This one's a twist (I didn't plan on writing about college students faking ADHD to get prescriptions because I didn't know about it). But it seems important.
3. Centers for Disease Control and Prevention (cdc.gov)	👍	No question. The CDC is the go-to resource for valid (but dry!) information about health issues. Amazing collection of statistics.
4. Labbe & Maisto (*Addictive Behaviors*)	👍	This one is just as authoritative as the rest, but it focuses on student opinions — students' needs and values — so it will give me another interesting angle to explore.
5. Lucke, Bell, Partridge & Hall (*EMBO Reports*)	👎	This one's iffy. The article was interesting, but the study was sponsored by a group whose Web site is covered with links to both nonprofits and corporations, so . . . No.
6. McCabe et al. (*Addiction*)	👍	This report by 5 researchers will be a good way to validate the information from Arria & DuPont, and it also looks at demographics for comparison (gender, race, etc.).
7. U. S. Drug Enforcement Administration (justice.gov/dea)	👍	What can I say? I'm not using any opinions from this source — only definitions that come straight from existing laws.

▶ *Talk Amongst Yourselves . . .*

Break into groups and discuss the decisions Mara has made about her sources. How sound is her reasoning for her decisions? What is she overlooking? To what extent do you agree with her decisions? How would you have done things differently?

▶ *Now You Try:* **Evaluating and Choosing Sources**

Okay, it's your turn again. Starting at the top of your list of *Yes* and *Maybe* sources from the end of Chapter 20, take note of the *deal-breaker* elements — elements whose absence would knock a source off your list. For example, Mara chose named author and reliability of publication as her deal-breaker elements. You might choose the same two elements, or you might add the date if currency is crucial. In this way, you can relieve yourself of reading a source or two that you're not going to use anyway.

Next, read through your remaining sources carefully. We really do mean *carefully* this time. No skimming — and no watching TV or surfing the Web while you're reading. Pay attention to what you're reading.

For each source, write down your evaluative notes — what the source's strengths and weaknesses are, what your reasons for or against using it are. When you're finished, you'll have a (tentative) source list for your essay. Why tentative? Because *everything* in writing is tentative until it's done!

So now you have reliable, relevant sources for your project. This is a big, big step in the research writing process, and you should feel good about the progress you've made so far. But don't rest on your laurels, feeling all proud and accomplished, for too long. It's time to learn how to *use* those sources in your own essay.

STEP 5 Understand Your Sources

The incoherent use of source material in college research writing is a tragedy. Strong words, you say? We think not.

This is what happens when students write essays that include chunks of source material they don't understand. And it's tragic because this particular condition is curable. But in order to cure it (or, better yet, prevent it), we first need to understand its causes. This horrible tragedy occurs for a few key reasons:

> When something is *incoherent*, it lacks coherence — in other words, it falls apart because it doesn't make sense. We discussed this back in Chapter 9, remember?

Common Causes of Source Incoherence

▶ **Procrastination** — putting off your research for so long that you literally don't have time to *read* your sources, let alone digest their meaning

▶ **Defeatism** — reading a complex or otherwise challenging text and giving up rather than engaging in active reading

- ▶ **Blind Trust in Authority** — assuming that because a particular chunk of text was written by a credible source, it must be exactly what's needed in your essay
- ▶ **Eyes-to-Fingers Syndrome** — looking at a chunk of source material while typing it without first inviting it to sit down in your brain for a visit
- ▶ **Noteaphobia** — an absolute and pathological refusal to take notes

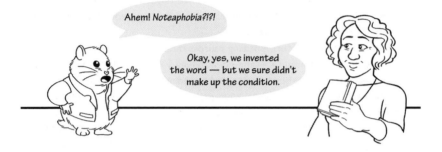

What these five causes have in common is a lack of investment on the part of the student. This lack of investment is most likely a fundamental underestimation of his or her own capabilities. *These scholarly articles are hard*, we hear students say. And our response is, *Yes, they are. But you're smart. You can do it.*

Ultimately, you want to understand your sources so that you will also understand how to *use* them in your essay. Remember, academic research really isn't about *input* (that is, filling your head with facts and opinions). It's about output — creating texts that tell your reader, *I do understand all of these facts and opinions well enough to use them ethically and effectively in supporting a point I want to make, thank you very much.*

Sounds great, doesn't it? So, how do you get there?

GO HEAD-TO-HEAD WITH YOUR SOURCES

The most important commitment you can make in understanding your sources is to set aside enough time to read them carefully and actively (i.e., recursively). In this way, you will convert some of the information in your sources — not all, but some — into *knowledge*. That conversion is the basis of understanding. Specifically, when you're reading scholarly sources for research, try to remember the following advice:

First, you need to recognize that once you've gone through the trouble of finding, evaluating, and choosing a source, you owe it to yourself to *read your source carefully.* And you really do need to think of it this way: it's not about "picking a quote" to jam into your essay somewhere, but about increasing your own knowledge base, expanding the shelves in that library of your mind. We sometimes lose sight of the fact that education is actually about learning — be sure to use your research experiences as opportunities to gain knowledge.

Second, *be honest with yourself about what you do or don't understand.* Never include a quote from a source if you can't put it into your own words without looking at it. In other words, even if you're planning to quote from a source verbatim, you should be able to state for yourself what the quote means.

Finally, *be skeptical of your sources.* Don't be bullied into believing that a source is beyond questioning just because the writing sounds sophisticated or because the author has credentials. What qualified authorities have is status. They also generally have a great deal of knowledge within their field of expertise. What your sources don't have is automatic correctness. Knowing a lot doesn't always equate to being right (a shocking concept, we know!). You have not only the right but also the responsibility to question what you're reading in order to understand it fully. Why? Because only when you understand it can you know whether you agree or disagree with it.

Remember, it's impossible to agree or disagree with something without first understanding it.

ENGAGE IN CRITICAL ANALYSIS

The kind of skepticism we just described also goes by the name **critical analysis**, and it's something that will be invaluable to you — and not just when it comes to understanding source material. It's also indispensable when you're reading the news, watching television, or listening to politicians talk.

To engage in critical analysis, you need to critique both the form and the content of what you're reading. After you are confident that you understand what you've read, examine the ways in which the *form* of the writing — perhaps it's a journal article, for example — shapes its *content*. (We began to touch on this in Chapter 3 and especially in Chapter 4 with our discussion of recursive reading. Now would be a good time to go back and review.) In other words, look at what you've read both subjectively and objectively. What does it say? How do you know that's what it says? What context does it appear in? How do you feel about what it says, and why?

Whether or not you are persuaded by a potential source is your subjective judgment, which is a perfectly valid way to begin. But you're not finished — subjective judgments alone are never enough for successful critical analysis. Remember always to pair subjective judgments with objective judgments. The most straightforward way to do this is to look your subjective judgments right in the eye and ask them, *Oh, yeah? Why?* If you ask (and answer!) this question several times until you've drilled down to the facts, then you will know that you understand both the source and your opinion about it.

Understanding Your Opinion About a Source

Practice! Critical Analysis

Remember Michael Byrne's essay "The Deep Sadness of Elk That Don't Run"? Sure you do! You read it *three times* back in Chapter 4. At the end of that recursive reading exercise, we asked you to answer two questions:

▶ What does the text mean?
▶ How do you know that's what it means?

Essentially, we were asking you to critically analyze the essay. Now we'd like you to take that analysis one step further and imagine that you're planning to use Byrne's essay as a source in an essay you're writing on the effects of introversion. After refreshing your memory about your answers to the two questions above, ask yourself a couple more questions:

▶ What specific points in the essay do I find convincing and useful? *Why?*
▶ What specific points in the essay do I *not* find convincing and useful? *Why?*

A Note on "Boring" or "Confusing" Sources

A word of caution: many of our students try to weasel out of real critical analysis by just telling us about how incredibly confusing or boring a piece of writing is. Now, to be fair, poor writing does exist, and there are pieces of writing that are needlessly long or impossibly confusing. However, we'd like to make two points.

First, "confusing" and "boring" are subjective judgments, so the person making such statements have an obligation to follow up with both an objective judgment (why is it confusing/boring?) and factual observation from the text to support that objective judgment. And second, you can rest assured that your professors will never have you read an essay or a story (or whatever) that is so confusing that the human mind cannot comprehend it, or so boring that no one has ever been able to finish it. If you find a text confusing or boring, don't assume that the piece of writing totally sucks — consider instead that you need to work harder to engage with the text. We are confident that it will make you a better person.

PARAPHRASE THREE TIMES

Finally, when you're wrestling with a tough idea in a source, we strongly encourage recursive note taking. It goes like this: when you've read a chunk of text from a source that seems as if it might be important (it may be a phrase, a sentence, or something longer), you should immediately read it again, think about it, set it aside, and then try to write the idea in your own words without looking at the source.

> If you follow all of the advice here in Step 5, you'll be in an excellent position to write an *annotated bibliography* of your sources. It's a great way to keep your research under control — as you'll see in just a page or two.

Once you're done, look at what you've written, think about whether it accurately reflects what the original source had to say, and (again without looking at the source) write it using different words and different phrasing. Repeat this process once more so that you have three different versions of the source idea — all of them entirely in your own words. Then you can compare them to the original source, and you'll know for sure that you understand it.

▶ *Let Us Show You:* Understanding Your Sources

Mara has decided to go through all the stages in the process of understanding her selected sources (also known as Step 5). She thought it would be a good idea to actually write down the evidence of her understanding, source by source.

> Clever! Sort of like the summary and review you wrote of "A Modest Proposal" back in Chapter 4, huh?

> I started writing down what I thought each source had to say, and then I wrote a brief analysis of the reliability and usefulness of each source so I wouldn't forget how I'm planning to use my sources.

Mara's process of critical analysis and note taking actually becomes a very helpful step in understanding her sources. She is creating what's known as an **annotated bibliography**: a complete citation of each source, followed by an objective summary and a thoughtful analysis. We're including here only the first entry in Mara's annotated bibliography. She has several more, but this will give you a sense of the kind of critical analysis she has done in order to understand her sources:

Sample of Mara's Annotated Bibliography

RESEARCH QUESTION
How has "study drug" use altered academic equality among students?

McCabe, Sean Esteban, et al. "Non-medical Use of Prescription Stimulants among US College Students: Prevalence and Correlates from a National Survey." *Addiction*, vol. 100, no. 1, Jan. 2005, pp. 96-106.

The study was on the relationship between non-prescription stimulant (NPS) use and students. It looked at demographics, institutional characteristics, and other substance abuse. About 6.9 percent of the subjects reported NPS use. Of those subjects, 4.1 percent reported use in the past year and 2.1 percent reported use in the past month. At individual colleges, use was between 0 percent and 25 percent. Over 80 percent of the colleges with rates of 10 percent or higher also had super competitive admissions standards and were located in the northeast or southern regions of the United States. Students at colleges with really competitive admissions were over 2.29 times more likely to report NPS use than students at less competitive schools. Males were 1.92 times more likely than females, and white students were more likely than Asian and African American students to report use. Sorority and fraternity members were 2.07 times more likely to report than non-members. Students who earned a B or lower GPA were more likely to be users than B+ or higher students.

This study gives insight on the "who" of NPS use. It provides hard data that males, white students, fraternity and sorority members, and students with lower GPAs have the highest rates of stimulant use. It clearly shows that NPS use is a problem, especially on highly competitive campuses. The survey had only a 52 percent return rate, and the use of self-reporting probably limits the accuracy of the research. It is also sort of outdated (2005), but it includes a large study sample (over 10,000 students). *Addiction* magazine is a respected publication on this issue.

▶ *Talk Amongst Yourselves . . .*

Find a partner in class and discuss Mara's analysis of her first source. How useful is it? What evidence do you see in this bibliographic entry that Mara truly understands what the source has to say? In what ways do you think her understanding of this information will be important in her essay? How good a job has she done of being *skeptical* about her source while at the same time being focused on *understanding* it?

▶ *Now You Try:* **Understanding Your Sources**

Take each of the sources that you selected in Step 4 of the research process and read each one recursively. Be sure to go head-to-head with each source, analyzing it critically in order to understand not only what the source says but also what it *means*. Then consider how you think the source might be useful in writing the research essay you've been prewriting.

For each source, do what Mara has done: first write down your understanding and your assessment of each source. Note that *understanding* and *assessment* are two different things, which is why the annotated bibliography is such a great tool: the first paragraph summarizes the source's ideas (which shows that you understand it), and the second paragraph discusses how and why the source is useful (which shows that you've assessed it). Be sure to show your results to a classmate or your professor for feedback.

> Will your professors always *require* you to write an annotated bibliography for your research writing? No. But writing one is never a bad idea, because annotated bibliographies are always helpful. So why not write one?

Once you've determined that each source is reliable, relevant, useful, and understandable, it's time to start mining your sources for the bits you'll use in your essay.

STEP 6 Take Good Notes

We often have students who do lots of research in preparation for their papers, which is something we are always delighted to hear. But occasionally when we ask them to show us their notes, they look at us like we've just asked to see their pet unicorn.

When we inevitably ask them why they think it was a good idea to do academic research without taking notes, the justification they give us usually goes something like this: they have good memories, they can remember pretty much every important detail they've run across as well as where they ran across it, and they've also jotted down a couple of specific phrases somewhere (they're never sure where) just in case they decide to quote something.

We hope this story has already caused you to realize an important truth on your own, but just in case you need a prompt, here it is: it's crucial that you take plenty of notes when you're doing research — and not just plenty of notes, but plenty of *good* notes. Quantity is important, but quality is absolutely vital, as you'll see in the advice and examples that follow.

KEEP TRACK OF YOUR SOURCES

The first step in ensuring the quality of your notes is to clearly differentiate among several different types of information that might be included in them. Generally speaking, there are three broad categories of notes you might take:

- ▶ your own thoughts about sources
- ▶ the ideas you read in sources
- ▶ the exact words of sources

It's imperative that when you sit down to draft your paper after engaging in research, you are able to determine with certainty which ideas are yours, which ideas come from Source A (or Source B, or whichever source), and — maybe most important of all — which notes represent not only the ideas but also the words of one of your sources.

Develop a Reliable System of Note Taking

A good, reliable system for labeling your notes will save you both time and trouble in the long run, and it's really not hard to set up. If you don't already have your own system, we have a few recommendations.

Reality Check! **Reliable Note Taking**

1. **Record complete publication data** for each source you consult. This includes at a minimum the author, title, publication, date, and page numbers — all of which you will need for the citations in your paper. Number each source (this is just for your notes, not for your paper).
2. **Write the source number at the top of the page** for each note you take. Trust us, you do not want to waste time trying to figure out which source a note refers to when it's time to write your paper. (If you're using only a few sources, you can cite the entire publication information at the top of each note.)

(continued)

3. **Just write notes normally when you're paraphrasing** (writing the source's ideas in your own words). This way you'll know that most of your notes are of the summary/paraphrase variety. Make sure you write down the number of the page or pages from which the ideas are drawn.

4. **Put quotation marks around exact words** from the source when you are writing them down so there will be absolutely no question whose words they are when you are writing your essay.

5. **Underline your own thoughts** when you're writing them down. (You may have a lot to say when you're taking notes on interesting sources.) That way you'll know they're *your* ideas.

▶ *Let Us Show You:* Taking Good Notes

The following page comes from the notes Mara has taken about one of the sources she selected back in Chapter 20 (see page 326). Because she recorded all of the necessary bibliographic information at the same time that she compiled her tentative list of sources, she can refer to this particular source (Labbe and Maisto) simply as #4. The Labbe and Maisto source is the fourth source on her list.

Sample of Note Taking

Mara's Academic Doping Essay — Source #4

This source is a study of student opinions about academic doping.

Its authors see academic doping as "a public health concern." (abstract)

The study analyzed three areas: "academic use, recreational use, and physiological effects." (abstract)

Recreational use will take me off-task — focus just on academic use and effects.

Up to 18.6 percent of college students use NPS (non-prescription stimulants) to help them study. (p. 727)

Students use the drugs to help them "concentrate better." (p. 727)

Some students claim the drugs help them "get their work done more efficiently." (p. 727)

Is it true that the drugs improve concentration & efficiency? Or do the students just think so?

▶ **Talk Amongst Yourselves . . .**

Break into groups and discuss Mara's notes. Based on the "rules" for reliable note taking that we gave you on pages 339–40, which elements in Mara's notes are the exact words from her source? Which elements are a summary or paraphrase of the source's ideas? Which elements are Mara's *own* ideas? How can you tell? Finally, how might Mara's careful attention to *quality* note taking help her when it comes time to use these sources in her essay?

▶ **Now You Try: Taking Good Notes**

Now that you understand your sources, you can mine them for the ideas, words, and data that will be most useful as support for the claims in your essay.

Take one of the sources you annotated back in Step 5 and go through it again, this time taking notes in which you carefully identify what's yours and what belongs to your source — as well as which source materials are *ideas* and which are *exact words*. Trust us when we tell you that this will be very important very soon.

And heck, once you've done that for one source, you might as well take good notes on the rest of them, right? You may want to show your notes to a classmate or your professor when you're done. Feedback can be useful at every step along the way.

STEP 7 Integrate Sources into Your Essay

Okay, here's the deal with writing research papers: it's all about the authorial relationship between you and your sources. You are the student who has done research and who is now writing an essay that uses that research. Your sources are all of the words, ideas, and data you have gathered to use in your essay.

When you write a research essay, you are integrating the writing that comes from your *sources* into the writing that comes from *you.*

Note that it's not the other way around: you're not integrating your ideas into someone else's ideas. This is *your* essay. As the person whose name is at the top of the page — as the author of your own essay — you have an obligation to be clear, honest, and thoughtful about everything in your paper. This includes acknowledging those parts of your essay that are not yours. Why? Well, you really don't want to commit plagiarism for this reason:

> Plagiarism is presenting the words, ideas, or data of another thinker or writer as if they were your own.

Therefore, you don't want to present words, ideas, or data from your sources without acknowledging that they're not your own.

A more positive take on the whole plagiarism situation might be put this way: an honest, careful writer will make sure to cite the source of any words, ideas, or data that he or she has borrowed. To meet your obligation to be clear, honest, and thoughtful — as well as to avoid plagiarism — you will make use of three common and reliable ways of integrating source material into your essay.

SUMMARIZING

When you summarize source material, you distill its essence and write that in your own words. A summarized source is one whose ideas, as represented in your text, will take up considerably less space on the page than they take up in the original source.

A summary within an essay might take a sentence or two in order to present an idea that covers a page or two pages or even an entire chapter in the original source. For example, Casey has volunteered to practice source-use skills by integrating some information from Chapter 20 of this book into his own paragraph about research.

As you know, a summary of an entire article will probably take up about a paragraph. Just a reminder.

> The idea of research always used to scare me. I would hear the word *research* and immediately get a picture in my head of a grouchy old man, maybe wearing a black robe and a white wig, glaring at anyone in his library who dares to speak above a whisper. I also pictured huge books, thousands of pages thick, full of words and ideas I'd never understand. But that was before I learned that research doesn't have to be so intimidating. As Lerych and Criswell point out, there's a clear process involved in research that can make the entire experience both organized and relatively painless (310).

Why is this considered summary? Because the borrowed idea takes up just one sentence at the end of this paragraph, but it refers to a bigger chunk of the content of Chapter 20.

Practice! Summarizing

Take a look at the second paragraph of this chapter. You know, right at the beginning of the chapter. The one that begins ... No? Okay, fine. Here it is:

Just as writing is both a process and a product, so is research. Whereas Chapter 20 focused on the process of researching, this chapter will focus on creating the product of your research. The essential ingredients that go into your research product — that make a research paper different from other essays — are the actual words, ideas, and data of the sources that you will ultimately include.

Now, we'd like you to read it again, think about what it says, read it one more time, think about it a little more, and then, without looking at it, write down the essential content of the paragraph in a single sentence, and entirely in your own words. When you're finished, compare your *summary* of the paragraph to the paragraph itself. Have you accurately and fairly represented the ideas of the paragraph in a briefer form? Show your summary to a classmate or your professor for feedback.

PARAPHRASING

When you **paraphrase** source material, you put it into your own words but do not shrink it down as you'd do in a summary. Paraphrased source material occupies roughly the same amount of space in your essay as it does in the original source. While it's tempting to think that paraphrasing might be easier than summarizing — because you're dealing with a smaller amount of source text — the opposite is true.

Understanding a *shorter* idea from a source is often more challenging than understanding a longer idea. It's harder to put a more specific idea into your own words. And generally, the more specific an idea, the more complex it is.

It is important when paraphrasing that you not look at the original source while you're writing. Doing so can result in unintentional plagiarism (which we'll discuss in more detail in Chapter 22). Given that any use of exact wording from a source must be enclosed within quotation marks, you need to be especially careful when paraphrasing *not* to borrow exact words.

Now, are we saying that you'll get in trouble if you paraphrase a passage from a source and your paraphrase happens to include the words "and so it was" in *precisely* the same order as they are used in the source? No, we're not — unless the words happen to be of key importance in the source, it's okay to repeat the generic phrasing of a few words in the same order. But to be on the safe side, you should enclose even an individual word in quotation marks if it seems particularly noteworthy or meaningful. Here's Casey's example of a paraphrase from Chapter 20:

> One of the most significant things I've learned about research is the importance of paying attention to what you do *before* you actually begin to research. Researching without first choosing a topic you're really interested in is just a disaster. But even having an interesting topic isn't really enough. I've learned, for example, that it's important to have in mind a good question that you want to answer before trying to find sources to use in a research paper (Lerych and Criswell 310).

This example is a paraphrase because the borrowed idea, contained exclusively in the last sentence, is specific enough that it takes up a roughly equivalent amount of space in the original source. Note that Casey has been careful to avoid using the exact words of the original and has therefore created a successful paraphrase.

Practice! Paraphrasing

This time we want you to look at *just the last sentence* of this chapter's second paragraph:

> The essential ingredients that go into your research product — that make a research paper different from other essays — are the actual words, ideas, and data of the sources that you will ultimately include.

Now we'd like you to read it again, think about what it says, read it one more time ... well, you know the drill. When you've read it and thought about it enough, write down the essential content in your own sentence, without looking at the original sentence. That's right — write it entirely in your own words. Be sure to include all of the important component ideas from the original. When you're finished, compare your paraphrase to the original sentence. Have you accurately and fairly represented the ideas of the original but in your own words, and from your own understanding? Show your paraphrase to a classmate or your professor for feedback.

QUOTING

When you **quote** source material, you have made a decision to use the exact words of the source, in the exact order in which they appear in the original. You can quote individual words, phrases, clauses, or entire sentences. In general, though, medium-length quotes (in other words, phrases or clauses rather than complete sentences) are preferred, for reasons we'll discuss a little later in this chapter (see "Avoiding 'Dropped' Source Material"). Quoted material must be enclosed within quotation marks, and you must take great care to ensure that you have faithfully and accurately represented the original author's words. Take it away, Casey:

> I'm actually learning to respect and even enjoy the research process. It's not easy, but it's also not the end of the world. Every time I complete another step in the research process, I get a little bit more comfortable. But I try not to relax too much; after all, it's "crucial" to stay "focused" — if you're not paying careful attention to what you're doing, "research can get out of control fast" (Lerych and Criswell 310).

This is quoted source material because the borrowed words are taken verbatim from the original. Casey takes great care to ensure that the quotes are accurate and that the entire original passage is enclosed in quotation marks. Failure to enclose verbatim borrowings in quotation marks is a form of plagiarism — even if the source of the text is acknowledged and cited (there's more on citation in Chapter 22 and Appendix B). So Casey has placed even individual borrowed words (*crucial* and *focused*) within quotation marks. Why? Because they seemed specific and important enough to be identified as coming from the original source.

Practice! Quoting

One more time, here's your new favorite paragraph in the whole wide world:

> Just as writing is both a process and a product, so is research. Whereas Chapter 20 focused on the process of researching, this chapter will focus on creating the product of your research. The essential ingredients that go into your research product — that make a research paper different from other essays — are the actual words, ideas, and data of the sources that you will ultimately include.

We know you've read it. We're pretty sure you understand it. Now we want to know what you think about it. Is there something new you learned in reading this paragraph? Is there something you agree with? Something you disagree with? Something you want to know more about? Overall, what's your reaction to this paragraph? Write it down in a single sentence.

Now, recognizing that what you've just written down is a claim, go back through the paragraph to look for support. Choose a brief quote that you think would support your claim well, and present it in a way that clearly supports your claim. Show your use of quoted evidence to a classmate or your professor for feedback.

AVOIDING "DROPPED" SOURCE MATERIAL

Regardless of whether you summarize, paraphrase, or quote, you should work hard to integrate the borrowed source material into your essay as seamlessly as possible. This skill takes some practice to master, but it is invaluable in many types of analytical and research writing.

One bad habit that many less successful writers have is what's called dropping source material. Let's say you're happily writing along in your essay, minding your own business, when it occurs to you, *Gosh, I haven't used anything from a source in quite a while.* So you look at your notes, find something that seems vaguely related to your topic, and type it into your paper. Then you go back to what you were writing about. The problem is that you haven't shown the reader a clear connection between the main point of your paragraph and the borrowed material. Check out this example that Casey wrote:

> Research in the age of ever-developing technology can be both a blessing and a curse. On the one hand, gaining access to information has never been easier: because of the Internet, a small-town student with limited social mobility and financial resources has just as much opportunity to consult academic sources as a legacy student at Harvard or Stanford. "It's pretty much anything and everything ever written or recorded anywhere by anyone at any time" (Lerych and Criswell 319).

Notice that in this example there is no grammatical connection between the borrowed source material (in this case, a quote) and the other sentences, and the logical connection is only loosely implied. This is called a **dropped quote**, and it is not an effective way to incorporate source material into an essay. Aside from being awkward and ineffective, dropping source material has another, more serious consequence: without placing source material in context and commenting on its purpose in your essay, you run the risk of using it in a misleading way. In Casey's paragraph above, for example, the quote appears linked to the idea that the Internet is entirely a positive force. But if we were to go back to Chapter 20 and read that quote in context, we'd discover that its purpose in the original text is to point out that the Internet can be *both* a positive *and* a negative force (the following passage is taken directly from page 319):

> For most of you, what will seem to be the easiest first step is to go directly to Google, type in your search term, and press "Enter." However, consider this: using the power of the entire Internet to locate information can be frustrating because *it's the whole Internet.* It's pretty much anything and everything ever written or

recorded anywhere by anyone at any time. It's a whole lot of stuff, and that can be both good and bad.

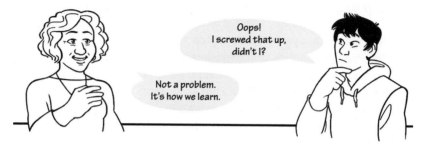

To avoid dropping source material, and also to avoid using source material in confusing or misleading ways, use a four-step cycle of development to integrate (or *blend*) direct quotes or paraphrases into your essay in order to methodically develop the idea you want to get across to the reader. You may recognize this process as a variation on the analytical paragraph structure that we discussed back in Chapter 10 and then practiced in Chapter 17.

How to Integrate Source Materials

1. **Introduce your own idea** into the paragraph before you introduce a quote or someone else's ideas. Remember that you are writing an essay, not making a patchwork quilt. Your voice and your idea should lead the reader smoothly and consistently through each paragraph.
2. **Use a signal phrase** or a sentence with a meaningful present-tense verb to lead into the quote. A phrase like "Smith agrees that . . ." or "Reyes emphasizes that . . ." or "Yamada rejects this idea by asserting . . ." will make a meaningful link between your own ideas and the ideas you're borrowing through quote or paraphrase.
3. **Use the borrowed quote** (or paraphrased idea) as a part of your sentence, not as its own sentence.
4. **Comment** on the borrowed material, **respond** to it, or **explain** it before you move on to your next idea. Don't assume that the source material means the same thing to readers of your paper that it does to you. They might interpret it differently. It is your job to lead them through your train of thought.

► *Let Us Show You:* **Integrating Sources**

Mara is moving right along with her research paper assignment. She has already started drafting parts of her essay by building analytical paragraphs that incorporate source material from reliable sources. Casey has agreed to look at and annotate one of her draft paragraphs.

ADHD stimulants are prescription for a reason. The U.S. Drug Enforcement Administration classifies the stimulants as Schedule II drugs because of their high potential for abuse and dependency. Other commonly known Schedule II drugs include morphine, cocaine, PCP, opium, and OxyContin. So how do so many students get these drugs? A study was done to research how easy it is to detect college students pretending to have ADHD symptoms. Thirty-one undergraduates who studied symptoms on the Internet were compared to twenty-nine students who actually had ADHD and fourteen who didn't have it and weren't pretending to have it. The three groups were given standard ADHD tests, which included symptom checklists, neurocognitive tests, and symptom validity tests. Overall, the undergraduates who were pretending to have ADHD were able to fool the tests (Berry, Ranseen, and Sollman 325). These findings show that it's surprisingly easy to get a prescription for stimulants. For those who don't have a prescription, a study showed that 62 percent of students with ADHD gave the medication to someone without a prescription (Arria and DuPont 419). While some students may not know that it's illegal to share or sell their own prescription drugs, it's relatively easy to get an ADHD prescription simply for the purpose of illegally giving stimulants to others.

Marginal annotations:

Here's the claim.

Nice paraphrasing here.

This is your question.

Hey! Good paraphrase.

Should this be in quotes?

Here's a source.

Your analysis? Or from the next source? Unclear.

Second source.

Good! Your commentary on how the source's ideas fit into your essay.

▶ Talk Amongst Yourselves . . .

Take a few minutes to write down your response to the questions below. Then break into groups of three and discuss your responses with each other.

How helpful do you find Casey's annotation of Mara's draft paragraph? Are there any points you disagree with? What suggestions would you have given Mara that Casey did not? What about the two suggestions Casey does make? Are these legitimate problems that need to be addressed, and if so, how should Mara go about addressing them?

▶ *Now You Try:* Integrating Sources

For this exercise, you'll need to take a step back from your *individual* sources and start to think about what they all add up to. So do that for a few minutes, okay? Then when you're done, do the following:

1. Review your annotated bibliography and notes from earlier in this chapter.

2. When you think of what you've learned from your sources in relation to your research question, what are some of the ideas that emerge? Write them down. (You've done this very thing before, on pages 75–76 back in Chapter 7.)

3. Take just one of those ideas and turn it into a *claim* (see Chapter 16, pages 230–31, for a refresher on claims).

4. Gather your source notes that contain the words, ideas, or data that you can most clearly and reasonably use to *support* that claim (reminder: Chapter 17, pages 245–57).

5. Draft a paragraph that uses the analytical paragraph structure of integrating source material (check out Chapter 9 or Chapter 17, or see "How to Integrate Source Materials" just a few pages back). Do your best to develop and support your claim by presenting and explaining both *what you've discovered* (information and ideas from sources) and *what you think about it* (your own analysis and interpretation of those sources).

If you've been keeping track of our journey through the steps in the research process, you have no doubt noticed that we have just finished the final step of that process.

Now there's one more thing left to do. But be aware that it's a doozy: making sure that you are using — and citing — your sources with ethics, integrity, and character. This important obligation is covered in Chapter 22, so turn the page!

Research and *Ethos:*
Good Rules for Ethical Writers

Rule #1: Use your best judgment in all
situations. There will be no additional rules.
— Nordstrom's Employee Handbook

The German Enlightenment philosopher Immanuel Kant — a guy so interested in ethics that there's a thing called Kantian ethics — said that you shouldn't do something unless you think everyone else should do it too. Well, okay, he didn't say it in those exact words, because then we would have put quotes around them (remember Chapter 21?), but still, that's his basic idea of ethics: rules that apply to *everyone.* We bring this up because we think it's healthy to consider Kant's idea if — or when! — you find yourself wondering what the point is of all these rules about academic integrity.

In general, rules are about ethics — standards of behavior that are valued by society, moral principles that are shared. One common ethical standard among societies is that it's wrong to steal. An offshoot of the *don't steal* ethical standard is the principle of academic integrity: *don't steal other people's ideas.* Try to imagine if everyone were to disregard the rules of academic integrity all the time. We'd never know the origin of ideas, much less whether what we were reading was even actually written by the person claiming to have written it. We'd never know whether someone writing about something was an expert or was just pretending to be an expert. And maybe even scarier is that we would never know whether what we were reading was the truth or a lie.

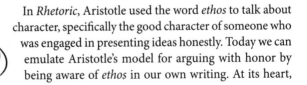

In other words, we think academic integrity is a social norm worth preserving. And we're not the only ones. Just ask your professor.

In *Rhetoric,* Aristotle used the word *ethos* to talk about character, specifically the good character of someone who was engaged in presenting ideas honestly. Today we can emulate Aristotle's model for arguing with honor by being aware of *ethos* in our own writing. At its heart, the quality of *ethos* in an argument is the author's presentation of himself or herself as both knowledgeable and honest. *Ethos* is about the process of transforming information into knowledge (or *authority*), and it's also about academic integrity (or *character*). These are two of the most important tools employed by ethical academic writers.

One of the most important tasks you'll perform as an ethical writer — a task that develops your reputation as an authority and as a writer of good character — is the careful and honest use of all sources in your writing.

Authoritative Source Use: Being Well Informed

One of the best ways to be an ethical writer is to be honest with yourself about what you know and what you don't know. In other words, be completely honest with yourself about how much *authority* you have on any given subject or in any given situation. You may recall that we discussed this in detail back in the "Understand Your Sources" section of Chapter 21.

If you've decided to write — or perhaps have been coerced into writing — about a topic that you aren't an authority on (which will happen fairly often in college), you'll need to become more knowledgeable, right? You'll need to do the research necessary to present your ideas with some credibility. In other words, it's your responsibility to become well informed about your subject before you write about it. That's a part of academic integrity.

Note that we're actually talking about the author's authority. The writer (the author) is the one who knows (the one with authority).

There are good reasons to conduct research (aside from the very good reason that you've been assigned to do so by a professor). The most important reason is that it's good to be informed about things before you give your opinion. If your research reconfirms what you already thought you knew, great. If not? Even better!

Another equally important reason to do research is that if you don't know too much about a topic but have to write about it, you can't just make stuff up. Well, you can — but it's really not a good idea. It will end in tears. Or maybe worse.

FAILURE OF AUTHORITY: BEING UNDER-INFORMED

Here's a question: What should you do if your assignment guidelines don't specify a required number of sources and you discover — after a careful selection and evaluation process — that only one source is really useful? Should you toss out all the other sources and rest your argument solely on that one excellent silver bullet of a source?

Sadly, no, you shouldn't.

Use More Than One Secondary Source

Even if your paper is quite short, you should follow this important rule: if you're going to use secondary sources, use more than one. (The only exception would be if you have been specifically assigned to do something different.) Why? Because using only one source results in a kind of plagiarism even if you are careful always to put verbatim borrowings in quotation marks and to cite every single summary and paraphrase (remember those from Chapter 21?).

Using only one secondary source forces you to rely too heavily on the words and ideas of that source. Remember the chat we had in the previous chapter (see pages 341–47) about integrating source ideas into your writing? If you rely on only a single point of view aside from your own, then you're not researching your topic — you're researching *just one source's view* of that topic. And relying too heavily on the ideas of a single source sounds dangerously close to that definition of plagiarism that we provided back in Chapter 21. Wait, what was that definition again? Oh, yes:

> Plagiarism is presenting the words, ideas, or data of another thinker or writer as if they were your own.

But, you may be thinking, *if I acknowledge that nearly everything in my paper came from that secondary source, I should be okay. After all, I'm not really pretending any of those ideas are actually mine.* As always, we admire your cleverness — but unfortunately, we must disagree with your premise.

See, when your professors ask you to write a paper, they're asking you to demonstrate your own understanding or interpretation of the subject matter. When they ask you to write a research paper, they're asking you to demonstrate your own understanding or interpretation of the subject matter *based on what you have learned by consulting sources.* At its heart, doing research is about demonstrating what you have learned, not demonstrating that you know how to use Ctrl-C and Ctrl-V.

Wait! I know what those commands mean . . . Ctrl-C is for "copy" and Ctrl-V is for "paste." And all-important Ctrl-Z is to undo something you shouldn't have done.

When too much of your paper isn't actually yours, then you have a problem with the spirit of academic integrity, even if you haven't violated the letter of the academic-integrity law. And one simple rule that can help you to avoid ever finding yourself in that situation is to ensure that you never, ever, under any circumstances, write a paper that makes use of only one lonely secondary source.

To show you what we mean, we offer the following paragraph. It cites its sources properly, but it uses those sources in a way that *lacks academic integrity* (read: this is a bad paragraph):

> Slowly but surely over the past decades, the average size of the Arctic ice cap has been shrinking. Last summer, Arctic sea ice reached the lowest point ever recorded. Things aren't looking better in Antarctica, either. The sheets of ice covering the land in Antarctica are melting at a fast pace. Even more worrying, a study released earlier this week showed that Antarctic permafrost is melting, too (Knapp). Permafrost is melting faster in the Arctic, too, and that's a cause for major concern. That's because permafrost in the Arctic contains large amounts of methane. As the Arctic permafrost melts, that methane then escapes into the atmosphere. Methane is a potent greenhouse gas — it traps significantly more heat than carbon dioxide. So as more methane is released into the atmosphere, it causes temperatures to rise faster, which causes more permafrost to melt, which releases more methane, which . . . you get the idea (Knapp). The result of the release of methane from permafrost "isn't just an environmental catastrophe. It's also an economic one" (Knapp). The economic impacts are "disparate," but we're already seeing them today. Carbon dioxide emissions are leading to smaller fish — which threatens the fishing industry (Knapp). Of course, the accelerated melting of ice on the Antarctic continent and on Greenland produces a bigger problem: rising sea levels (Knapp). Some scientists have even suggested that such a sea level rise might end up flooding Miami by the end of the century. Whether the situation will be that dire remains to be seen, but when it comes to sea level rise, "past models have turned out to be too conservative" (Knapp). That is, sea level keeps rising faster than climate scientists have predicted — which makes numbers about the future "that much more worrisome" (Knapp).

If this paragraph appeared in an essay of yours, that essay wouldn't really be *yours*, see? Every single sentence is either a paraphrase or a quote from the only secondary source the writer consulted. Missed that? Read the paragraph again, very carefully. By the end of the paragraph, we have a fairly good idea of the information that someone named Knapp has gathered and analyzed — but we don't have a clue what *the writer* thinks about any of it.

Important Note! This isn't a problem when your only source is a primary source. When you use a painting or a poem or an important document or a scientific experiment as your sole source — in short, when your only source is an original artifact instead of an interpretation or commentary or other scholarly discussion — you're okay: the source material is the subject that you're writing about, and you yourself are the scholar. Thus you are your own secondary source. And no, this wouldn't mean that you have to cite yourself. That would just be silly.

But if your only source is a secondary source, you end up essentially restating that scholar's ideas instead of coming up with any of your own. So when you're writing with secondary sources, you really should make meaningful use of at least two sources. As soon as you incorporate the words and ideas of a *second* secondary source, you are automatically balancing the ideas in your essay and upping the ante on your own participation: someone will need to referee the thoughts of these two sources by analyzing, interpreting, comparing, and contrasting — and that referee might as well be you, since it's your essay.

Avoid Patchwork Plagiarism

It's possible for some beginning writers to get into trouble with what we call *regurgitative plagiarism* (vivid language, isn't it?) even when they're using more than one secondary source. In such cases, the term that's generally applied is **patchwork plagiarism**.

This is the result of the writer stringing together words, ideas, and data from multiple sources without really bringing his or her own brain to the party. It doesn't take too much thinking to realize that such a paper wouldn't pass the "demonstrate your own understanding or interpretation" test, would it?

Here's an example paragraph in which the writer uses multiple sources, and every use (including paraphrased ideas and data) is cited properly. See if you can determine why this paragraph still lacks academic integrity as a result of patchwork plagiarism:

"The Arctic is global warming's canary in the coal mine. It's a highly sensitive region, and it's being profoundly affected by the changing climate. Most scientists view what's happening now in the Arctic as a harbinger of things to come" ("Global Warming Puts the Arctic on Thin Ice"). "As the Arctic permafrost melts, that methane then escapes into the atmosphere. Methane is a potent greenhouse gas — it traps significantly more heat than carbon dioxide. So as more methane is released into the atmosphere, it causes temperatures to rise faster, which causes more permafrost to melt, which releases more methane, which . . . you get the idea" (Knapp). This release of methane has both economic and environmental consequences, touching everything from our food supply to sea levels. "A group of environmental researchers earlier this month demonstrated that for every degree Celsius average global temperatures rise, we can expect there to be a 2.3 meter rise in sea levels. As that rise increases, some coastal cities may not be able to be saved and will have to be evacuated completely. Some scientists have even suggested that such a sea level rise might end up flooding Miami by the end of the century" (Knapp). "But there might be a less dramatic reason than polar ice melting for the higher ocean level — the higher temperature of the water. Water is most dense at 4 degrees Celsius. Above and below this temperature, the density of water decreases (the same weight of water occupies a bigger space). So as the overall temperature of the water increases it naturally expands a little bit making the oceans rise" (Brain).

This paragraph has actually used multiple sources to present various pieces of information — and that's good. But once again, every sentence is simply paraphrased or quoted source material. There is absolutely *no* commentary from the actual "author" of this paragraph. In fact, the "author" has no authority here — everything presented in the paragraph comes from someone else.

Bottom line: if all you're doing is typing up someone else's ideas, you're not writing an essay.

Integrity: Being Honest with Yourself

For a writer to have good *ethos* (a good, credible character, remember?), authority is necessary but not sufficient. The ethical writer also needs integrity.

Integrity comes from the Latin *integritas*, meaning "completeness" or "wholeness." Basically, if one has integrity, one is honest, sincere, and virtuous. Read on.

When a thing has integrity, nothing is missing from it; it is unbroken, unmarred, uncorrupted . . . do you see where we're going with this? If a person (or a person's work, such as an essay) has integrity, then that person (or work) is clean and whole and without — well, without *sin*.

Academic integrity is both a general and a specific term. Often when students hear the term, they think primarily of its specific, narrow meaning, which essentially is doing your work without cheating or plagiarizing. And at this point, you can probably see the connection between *integritas* and *not cheating* — after all, if you've been breathing on the planet for more than the last week or two, you're aware that cheating and plagiarizing are activities associated with concepts like corruption, sin, and dishonesty. You understand that to purposely cheat or plagiarize is wrong and would mark you as lacking academic integrity.

But what you may or may not understand at this point is that it's possible to lose track of your integrity without meaning to.

STAYING OPEN-MINDED

One way you can maintain your integrity is to make sure that you maintain an *open mind* while you're consulting the sources that qualify you to write about your topic. In other words, set aside your preconceived notions when researching a topic and give full consideration to what your sources are saying. (*Hint:* You can do this by following Steps 4–7 of our patented seven-step research process — we went over them in Chapter 21. See how much we care about you?)

Going into your research believing that you already know the answers — or even worse, going out of your way to find and use *only those sources that support your preconceived opinion* — will likely result in a biased argument. And bias is a serious obstacle to academic integrity, as you know from our discussion in Chapter 20. This openness, or fairness of character, is so important that we've discussed it in a variety of ways throughout this book.

The Importance of Openness in Writing

▶ Viewing your initial thesis in any essay as a *working thesis* (Chapter 7, pages 82–85) means knowing that your thesis can — and should, and probably *will* — change as you learn.

▶ Being aware of the various ways that writers make assumptions about their arguments (Chapter 17, pages 247–48) means that you are open to the assumptions of your reader.

▶ Being open to the reader's assumptions helps you to avoid committing logical fallacies (Chapter 18).

▶ Being open to the reader's needs and values helps you to avoid committing fallacies of *pathos* (Chapter 19, pages 295–300).

Ethical writers — writers of good character — demonstrate an openness to all possible sides of an argument. Does that mean you have to give equal time to ideas you disagree with? No. (See our discussion of rebuttals on pages 258–59 in Chapter 17.) But it does mean that you owe it to yourself and your reader to consider opposing viewpoints. Then you can rest assured that your conclusions have taken into account what others have to say. Considering others' views can only strengthen your own views, either by making your point of view more inclusive or by providing you with an opportunity to explain your reasons for disagreeing.

AVOID UNINTENTIONAL PLAGIARISM

Even when you're open-minded about what you're learning from your sources, how you use them can get you into trouble. And even when you're careful to avoid the regurgitative plagiarism and patchwork plagiarism that result from careless or thoughtless consideration of source material, you can still have a problem with the careless or thoughtless use of source material. It typically goes something like this:

Unintentional Plagiarism: How It Happens

▶ While incorporating source material into your essay, you run across an idea in your notes that you want to use, but you're not sure which source it came from. You **use it anyway without citing it** because you don't know which source to cite.

▶ While incorporating source material into your essay, you run across a really great phrase in your notes. You use it and cite it — but you don't realize it was taken word-for-word from the source (because *that* isn't in your notes), so you **don't put it in quotation marks**.

▶ You copy and paste a paragraph of source material into your notes for consideration. A week later, your idea about considering that material has slipped your mind, and you **insert the whole paragraph** into your essay, unconsidered and without paraphrasing because you don't remember that it isn't your idea. This problem is related to the previous one, but this one's worse because it can't be fixed with a set of quotation marks. The good news? You can avoid this problem by never, ever using Ctrl-C, Ctrl-V in your research.

We trust you're seeing the pattern here. It all comes down to *bad note taking.* This is why we were so insistent back in Chapter 21 that you develop a good system of taking notes for research writing. Bad note taking leads directly to unintentional plagiarism.

One more time: whenever you present the words, ideas, or data of a source as if they were your own, you're committing plagiarism — *whether you mean to or not.* Each of the examples we've just given constitutes plagiarism, because in each case, you are presenting someone else's words or ideas without acknowledging that those ideas, or that data, or those exact words, came from another source.

The most important thing to know about plagiarism is this: it might be unintentional, but it's still plagiarism. So don't do it, okay?

Character: Being Honest with Your Reader

Writers of integrity are always honest with themselves throughout the research process, as we've discussed already. But of course, writing isn't just about the writer. Writers of good character exhibit thoughtful consideration of and respect for their *readers* by being honest with them as well. The two major types of dishonesty that will torpedo a writer's relationship with the reader are misuse of authority and intentional plagiarism.

DISHONEST OR MISLEADING USE OF AUTHORITY

Dishonest or misleading use of authority, also known as a **fallacy of ethos**, comes from a writer making a bad assumption about a source. In such fallacies, the writer misuses expert opinion to support claims in an argument. Generally, these errors involve bad judgments about the writer's — and the reader's — trust in an authority. Bottom line? You are obliged to demonstrate the authority of all source material you present. Otherwise, your *ethos* — your good character — suffers.

Simply finding sources that agree with you does not necessarily make your argument valid. When you use a source created by a person who is an authority on something, you must be careful not to engage in **faulty use of authority**. Several problems with authorities are possible: An authority may represent a "renegade" or generally unaccepted view. Or the authority may be biased. The most difficult problem is probably using an authority who is respected in *a* subject but *not* in the subject of your argument — for example:

> Lynne is justifiably famous for her ability to recite all of the auxiliary verbs in the English language in order in under five seconds. Therefore, I will be citing her as an expert on the use of indirect object pronouns in Portuguese for my Linguistics 101 paper.

Quoting out of context sounds exactly like what it is: using a quote in a way that misrepresents its original meaning. Sometimes this fallacy is the result of deliberate dishonesty, such as when a politician makes a campaign ad that includes video of an opponent saying something horrible — purposely cutting out the beginning of the opponent's sentence, which was something like "I do not believe that [horrible thing]." At other times, this fallacy is the result of misunderstanding the larger context of the original quote. One of the most famous examples of this fallacy emanates from this quote from Albert Einstein: "God does not play dice." Do you think this means something religious? Or do you understand it in another way?

When placed in the broader context of Einstein's complete statement, one can see that Einstein was making not a religious argument but a scientific one. He was speaking about quantum mechanics, which he thought was flawed because it allowed randomness to exist in the universe. Basically, he was arguing that everything that happens has an identifiable cause. For instance, apples don't fall from trees randomly — they do so because they are ripe, or because the wind is blowing, or because someone is shaking the tree's branches, triggering gravity to kick in and do its thing. In the context of his whole statement, "God" is a figure of speech, not a declaration of his spiritual leanings.

Card stacking is a type of lying in which information is deliberately left out. It is the result of unfairly presenting only one side of an issue in order to manipulate an audience. This strategy makes a position seem like it's "just the way things are" when in fact the arguer is working hard to edit the information presented to the audience. In academic writing, this tactic generally involves *cherry-picking* evidence from sources — meaning that the writer presents only the pieces of evidence that support his or her argument but conveniently leaves out all evidence to the contrary. Can you find evidence of both card stacking and cherry picking in this example?

> The government needs to drug-test all welfare recipients because 2 percent of people who receive public benefits in Florida have failed a drug test. It's wrong for people who get money from tax dollars to use drugs.

What the example doesn't tell you is that studies show that 8 percent of the general population uses drugs, so those tested for public assistance funding in Florida actually used drugs at a rate that was significantly *less* than the rate for the public at large. Not to mention that the drug-testing program for the state of Florida was extraordinarily expensive and demonstrably inaccurate and is widely regarded as a failure. Oh, and the example also fails to mention that plenty of people who aren't "welfare recipients" also "get money from tax dollars" — for instance, everyone who works for the federal, state, or local government (elected officials, judges, cabinet secretaries, bureaucrats, teachers, police officers, firefighters, etc.). Based on the reasoning in this example, shouldn't all of *those* people be drug-tested as well?

Reality Check! Fallacies of Authority

► **Faulty use of authority:** Have you presented information from an unreliable source?

► **Quoting out of context:** Have you misrepresented the meaning of a source?

► **Card stacking/cherry picking:** Have you unfairly presented only one side of the argument by ignoring relevant evidence that hurts your position?

Practice! Fallacies of Authority

See if you can determine which authoritative fallacy is doing its utmost to destroy the integrity of each of the following arguments:

1. According to the International Association of Medical Professionals, "homeopathic treatments are ... more effective than a placebo."

2. If you're planning to set up an individual retirement account, you should seriously consider investing in Trustworthy Mega-Bank — the only retirement investment recommended by Tiger Woods.

3. Although no evidence of the effectiveness of this policy exists for North Carolina, the data from certain provinces in France suggest that nearly 30 percent of those who volunteered to take the survey favor this policy. Therefore, it's the right move for North Carolina.

INTENTIONAL PLAGIARISM

Writers who commit abuses of *ethos* such as those we've just described run the risk of damaging their relationship with the reader. But the absolute worst way for writers to betray their readers, the most egregious way to violate their *ethos* as writers, is to lie about where the content of their essays comes from.

The truth is, we hate to even mention **intentional plagiarism**. We like to believe that all college students are inherently ethical because we like to believe that people in general are all inherently good. That's just how we roll.

But sad and sometimes bitter experience has taught us that, yes, occasionally students plagiarize on purpose. We understand that intentional plagiarism only rarely happens because the plagiarist is truly a bad person who wants to. Students who knowingly plagiarize — that is, who plagiarize with full awareness that they're copying someone else's work and turn it in as if they had written it — usually do so in response to other conditions aside from innate evil.

For example, they *procrastinate* so long on an assignment that in the end, with only a few hours left to complete the entire paper and nothing to show for it, they desperately find something on the Internet that they can copy and paste, hoping that they won't get caught. (Generally they do, by the way.) Or perhaps a student is so *confused* about an assignment, so unsure of how to complete it — and unwilling or afraid to ask for help — that he or she just panics and turns in someone else's work that looks like it might meet the assignment.

The problem is that even if you're out of time, or desperate, or panicky, you don't have the right to pretend you wrote something that you didn't write. Or at least, you don't have the right to do that without enduring harsh consequences.

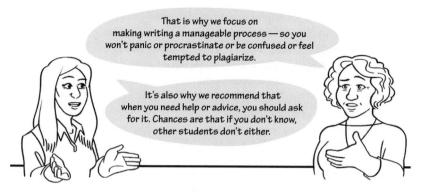

If someone chooses to plagiarize after all of our advice and examples, after all of our instruction and warnings — particularly here in the research section of our book, that is, Part 6 (Chapters 20–22) — then we are left only to wonder: is that person just dense, or is that person a jerk?

Neither is a good thing to be. And we're glad *you* aren't such a person, dear reader. Next we'll show you how to prove it.

Ethics and Source Use: Citation

At the heart of ethical, research-backed writing is the practice of **citing sources**. To cite a source simply means to acknowledge the original source of any words, information, or ideas each time you use them.

WHY CITE SOURCES?

Reason #1 for citing a source is the one everyone knows: *you don't want to be accused of plagiarism.* This accusation can lead to your failing an assignment or a course, being brought up on disciplinary charges at your college, and even being expelled. None of these things are good. But two other reasons are less commonly considered — and we would argue that they are even more important than avoiding prosecution.

Reason #2 is that *it's helpful to your reader when you cite your sources*. Think about it: you're writing along in your essay when you suddenly mention a study or a set of statistics or some other interesting tidbit you gleaned from a source. Your reader is intrigued and wants to know where to find more about this topic. If you've properly cited the source of the tidbit, then your reader will happily discover how to find the source and therefore will be likely to find more information on whatever was so intriguing.

Reason #3 — and the most important reason to cite your sources — is that *it shows the proper respect for the author of the words, ideas, or data you're using*. Anyone who puts his or her time, effort, training, and talent into creating something ought to be acknowledged as its creator. It could be a poem, a symphony, a piece of software, an original mathematical proof, a study of adolescent behaviors, or a jet-engine design — whatever is an original thought, argument, or expression. You would probably feel violated and abused — if not outraged — if you discovered that someone else was presenting your work as if he or she had created it instead of you. And you would be justified in feeling that way.

Now that we've cleared up the question of *why*, there's another question you're no doubt dying to ask: *Exactly how do I go about citing sources so as to avoid charges of plagiarism, help my readers, and respect those from whom I've borrowed?*

HOW TO CITE SOURCES

We're glad you asked. We have a quick and easy answer, a longer and more complex answer, and a piece of helpful advice. Let's take them in that order, shall we?

The quick and easy answer is that you cite sources by making sure that each and every time you borrow any words, ideas, or data you acknowledge their source by indicating in your essay where they came from — at the end of whatever content you've borrowed. Remember what Casey did in Chapter 21 when he paraphrased text from Chapter 20? Here it is again:

> One of the most significant things I've learned about research is the importance of paying attention to what you do *before* you actually begin to research. Researching without first choosing a topic you're really interested in is just a disaster. But even having an interesting topic isn't really enough. I've learned, for example, that it's important to have in mind a good question that you want to answer before trying to find sources to use in a research paper (Lerych and Criswell 310).

Okay, that's the quick and easy answer. Let's move on to the longer and more complex answer.

Every single time you summarize, paraphrase, or quote, you need to clearly acknowledge the source. We cannot stress this enough. That's why we're saying it over and over and over and . . .

Components of Citation

There are several different methods of citing sources in academic research writing. These methods are often referred to as styles or formats of citation.

Even though there are some differences among citation styles, most are designed around two required elements:

▶ the *reference* (the acknowledgment of a specific use of source material within the essay)
▶ the *bibliography* (the list of complete information about each source at the end of the essay)

Many but not all citation styles make their references through what is called in-text citation or parenthetical citation. This involves acknowledging the source by placing identifying information in parentheses right in the text of the essay at the end of each source use. We provided an example from Casey on the facing page. Here's another example, taken from Mara's academic doping essay that appears a bit later in this chapter:

> Of a sample of students from 119 four-year colleges, 6.9 percent reported NPS use (McCabe et al. 98).

At the end of the essay is a bibliography page that includes an alphabetized listing of all of Mara's sources, with complete publication data for each source. Depending on the citation style used, this page might be titled *Bibliography, Works Cited,* or *References.* Mara's works cited list appears on page 368 and is an excellent example of how sources are listed in a bibliography.

And as for that final piece of helpful advice we promised . . . here you go.

Styles That Use In-Text Citation

▶ MLA parenthetical citation (for English and humanities classes)
▶ APA parenthetical citation (for many social science and science classes)
▶ *Chicago*/Turabian footnotes/endnotes (for some disciplines in both the humanities and the social sciences)

For more complete information about writing and citing for different disciplines, see Appendix B.

Reality Check! The Ethical College Research Paper

▶ Does the essay have a clear thesis, or main point, that's appropriate for the assignment?

▶ Is that thesis well supported with relevant, meaningful, factual evidence?

▶ Is the thesis developed through appeals to the reader's needs and values?

▶ Does the essay make use of valid, authoritative sources to back its claims?

▶ Are source materials integrated fairly and understandably into the essay?

▶ Are all borrowings of words, ideas, or data from sources cited clearly within the text?

▶ Is the paper's bibliography complete, accurate, and usefully presented according to format?

▶ *Let Us Show You:* Ethical Use and Citation of Sources

Now that Mara knows the steps to writing an essay, writing one is not as big of a deal as it used to be. Look:

Stuff Mara Knows How to Do Now

▶ Understand the assignment (Chapter 5)

▶ Brainstorm for a topic (Chapters 5 and 6)

▶ Find, evaluate, and narrow valid sources (Chapter 20)

▶ Select, read, understand, and record source ideas (Chapters 4 and 21)

▶ Develop a working thesis (Chapter 7)

▶ Draft meaningful, appropriate paragraphs (Chapters 8, 9, and 11)

▶ Integrate source material analytically (Chapters 10 and 21)

▶ Make a solid, logical argument (Chapters 16, 17, and 18)

▶ Consider how the essay might appeal to the reader (Chapters 2 and 19)

▶ Revise a draft for its content (Chapters 12 and 13)

▶ Organize a draft for its structure (Chapter 14)

▶ Edit a draft for coherence and precision (Chapter 15)

As a result of her new knowledge and skill, Mara has completed her draft research essay, and Casey has agreed to review it.

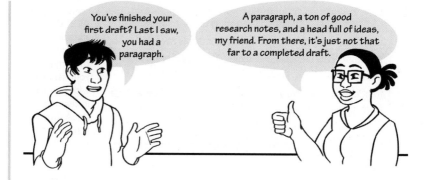

Mara Johnson

November 16, 2015

Professor McGonagall

English 101

Research Essay (Revised Draft)

Academic Doping: Not So Smart

Attention Deficit Hyperactivity Disorder (ADHD) is one of the most common childhood disorders, and often carries into adulthood. According to the Centers for Disease Control and Prevention, ADHD can mean you have trouble paying attention, controlling impulsive behaviors, or being overly active. The high rates of ADHD in the United States have led to a huge range of ADHD medications in society, and having a prescription is common. The combination of easily accessible ADHD stimulants, academic pressures, and false beliefs has led to a new type of drug abuse among students. Commonly known as "study drugs," non-prescription stimulants (NPS) are taken by college students without ADHD in order to get ahead in the competitive world of academics, but they have lesser known uses and effects as well. While some students are more likely than others to illegally use these drugs, most students think that they are academic performance enhancers. However, studies have shown that they may do more harm than good and that students use them for reasons other than studying.

Starts out with strong, authoritative information, but maybe avoid saying "you" since the reader doesn't necessarily have ADHD.

Is using quotes around commonly known phrases okay?

Should anything here be cited?

(continued)

The number of students taking study drugs is surprising in itself. When looked at closely, the numbers show specific patterns of NPS use among students. Of a sample of students from 119 four-year colleges, 6.9 percent reported NPS use (McCabe et al. 98). Smaller surveys have found numbers as high as 18.6 percent of students (Labbe and Maisto 727). Certain factors can identify a student as more likely to be one of these users. For example, colleges with very competitive admissions standards have higher rates of use. Students at these colleges were over 2.29 times more likely to report NPS use than students at less competitive schools. Students in sororities or fraternities are also more likely to be users, as are male or white students (McCabe et al. 101). These studies offer insight into who exactly uses NPS, clearly showing that NPS use exists in significant numbers, especially on highly competitive campuses.

ADHD stimulants are prescription for a reason. The U.S. Drug Enforcement Administration classifies the stimulants as Schedule II drugs because of their high potential for abuse and dependency. Other commonly known Schedule II drugs include morphine, cocaine, PCP, opium, and OxyContin. So how do so many students get these drugs? A study was done to research how easy it is to detect college students pretending to have ADHD symptoms. Thirty-one undergraduates who studied symptoms on the Internet were compared to twenty-nine students who actually had ADHD and fourteen who didn't have it and weren't pretending to have it. The three groups were given standard ADHD diagnostic tests, which included symptom checklists, neurocognitive tests, and symptom validity tests. Overall, the undergraduates who were pretending to have ADHD were able to fool the tests (Berry, Ranseen, and Sollman 325). These findings show that it's surprisingly easy to obtain a prescription for stimulants. For those who don't have a prescription, a study showed that 62 percent of students with ADHD gave the medication to someone without a prescription (Arria and DuPont 419). While some students may not know that it's illegal to share or sell their own

---

Margin annotations:

All of these statistics are integrated smoothly into your sentences with correct in-text citation (MLA format, as assigned).

Are they more likely to use the drugs? Or just more likely to report using the drugs?

Good tone! It is conversational and informative.

Is this maybe a scare tactic? Like, trying to suggest that NPS is as dangerous as the rest of the list?

Every paragraph ends with your own idea, which is good.

prescription drugs, it's relatively easily to get an ADHD prescription simply for the purpose of illegally giving stimulants to others.

While certain factors can predict NPS use, and the drugs are easy to get, there are underlying reasons as to why students are taking them to begin with. Students may think they will get certain effects from using NPS. Academically, students use the drugs because it "helps people concentrate better," "makes people feel more focused," and "helps people get their work done more efficiently" (Labbe and Maisto 727). However, these are only beliefs held by students and may not be physically true. Studies show that students with lower GPAs have the highest connection to stimulant use (McCabe et al. 99). This conflicting information suggests that students have false beliefs regarding NPS use. According to the *Journal of Addictive Diseases*, "[n]ew research has demonstrated that performance improvements related to methylphenidate administration in healthy volunteers are highly variable and might be dependent on baseline cognitive ability," showing that study drugs may not be effective in the first place. NPS use is not limited to just academic reasons either. A lot of people don't realize that "many students use these drugs nonmedically to enhance their experience of partying and getting high on other substances," creating a hidden side of NPS use (Arria and DuPont 419). Students don't always just use NPS for harmless reasons like to help them study.

Whether it is happening for academic or social reasons, this type of non-prescribed Schedule II drug use creates many reasons to classify it as outright abuse. The drugs are easy to access, distribute, and buy — all of which are illegal to do without a valid prescription, which is also easy to get with fake ADHD symptoms. Although they are Schedule II drugs, there is very little control over their circulation among students. While there is a wide variety of reasoning behind NPS use, nothing makes it less harmful.

> These quotes are integrated but a little hard to read — maybe you could paraphrase some of them?

> This quote is well integrated into your own sentence.

> Good presentation of the thesis after all that expert evidence.

(continued)

If it works, it creates an unfair advantage for some students, much like doping in sports. Socially, it's used in party settings alongside other dangerous substances — not for the reasons stimulants were originally intended to be used. Society often sees the use of "study drugs" as harmless academic support, but it should be taken as seriously as any drug abuse out there.

The conclusion is good, but the claim about harm is not well supported: you don't present the negative effects of these drugs. But maybe that's not your point? Make this stronger?

Works Cited

Arria, Amelia, and Robert DuPont. "Nonmedical Prescription Stimulant Use among College Students: Why We Need to Do Something and What We Need to Do." *Journal of Addictive Diseases*, vol. 29, no. 4, Oct. 2010, pp. 417-26.

Berry, D., et al. "Detection of Feigned ADHD in College Students." *Psychological Assessment*, vol. 22, no. 2, June 2010, p. 325.

Centers for Disease Control and Prevention. "Facts about ADHD." *Centers for Disease Control and Prevention*, Centers for Disease Control and Prevention, 16 July 2013, www.cdc.gov/ncbddd/adhd/facts.html. Accessed 8 Aug. 2013.

Labbe, Allison K., and Stephen A. Maisto. "Development of the Stimulant Medication Outcome Expectancies Questionnaire for College Students." *Addictive Behaviors*, vol. 35, no. 7, July 2010, pp. 726-29.

McCabe, Sean Esteban, et al. "Non-medical Use of Prescription Stimulants among US College Students: Prevalence and Correlates from a National Survey." *Addiction*, vol. 100, no. 1, Jan. 2005, pp. 96-106.

U.S. Drug Enforcement Administration. "Drug Scheduling." *DEA/Drug Scheduling*, U.S. Department of Justice, www.justice.gov/dea/druginfo/ds.shtml. Accessed 11 July 2013.

Your list of works cited looks good. All of your sources are completely identified and listed in alphabetical order. And you used the hanging indent — very helpful!

▶ *Talk Amongst Yourselves ...*

Find a partner and review Mara's essay using the *Reality Check!* box on page 364. Then discuss Casey's annotations. Which do you agree with? All of them? Some of them? None of them? Is there any additional feedback you'd give Mara? And perhaps most important, what can you learn from Mara's draft that will help you in drafting your own research paper? Why is that "most important"?

▶ *Now You Try:* **Ethical Use and Citation of Sources**

Remember that paragraph you wrote at the end of Chapter 21 (see page 349)? You know, the one that integrated sources into your own ideas by way of the analytical cycle of development? Sure you do!

Now we'd like you to go back to that paragraph and review it in order to assess your own good *ethos* as a research writer (note that these questions echo those in the checklist on page 364).

▶ Does your paragraph have a clear claim, or main point, that's appropriate to the assignment?

▶ Is that claim well supported with relevant, meaningful factual evidence?

▶ Is the claim developed through appeals to the reader's needs and values?

▶ Does the paragraph make use of valid, authoritative sources to back its central claim?

▶ Are source materials integrated fairly and understandably into the paragraph?

▶ Are all borrowings of words, ideas, or data from sources cited clearly within the text?

▶ Are citations complete, accurate, and usefully presented according to format?

If you find your paragraph wanting in any of the above respects, revise it. And if you're asking yourself if, after this revision, you're done, the answer, dear student, is not quite yet.

The next step is this: now that you are armed with a solid research-backed paragraph to use as a model, go back to the original assignment on page 349, choose a different idea from the list you created in step 2 — an idea other than the one you already wrote about — and then go through the whole process again. Yes, that's right — we'd like you to practice writing more research-backed paragraphs because it's such an important skill.

We're willing to bet that you'll find writing a second paragraph a bit easier than writing the first one. Maybe even a lot easier. And when that happens — when you make that discovery — well, we won't blame you if you decide to just keep writing paragraphs. Before you know it, you'll have an entire research essay, just like Mara!

And One More Thing: *Ethos* and Language Use

Aristotle talked about *ethos* as having three components. The first of these is *being well informed*, which we discussed in detail in the first part of this chapter. The second component is *open-mindedness*, which we spent another big chunk of this chapter talking about. The final component in Aristotle's system of *ethos* is *careful consideration of the reader*.

Aristotle's word for being well informed is *phronesis*, which means "ownership of practical skills and wisdom." For open-mindedness it's *arete*, which roughly means "virtue" or "goodness." And his word for carefully considering the reader is *eunoia*, which means "beautiful thinking."

To achieve Aristotle's final ethical goal — careful consideration of the reader, or *eunoia* — it helps to remember the role of the reader in creating the meaning of what you've written. For a reminder about considering the reader's needs, see Chapter 2 and Chapter 19.

The ethical writer will employ a *tone* (mood or attitude) that is appropriate to the readership, the topic, the situation, and the argument itself. In other words, if you're an ethical and honest writer, you will be mindful of the communication triangle — you remember that, right? For a refresher on achieving the appropriate tone, see Chapter 15, pages 212–14.

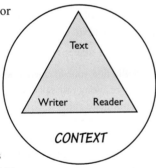

A final, crucial part of doing your very best to achieve a good relationship with your reader is to communicate as clearly and understandably as possible. The more work *you* do to write clearly, the less work your *reader* has to do to understand what you've written. Writing clearly means that you employ standard grammar, create sentences with structural integrity, and use punctuation carefully. If you need to work on any of these issues in your own writing, then be sure to make use of Part 7 of this book, coming up next!

Quick Help for Writing Clearly

▶ Proofreading advice: Chapter 23, page 375
▶ Problems with grammar and word usage: Chapter 24
  • misusing verbs, pronouns, and prepositions
  • commonly confused words
▶ Problems with sentence structure: Chapter 25, page 408
  • fragments and run-on sentences
  • shifts and mixed constructions
  • dangling and misplaced modifiers
▶ Problems with punctuation: Chapter 26, page 422

PART 7

Fine-Tuning the Text

Writing with Style:
Proofread for Clarity and Precision

> I do not think you can start with anything precise. You have to achieve such precision as you can, as you go along.
> — Bertrand Russell

If you have been reading this book in order, then you are already familiar with the idea of *ethos* in writing. But in case you're skipping around the chapters — not that there's anything wrong with that — here's a quick refresher: the writer establishes good *ethos* by demonstrating good and ethical character.

As we discussed at length in Part 6, "Researching Effectively" (Chapters 20–22), writers can establish good *ethos* by becoming knowledgeable about the topics they're covering and by being honest about where their knowledge comes from.

An equally important aspect of *ethos* is thoughtful consideration of the reader. Ethical writers do everything they can to make their writing as understandable as possible. Achieving this quality is largely a matter of careful use of the language: a writer who considers the reader thoughtfully realizes that clear, precise, correct writing is more helpful to the reader than muddled, vague, or sloppy writing. Therefore, the ethical writer employs standard grammar, effective sentence structure, appropriate word usage, accurate spelling, and meaningful punctuation in order to be considerate of the reader.

After you've done your research, gathered your thoughts, constructed your argument, used your sources honestly, revised for content and structure, and edited for coherence — well, then it's time to proofread in order to find and correct errors in spelling, punctuation, and mechanics, as well as typographical errors and any grammatical or word-choice problems you've missed in earlier edits.

This chapter will focus on proofreading — both *why* we do it and *how* to do it. The subsequent chapters in Part 7 will focus on specific types of problems that are commonly identified during proofreading and how to correct them:

▶ Chapter 24 — Problems with grammar and word usage
▶ Chapter 25 — Problems with sentence structure
▶ Chapter 26 — Problems with punctuation

Proofreading Matters

We know what you're thinking: *Come on, we did prewriting and drafting and revision and even editing. Seriously, we need to* proofread *now?*

Yes, you do. You really do. Your ideas *are* arguably more important than your grammar. But at the same time — take a look at this:

> By using correct grammar, or what linguists call the grammar of Standard English in which we will get too later it is an important part of academic and professional writing. Reading our students essay's alot of them have grammar problems such as, the kind's of problems that plague this paragraph, this section of the book we hope, will justify our need to ruthlessly impose our will upon you talking about grammar.

> Ouch!
> Seriously, that's
> just awful.

This paragraph is hard to read because it is grammatically incorrect. Or more accurately, it is not written in Standard English.

USE STANDARD ENGLISH

Standard English is the version of the English language used in academic and professional writing. All dialects of a language are logical and help us communicate, but Standard English just happens to be the variety of English used in academic and professional settings. It is the version of our language that is used in newspapers, books, and magazines.

It is called *standard* because it is the standard for correctness, *not* because it is the form of English heard in everyday situations. People talking in line at the bank or text messaging almost definitely are not using Standard English. And since what we see and hear most frequently is what *sounds* correct to us, then it makes sense to assume *everyday* English is the same thing as *Standard* English. But it isn't.

Not that we are suggesting that there is something wrong with you if you don't use Standard English all the time. Our goal is for you to learn it so that you can choose when to use it (mainly when you are writing something for school or for work) and when not to use it (when you're writing an e-mail to your mom, for example, or texting your best friend).

> When you address different audiences, you most likely will use different levels of formality, and possibly even two different dialects. That's normal and reasonable.

If you're going to miss class because you need to attend a job training session out of town, you will write two very different messages to your professor and your best friend.

Professor Higgins, I am sorry to say that I will need to miss class on Thursday to attend a mandatory training session for my job. I will make sure to get notes from a classmate and to see you during office hours on Friday to pick up any materials I may have missed. Thank you, Casey N. Pointe (Environmental Science, 9:00)	Hey Mara! I totally hafta do this ridonkulous training thing for work on Thurs (don't wanna, gotta do it, what can I say?) Could you take Enviro notes for me? I'll catch up with you Fri if that's cool. C.

In other words, Standard English is like a gorgeous pair of shoes that seem to have been made just for your little black dress (or tuxedo) of college writing. You probably won't want to wear them all the time — in fact, you'd look silly wearing them to the gym or while you're cleaning your house — but without them, your dressy outfit just won't make as much fashion sense. We'd like to show you how to wear those shoes with style and poise, so that when the time is right, you'll have no trouble making the whole outfit work.

THE RULES — AND VIOLATIONS — OF STANDARD ENGLISH

Basically, you need to learn the rules of Standard English so that you can choose when and where to follow them or to break them. Right now, you might not know the rules well enough to be able to do that. Here are some sentences with violations of Standard English that we see and hear all the time. They are so prevalent in everyday speech and writing that many of you will probably not see the problems. But don't worry — we'll help you out at the end of this chapter.

Practice! Violations of Standard English

Each of the following sentences contains at least one violation of the rules of Standard English. Try your hand at identifying and correcting the errors.

1. The room in which the class is held in is stuffy.
2. Bob try's hard, but struggles with chemistry any ways.
3. Just between you and I, grammar is kind of interesting.
4. Yesterday, I seen a new kind of M&M's at Safeway.
5. I am doing a load of laundry, do your socks need washed?
6. Laura, who we did not invite to the party is not speaking to any of us.
7. One should always read their syllabus before class.
8. Gary use to work at the roller rink, but now he doesnt.
9. Mowing the lawn, the grass was too wet and clogged the mower.
10. I eat nails for breakfast, it makes me tough.

Just because you might not see problems in these sentences does not mean that other people won't — especially in academic and professional settings. Think of it this way: language, especially written language, is like a contract — and grammar is like the key to a code we all use. It's a set of shared understandings about how words actually communicate meaning. We can sometimes get away with minor glitches in the code and still be understood. But bigger errors, or persistent errors, put us in violation of the contract.

In a memorable episode of the classic "TV show about nothing," *Seinfeld*, George becomes enraged when a pigeon and a squirrel violate an implied contract that states that however close they come to the tires of a vehicle, they will always get out of the way at the last minute.

Wait, what?
You can't do that!

Language is similar. Whenever you pick up a book and read a sentence.

See what we did there, in that last sentence? We broke the contract. You were expecting another clause — another idea to finish the sentence — and we didn't give you one.

Whenever you pick up a book and read a sentence, even if you're not aware of it, you expect that sentence to conform to the rules of Standard English. And your reader expects the same of your writing. Every time you start writing in an academic or a professional setting, you are automatically signing the contract, whether you want to or not. And proofreading is the best way to ensure that you're living up to your end of the bargain.

The Process of Proofreading

So how should you go about proofreading? What kinds of things should you look for? Well, when you're ready to proofread for sentence structure, grammar, punctuation, and spelling, we recommend that you begin by using your computer's built-in tools for writers.

USE YOUR COMPUTER: SPELL-CHECKING AND GRAMMAR CHECKING

The spell-check function on your word-processing program will catch a lot of common spelling errors that you might miss on your own. It isn't perfect, though, so we have some suggestions for using it wisely.

> *Reality Check!* **Responsible Spell-Checking**
> ▶ Don't automatically accept a suggested spelling from your spell-checker — spell-checkers are often wrong, as in the case of telling Lynne to change her last name to "lurch," or recommending that Allison change her first name to "allusion."

(continued)

> ▶ If you're unsure whether your computer knows more than you do (is it really "canceled," not "cancelled"?), check an alternate source, such as an actual dictionary.
> ▶ Don't fool yourself into thinking that spell-checking is a valid substitute for proofreading. Your computer doesn't know which word you meant to use.

That last point is really important, so please take a moment to read it again. Seriously.

Because your computer is not as smart as you are, it cannot figure out what you meant to say in context. All it knows is what you typed and whether those combinations of letters are actually words. As a result, it won't catch errors like this:

I thing you should defiantly ask for there permission.

Even though there's not a single misspelled word in the above sentence, it still has three errors that can be classified as spelling errors and that must be corrected by a human in the following way:

I **think** you should **definitely** ask for **their** permission.

Your computer's word-processing program probably also has a grammar checker. It's the thing that underlines words and phrases and whole sentences in green to indicate that you've made a grammatical error. The thing is, though, the grammar-check function (at least the one in Microsoft Word) is sometimes wrong. It may tell you that a sentence you've written is incorrect when it actually isn't. This is because your computer has a lot of information in its memory, but it doesn't really have knowledge or experience, and it certainly doesn't have wisdom. It can't tell the difference between doing something fresh and interesting with language and doing something wrong with language.

> The grammar-check function can be a good tool, especially for beginning writers or writers who aren't quite comfortable with their language skills. But remember: just like the spell-checker, the grammar checker needs to be used wisely. Don't let it bully you!

USE YOUR BRAIN: ACTUAL PROOFREADING

After you've used your spell-checker to catch simple errors — and either ignored your grammar checker or used it very skeptically — it's time for you to proofread your draft yourself in order to identify and correct the errors that your computer didn't, or couldn't, catch. (Yes, we know this step's a drag, but it's worth it.) A few tips:

Revise and edit in stages. Be willing to rewrite (and rewrite) so that your eye will be able to detect increasingly sophisticated errors. Recognize that when you're focusing on problems with content, you may not notice structural issues; when you're addressing concerns with coherence, you might have a hard time seeing imprecise language use.

Keep valuable reference materials on hand. It's important to have reference resources — dictionaries and grammar handbooks, for example — available to use when you're revising and editing your work. Note that this book might very well be one such resource. Just look at what we have for you!

- ▶ Basic grammar and punctuation (Appendix A)
- ▶ Citation of research sources (Appendix B)
- ▶ Common problems with grammar (Chapter 24)
- ▶ Common problems with sentence structure (Chapter 25)
- ▶ Common problems with punctuation (Chapter 26)

We cannot stress enough how important it is that you **have fresh eyes read through your draft carefully** to catch any remaining errors. *And where am I going to get those fresh eyes?* you may be wondering. Well, you can start with your own. They'll be fresh enough if you proofread your draft after some time away from it — at least a few hours.

Reading with Fresh Eyes

After you've read something you've written 5, 10, or 15 times, your eyes won't see mistakes you've made.

Your brain will register what you MEANT TO write rather than what you DID write.

Even if you've set aside your draft and come back to it with fresh eyes, it's a good idea to get another person — or a few other people — to proofread your work for you. If they're careful, they'll almost certainly catch something that you would swear wasn't there when you read it yourself.

Finally, **read your essay backwards** (that is, from end to beginning, sentence by sentence) before turning it in. We know that sounds weird, but trust us, reading backwards works. It allows you to focus on surface-level problems like spelling and typographical errors without being distracted by your brilliant content.

Remember this paragraph from earlier in the chapter? Sure you do! It's the paragraph that nearly drove poor Grammster out of his mind back on page 376.

By using correct grammar, or what linguists call the grammar of Standard English in which we will get too later it is an important part of academic and professional writing. Reading our students essay's alot of them have grammar problems such as, the kind's of problems that plague this paragraph, this section of the book we hope, will justify our need to ruthlessly impose our will upon you talking about grammar.

Now we want you to read a version of the paragraph that has been proofread using all of the strategies we've presented so far. All instances of nonstandard English have been edited for correctness. In other words, all of the actual mistakes (violations of the rules of Standard English) have been fixed, and the paragraph is now grammatically correct. (If any of the grammatical terms used below freak you out, remember that you can always look them up in Appendix A or in the chapters mentioned in the annotations.)

~~By~~ Using correct grammar, or what linguists call the grammar of Standard English, ~~in~~ which we will get ~~too~~ **to** later, ~~it~~ is an important part of academic and professional writing. ~~Reading our students essay's alot~~ **A lot** of ~~them~~ **our students' essays** have grammar problems, such as~~;~~ the kind~~'~~**s** of problems that plague this paragraph; this section of the book, we hope, will justify ~~our need to~~ **the way we've** ruthlessly impose**d** our will upon you **by** talking about grammar.	Removed "by" and "in" to correct mixed constructions. Corrected misused word "too" and incorrect shift. Deleted dangling modifier. Inserted subject ("our students' essays"). Deleted unnecessary comma & possessive Corrected comma splice by adding a semicolon and a comma. Corrected misplaced modifier. Inserted necessary preposition.

And voilà! Here's a cleaned-up version of the paragraph:

Using correct grammar, or what linguists call the grammar of Standard English, which we will get to later, is an important part of academic and professional writing. A lot of our students' essays have grammar problems, such as the kinds of problems that plague this paragraph; this section of the book, we hope, will justify the way we've ruthlessly imposed our will upon you by talking about grammar.

Okay, it might be correct now, but it's still not really very good, is it?

Beyond Rules and Violations: Writing to *Express*, Not to *Impress*

Our revised paragraph may technically be free of errors now, but it's still awkward. We can picture the reader squinting while reading, or maybe frowning a bit, in an attempt to decipher what we really meant to say. That's because writing with clarity and precision is about more than just correctness according to the rules of Standard English — it's also about *style*.

The word style refers to a writer's diction (word choice) and syntax (sentence structure). Each writer has his or her individual style. We all have our own favorite words and phrases, for example. But there is also such a thing as a solid academic style in writing. To establish yourself as a reader-friendly writer of academic essays, you'll certainly proofread to ensure that you haven't left any actual errors of grammar or punctuation. But you will also pay attention to the elegance and simplicity of your style. And the best way to write simply and elegantly is to remember that good writers write to *express*, not to *impress*. In other words, you should focus on what you're trying to communicate rather than on trying to sound like you're communicating something.

Wondering how you can accomplish that simple, elegant style? We thought you'd never ask!

First, and most important, **read consciously** with an eye toward understanding why clear writing is clear and why unclear writing is unclear. If you feel that a particular phrase is clear or unclear, don't stop there: think about it. Ask questions. Answer those questions. Figure it out.

> I think that paragraph sounds so awkward because it wanders away from the point.

> The different parts of some of the sentences also seem to be in the wrong order. I can't figure out whether it really says what it wants to mean.

Then, make sure you **read your essay aloud** so that you can hear your ideas and your expression of those ideas. Note that this is particularly important if you are an auditory learner (a person who learns better from listening than from watching or reading). Whenever you catch yourself zoning out or frowning or stumbling over your own words — well, each of those reactions is an indication that you have some adjustments to make in order to be clear and precise.

And how, exactly, do you make those adjustments? Well, when you stumble over or frown at something in your writing, you should ask yourself, *What did I really mean to say?* This sometimes works better if you do it while reading aloud. When you hear yourself say something odd like, *Using the dishwasher, dinner cleanup it wasn't that bad this time compared to last*, just stop and ask yourself, *Okay, seriously, what am I trying to say?* And then the answer will come to you: *Well, I'm trying to say that the last time we had a dinner party, the cleanup was hard, but it was better this time because we used the dishwasher.* Now, you might still want to edit that down a bit for wordiness — maybe to something like, *Cleanup after our last dinner party was much easier than after the previous one because this time we used the dishwasher.* See how much better that is? And all because we simply asked what idea we're trying to express.

Remember that paragraph about Standard English? The one we proofread and edited for correctness? Well, you'll be pleased to know that we've followed our own advice and done another edit, this time with an eye toward a more elegant style:

Using ~~correct~~ grammar **correctly**, or **using** what linguists call the grammar of Standard English, ~~which we will get to later,~~ is an important part of academic and professional writing. ~~A lot of our students'~~ **Many, if not most, student** essays ~~have~~ **contain errors in** grammar ~~problems~~ **and usage,** ~~such as the kinds of~~ much like the problems **that plagued the earlier draft** of this paragraph. **In** this section of the book, **we will discuss the importance of Standard English in college writing**. ~~we~~ **We** hope you will find that **the advice and examples that follow make up for the way that,** ~~will justify the way~~ we've ruthlessly imposed our **grammatical** will upon you ~~by talking about grammar.~~	Adverb (*correctly*) modifies *using.* Wordy. Eliminate casual tone. Fresher, more precise phrasing. Two ideas need two sentences. Adds precision. *Make up for* fits the tone better than *justify.* Cut wordy phrase.

And here's our significantly more elegant version of the paragraph again, all cleaned up and ready to go — and in case you're tempted to think we haven't really changed it much, you can compare it to the original:

Original

By using correct grammar, or what linguists call the grammar of Standard English in which we will get too later it is an important part of academic and professional writing. Reading our students essay's alot of them have grammar problems such as, the kind's of problems that plague this paragraph, this section of the book we hope, will justify our need to ruthlessly impose our will upon you talking about grammar.

Improved

Using grammar correctly, or using what linguists call Standard English, is an important part of academic and professional writing. Many, if not most, student essays contain errors in grammar and usage, much like the problems that plagued the earlier draft of this paragraph. In this section of the book, we will discuss the importance of Standard English in college writing. We hope you will find that the advice and examples that follow make up for the way that we've ruthlessly imposed our grammatical will upon you.

We've covered quite a bit of territory in this chapter that we think you'll find really useful in proofreading your own writing. So much territory, in fact, that you'll probably appreciate a handy list of things to consider when you're giving that essay a final go-round before submitting it to your professor for a grade.

Reality Check! Proofreading

► Have I used the spell-checker wisely?
► Have I turned off the grammar checker (or at least used it thoughtfully)?
► Have I edited and proofread in levels, finding and correcting different types of errors?

- ▶ Have I made good use of reference resources when I should?
- ▶ Have I ensured, one way or another, that fresh eyes have seen my paper?
- ▶ Have I read my essay backwards to catch those last few surface-level glitches?
- ▶ Have I read my paper consciously to catch unclear passages?
- ▶ Have I read it aloud to hear any problems that I couldn't see?
- ▶ Have I responded to any awkward passages by asking myself what I meant to say?

▶ *Let Us Show You:* Proofreading

Remember Casey's essay about plagiarism? We certainly hope so: he worked on it throughout Parts 2, 3, and 4 (prewriting, drafting, and revising). Before he turned it in for credit in class, he made sure to take that all-important final step of proofreading carefully, using the Proofreading checklist we just gave you.

> Look how many errors I caught in just one paragraph! And this was *after* I already thought I was done. Good thing I did this before turning it in!

As a result, the college still **~~focusses~~ focuses** on plagiarism **~~as a kind of~~** intellectual theft, which makes sense because school is built upon this idea of "intellectual property." Professors at universities are hired partly because **~~of~~ they will do** research and **create** original ideas. But when you think about it, their ideas aren't original, because they learned from their professors. Sometimes I think **~~its~~ it's** very hard to tell where the line is between learning **from someone** and plagiarizing someone's idea, and honestly I think professors are probably more likely to **~~plagiarize~~ cross that line** than students because professors don't usually credit their sources when they're teaching.

▶ *Talk Amongst Yourselves . . .*

After reviewing the changes Casey made to this paragraph as a result of proofreading, get together with a partner and look at each change individually. Can you identify what problem Casey was solving with each correction? Are there any changes that don't actually correct a problem? Are there other errors that Casey didn't catch?

▶ *Now You Try:* **Proofreading**

If you have a draft essay that has already been through the larger revision process — that is, you've revised it for content, structure, and coherence — you can now use the Proofreading *Reality Check!* box on pages 386–87 to catch any surface-level errors that are cluttering up the clarity and elegance of your writing.

Even if you don't have a revised draft handy, you can take a completed piece of writing — say, something you've already turned in for this class, or even something you wrote for a previous class — and proofread it carefully.

Be sure to ask for help from your instructor, a classmate, or a writing consultant (at your campus writing center) if you're not sure whether that mistake you've found is actually an error that needs correcting.

Chapter 24

Grammar and Usage: Make Your Words Behave

> First they came for the verbs, and I said nothing because verbing weirds language. Then they arrival for the nouns, and I speech nothing because I no verbs.
> — Nancy Lebovitz

Sometimes writers create problematic sentences by using words ungrammatically or in non-standard ways. The vast majority of the time, the words being abused are either verbs or pronouns, which is why much of this chapter is devoted to discussion of problems with these parts of speech. But we'll also clue you in to some common problems with adjectives, adverbs, and prepositions — as well as the pernicious problem of commonly confused words.

I *love* this chapter.

Problems with Verbs: Voice, Mood, Form, Agreement

It's common for student writers to use weak, passive, or otherwise backward verbs instead of strong, muscular, assertive verbs. Active and assertive verbs liven up sentences; weak, passive verbs obscure meaning, creating error in voice.

ERRORS IN VOICE

Verb voice is a grammatical term referring to the relationship between the action that the verb describes and the subject and object of the verb. In other words, it's about the relationship between the person or thing that *acts* and the person or thing that *receives* the action.

Use the Active Voice

The distinction between the **active voice** and the **passive voice** in grammar is simple: either the subject of the sentence is *active* (it's doing something, as in "students solve puzzles") or it's *passive* (it's being acted upon, as in "they are given answers").

389

Active or passive voice has nothing to do with verb *tense*, which indicates whether something happened in the past, present, or future. Rather, it has to do with whether the verb is preceded by an *active subject*, someone or something that is doing what the verb says.

This distinction actually goes beyond grammar because it points out whether the subject of the sentence is being active or passive. The *active voice* directly states who is doing what:

A giant tidal wave swept my village out to sea.

active voice

This sentence is active because the subject comes first in the sentence, followed by the verb and then the direct object. The *passive voice* expresses action indirectly:

My village was swept out to sea by a giant tidal wave.

passive voice

This sentence is passive because the thing being acted upon (*village*) comes first in the sentence, followed by the verb (*was swept,* a weak linking verb) and then finally by the thing doing the action (i.e., the agent, *tidal wave*).

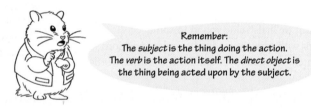

Remember:
The *subject* is the thing doing the action.
The *verb* is the action itself. The *direct object* is
the thing being acted upon by the subject.

The moral of the story is use the active voice whenever you can. The passive voice is grammatically correct, but it's less clear. It can result in sentences like these:

A good time *was had* by all.

[*vague*]

Native Americans *were placed* on reservations.

[*Who placed them there?*]

The priceless vase in the dining room *was broken.*

[*Who broke it?*]

Any reader with the slightest touch of skepticism would recognize the problem in these sentences: unless the subject is truly not known (which is a possibility only in the third example — perhaps everyone arrived home to discover the broken vase and nobody involved has any idea how it happened), the reader will find that each sentence tries to weasel out of assigning or accepting responsibility. Writers who avoid directly stating *who did what* undermine their own credibility.

Instead of being passive and unclear, be direct with specific nouns and active verbs:

Everyone had a good time.

The U.S. government placed Native Americans on reservations.

I broke the priceless vase in the dining room.

Active voice and active verbs really do make sentences sound better. The sentences are so much clearer, it's almost like they weigh less.

Use Strong Verbs

While we're on the subject of voice, a related issue is using *strong* verbs rather than *weak* verbs. Strong verbs show clear action. Weak verbs take no action. For example, many writers abuse the weak or linking verb *to be* by using it to weaken or obscure the action in a sentence:

Sylvia was resistant to surrendering her passport even though she was in violation of international law.

This sentence would be stronger, more direct, and more concise without the use of *to be*. Instead, the writer should consider what action is really implied by the passive verb phrases *was resistant to* and *was in violation of*:

Sylvia *resisted* surrendering her passport even though she *had violated* international law.

However, you will use a weak or linking verb (in a form of *to be*) when you want to define or describe a subject with a *subject complement*. Here's an example of a weak or linking verb used appropriately:

Wanda and Gretel are excellent gymnasts.

    subject   linking   complement
               verb

In this case, the writer could not use a stronger and more direct verb than *are*. Such a verb doesn't exist. The writer can't, for example, say *Wanda and Gretel*

> Rather than expressing action,
> linking verbs express what the subject of the sentence
> is, was, or will be. Complements are words that describe
> or define the subject. See Appendix A for more.

gymnasticate excellently because (bummer!) there's no such verb as *gymnasticate*.

ERRORS IN MOOD

Verb mood is a grammatical term referring to a form of verb used for a specific function in a sentence.

In English there are three moods: the **indicative** (used almost all the time), the **imperative** (employed in commands that use the implied *you* as the subject; see "Sentence Purpose" in Appendix A), and the **subjunctive** (used in expressing wishes, requests, and conditions contrary to reality). Of these three, the subjunctive is the one most likely to cause you trouble.

Use the Subjunctive Correctly

So how do you know when to use the subjunctive mood? Fortunately, it's quite simple. There are really only three situations in which you need the subjunctive:

1. Conditions contrary to reality that begin with the conjunction *if*

If Della <u>were</u> the Jolly Green Giant, she <u>would never eat</u> vegetables.

subjunctive [*not* was]   conditional
mood of
to be

The sentence above is correct because Della is not actually the Jolly Green Giant, and she likely will never *be* the Jolly Green Giant. Therefore, the sentence is expressing a condition contrary to reality.

Be careful, though! The mere existence of *if* doesn't require the subjunctive. When *if* is used to indicate what *might happen* rather than what is contrary to reality, you need the indicative mood.

If she <u>was</u> such a good musician, why didn't she win the competition?

indicative
mood of *to be*

2. Conditions contrary to reality that express a wish

I wish that my textbook <u>were</u> made of chocolate.

subjunctive
[*not* was]

This wish is contrary to reality because the textbook, sadly, is not actually made of chocolate — and it never will be made of chocolate. Note that a wish of a more realistic nature typically uses the **conditional** rather than the subjunctive:

I wish that Albert <u>would do</u> my homework for me.
　　　　　　　　conditional

3. **Requests or commands in clauses beginning with the relative pronoun *that***

My mother requests that all of her children <u>be</u> ready for the zombie apocalypse.
　　　　　　　　　　　　subjunctive
　　　　　　　　　　　　[*not* are]

We recommend that Gonzalez <u>kiss</u> his job goodbye.
　　　　　　　　　　subjunctive
　　　　　　　　　　[*not* kisses]

ERRORS IN FORM

Problems with verb forms occur when the behavior of the verb or **verbal** in the sentence is misunderstood or ambiguous.

Check this out:

Elliot's job is picking up.

You might be asking yourself: Does Elliot pick up things for a living? Or is he getting busier at work, so things are picking up? This sentence doesn't give us enough context to understand its subject, so it's impossible to tell whether *picking* is a gerund (noun) or a verb.

> A *verbal* is a form of a verb that is behaving like an adjective or a noun. Read more about verbals in Appendix A.

Two Troublesome Verbs: *Use* and *Suppose*

By far the most common problem with verb form involves the verbs *to use* and *to suppose*. Why these two verbs? It has to do with how we use them when we talk. We often use them as past participles (*used, supposed*) preceding an infinitive (*to go, to be, to have,* etc.) to create sentences such as *I used to go* and *I'm supposed to go.*

However, in speech it can sound like people are not using the past participial form of the verb. Instead, their sentences sound like *I use to go,* or *I'm suppose to go.*

Here are some more examples of this verb error:

I use to work at a coffee shop.

Gretchen, you were not suppose to be in there.

In these examples, *use* and *suppose* need to be past participles. (Think about it: we know from the rest of the first sentence that working at the coffee shop happened in the past.) The verbs need to be in the past-tense form, like this:

I *used* to work at a coffee shop.

Gretchen, you were not *supposed* to be in there.

SUBJECT-VERB AGREEMENT ERRORS

A sentence is like a family: a bunch of individuals living in close quarters who sometimes have to make adjustments in order to get along. If the subject and the verb don't get along with each other, the whole sentence is over. Consider this sentence:

Verbs has to agree with their subjects.

The subject of the sentence (*Verbs*) is a plural noun. However, the verb (*has to agree*) goes with a singular noun. Thus this sentence illustrates its own point: verbs must agree with their subjects in number in order to make sense. Get it?

One common agreement error of this kind happens in passive constructions, like this one:

There is too many commercials on TV.

The writer of this sentence thought that the word *there* was the subject, when it's really the phrase *too many commercials*. Yes, we know, normally the subject of a sentence comes before the verb, but there are a few exceptions — most notably in some sentences that begin with *there* or *it*. If we rearrange this sentence so the subject comes before the verb, it's easier to recognize the subject:

Too many commercials is on TV.

And now you can probably see that this sentence should be revised in one of these ways:

Too many commercials *are* on TV.

There *are* too many commercials on TV.

In most cases, speakers of English as a first language do not have trouble with subject-verb agreement. There are a few exceptions, though. Look at these sentences, for example:

Sentences with Subject-Verb Agreement Problems

1. There is quite a few cars on the freeway today.
2. High levels of stress causes me to consume Reese's Pieces.
3. The committee like the third applicant best.
4. The bowl of cherries were on the counter, waiting to be eaten.

5. Neither Bob nor John like watching football.

6. Everyone want a ride in my new car.

All of these sentences have a problem with subject-verb agreement. Each problem results either from misunderstanding what the subject actually is (as in sentences 1, 2, and 4) or from misidentifying the subject as singular when it's really plural, or vice versa (as in sentences 3, 5, and 6). The sentences should actually look like this:

Sentences with Subject-Verb Agreement Problems Corrected

1. There *are* quite a few cars on the freeway today.

2. High levels of stress *cause* me to consume Reese's Pieces.

3. The committee *likes* the third applicant best.

4. The bowl of cherries *was* on the counter, waiting to be eaten.

5. Neither Bob nor John *likes* watching football.

6. Everyone *wants* a ride in my new car.

And just in case you think we're keeping all the fun grammar exercises for ourselves, here are a whole bunch we made just for you. Have fun!

Practice! Problems with Verbs

Edit the following sentences to correct any problems with verb mood, voice, form, or agreement that you can find. Not every sentence will have an error.

1. The bowl of petunias on the counter are quite fragrant.
2. There's not a lot of people at the mall today.
3. The French Club meet at Tully's on Tuesday afternoons.
4. I wish I was an Oscar Mayer wiener.
5. Susan asks only that her next boyfriend brushes his teeth regularly.
6. Dorris and Cletus are very good writers.
7. John is in vocal opposition to the war.
8. For as long as I can remember, the laundry has been done by my mother.
9. Susan's face looked slightly jaundice.
10. I use to have a parakeet.

Problems with Pronouns: Agreement, Reference, Perspective, Case

Pronouns are very useful, but they need to follow a few rules:

▶ They need to agree with their **antecedents**;

▶ They need to actually *have* **clear antecedents**; and

▶ They need to be used in the right **case**.

ERRORS IN PRONOUN AGREEMENT

Stop us if you've heard this one before. A sentence is like a family: a bunch of individuals living in close quarters who sometimes have to make adjustments in order to get along. If a pronoun in a sentence doesn't agree with the noun it replaces (called its antecedent), the whole sentence is over.

And no, you're not losing your mind: you did read the same analogy just a couple pages back. (To be fair, we told you to stop us if you'd heard it before.) You're hearing it again because the problem that *pronouns* can have with agreement is very similar to the problem that *verbs* can have with agreement — for instance:

A pronoun must agree with their antecedent.

If you get the joke, you may not need to read this section. If you don't get it, here's the explanation. In the sentence, the word *pronoun* is singular — that is, it's *one* pronoun, not multiple pronouns. Therefore, it does not agree with *their*, the pronoun that refers back to it, because *their* is plural.

Just as a subject must agree with its verb in number, a pronoun must agree in number with the noun or pronoun that it refers back to.

Practice Good Pronoun Agreement

What can be done about errors in pronoun-antecedent agreement? you ask. Take a look at the following sentence:

If a student wants to pass English 101, they will need to become an expert in sentence diagramming.

This sentence might sound fine to you, but it isn't. *They* is a plural pronoun, so it can't logically be used to refer to *student*, which is a singular noun.

There are three good solutions to the problem: (1) change the antecedent; (2) change the pronoun; or (3) reword the sentence to eliminate the pronoun.

1. If *students* want to pass English 101, <u>they</u> will need to become experts in sentence diagramming.

2. If <u>a student</u> wants to pass English 101, *he or she* will need to become an expert in sentence diagramming.

3. <u>To pass English 101,</u> *a student* will need to become an expert in sentence diagramming.

As we mentioned at the beginning of this section, pronouns must agree with their antecedents. Even in a sentence with a string of pronouns all referring back to one antecedent, this agreement must continue. Consider this sentence:

When a person is crossing the street, he or she should always look both ways or they run the risk of being hit by a car.

Don't see the problem? Keep looking. This sentence has multiple pronouns that all have the same antecedent: *one*, a singular noun. The rule says singular nouns have to be replaced by singular pronouns. *He or she* replaced *one*, so that's good — *he or she* is singular. But later in the sentence there's a *they*! Since *they* is plural, it does not agree with the singular noun. Both pronouns in the sentence need to be singular:

When a person is crossing the street, he or she should always look both ways or he or she runs the risk of being hit by a car.

Style with Pronoun Agreement

Here's a twist: the corrected sentence you just read uses pronouns correctly, which is a good thing, but it also repeats *he or she* a lot. That can get annoying. If you use multiple-word phrases such as *he or she* too many times in one sentence — or in a group of sentences — your sentence style might suffer. In other words, your grammar won't be wrong, but your reader won't be happy. To keep your reader sailing along smoothly, you'll want to correct the problem using method 1 or 3 on page 396: either change the antecedent or reword the sentence to eliminate the pronoun.

When *people are* crossing the street, *they* should always look both ways or *they* run the risk of being hit by a car.

When *a person* is crossing the street, *he or she* should always look both ways *or run the risk* of being hit by a car.

UNCLEAR PRONOUN REFERENCE

As you now know, a pronoun must agree with its antecedent in number and gender. But a pronoun must *have* a specific antecedent in the first place. In other words, you should not use a pronoun (especially *this, that, they*, or *it*) to refer to an entire clause or a vague idea; also, the person or thing that it refers to should be easily identifiable. Here are some examples of pronoun references that are vague or unclear:

The food at this restaurant is disgusting. They should improve it.

All of this is important. It is why we must act now.

Susan told Bethany that she was in trouble.

These sentences could all be made clearer if the writer specified what the pronouns refer to. A pronoun should clearly refer to some specific person, place, thing, or idea. If the surrounding sentences don't make clear what exactly the pronoun in a sentence refers to, then that sentence will need to be rewritten. The preceding examples of vague or unclear pronoun reference could be improved like this:

> The food at this restaurant is disgusting. *The chef* should improve it.

> *This injustice* is why we must act now.

> *Bethany* was in trouble, and Susan told her so.

The second sentence still might not be specific enough, depending on the context. The surrounding sentences should make crystal clear which specific injustice the writer is referring to and why it requires action.

SHIFTS IN PERSPECTIVE

You may already be familiar with the terms *first person*, *second person*, and *third person*. Maybe you discussed the significance of the unreliable first-person narrator or the limited third-person point of view in one of your high school English classes. Basically, these "persons" are three different perspectives from which we can write or speak.

▶ **First person:** *I saw Molly Ringwald at the mall last week.* First-person pronouns are *I/me/mine* (singular) and *we/us/ours* (plural).

▶ **Second person:** *You saw Molly Ringwald at the mall last week. You* is the only second-person pronoun. It works for both singular and plural as well as both subjective and objective cases. It only changes for the possessive case: *yours.*

▶ **Third person:** *Jon Cryer saw Molly Ringwald at the mall last week.* The third person has an objective view of things and talks not about what *I* (the speaker) did or what *you* (the reader) did, but about what some *third party* did. So the third-person pronouns are *he/him/his, she/her/hers, they/them/theirs,* and *it/its.* Other nouns and proper nouns (e.g., *the barista, that girl, Randolph Smith, Dr. Jones*) are also in the third person.

Much of this book is written in the first-person plural — with the pronoun *we.* That's because *we* — Allison and I — are talking to you together.

Problems can arise when you shift perspective from one person (such as first person, *I*) to another (such as second person, *you*) without realizing what's happened.

> I saw Molly Ringwald at the mall and you wouldn't believe how pretty she was.

If you start writing from a first-person perspective, stay there — and the same with the second-person and third-person perspectives. Otherwise your writing will become unclear.

> *I* saw Molly Ringwald at the mall and *I* couldn't believe how pretty she was.

Avoid the Rhetorical Use of *You*

Shifts in perspective are very common. You might make them — or read them — regularly, especially the very popular rhetorical use of *you* (using *you* to stand in for "all people" or "people in general"). Still, popularity doesn't make these shifts correct or standard. Take a look at this example:

> The other day I went to dinner at Parma, where you have your choice of soup or salad.

Wondering why this sentence is incorrect? Take a look: the speaker begins in the first person (*I went*) and then shifts into the second person (*you have*). The problem is that the writer is using *you* rhetorically. It's not that the speaker went to dinner at Parma where you and you alone, dear reader, had your choice of soup or salad — presumably everyone who goes to that restaurant has a choice of soup or salad. So the sentence could be fixed in a few different ways:

> The other day I went to dinner at Parma, *where I had* my choice of soup or salad.

> The other day I went to dinner at Parma, *where the choices are* soup or salad.

> The other day I went to dinner at Parma, *which offers a choice* of soup or salad.

The key, really, is to avoid rhetorical use of the pronoun *you*. In other words, don't use *you* when you really mean "everyone" — use it only if you actually mean the person you're addressing.

> When we use *you* in this book, which we do all the time, we're not using it rhetorically. We're really talking to you. Yes, *you*.

PROBLEMS WITH PRONOUN CASE

Some pronouns change form depending on whether they are in the subject or the object position. Personal pronouns — and the relative pronoun *who* — will always be in either the **subjective**, the **objective**, or the **possessive case**, depending on their place or function in a sentence.

If a pronoun is the *subject* of a verb — as in the sentence *I like cake*, for instance — it will be in the subjective case. If a pronoun is the *object* of a verb or preposition — for instance, *Bob baked **me** a cake*, or *Bob gave the cake to **her*** — it will be in the objective case.

It works like this:

To whom should we give the cake?
<u>To whom</u>   <u>we</u>   <u>cake</u>
objective   subjective   object
case   case

Who wants cake?
<u>Who</u>   <u>cake</u>
subjective   object
case

Whose cake is this?
<u>Whose cake</u>
possessive subject
case

To see why the first sentence needs *whom* and the second sentence needs *who* — even though both pronouns appear to be in the subject position — all you have to do is rewrite each question as a statement and plug in a personal pronoun:

We should give the cake to **she**.
[*Um, no.*]

We should give the cake to **her**.
[*Yes!*]

Him wants cake.
[*Not so much, no.*]

He wants cake.
[*That works!*]

> Use the subjective-case *who* when you need a subject, and use the objective-case *whom* when you need an object. That's the secret to using *who* and *whom*!

Practice! Problems with Pronouns

Edit the following sentences to fix any problems that you find with pronoun-antecedent agreement, pronoun reference, pronoun perspective, or pronoun case.

  1. Everyone has a right to their own opinion.
  2. Egypt will be holding their presidential election next week.

3. A student can improve his or her grades if they study for a short period daily.
4. In my third-grade spelling bee, you had to spell "cattywampus," which nobody could do.
5. Wallace threw the ashtray at the mirror and broke it.
6. Just between you and I, Trader Joe's is overrated.
7. Whom is that man lurking in the corner?
8. Who's cat is that?
9. Bob gave Todd and I the wrenches.
10. I am the kind of person who minds their p's and q's.

Problems with Prepositions

Have you ever tried to learn a new language? If you are a native speaker of English, imagine for a minute that you aren't. Having learned impeccable English grammar and loads of vocabulary, how would you make sense of statements like *It's raining cats and dogs* or *Wilma kicked the bucket*? How would you know that it's standard to write, "I agree with the decision," but not to write, "I agree to the decision"? These phrases are **idioms**, set phrases that exist in a particular language and follow no easily specified grammatical rules.

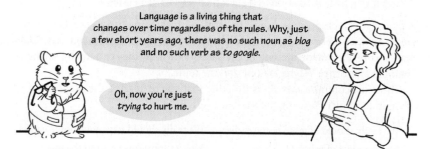

Language is a living thing that changes over time regardless of the rules. Why, just a few short years ago, there was no such noun as *blog* and no such verb as *to google*.

Oh, now you're just trying to hurt me.

Language is created by its speakers. Think of it as a mutually agreed-upon contract. (Remember that idea from Chapter 23?) We understand each other because we agree to use the same words to mean the same things. We would be violating that unofficial contract if we suddenly began referring to paragraphs as "banana slugs."

However, if you and all of your friends began using the word *dinglehopper* in place of the word *fork*, depending on how many friends you have, and in how many parts of the English-speaking world they live, there is a slim chance that *dinglehopper* could eventually work its way into the dictionary. That's because the people who write the dictionaries aren't creative writers — they're reporters. They don't make up words or even decide which words get to exist; they simply pay attention to what the native speakers of a language are saying and then write that down.

Preposition use is largely idiomatic. There is no grammatical reason for using "fascinated by" rather than "fascinated about," but frankly it just sounds weird if you don't. Why is it standard to say "I worked hard on my paper" rather than "I worked hard for my paper"? Sadly, the answer is simply that the standard idiom requires the use of *on*. It's not about logic. It's not even about clearly defined rules. Rather, it's about absorbing (if you're a native speaker) or memorizing (if you're not). Following are some sentences that contain commonly misused prepositions. See if you can spot and correct them.

There must be some explanation to the mess in the hallway.

Karen has a strong belief on the value of hard work.

Both kids are fully capable to do the work.

Mr. Wingo intends on throwing a barbecue next Friday.

Yes, Mimi, but my situation is terribly different than yours.

ERRORS BASED ON MISHEARD PREPOSITIONS

A final error in preposition use is the result of mishearing the way certain words are pronounced. For example, you might *think* you're hearing someone say, "Batman and Bruce Wayne are one in the same," but what they're actually saying is "Batman and Bruce Wayne are one and the same."

The most common mix-up is thinking that you're hearing the preposition *of* when in fact you're hearing the auxiliary verb *have*.

We really should of gone home earlier.   We really should *have* gone home earlier.

Melissa must of missed the bus.   Melissa must *have* missed the bus.

You'll learn more about similar kinds of errors soon, in the section on commonly confused words, which is coming right up. But first . . .

Problems with Adjectives and Adverbs

In simplest terms, an adjective is used to modify (or describe) a noun or pronoun, whereas an adverb is used to modify a verb, an adjective, another adverb, a phrase, a clause, or an entire sentence. In other words, if the word modifies a noun or pronoun, then it's an adjective; if it modifies anything else, it's an adverb. (If you are unclear about the uses of adjectives and adverbs, refer to Appendix A, pages 447–49, for a refresher.)

Check out the two sentences below. Is one of these sentences correct? Are they both correct? Are they both incorrect?

My dog smells bad.

My dog smells badly.

In fact, they're both correct, but they mean two entirely different things. In the first sentence, the adjective *bad* describes the noun *dog* — so the sentence means that the dog stinks. In the second sentence, the adverb *badly* describes the verb *smells* — so the sentence means that the dog's nose doesn't work very well. See the difference?

USE COMPARATIVE AND SUPERLATIVE ADJECTIVES CORRECTLY

Another fairly common problem with adjectives is the misuse of comparative and superlative forms. A **comparative adjective** is the *-er* form of an adjective (*stronger, sillier, quicker*) and is used to make a comparison between two nouns:

Edward is *cuter* than Walt.

Writing is *harder* than reading.

This tuna is *fishier* than the salmon.

A **superlative adjective** is the *-est* form (*cleanest, bravest, dumbest*) and is used to highlight one noun from among a group of three or more:

Edward is *the cutest* of all the puppies.

Writing is *the hardest* task in this class.

This tuna is *the fishiest* I've ever tasted.

The problem with comparatives and superlatives occurs when a writer confuses their uses. See if you can correct these errors in comparative and superlative adjective use:

Compared to Walt, Edward is the cutest.

Writing is the harder of all the tasks in this class.

We had both tuna and salmon, and the tuna was the fishiest.

And hey, here's a fun rule. When creating a comparative or a superlative, you can generally just add -*er* or -*est* to the end of a one-syllable or two-syllable adjective:

- smart, smarter, smartest
- witty, wittier, wittiest
- grouchy, grouchier, grouchiest

But once you get up to three or more syllables, it's best to use the adverbs *more* and *most* to indicate the comparative and superlative:

- difficult, more difficult, most difficult (*instead of* difficulter *or* difficultest)
- beautiful, more beautiful, most beautiful (*not* beautifuller *or* beautifullest)

And now, here are the answers to our mini-quiz:

Compared to Walt, Edward is the cuter one.

Writing is the hardest of all the tasks in this class.

We had both tuna and salmon, and the tuna was fishier.

Commonly Misused / Confused Words

Often when writers choose — and use — the wrong word for a particular situation, the misused word is a **homophone**. That is, the word sounds exactly the same as another word that means something else. For example, the writer confuses *to* for *too* or *two*, or *there* for *their* or *they're*.

Even more interesting, many commonly confused words are *almost* homophones — that is, they sound *almost* the same but not quite. Here are some of the more frequently misused pairs of homophones or near homophones:

> The word *homophone* is Greek: *homo* means "same," and *phone* means "sound." So homophones are words that sound the same.

Homophones and Almost Homophones

accept/except	council/counsel/consul
advice/advise	elicit/illicit
affect/effect	eminent/imminent
allusion/illusion	its/it's
capital/capitol	loose/lose
censor/censure	passed/past
cite/sight/site	precede/proceed
coarse/course	principal/principle
complement/compliment	set/sit
conscience/conscious	sense/since

than/then	weather/whether
their/there/they're	who's/whose
to/too/two	your/you're

Note: If you're using one of the words in the list above and you're not absolutely sure that you have the right one, look it up in a dictionary.

And finally, there are pairs of words that are commonly confused not because they sound alike but because their meanings are similar, or because the words are related to each other in a way that is genuinely confusing. Take, for example, the words *amount* and *number*:

My nephew Winston has an incredible amount of Legos.

I can't even begin to figure out the number of money we spent.

Amount refers to an uncountable quantity, while *number* is reserved for things that can be counted. We can count Legos, so the first sentence should use *number*. We can't count money (we can count units of money, like dollars or euros or loonies, but we can't actually count *money* because it makes no sense to say, *I have six moneys*). So the words *amount* and *number* are both misused in the example sentences. Here those sentences are again, corrected:

My nephew Winston has an incredible *number* of Legos.

I can't even begin to figure out the *amount* of money we spent.

Other commonly confused words in this category include the following:

Words Commonly Confused Based on Meaning

beside/besides	**beside** means *next to*; **besides** means *except* or *also*
between/among	**between** refers to two objects; **among** refers to three or more
can/may	**can** means *to be able*; **may** means *to be allowed*
emigrate/immigrate	one **emigrates** from one place to **immigrate** to a new one
farther/further	**farther** describes concrete distance; **further** is abstract
fewer/less	use **fewer** for countable nouns and **less** for uncountable nouns
imply/infer	to **imply** is to hint; to **infer** is to perceive the hint
that/who	use **that** to refer to things and **who** to refer to people
well/good	**well** is an adverb; **good** is an adjective

If the word you're looking for is not here, either look it up in a dictionary or google "commonly confused words" and get whole big lists of words with their definitions. And there's nothing cooler than a big list of words.

Reality Check! Grammar and Usage

▶ Have you reviewed your use of verbs to ensure that they're in the active voice whenever possible?

▶ Have you checked the appropriateness of your verbs' mood and form?

▶ Have you confirmed that all of your verbs agree with their subjects in number (singular/plural)?

▶ Have you checked your use of pronouns to ensure that they agree in number with their antecedents?

▶ Have you identified a clear reference for each of the pronouns you've used?

▶ Have you avoided shifting pronoun perspective (first person, second person, third person)?

▶ Have you taken care to use the appropriate pronoun case (subjective, objective, possessive) for each situation?

▶ Have you reviewed your draft carefully to ensure idiomatically correct use of prepositions?

▶ Have you checked to make sure that you are using adjectives and adverbs appropriately?

▶ Have you done a close reading for commonly confused words (and looked in a dictionary for those you're not sure of)?

▶ *Let Us Show You:* Proofing for Grammar and Usage

Remember Mara's draft essay about academic doping? She worked on it when she was doing all that academic research throughout Chapters 20, 21, and 22. At one point in her process, Mara was so wrapped up in the *content* of her draft that she shortchanged the *presentation.*

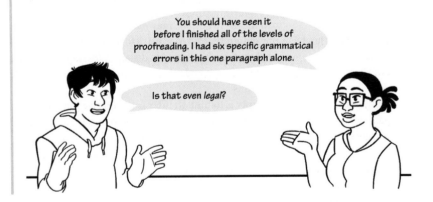

> You should have seen it before I finished all of the levels of proofreading. I had six specific grammatical errors in this one paragraph alone.

> Is that even *legal?*

While certain factors can predict NPS use ~~can be predicted by certain factors~~, and the drugs are easily accessible, there are underlying reasons as to why students are taking them to begin with. Students may hold particular outcome expectations, beliefs that a certain ~~affect~~ effect will result ~~with~~ from using NPS. Academically, students use the drugs because they help people "concentrate better," "feel more focused," and "get their work done more efficiently" (Labbe and Maisto 727). However, these are only beliefs held by students and may not be ~~physical~~ physically true. Studies show that students with lower GPAs have the highest connection ~~with~~ to stimulant use (McCabe et al. 99). This conflicting information suggests that students have false ideas regarding NPS use. According to the *Journal of Addictive Diseases*, "[n]ew research has demonstrated that performance improvements related to methylphenidate administration in healthy volunteers are highly variable and might be dependent on baseline cognitive ability," suggesting that study drugs may not be effective in the first place. NPS use is not limited to purely academic reasons either. Not often realized, "many students use these drugs nonmedically to enhance their experience of partying and getting high on other substances," creating a hidden side of NPS use (Arria and DuPont 419). The reasons that students use NPS ~~is~~ are not always as benign as simple study aids.

▶ *Talk Amongst Yourselves . . .*

After you have reviewed the changes Mara made to this paragraph as a result of proofreading for errors of grammar and usage, work with a partner to examine each change individually. Can you identify the particular problem Mara solved with each correction? Are there any changes that *don't* actually correct a problem? Are there other errors that Mara didn't catch?

▶ *Now You Try:* Proofing for Grammar and Usage

Take any draft essay you're working on (or, again, even one you're not currently working on) — as long as you've taken it through revision for content, structure, and coherence — and review it for its grammatical soundness. Use the Grammar and Usage *Reality Check!* box on page 406, just as Mara did, to identify and resolve any problems you find in the way you're using words. As always, be sure to ask for help from your instructor, a classmate, or a writing-center consultant if you're not sure whether you're catching every error or correcting all errors appropriately.

Chapter 25

Solving Sentence Structure Problems: Build a Solid Foundation

> I like the construction of sentences and the juxtaposition of words — not just how they sound or what they mean, but even what they look like.
> — Don DeLillo

Just like essays and paragraphs, sentences have structure. But unlike essays and paragraphs — whose structures are loosely based on the idea of a beginning, a middle, and an end — sentences are structured according to actual rules. And the number one rule of sentence structure is that the basic structural unit within a sentence is a **clause**, a group of words with a subject and a predicate.

Yes, there are rules involved in writing complete sentences. In this chapter, we'll cover some common problems students have with sentence structure, and we'll show you how to avoid mistakes that will make your sentences unclear or confusing. You can also find helpful definitions and examples in Appendix A (see pages 451–55).

Problems with Clauses, Part 1: Fragments

To be a complete sentence, a group of words must contain at least one independent clause (a clause that can stand alone as a sentence if it wants to). That is, a sentence must either *be* an independent clause or *contain* an independent clause.

SENTENCE FRAGMENTS

Sentence fragments are incomplete sentences. More specifically, a fragment is a group of words that wants to be a sentence but can't because it is in some way incomplete.

Most often, a sentence fragment is an incomplete clause. It might lack a subject:

waited all night long to get tickets to the concert.

Or perhaps it's missing a predicate:

The troll that lives under the bridge.

Could be it's missing both a subject *and* a predicate:

running toward the carnival with reckless abandon.

All three of these examples lack an independent clause — each attempt is missing something crucial to *clause*-ness: a subject, a predicate, or both.

A fourth type of fragment exists as well: a dependent clause presented as if it were a complete sentence.

Although Lynne is truly excited about grammar.

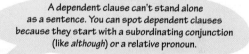

A dependent clause can't stand alone as a sentence. You can spot dependent clauses because they start with a subordinating conjunction (like *although*) or a relative pronoun.

FIXING FRAGMENTS

Just as there are several ways to create a fragment, there also are several ways to fix a fragment. Common sense will tell you that if your clause is only a fragment, then you should just add whatever is missing to correct the problem, and that's true — but we think the best way to try to correct a fragment is to ask yourself what you're trying to say. The answer to this question almost always implies the solution to the problem.

Waited all night long to get tickets to the concert. [*Who waited all night?*]

Corrected: **Steph and James waited all night long to get tickets to the concert.**

The troll that lives under the bridge. [*What about him? What did he do?*]

Corrected: **I'm thinking of singing a song to the troll that lives under the bridge.**

Corrected: **The troll that lives under the bridge keeps trying to drink my milkshake.**

Fixing Fragments

When you write a fragment, you don't do it in a vacuum; you do it in the context of a sentence, a paragraph, or an essay. So the best way to fix a fragment is to take a look at that context and then ask yourself what you can do to make the idea in your head clearer to your reader.

Problems with Clauses, Part 2: Run-On Sentences

We occasionally come across students who think that a run-on sentence is simply a big sentence — a sentence that seems to go on for longer than they're comfortable with. But a run-on sentence has a more specific problem than just being too long.

Here is why: a **run-on sentence** occurs when a writer "runs" two or more sentences together as one. More precisely, it runs two or more independent clauses together without properly joining them with the right words or punctuation. Independent clauses must be connected to each other in one of the following ways:

▶ by using a **period** to create two sentences
▶ by using a **semicolon** (or sometimes a **colon** or a **dash**) to create a compound sentence
▶ by using a **comma** plus a **coordinating conjunction** to create a compound sentence
▶ by beginning one clause with a **subordinating conjunction** to create a complex sentence

If a writer fails to use a conjunction with the comma, or uses a comma in place of a semicolon — or, even worse, uses no punctuation or conjunction at all between independent clauses — then the result will be a run-on. There are two types of run-ons: fused sentences and comma splices.

You can review the "Punctuation" section of Appendix A (pages 459–65) for more help. And maybe take a look at conjunctions in the "Parts of Speech" section (pages 449–50) while you're at it.

FUSED SENTENCES AND COMMA SPLICES

A **fused sentence** is the classic run-on: two complete sentences that are punctuated as if they were a single sentence. They are quite literally fused together without the appropriate and necessary internal punctuation or conjunction. Can you spot where the two independent clauses are fused in the following example?

I'm not bad I'm just drawn that way.

A **comma splice** is a fused sentence with a twist: the two independent clauses are spliced together with a comma when stronger punctuation is needed. In fact, many comma splices are the result of a writer trying to fix a fused sentence with the wrong punctuation.

You win some, you lose some.

Leave the gun, take the cannoli.

FIXING RUN-ON SENTENCES

You may be experiencing some grammatical heartbreak right now. On the one hand, you know the unfortunate clauses in each of those run-on sentences are doomed to fail if they don't separate. On the other hand, the clauses really want to be with each other. So what's a writer to do? Don't worry — only one of the three available options involves breaking up the clauses and letting them go their separate ways.

Option 1: Use a period to create two sentences. This option will fix the problem, but a period may be too harsh and final.

> I'm not bad. I'm just drawn that way.
>
> You win some. You lose some.
>
> Leave the gun. Take the cannoli.

Option 2: Use a semicolon (;). A semicolon is stronger than a comma, so it can separate two grammatically complete sentences, but it is more permeable than a period, which means it can still let the lovers — er, sentences — be closer together. Note that in contemporary usage, the dash (—) is often used in place of a semicolon. (And in certain cases where the second clause serves as an explanation of the first clause, a colon can replace the semicolon.)

See if you can figure out why the colon is a valid option for sentence 1 but not for sentences 2 and 3 in the examples that follow.

1. I'm not bad; I'm just drawn that way.
   I'm not bad — I'm just drawn that way.
   I'm not bad: I'm just drawn that way.

2. You win some; you lose some.
   You win some — you lose some.

3. Leave the gun; take the cannoli.
   Leave the gun — take the cannoli.

Option 3: Use a conjunction. You could insert a coordinating conjunction after the comma, or begin either of the two clauses with a subordinating conjunction. Conjunctions allow the two sentences to be united as one, but be careful: any time you add a word to a sentence (as this option requires), you change the sentence's meaning— which can be a good thing or a bad thing. Use your judgment.

See if you and a classmate can explain to each other how the use of different conjunctions changes the meaning of each of the following sentences.

1. I'm not bad, but I'm drawn that way.
   While I'm not bad, I'm drawn that way.

2. You win some, and you lose some.
   Although you win some, you lose some.
3. Leave the gun, but take the cannoli.
   If you leave the gun, take the cannoli.

Practice! Fixing Fragments and Run-On Sentences

Edit the following sentences to fix fragments and run-ons.

1. Jennifer has a dog, his name is Lou.
2. Eating pizza, drinking beer, and playing Scrabble. What a fun evening.
3. We have been snowed in for two weeks, I am getting cabin fever.
4. Texting while driving is dangerous. Just as dangerous as driving drunk.
5. Holden isn't misanthropic he is just honest.
6. Sometimes you feel like a nut, sometimes you don't.
7. The kind of feeling you get when you are all alone on a dark, stormy night.
8. Documentaries about ravens that really make you think about animal intelligence.
9. The best part of fall is when pumpkin spice lattes become available, I look forward to it every year.
10. The rain cut short our camping trip. Which otherwise was fun.

Problems with Sentence Structure and Purpose

All sentences have both *structure* and *purpose*. But sometimes things go haywire midway through a sentence, resulting in confusion for the reader — and, if we're being honest, confusion for the writer as well. These problems can be sorted into three categories: shifts, mixed constructions, and faulty parallelism.

If you aren't quite sure what sentence structure and sentence purpose are all about, you might want to review the relevant sections of Appendix A (pages 457–58) before moving on.

PROBLEM 1: SHIFTS

Sentences sometimes take abrupt grammatical turns or go in directions that aren't consistent with the way they began, making them confusing or just plain weird. For instance, if a sentence begins as a statement (also known as the declarative mode), it's best for the sentence to continue that way and not turn into a question (a.k.a. the interrogative mode). If it doesn't, we call this problem a **shift**, and it can be a really awkward problem.

But don't worry. In this section we'll explain the kinds of shifts that can happen, how to spot them, and how to fix them.

Avoid Shifts from Statement to Question

A sentence that begins in the declarative mode — that is, as a statement — should not end as a question. Avoid sentences like this:

> We asked Gina did she want to take the train or the bus?

Instead, keep the sentence as a statement all the way to the end:

> We asked Gina if she wanted to take the train or the bus.

Avoid Shifts from Direct to Indirect Quotation

A **direct quotation** is a word-for-word copy, enclosed in quotation marks, of what someone else has said or written. An **indirect quotation** (also known as *reported speech* because it's someone's words reported by someone else) is not word-for-word and therefore is not enclosed in quotes. Both direct and indirect quotations are fine, but a sentence should not shift from one type of quotation to the other. Avoid sentences like this:

> Bob said that he was starved and let's go get burgers.

Instead, you should choose either direct or indirect quotation and be consistent:

> **Direct quotation**: Bob said, "I'm starved. Let's go get burgers."

> **Indirect quotation**: Bob said that he was starved and that we should go get burgers.

PROBLEM 2: MIXED CONSTRUCTIONS

A **mixed construction** is, simply put, a sentence that just doesn't make sense. It usually doesn't make sense for one of two reasons: either it loses its sense of direction midway through, or its ideas lose their logical connection to each other at some point.

The first cause of a mixed construction is that the writer begins a sentence one way, gets distracted, and then finishes it another way, resulting in a sentence that is grammatically tangled. To fix such a sentence, read it aloud and try to untangle its structure.

Here's an example of a mixed construction:

> Because coffee keeps me awake at night if I drink it in the afternoon is the reason why I stick to tea after lunch.

What exactly is the reason I stick to tea after lunch? It's the fact that *coffee keeps me awake at night*, not the fact that *because coffee keeps me awake at night*. We could fix the sentence in one of these ways:

> Because coffee keeps me awake at night if I drink it in the afternoon, *I stick to* tea after lunch.

> Coffee keeps me awake at night if I drink it in the afternoon, *so I stick to* tea after lunch.

Here's another example of a mixed construction:

> By making *Infinite Jest* required reading it will cause some students to want to drop the class but will help others discover their new favorite writer.

Can you tell what is making students want to drop the class or helping them to discover a writer? We might correct this mixed construction like this, by making the emphasis clearer:

> Making *Infinite Jest* required reading will cause some students to want to drop the class but will help others to discover their new favorite writer.

The second cause of a mixed construction is that the ideas within a sentence have no logical connection to each other.

> The flu is where a person has a runny nose, sore throat, and fever.

Do you see the problem here? The flu isn't a *place*; it's a *virus*. So it's illogical to define the flu as a place (*is where*). Here's the fix:

> The flu *causes a person to have* a runny nose, sore throat, and fever.

Okay, here goes. The motorcycle riders wear *helmets*, not *responsibilities*, right? So the sentence could be: <u>Motorcycle riders</u> in the United States are now responsible for wearing helmets.

Try fixing this mixed construction: *Helmets are a responsibility now worn by most motorcycle riders in the United States.*

PROBLEM 3: FAULTY PARALLELISM

When you need to list or compare ideas in a sentence, it is best to present these ideas so that they parallel each other grammatically. For example, if you want to explain that you did three things last night — you went to the roller rink, you won the roller derby, and you took home the team trophy — you should present each idea in a form that matches the grammatical form of the other two ideas (e.g., they're all clauses, they're all phrases, or they're all nouns). If one idea fails to match the others — if, for example, the first two ideas are complete predicates (*went to the roller rink, won the roller derby*) and the third is just a noun phrase (*the team trophy*) — it creates what is called **faulty parallelism**:

> Last night I went to the roller rink, won the roller derby, and the team trophy.

You might be wondering, *What's the problem? I won the derby for my team, so I won the trophy. The sentence makes sense, right?* Well, yes and no. We can see that you meant that you won both the derby and the trophy; however, the sentence is unbalanced. The phrases *went to the roller rink* and *won the roller derby* both contain past-tense verbs and direct objects, whereas *the team trophy* contains only a direct object. So the constructions are not the same.

> Last night, I went to the roller rink, won the roller derby, and ⊘the team trophy.
>   verb   object   verb   object   [missing verb]   object

It's clear that the second object goes with *won*, but for this sentence to be parallel, *the team trophy* will need a verb, too. You could achieve parallelism by writing this instead:

> Last night I went to the roller rink, won the roller derby, and *took home* the team trophy.

Here are a few more examples of faulty parallelism. Work with a partner to see whether you can figure out why the first sentence in each pair contains an error in parallelism and the second sentence does not.

1. I wanted not only to ride a pony but also have one of my own.

   I wanted not only to ride a pony but also to have one of my own.

2. It is better to have loved and lost than never loving at all.

   It is better to have loved and lost than never to have loved at all.

3. Stacy told Bob either to fish or cut bait.

   Stacy told Bob either to fish or to cut bait.

Now it's time for you to put your knowledge of sentence structure problems and sentence purpose confusions to the test.

> ### *Practice!* **Problems with Sentence Structure and Purpose**
> Edit the following sentences to fix shifts, mixed constructions, and faulty parallelism.
>
> 1. Last weekend I saw a movie, went out to dinner, and a party.
> 2. Gilbert said he'd like to read the book and could he please have a copy.
> 3. The students wondered would they have a test on Chapter 43.
> 4. The kids wanted to either go to Disneyland or Dollywood for spring break.
> 5. Reading, drawing, dancing, and a moderate workout are all good ways to unwind.
> 6. Corvids not only use tools, but they also remember faces.
> 7. Sarah said she had locked her keys in her car and what is the number of a locksmith.
> 8. I wonder why is the grocery store so busy today?
> 9. The reason the car is making that funny noise is because the alternator is wearing out.
> 10. By wearing a wide-brimmed hat, it can help you avoid a sunburn.

Problems with Phrases: Dangling and Misplaced Modifiers

Neither as weighty as a clause nor as delicate as an individual word is a unit of expression called a phrase. A **phrase** is a group of words that often lacks a subject and always lacks a complete verb.

Very often, phrases act as modifiers. Modifiers do what it sounds like they do: they change (or describe) other elements of a sentence. **Adjectives** change (or describe) nouns or pronouns, and **adverbs** change verbs or adjectives or other adverbs. Modifying phrases are almost always either verbal (gerunds, participles, and infinitives) or prepositional. (If these technical names are unfamiliar, pages 455–56 in Appendix A will help clarify things.)

Most problems with phrases revolve around modifying phrases. Like parasites, modifiers always have to be attached to something, and they should be placed as close as possible to what they modify; if they aren't placed closely enough to what they are actually supposed to modify, they will latch onto something closer and modify that. This creates confusing sentences.

DANGLING MODIFIERS

A modifying phrase at the beginning of a sentence will always modify the subject of that sentence. When the subject of a sentence is not what the modifying phrase describes, that phrase becomes a **dangling modifier**. Check out the examples on the next page.

Walking into the house, garbage was strewn across the floor.

As a citizen of this town, a new high school needs to be built.

Eating the candy bar, it tasted like heaven.

Each of these sentences contains a dangling modifier. The phrase *walking into the house* should modify a person, but as the first sentence stands, the phrase modifies *garbage*. Something similar occurs in the other examples.

Walking into the house, *garbage* was strewn across the floor.

As a citizen of this town, *a new high school* needs to be built.

Eating the candy bar, *it* tasted like heaven.

There are two ways to fix a dangling modifier. Option 1: you can add a subject and complete verb to the phrase, thus turning it into a clause; or, option 2, you can insert the subject that is logically modified by the phrase immediately after the phrase. The first example could be fixed in either of these ways:

When Michael walked into the house, garbage was strewn across the floor.
option 1

Walking into the house, Michael could see that garbage was strewn across the floor.
option 2

So fixing dangling modifiers is like fixing fragments. You have to ask and answer questions.

Right. *Who* walked into the house? *Michael* walked into the house.

And for the other sentences: *Who* is a citizen of the town? *Who* is eating the candy bar?

As a citizen of this town, I think we need to build a new high school.

<u>subject changed</u>

Eating the candy bar, Grammster thought it tasted like heaven.

<u>subject changed</u>

MISPLACED MODIFIERS

A **misplaced modifier** is simply a modifying word, phrase, or clause that is placed too far from what it modifies, creating a vague or incorrect modification. To correct a misplaced modifier, simply place it right next to the word it should modify.

I *only* want to eat candy for the rest of my life.

The word *only* in this sentence should modify *candy*, not *want*. How about this instead?

I want to eat *only* candy for the rest of my life.

Perfect! *Only* is now in a position to modify just the word that it should modify: *candy*.

Now let's take a look at a sentence that has misplaced an entire prepositional phrase:

The soup on the counter in the bowl smells like cream of mushroom.

Can you see the problem? The soup should be in the bowl, not on the counter. The prepositional phrase *on the counter* should modify *bowl*, not *soup*.

The soup *in the bowl* on the counter smells like cream of mushroom.

See how that works? Now test your knowledge of all that you've learned about misplaced modifiers (words and phrases) as well as dangling modifiers.

Practice! Problems with Modifiers

Correct any dangling or misplaced modifiers in the following sentences.

1. Stephanie learned that all sixth-grade boys are not bullies.
2. A desk clerk showed me to my room with a unicorn tattoo.
3. To play bridge like a professional, a good memory is required.
4. Bob admitted that he had cheated on his taxes after repeated questioning.
5. Arriving almost an hour early, none of the food was prepared.

(continued)

6. I can't believe we almost ate the whole cake.
7. Watching the movie, a scary scene made me cover my eyes.
8. George didn't even understand one word Roger said.
9. Tickling the dog, Susan's shirt ended up smelly and torn.
10. The house near the river with the big satellite dish on the roof is Amy's.

Reality Check! Sentence Structure

▶ Have you identified and corrected any fragments in your writing?

▶ Have you identified and corrected any run-on sentences (comma splices or fused sentences)?

▶ Have you avoided any confusing or distracting shifts in the purpose of each sentence?

▶ Have you identified and fixed any mixed constructions?

▶ Have you made sure that all lists and comparisons are presented in parallel grammatical forms?

▶ Have you resolved any dangling modifiers by including the subjects they're meant to modify?

▶ Have you moved any misplaced modifiers to their more appropriate placements?

▶ *Let Us Show You:* Proofing for Sentence Structure

You do remember Mara's essay about academic doping, right? She worked on it throughout Part 6 — and you saw her proofread a paragraph for grammar and usage issues in Chapter 24 (see pages 406–7). Before she turned in the essay to her professor for credit in class, she also made sure to fine-tune her sentence structure by referring to the Sentence Structure checklist above.

I went through my academic doping paper again for sentence errors — look how many I fixed in just one paragraph. There was a comma splice in the very first sentence!

Hey, at least you caught it!

ADHD stimulants are prescription for a reason, the. The U.S. Drug Enforcement Administration classifies the stimulants as Schedule II drugs for their high abuse and dependency potential. Other commonly known Schedule II drugs include morphine, cocaine, PCP, opium, and OxyContin. So how do so many students obtain these drugs? A study was done to research the detection of feigned ADHD symptoms in college students. Thirty-one undergraduates who were coached about the symptoms via Internet information were compared to twenty-nine correctly diagnosed undergraduates and fourteen neutral undergraduates. Given The three groups were given standard ADHD diagnostic tests, including symptom checklists, neurocognitive tests, and symptom validity tests. Overall, the malingering undergraduates were able to produce a positive diagnostic profile (Berry, Ranseen, and Sollman 325). It These findings reveal that it is surprisingly easy to obtain a prescription for stimulants, for. For those who don't have a prescription, a study showed that 62 percent of students with ADHD diverted the medication to someone without a prescription (Arria and DuPont 419). While some students may not know that it is illegal to share or sell their own prescription drugs, others may easily gain an ADHD prescription simply for the purpose of simply illegally distributing stimulants.

▶ *Talk Amongst Yourselves ...*

After you have reviewed the changes Mara made to this paragraph as a result of proofreading for sentence errors, work with a partner to look at each change individually. Can you identify what problem Mara solved with each correction? Are there any changes that *don't* actually correct a problem? Are there other errors that Mara didn't catch?

▶ *Now You Try:* Proofing for Sentence Structure

Take any draft essay you're working on (or, again, even one you're not currently working on) — as long as you've taken it through revision for content, structure, and coherence — and, just as Mara did, use the Sentence Structure *Reality Check!* box on page 420 to identify and resolve any problems you find in your sentence structures. As always, be sure to ask for help from your instructor, a classmate, or a writing-center consultant if you're not sure whether you're catching every error or correcting all errors appropriately.

Chapter 26

Solving Problems with Punctuation: Form Healthy Relationships Between Words

> Commas in the *New Yorker* fall with the precision of knives in a circus act, outlining the victim.
> — E. B. White

When punctuation is used correctly, it makes sentences easier to read and can often clarify the meaning of otherwise unclear sentences. Why? Because punctuation shows readers how words, phrases, clauses, and sentences are related to each other.

You've probably seen the punctuation jokes that were popular a few years ago. Come on, you remember — stuff like: *A simple comma is the difference between "Let's eat, Grandma" and "Let's eat Grandma."*

All joking aside, though, we aren't going to cover all of the punctuation errors and rules that we can think of here because that would take forever. But we will present the errors we see most often in student writing and show you how to easily fix those errors. And Appendix A is always there to remind you of the relevant punctuation rules.

The most common mistakes students make with punctuation are either sentence-structure errors involving the misuse of terminal or internal punctuation, or non-structural errors involving the use of grammatical/mechanical punctuation.

Common Problems with Terminal Punctuation

Terminal punctuation refers to punctuation that terminates, or ends, a sentence. There are three terminal punctuation marks:

Terminal punctuation marks

exclamation point   question mark   period .

The most common errors in terminal punctuation use involve the first two punctuation marks.

Use an **exclamation point** only if the sentence is truly an exclamation. These almost never occur in academic writing, so if you're wondering whether what you're writing is truly an exclamation, it probably isn't. For example:

> Bottled water is too expensive! We should stop buying it! We should filter tap water instead!

You're not really that excited about bottled water, are you? Yes, that's what we thought. Save your exclamation points for when they're necessary:

> As Barney walked through the door of his condo after a long day of work, thirty tipsy friends wearing orange-and-pink-striped party hats jumped out from behind the furniture and screamed, "Surprise!"

A common mistake — and we're not exactly sure why it happens — is neglecting to use a **question mark** after a sentence that is a question. Make sure you make a distinction between questions and statements by using the appropriate end punctuation. For example:

> Why, do you think, is grammar part of the English 101 curriculum. It seems useless and unnecessary.

Clearly the first sentence is an actual question, so it needs to be punctuated as one:

> Why, do you think, is grammar part of the English 101 curriculum? It seems useless and unnecessary.

I sincerely hope you weren't making fun of me with that last example. Anyway, for extra help with terminal punctuation marks, refer to page 459 in Appendix A. You might want it for the exercise below.

Practice! **Terminal Punctuation Marks**

Add end punctuation to the following sentences. Be prepared to explain your choices.

1. Oh Mylanta, this meal is to die for
2. Are you paying attention to the weather forecast
3. I wonder who will win the Super Bowl this year
4. Why did the chicken cross the road

(continued)

5. Watch out, there is an earwig in your hair
6. Casey wrote an essay and revised it several times
7. Did you know that there is a raccoon in your garage
8. Are you going to answer the phone
9. The lawn is turning brown
10. Black bears are more afraid of you than you are of them

Common Problems with Internal Punctuation

Internal punctuation functions *within* a sentence (as opposed to terminal punctuation, which separates sentences from each other). There are three major internal punctuation marks — the comma, the semicolon, and the colon — as well as two others we've used in this very paragraph: parentheses and the dash.

Internal punctuation marks

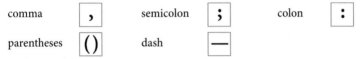

comma **,**   semicolon **;**   colon **:**

parentheses **( )**   dash **—**

On the following pages we identify several of the most common problems with internal punctuation marks. If you'd like to read a lot more about them and see guidelines for how to use some of them, take a look at pages 460–64 in Appendix A.

COLONS AND SEMICOLONS

They look similar, and they both help to separate two or more parts of a sentence. However, the truth is that the colon and the semicolon serve quite different functions in sentences.

Semicolons and Lists

If a list is introduced by an independent clause, use a colon — not a semicolon — after the clause. Semicolons should never be used to introduce quotations or lists.

Confused about semicolons and lists?
When each example in a list is lengthy, use a semicolon instead
of a comma to separate the items. It's just clearer that way.
We cover this in Appendix A.

This sentence, for example, uses the semicolon incorrectly:

Allison's desk is covered with these things; ungraded papers, unsharpened pencils, and unread books.

As long as the sentence before the list is a complete independent clause, use a colon to introduce the list:

Allison's desk is covered with these things: ungraded papers, unsharpened
<u>   independent clause   </u>   <u>list (not an independent clause)</u>

pencils, and unread books.

Colons and Lists

You may have heard that you should *always* put a colon before a list. This is incorrect. A colon should precede a list only if the list is introduced by a complete independent clause. If the list is *part of* an independent clause and not *introduced by* one, a colon should not come before it.

So don't use a colon in a sentence like this one:

Remember, a clause is independent if it can stand alone as a sentence.

My favorite kinds of candy are: Reese's Peanut Butter Cups, Red Vines, and Hershey's Cookies 'n' Creme bars.

Instead, just allow your clause to complete itself without breaking it up with a colon:

My favorite kinds of candy are Reese's Peanut Butter Cups, Red Vines, and
<u>   independent clause   </u>   <u>list that is part of the independent clause</u>

Hershey's Cookies 'n' Creme bars.

Semicolons with Phrases and Clauses

The general purpose of a semicolon is to join independent clauses in a sentence — that is, the semicolon joins two or more groups of words that could stand alone as sentences if they wanted to. To put it another way, if you could use a period after the first group of words and start a new sentence, then you can also use a semicolon.

If an element in a sentence can't stand alone as its own sentence (such as a phrase or a dependent clause), don't separate it from the rest of the sentence with a semicolon. Instead, use a comma. For example, the following would be incorrect:

Her hair frizzy and matted; Bridget Jones kept her cool as Mark Darcy entered the hotel lobby.

This is the appropriate way to join that introductory phrase to the rest of the sentence:

Her hair frizzy and matted, Bridget Jones kept her cool as Mark Darcy
<u>   </u>   <u>   </u>
     phrase   independent clause

entered the hotel lobby.
<u>   </u>
   independent clause

COMMAS

For some reason, these friendly little squiggles cause students (and — let's face it — the rest of the population) a lot of confusion. Here's the bottom line: commas are very brief pauses that help readers make meaning out of the elements of a sentence.

> Colons and semicolons offer longer pauses, while periods, exclamation points, and question marks bring sentences to a dead stop.

Commas and Independent Clauses

When two independent clauses (complete sentences) are connected with a coordinating conjunction (*and*, *but*, *so*, etc.), place a comma before the conjunction. For example:

Julia wanted to be a neurosurgeon, **but** her father thought stand-up comedy was a wiser choice.

Here's a useful tip: there are only seven coordinating conjunctions in English, and you can memorize them by using the acronym FANBOYS:

For **A**nd **N**or **B**ut **O**r **Y**et **S**o

Most people remember to use a comma with a coordinating conjunction when the clauses are long but forget to do so when the clauses are short:

The sky opened up and it began to rain.

Can you spot where the comma belongs in that sentence? Yeah, we thought you could.

The sky opened up, **and** it began to rain.
<u>   </u>   <u>   </u>
  independent clause   independent clause

Commas and Other Coordinating Conjunctions

You don't need to use a comma with every coordinating conjunction — only with those that join independent clauses. When you have a compound subject (*Terrence and his sister*) or a compound predicate (*were laughing and living it up*), commas are not just unnecessary but incorrect. Here are some examples of unnecessary commas:

> I mowed the lawn, and watered the flowers.

> The elephant trainer, and the elephant were good friends.

> Jessica gave us some lemonade, and snickerdoodles.

The incorrectly used commas in these sentences divide elements that need to stay together. Thus the commas should be removed:

> I mowed the lawn **and** watered the flowers.
> <u>compound verb</u>

> The elephant trainer **and** the elephant were good friends.
> compound subject

> Jessica gave us some lemonade **and** snickerdoodles.
> compound object

Avoid Putting Commas Between Subjects and Verbs

A comma should not be used to separate a subject from its predicate. This creates a confusing break in a sentence. For example:

> The reason I like cats better than dogs, is that they are smarter.

Remove the comma to maintain the coherence of the sentence:

> The reason I like cats better than dogs is that they are smarter.

There are exceptions to this rule, though. Check out the next section.

Commas and Internal Phrases

When a **nonrestrictive** phrase or clause (for example, the clause *who owns the scooter*) appears between a subject and a predicate (e.g., *Jane rocks*), you need not just one but <u>two</u> commas to set off the phrase or clause. Put one at the beginning of the phrase or clause and one after it: *Jane, who owns the scooter, rocks.*

> Nonrestrictive information
> is "extra" information — something that
> you don't need to know in order to understand
> who or what the sentence is about.
> It doesn't "restrict" understanding.

Here's another way to think about this: if a phrase or clause is not essential to understanding who or what a sentence is about, make sure you enclose the entire phrase or clause with commas. Punctuating one side but not the other is a common mistake.

Both of the following sentences use commas incorrectly (or only partly correctly, which is just another way of saying incorrectly):

Blake's brother Ralph an accomplished violinist, is performing tonight at Stuart's Coffee House.

Blake's brother Ralph, an accomplished violinist is performing tonight at Stuart's Coffee House.

We can correct this problem by setting off the *entire nonrestrictive phrase*:

Blake's brother Ralph, <u>an accomplished violinist</u>, is performing tonight at
nonrestrictive phrase
Stuart's Coffee House.

Remember also that this rule applies to nonrestrictive clauses as well as phrases. For example, each of the following sentences is incorrectly punctuated:

My mother who loves playing bingo does not enjoy high-stakes poker.

My mother, who loves playing bingo does not enjoy high-stakes poker.

My mother who loves playing bingo, does not enjoy high-stakes poker.

Instead of using no commas or just one comma, set off that entire nonrestrictive clause with a comma at each end:

My mother, <u>who loves playing bingo</u>, does not enjoy high-stakes poker.
nonrestrictive clause

The *bingo* part of the sentence is nonrestrictive because we would still know who *my mother* is even if we didn't know she likes playing bingo. But (!) changing the subject changes the equation:

> My friend <u>who loves playing bingo</u> does not enjoy high-stakes poker.
>   restrictive clause

See what happened there? When the subject becomes *friend* instead of *mother*, everything changes. Because we assume that the writer has only one mother but multiple friends, the clause *who loves playing bingo* becomes **restrictive**. That is, it restricts the meaning of the sentence by letting us know which friend we're talking about (the one who loves playing bingo).

Commas and Introductory Material

Without a break between introductory material and main clauses, sentences can be confusing or difficult to read. A comma should always come after an introductory phrase. The following sentence is incorrect because there needs to be more separation between the sentence and the phrase that introduces it:

> While watching the documentary don't forget to take notes.

Correct it by placing a comma after the introductory phrase:

> <u>While watching the documentary</u>, don't forget to take notes.
>   introductory phrase

A comma should also come after an introductory dependent clause in a sentence. For example, the following sentence is incorrectly punctuated:

> Since you are being so friendly I will offer you a refreshing cup of chamomile tea.

But this one is correct:

> <u>Since you are being so friendly</u>, I will offer you a refreshing cup of
>   introductory phrase
> chamomile tea.

If you're confused about phrases and dependent clauses, go spend a little time with them on pages 455–56 in Appendix A.

Practice! Internal Punctuation Marks

Add or delete semicolons, colons, and commas as needed in the following sentences.

1. Coffee isn't better than tea, it's just different.
2. There are two kinds of run-on sentences, fused sentences and comma splices.

(continued)

3. Three plants with beautiful winter foliage in the Northwest are: heather, hellebores, and Oregon grape.

4. Mom I don't want to clean my room.

5. Although it is only August; it already feels like fall.

6. Four fun summer activities are, hiking, biking, water skiing, and rafting.

7. After a long dry spell; the sidewalks give off a sweet odor when the rain falls.

8. One thing is clear, meat should not be left on the counter for long periods of time.

9. Susan of course, will not be joining us at the circus this evening.

10. Cats are girls, dogs are boys.

Common Problems with Grammatical and Mechanical Punctuation

Grammatical and mechanical punctuation marks (also called nonstructural punctuation marks) don't affect the overall structure or purpose of a sentence the way that internal and terminal punctuation marks do. Nevertheless, using them correctly is important if you want your reader to understand your meaning.

In this section we cover a few common problems with the most often used grammatical and mechanical punctuation marks.

Grammatical and mechanical punctuation marks

hyphen   **–**   apostrophe   **'**   quotation marks   **" "**

Complete guidelines for how to use apostrophes and quotation marks appear in Appendix A, on pages 464–65.

HYPHENS VS. DASHES

Use a hyphen only between two words that you are turning into one (such as *blue-green*), not between two parts of a sentence (such as *I went-you saw me*). That second example uses a hyphen when it really needs a dash. The next example does, too:

This wine-it sort of tastes like dirty feet.

And here's the corrected version, with an actual dash:

This wine — it sort of tastes like dirty feet.

The confusion between the hyphen and the dash most likely stems from the fact that they are the same key on the keyboard. However, a dash is *two hyphens* (also known as an em-dash because it's the width of the letter *m*) joined together (—), whereas a hyphen is just, well, itself (-).

Here's a hint: when you want a hyphen, hit the hyphen key without hitting the space bar first. When you hit the space bar both before and after a hyphen, you get a dash.

QUOTATION MARKS

We've noticed that students are often confused about how to use quotation marks with other punctuation marks.

Using Commas with Quotation Marks

A common error is thinking that you *always* need to use a comma with quotation marks. Here's a trick: remove the quotation marks and then ask yourself, *Is a comma necessary to create a correct sentence?*

For example, read the following sentence and decide whether you would use a comma if the title weren't in quotation marks:

"The Love Song of J. Alfred Prufrock," is one of my favorite poems.

We're hoping that your decision was, *Why, no, I certainly wouldn't use a comma there.* This is the correct version of the sentence:

"The Love Song of J. Alfred Prufrock" is one of my favorite poems.
                                       ^

Using Other Punctuation Marks with Quotation Marks

Here are some more helpful punctuation rules about where to place other punctuation marks with quotation marks.

Generally, commas go inside the quotation marks and semicolons go outside the quotation marks, like this:

One label says "hand wash," but the other says "dry clean only"; I can't decide what to do.

Terminal punctuation marks typically go inside the quotation marks, like this:

> Billy asked, "Should we go trick-or-treating?"
> Stan answered, "I don't see why not."

But there's an exception to that last rule: if an entire sentence and not just the quoted part is an exclamation or a question, place the terminal punctuation outside the quotation marks, like this:

> Did Regina actually say, "I am a vampire slayer"?

In this sentence, the question mark goes outside the quotation mark because it's not *Regina* but the writer of the sentence who's asking a question, so the entire sentence is a question. (You can see this exception in action in this very book — check out the title of Chapter 19.)

Keeping in mind the exception to the terminal-punctuation rule, see if you can figure out whether anything is wrong with either of these sentences:

> "Why didn't you list that among our assets"? the Dread Pirate Roberts asked.

> I was so excited when the queen said "hello!"

Both of these sentences are punctuated incorrectly. In the first case, the quote itself is the question, so the question mark belongs inside the quotation marks. In the second, it's not the queen who is excited but the "I" who is talking about the queen; therefore, the entire sentence is the exclamation.

> "Why didn't you list that among our assets?" the Dread Pirate Roberts asked.

> I was so excited when the queen said "hello"!

Avoid Using Quotation Marks Ironically

Finally, we'd like to address a fairly recent development in the misuse of quotation marks: the ironic quotation — you know, when you use your fingers to put "quotes" around "something" ironically (i.e., air quotes).

In many situations, it's fine to use ironic quotation marks — which essentially say, *Hey, I'm kidding! I don't really mean this!* But in academic and professional writing, the ironic use of quotation marks is confusing at best. For example, using ironic quotation marks around words in a research essay that also includes real quotes from sources is probably a bad idea.

At worst, these ironic quotation marks are insulting to the reader because they're a form of sarcasm that may not be appropriate to the writing task at hand. So it's best to avoid them when writing for school or work.

> If random words are quoted but not cited in a student essay, I have a hard time knowing what's from a real source and what isn't. Generally, it's not a good idea to frustrate your professor or make her wonder what you're up to.

APOSTROPHES

Here's the truth: not every word that ends in -s needs an apostrophe. In fact, the only words ending in -s that need apostrophes are those that are possessive. You can't make a noun plural or change the tense of a verb with an apostrophe. On the other hand, a possessive (as in *Randolph's mustache*) does need an apostrophe before the final -s.

To demonstrate, we give you the following sentences that use apostrophes incorrectly:

Fossil's are fascinating, and that is why David love's finding them.

The burglar hide's in the bush's.

And here are the corrected versions:

Fossils are fascinating, and that is why David *loves* finding them.

The burglar *hides* in the *bushes*.

Create Correct Possessives and Contractions

A possessive shows ownership (*Jane's scooter*) while a contraction turns two words into one (*do not = don't*). If you leave an apostrophe off a possessive noun, the noun will look plural and will most likely create confusion in your sentence. If you leave an apostrophe out of a contraction, it will cease to be a word at all.

For example, the following sentence is missing not one, not two, not three, but *four* apostrophes. Can you spot all four errors?

Im really tired today, so I dont think Ill go to my friends house after all.

Yep, you got it. Here's how that sentence should be punctuated:

I'<u>m</u> really tired today, so I <u>don</u>'t think I'<u>ll</u> go to my <u>friend</u>'s house after all.

contraction   contraction contraction   possessive
(for *I am*)   (for *do not*) (for *I will*)

Avoid Apostrophes with Possessive Pronouns

Note that just because some possessive pronouns (such as *yours, ours,* and *theirs*) end in *-s,* that doesn't mean they need possessive apostrophes. For instance, the following sentence is punctuated incorrectly:

Is that cow your's — the one flicking it's tail?

Neither of the possessive pronouns should have an apostrophe:

Is that cow your*s* — the one flicking it*s* tail?

Now's your chance to demonstrate your understanding of how to use nonstructural elements of punctuation. Knock yourself out!

Practice! Grammatical and Mechanical Punctuation Marks

Correct problems with apostrophes and quotation marks in the following sentences.

1. Mocha's cost more than latte's.
2. I really "enjoy" reading about grammar.
3. George run's faster than his wifes brother.
4. Shakespeare writes ",A rose by any other name would smell as sweet".
5. Youre forgetting that its Sunday. Theres no mail on Sundays'.
6. Three family's live in that house, which is why it look's so well maintained.
7. I overheard my neighbor saying that "she wants to move."
8. Tonys favorite color is light pink.
9. Dont look now, but the dogs' are digging hole's in the yard.
10. "'Twas brillig, and the slithy toves / Did gyre and gimble in the wabe," writes Lewis Carroll in "Jabberwocky".
11. Jims ex-girlfriend work's at the Crab Shack.
12. The students books arrived late, so the professor had to improvise.
13. Tims car is running on it's last leg's.
14. Why did he say, "Well, that depends?"

In the following exercise, you can practice the chapter's lessons about terminal, internal, and grammatical/mechanical punctuation — all in one place! Have fun!

Practice! Punctuation

Fix the punctuation errors in the following sentences.

1. Over there-thats where we keep the lawn mower.
2. Im here to do two things; kick kneecap's and chew bubble gum.
3. Where did you put the tweezers.
4. The film, an Oscar winner last year was boring and offensive.
5. Rondy went outside to shoe the horse, and light the barbecue.
6. The first rule of fight club is, dont talk about fight club.
7. Raspberry jam taste's really good but snozzberry jam is scrumdiddlyumptious.
8. Latte's are getting increasingly expensive so I switched to black coffee.
9. In my vegetable garden, I want to grow: corn, beans, and peas.
10. George Orwell's famous essay, "Politics and the English Language" is included in the book.

Reality Check! Avoiding Common Punctuation Errors

▶ Have you checked the end of each sentence for correct and appropriate terminal punctuation?

▶ Have you used the heavy internal artillery (colons, semicolons, and dashes) correctly and appropriately?

▶ Have you used commas within sentences wherever they are needed for clarity and precision?

▶ Have you avoided using commas where they don't belong?

▶ Have you ensured the standard usage of grammatical and mechanical punctuation?

▶ *Let Us Show You:* Proofing for Punctuation

After Casey revised his essay about plagiarism for content, structure, and coherence, he needed to review it for punctuation errors. He used the Avoiding Common Punctuation Errors *Reality Check!* box to give him a head start.

Here's Casey's introduction with all of the punctuation errors and corrections marked (and with Casey's explanations).

A while ago I had a conversation with a friend about a movie we both saw. Because I had also read an interesting interpretation of the movie somewhere, I presented that idea to my friend to see what she thought of it. It never occurred to me that I had a duty to tell her the source of the idea. I don't think I was being dishonest and trying to trick my friend into thinking I'm smart; I was just sharing an interesting piece of information from a source I honestly didn't even remember. At that moment at least, the idea itself was more important than where it came from. This idea made my friend see the movie in a whole new way, so it didn't matter whether it was my idea or not. This makes me wonder why college professors care so much about acknowledging sources of information? This story makes me question the plagiarism rules at colleges and universities today.	I removed a comma. I added a comma. I took out a colon. The comma here was wrong. I needed a semicolon. The original exclamation point was too much. I needed a semicolon instead of a comma here. I think this question mark could just be a period.

▶ *Talk Amongst Yourselves . . .*

Review the changes Casey made to this paragraph as a result of proofreading for problems with punctuation. Then get a partner and look at each change individually. Can you explain why Casey made each change? Are there any changes that *don't* actually correct a problem? Are there other errors that Casey didn't correct? What do you think of Casey's dilemma about the question mark near the end? Is he correct in his suspicion that it should be a period instead? Why or why not?

▶ *Now You Try:* **Proofing for Punctuation**

Take any draft essay you're working on (or, again, even one you're not currently working on) — as long as you've taken it through revision for content, structure, and coherence — and, just as Casey did, use the Avoiding Common Punctuation Errors *Reality Check!* box on page 435 to identify and resolve any problems you find with your use of punctuation. As always, be sure to ask for help from your instructor, a classmate, or a writing-center consultant if you're not sure whether you're catching every error or correcting all errors appropriately.

APPENDICES
The Writer's Toolkit

Basic Grammar and Punctuation Reference

First of all, we want to be clear: this appendix is not an exhaustive grammar reference. There are terrific whole books devoted to describing English grammar in detail, but this appendix is not one of those books. If you are in need of such an exhaustive reference, we strongly recommend that you get your hands on any one of the very good grammar reference books available. For the record, our favorite such book is Diana Hacker's *A Writer's Reference* (Bedford/ St. Martin's).

This appendix is designed to provide a description of only the most basic elements of English grammar and punctuation, and in the briefest and clearest way possible. Its intent is to give you the terminology you need if you want to talk about why and how a particular sentence works (or fails to work).

The Parts of Speech

The parts of speech are the labels we give to words that indicate their function within a sentence. There are eight parts of speech in English: nouns, verbs, pronouns, adjectives, adverbs, prepositions, conjunctions, and interjections. The part of speech is determined by how a word is **used** in a sentence; it is not determined simply by what the word **is**.

NOUNS

A **noun** is a word that represents a person, place, thing, or concept. In a sentence, a noun always answers the questions *Who?* or *What?*

Three Types of Nouns

Nouns come in three varieties: common, proper, and collective.

Most nouns are **common**, meaning that they refer to common persons, places, things, or concepts. A **proper noun** refers to a particular person, place, thing, or idea and is capitalized to indicate the specific nature of what it refers to. Nouns can also be **collective**, which means that they are singular words that refer to multiple persons, places, things, or concepts.

Three Types of Nouns

Type	Common	Proper	Collective
Person	stockbroker	the Dalai Lama	team (of athletes)
Place	kitchen	the Louvre	row (of houses)
Thing	motorcycle	the Parthenon	bunch (of grapes)
Concept	fidelity	Manifest Destiny	plethora (of responsibilities)

Do a Noun Test

There are three tests to determine whether a word is functioning as a noun.

1. Most common nouns can be used in the plural. Thus, if a word can be used correctly in the plural form, it's most likely a noun.

The *child* plays with the *toy*.

The *children* play with the *toys*.

2. In addition, most common nouns can be preceded by the articles *a*, *an*, or *the*. If an article directly in front of a word sounds correct and makes sense, then the word is most likely a noun.

Historians like to read books. The historians like to read the books.
<u>noun</u>   <u>noun</u>   <u>article + noun</u>   <u>article + noun</u>

3. Finally, if we can correctly replace a word with a **personal pronoun** (*I, you, he, she, it, we, they, me, him, her, us,* or *them*), then that word must be a noun. Remember that personal pronouns take the place not only of the noun but also of any of the words that modify that noun:

My aunt believes in tiny little elves. She believes in them.
<u>noun</u>   <u>noun</u> <u>pronoun</u>   <u>pronoun</u>

VERBS

A **verb** is a word that expresses action or state of being. In a sentence, a verb always answers the questions *Does/is what? Did/was what?* or *Will do/be what?*

Three Types of Verbs

1. Verbs can be **transitive**, which means they transfer action from a *subject* (a noun that's doing something) to an *object* (a noun that the subject is acting upon).

Victor Gonzalez *plays* the piano.
<u>subject</u>   <u>transitive</u> <u>object</u>
             verb

2. Verbs can be **intransitive**, which means they express a subject's action but don't transfer it to an object.

<u>Victor Gonzalez</u> <u>*plays*</u> <u>beautifully.</u>
    subject   intransitive adverb
            verb

3. Verbs can also be **linking**, which means they express state of being by equating a subject to a complement (a noun or an adjective that defines or describes the subject).

<u>Victor Gonzalez</u> <u>*is*</u> <u>an excellent pianist.</u>
    subject   linking   complement
          verb

Many verbs can serve as either a transitive or a linking verb depending on their context:

He <u>tasted</u> the muffin that was half-price.
   transitive

The half-price muffin <u>tasted</u> terrible.
             linking

I <u>smelled</u> the dry erase marker.
  transitive

The dry erase marker <u>smelled</u> awful.
          linking

Verb Tense and Agreement

All verbs have **tense** — that is, they indicate the time of the action or state of being in some form of the present, past, or future.

Simple Verb Tenses

Type	Simple present	Simple past	Simple future
Transitive	John *throws* a punch.	I *ate* my gum.	Sylvia *will break* your heart.
Intransitive	Rover really *stinks*.	The lilacs *bloomed*.	Your birds *will fly* south.
Linking	Ignorance *is* bliss.	Rupert *seemed* moody.	That tie *will look* funny.

In addition to the simple verb tenses shown in the chart on page 441, English has progressive tenses (*-ing*), perfect tenses (*have/had*), and perfect progressive tenses (*have/had* + *-ing*), as well as a conditional mood.

Depending on whether you consider the conditional to be a tense (and for the record, we do), the English language has either twelve or sixteen verb tenses in all, as shown in the following chart.

All Verb Tenses

TENSE	Present	Past	Future	Conditional
Simple	I think	I thought	I will think	I would think
Progressive	I am thinking	I was thinking	I will be thinking	I would be thinking
Perfect	I have thought	I had thought	I will have thought	I would have thought
Perfect progressive	I have been thinking	I had been thinking	I will have been thinking	I would have been thinking

Note that certain forms of verbs, such as present participles (*-ing* verbs), can't function as a complete verb unless they have help from an auxiliary verb. *Walking* isn't a verb, for example, unless it has help: <u>*is walking*</u> or <u>*was walking*</u>.

Gretchen <u>singing</u> a song.
[Nope]

Gretchen <u>was singing</u> a song.
[Okay]

A verb also must agree with its subject in both **number** (singular/plural) and **person** (first person, *I/we*; second person, *you*; third person, *he/she/it/they*). For instance, it probably comes as no shock that it's better to say "I am mad" than "I are mad." This is because *are* doesn't agree with a first-person singular subject (*I*), whereas *am* does.

Identifying Verbs

And finally, when you're trying to identify the verb in a clause, there are two slightly tricky situations to keep in mind.

First, sometimes an adverb or two might sneak in between the parts of a multi-word verb. These adverbs are <u>not</u> a part of the verb.

Gretchen <u>was</u> very beautifully <u>singing</u>.

      part   adverbs   part
     of verb   of verb

And second, a verb may sometimes be joined to another word through a compound such as *cannot* or a contraction such as *isn't* or *he's*:

> While Gretchen *was* indeed *singing* a song, Luther *was* not *enjoying* the performance.

> Gretchen*'s* an excellent singer, but Luther still *isn't* impressed.

The adverbs in the first example (*indeed* and *not*) are <u>not</u> considered a part of the verbs (*was singing, was enjoying*). In the second example, the verb *is* is reduced to *'s* through a contraction; although it has become smaller, *is* remains the verb in the first part of the sentence.

PRONOUNS

A **pronoun** is a word that takes the place of a common, proper, or collective noun in a sentence. Its essential function is to simplify sentences by eliminating the need to repeat nouns. Without pronouns, for example, the following sentence would have to repeat the subject (*an apple*) in the second independent clause instead of using the simpler *it*:

> An apple fell from the tree, and it conked Bobby on the head.

Even a fairly uncomplicated sentence would be rendered ridiculous if we didn't have pronouns to reduce repeated nouns. Check it out:

> Cindy likes Cindy's new computer, but Cindy doesn't like the computer's operating system.

> Cindy likes <u>her</u> new computer, but <u>she</u> doesn't like <u>its</u> operating system.

         pronoun   pronoun   pronoun

Eight Types of Pronouns

There are eight types of pronouns: personal, indefinite, demonstrative, relative, interrogative, intensive, reflexive, and reciprocal.

1. Personal pronouns are by far the most commonly used of all the pronouns. They are called personal because they typically take the place of otherwise named or identified persons in a sentence (*Cindy* becomes *she*, for example). But personal pronouns also take the place of specific things or concepts (*computer* becomes *it*, for example). Personal pronouns carry **number** so that they can accurately represent whether the nouns they replace are singular or plural:

Bob asked the children to stop screaming.

He asked them to stop screaming.
<u>pronoun</u>   <u>pronoun</u>

Personal pronouns also carry person, case, and gender.

They carry **person** so that they can accurately reflect whether the nouns they replace refer to the speaker of the sentence (first person: *I/we*), the receiver of the speaker's sentence (second person: *you*), or persons or things that are neither the speaker nor the receiver (third person: *he/she/it/they*):

I think we should leave before things get ugly.
first person

Are you really planning to buy a time-share condo?
second person

He tried to argue, but they weren't interested.
third person

Personal pronouns will take on a specific **case** depending on their function within a sentence: when a pronoun plays the role of a subject in a sentence, it must take the **subjective case**; when it plays the role of an object in a sentence, it must take the **objective case**; and when it takes the place of a noun that is possessed by a person in a sentence, it must take the **possessive case**.

We are probably in deeper trouble than we thought.
subjective

Will the manager really kick us out?
objective

No, that suitcase full of money isn't ours.
possessive

Pronoun Case

PRONOUN	Subjective case	Objective case	Possessive case
First-person singular	I	me	mine
First-person plural	we	us	ours
Second-person singular/plural	you	you	yours

PRONOUN	Subjective case	Objective case	Possessive case
Third-person masculine singular	he	him	his
Third-person feminine singular	she	her	her/hers
Third-person neutral singular	it	it	its
Third-person plural	they	them	theirs

And finally, the third-person singular pronouns also have **gender**, which communicates whether the noun that the pronoun refers to is masculine, feminine, or neuter:

She respectfully asked *him* to put *it* down on the side table.

2. Indefinite pronouns are similar to personal pronouns, but instead of taking the place of a specific noun, they take the place of an unknown (or indefinite) person, place, or thing (*anyone, everybody, something,* etc.).

An important grammatical quirk of most indefinite pronouns is that even when they logically refer to something plural, they are treated as singular grammatically. The indefinite pronoun *everyone,* for example, clearly refers to multiple people, yet in a sentence, it is treated as if it refers to one person. All of the pronouns that end in *–one, -body,* or *–thing* are treated as singular.

Also keep in mind that an indefinite pronoun that precedes a prepositional phrase is treated as singular if the object of the prepositional phrase is singular, and as plural if the object is plural. The chart below gives a bunch of examples of what we're talking about.

Indefinite Pronouns

Indefinite pronouns treated as singular or plural depending on what they refer to	
Singular	Plural
half (of the book)	half (of the programs)
all (of the water)	all (of the clowns)
most (of the day)	most (of the puppies)
some (of the music)	some (of the hammers)
any (of the money)	any (of the pumpkins)
none (of the ice cream)	none (of the ideas)

3. Demonstrative pronouns are also similar to personal pronouns, but they are used to point to (or demonstrate) the nouns for which they substitute. There are only four demonstrative pronouns — two are singular (*this* and *that*), and two are plural (*these* and *those*). Note that they function as pronouns only if they actually take the place of a noun; if they precede a noun, they function as adjectives.

These are the best peaches I've ever had.
<u>pronoun</u>

Is he really going to wear that shirt?
<u>adjective</u>

4. Relative pronouns always signal the beginning of a new dependent clause. The list of relative pronouns is relatively short: *who, which, that, what, when, where, why,* and *how*, as well as the other forms of those words (*whom, whoever, whomever, whose, whichever, whatever, whenever, wherever*).

These words are relative pronouns only when they are used to begin a dependent clause that is joined to an independent clause in a sentence.

Ludwig wants to know why Harriet is laughing.
    independent   relative
      clause   pronoun

He who laughs last laughs longest.
   relative   independent
  pronoun   clause

It's terribly funny that you should ask.
  independent relative
    clause   pronoun

There is no good explanation for how he ended up on the roof.
      independent   relative
       clause   pronoun

5. Interrogative pronouns are almost the same as the list of relative pronouns, but unlike relative pronouns, interrogative pronouns are used to ask questions (or to interrogate).

When will the pizza get here?

Whom did the mayor invite to the reception?

6. Intensive pronouns are created by adding the suffix *-self* or *-selves* to the possessive or objective forms of personal pronouns (*her, it, them*, etc.). They are used to emphasize (or intensify) the subject to which they refer.

Wanda *herself* told us to arrive early.

Of course they don't understand: I *myself* am confused by what I said.

They *themselves* were the source of the leak.

7. Reflexive pronouns are the same words as intensive pronouns, but they are used as objects that refer directly back to the subject of the sentence they appear in.

Oh, dear, I'm afraid Stefan has hurt *himself* again.

Edith certainly likes *herself*, doesn't she?

8. Reciprocal pronouns function in the same way as reflexive pronouns, but they are used for mutual reference when the subject is plural.

The *boys* are always hurting *each other*.

You two should try to be nice to *one another*.

ADJECTIVES

An **adjective** is a word that modifies, or describes, a noun or pronoun. Within sentences, adjectives always answer the questions *Which one? What kind?* or *What's it like?*

Three Forms of Adjectives

Adjectives have three forms: positive, comparative, and superlative.

1. The **positive** or base form of an adjective positively describes a quality of a noun or pronoun.

Sylvia is wearing her *purple* sneakers again.

2. The **comparative** form of an adjective is used to compare two nouns, and it either ends in *-er* or is preceded by the word *more*. Generally, the *-er* rule applies to adjectives that are only one or two syllables in their positive form; longer words typically receive the *more* treatment. Note that the common adjectives *good* and *bad* are irregular and therefore don't follow the standard *-er* rule.

That's okay; I'll use the *older* laptop for my homework.

Bali was even *more beautiful* than I imagined it would be.

Mario's lasagna is infinitely *better* than mine.

3. The **superlative** form of an adjective is used to compare three or more nouns; it either ends in *-est* or is preceded by the word *most*. The same rules and exceptions apply to it as to the comparative form:

> This is not the *toughest* class I've ever taken.

> I will say, though, that it's the *most challenging* class I've had.

> It's definitely not the *worst* experience in the world.

Note that some forms of verbs (such as present and past participles) and some types of pronouns (such as possessive and demonstrative) function as adjectives, although pronoun-adjectives do not take comparative or superlative forms.

> Please give the *crying* child some *cooked* carrots.

> I think *her* neurosis was exacerbated by *those* phone calls.

ADVERBS

An **adverb** is a word that modifies, or describes, a verb, an adjective, another adverb, or even a whole clause or sentence. An easier way to remember what adverbs do is that they modify or describe anything but a noun or pronoun. Within sentences, adverbs always answer the questions *When? How? Where? In what way?* or *To what extent?*

> He ran today.
>   [When?]

> He ran swiftly.
>   [How?]

> He ran here.
>   [Where?]

> He ran clumsily.
>   [In what way?]

> He ran constantly.
>   [To what extent?]

Many — but not all — adverbs are constructed by adding *-ly* to an adjective (as in the case of *swiftly*, *clumsily*, and *constantly* in the preceding examples). Be careful about relying too heavily on this "rule," though. For one thing, not all words that end in *-ly* are adverbs (*lovely* and *ugly*, for example, are adjectives). And for another thing, the most commonly used adverbs are not formed by modifying existing adjectives — they are their own words, including such easy-to-overlook words as *not*, as well as other limiting adverbs. Examples of these limiting adverbs are italicized in the following sentences:

Come to see me *first*.

Juliette *just* wants an answer.

I do*n't* have seafood *very often*.

Like adjectives, many descriptive adverbs — but not limiting adverbs — can take comparative and superlative forms:

Stan responded *more patiently* than Stephanie deserved.

Bruno's table was set the *most elegantly* among all those in the competition.

PREPOSITIONS

A **preposition** is a word that demonstrates the relationships, or positions, between and among other words in a sentence. A preposition begins a prepositional phrase, which consists of the preposition itself followed by a noun or pronoun and its modifiers. There are many prepositions — at least fifty — but the most common are *about, after, as, at, before, by, during, for, from, in, of, on, to, under,* and *with*.

Prepositions show relative positions in time and space, as well as conceptual relationships, between nouns or pronouns in a sentence.

Why don't you come over after school?

temporal relationship

Whose slippers are under the table?

spatial relationship

We will provide amenities for your convenience, of course.

conceptual relationships

Prepositions dealing with space are the most common and are sometimes referred to as **squirrel words**. These prepositions show anything a squirrel can do to a tree (try not to think about that too hard): a squirrel can go *up* the tree, *down* the tree, *to* the tree, *from* the tree, *over* the tree, *under* the tree, *in* the tree, *out of* the tree, and so on.

CONJUNCTIONS

A **conjunction** is a word that joins together words, phrases, and clauses within a sentence. There are two types of conjunctions: subordinating and coordinating.

1. Subordinating conjunctions are both simpler and more complex than coordinating conjunctions, so we'll start with them. Subordinating conjunctions are used almost exclusively to join clauses together, but they do it in a particular way. The word *subordinate* means "lesser than" or "beneath." A clause that is subordinated (that is, a clause that begins with a subordinating conjunction) is called *dependent*, which means it cannot stand alone as a sentence — it is less than a sentence.

To be part of a complete sentence, a dependent clause needs to be joined to an independent clause. In this way, subordinating conjunctions are functionally identical to relative pronouns — and in fact, the relative pronouns are often included on lists of subordinating conjunctions. There are many subordinating conjunctions — too many to remember easily — but the most common ones, in addition to the relative pronouns, are *after, although, as, because, before, if, since, unless, until, when,* and *while*.

Warren will visit you in the hospital *if* you promise not to cry.

After we eat dinner, let's watch TV *since* there's nothing better to do.

2. Coordinating conjunctions, like subordinating conjunctions, can be used to join clauses together. But a clause that begins with a coordinating conjunction can still stand alone as a sentence (the word *coordinate* means "equal"). Perhaps the best thing about coordinating conjunctions is that there are only seven of them in the English language, so they're very easy to remember, especially if you use the mnemonic device FANBOYS (*for, and, nor, but, or, yet, so*).

Ms. Trillin isn't going to believe your story, *so* don't even try.

Several small animals gathered in the front yard, *and* I sat down to watch them.

In addition to joining clauses, coordinating conjunctions are often used to join smaller sentence elements such as words and phrases:

Over the river *and* through the woods to grandmother's house we go.

Not one *but* two of my friends canceled on me for Friday night.

I think you should go with stilettos *or* Crocs — it's your call.

To go one step further, **correlative conjunctions** are paired variations on the simple coordinating conjunctions (*both/and, either/or, neither/nor, not only/but also*) and can be used in the same ways as single coordinating conjunctions:

Both measles *and* mumps are on the rise in some countries.

Either that wallpaper goes, *or* I do.

INTERJECTIONS

An **interjection** is a word that has no clear grammatical relationship to any other words in a sentence. Its function is essentially the same as that of spices in food — it adds flavor. An interjection is set off with an exclamation point or a comma. Most interjections demonstrate a level of emotional content within the sentence; interjections such as *wow* and *ouch*, for example, clearly hint at the mood of the speaker.

> *Yikes!* Did you see that bear?

The most difficult interjections to identify in their natural habitat are mild interjections such as *oh*, *well*, and *please*:

> *Oh*, pass the guacamole, *please*.

The Parts of the Sentence

A **sentence** is a complete grammatical structure that communicates information. Some sentences are simple, consisting of a single clause (for example, *I study grammar*), while others are much more complicated (for example, most of the sentences in this book). A clause, and therefore a simple sentence, is a group of words containing a subject and a predicate.

SUBJECTS

A **subject** is a noun or pronoun that answers the question *Who or what takes action or is described in this sentence?* A subject can be single or compound:

> My <u>dog</u> chews the furniture.
> single subject

> <u>Tracy and her friends</u> bought me a fondue pot.
> compound subject

It's often useful to identify both the **complete subject** (the subject plus any modifiers attached to it) and the **simple subject** (the heart of the complete subject). In the following example, the complete subject is in italics and the simple subject — which is part of the complete sentence — is underlined.

> *The <u>reason</u> for her rejection* is fear of commitment.

It's also useful to remember that the simple subject of a clause can never appear inside a prepositional phrase. It may be tempting to think that the simple subject — which is part of the complete sentence — in the following sentence is *sisters*, but that's not the case:

> <u>Both of my sisters</u> pulled my hair.
> prepositional
> phrase

PREDICATES

A **predicate** is a complete verb plus any objects, complements, or modifiers. The predicate answers at least one question (*What does the subject do?*) and potentially answers several others (*to whom/what? for whom/what? when? where? why?*), depending on the type of verb as well as the presence of objects or complements and modifiers.

Complete Verbs

The **complete verb** of a clause is the main verb (the action or state of being itself) plus any auxiliary verbs that are attached to the main verb in order to further define its tense or condition. Sometimes a verb is a single word, while at other times it is two, three, or more words. Remember, though, that an adverb is not a part of the verb — even when it sandwiches itself between the verb parts:

Steve *is* crazy.

That new Porsche *would have made* me very happy.

I *have* rarely *given* interviews, and I *am* not *planning* to start now.

[*rarely* and *not* are adverbs]

Remember that verbs can be **transitive** (meaning that they transfer action from a subject to a direct object, as in *Scruffy ate my shoe*), **intransitive** (meaning that they express action but do not transfer the action to a direct object, as in *Scruffy ate quietly*), or **linking** (meaning that they express state of being, as in *Scruffy seems unhappy*).

OBJECTS

There are two types of objects in sentences: direct and indirect.

1. The **direct object** is the noun or pronoun that receives the action of the transitive verb:

My dog chews the *furniture*.

An easy way to locate the direct object in a sentence that contains a transitive verb is to ask: *The subject verbs what?* In the example you just read, the question would be: *My dog chews what?* The answer, of course, is *the furniture*, which is the direct object.

2. The **indirect object** is the noun or pronoun on whose behalf the action of the transitive verb is taken. It appears between the subject and the direct object:

Tracy and her friends bought *me* a fondue pot.

An easy way to locate the indirect object in a sentence that contains one is to ask: *To whom or for whom does the subject verb the object?* In the preceding example, the question would be: *For whom did Tracy and her friends buy a fondue pot?* And the answer is *me*, which is the indirect object.

COMPLEMENTS

There are two types of complements in sentences: subject and object. A **subject complement** is a noun or an adjective that follows a linking verb and either describes or defines the subject:

> Steve is *crazy*.

> Steve is a *drummer*.

An easy way to locate the subject complement in a sentence that contains a linking verb is to ask: *The subject equals what?* For each of the examples above, the question would be: *Steve equals what?* The answers, of course, are *crazy* and a *drummer*, which are the subject complements.

An **object complement** is a noun or an adjective that follows — and renames, defines, or describes — the direct object:

> The committee elected Smithers president.
> direct   object
> object complement

> That new Porsche would have made me happy.
> direct object
> object complement

An easy way to locate the object complement in a clause that has one is to ask: *The direct object equals what?* For these two examples, the questions would be: *Smithers equals what?* and *I (me) equal what?* The answers, respectively, are *president* and *happy*, which are the object complements.

Objects and Complements: Eight Rules to Memorize

1. **Direct objects** follow transitive (action) verbs. They are acted upon by the subject:

> Steve passed the ball.

> Bryn read a story.

> Sue baked dinner.

> Ryan tasted the fried chicken.

2. **Indirect objects** come between the transitive verb and the direct object. They benefit from the action:

Steve passed <u>Sue</u> the ball.   Sue baked her <u>family</u> dinner.

Bryn read the <u>class</u> a story.   Sally gave <u>Amy</u> a Porsche.

3. All **transitive verbs** take direct objects:

Steve hit the <u>ball</u>.

Some transitive verbs also take indirect objects (but most don't):

Steve hit <u>Sue</u> the ball.

4. **Subject complements** follow linking (state of being) verbs. They can define the subject:

Jeff is a <u>minister</u>.   Tom became a famous <u>lawyer</u>.

The sculpture resembled a giant <u>bean</u>.   My new car is a <u>Porsche</u>.

Or they can describe the subject:

Sushi is <u>delicious</u>.   Kendall became <u>grumpy</u>.

Sara seems <u>sleepy</u>.   The fried chicken tasted <u>fantastic</u>.

5. All **linking verbs** are followed by subject complements. (Just try to remove the complements from any of the example sentences in #4 above.)

6. **Object complements** follow and describe direct objects:

Grammar makes me <u>giddy</u>.

Not all direct objects take object complements; in fact, most don't.

7. **Intransitive verbs** express action but aren't followed by objects or complements:

Lambert <u>whistles</u> exceptionally well.   The children <u>played</u> all afternoon.

8. **Some verbs** can be transitive, intransitive, or linking depending on their function in the sentence.

Transitive versus intransitive:

Wanda <u>flew</u> a kite.   Wanda <u>flew</u> into a rage.
     transitive   intransitive

Transitive versus linking:

Louise <u>felt</u> my forehead.   Louise <u>felt</u> sick.
     linking   transitive

CLAUSES

Any group of words containing a subject and a predicate is a **clause**. There are two types of clauses: independent and dependent.

1. Independent clauses can stand alone as complete sentences if they want to — but they don't have to. Independent clauses begin either with no conjunction or with a coordinating conjunction.

Sally has a headache.

clause that begins with no conjunction

But William feels fine.

clause that begins with a coordinating conjunction

2. Dependent clauses, on the other hand, cannot stand alone as complete sentences. Dependent clauses (also known as subordinate clauses) begin with either a subordinating conjunction (e.g., *although*) or a relative pronoun (e.g., *which*). Remember that even though a dependent clause cannot stand alone as a complete sentence, it is still a clause because it has a subject and a predicate.

Although she's happy, I am miserable.

subordinating
conjunction

The roof is leaking, which is unfortunate.

relative pronoun

PHRASES

Aside from words and clauses, sentences are made of **phrases** — groups of related words that function as units within sentences but that cannot be clauses because they often lack a subject and always lack a complete verb. The two most common types of phrases are prepositional and verbal.

1. Prepositional phrases always begin with a preposition and end with a noun or pronoun, which may have modifiers:

In fact, I bought one of those funny hats.

prepositional   prepositional phrase
phrase

When both prepositional phrases in this sentence are removed, only the core elements of the sentence remain: the subject (*I*), the verb (*bought*), and the direct object (*one*).

2. Verbal phrases are made of forms of verbs that cannot function as complete verbs. There are three types of verbal phrase: participial, gerund, and infinitive.

a. Participial phrases consist of a present (-*ing*) or past (-*ed*, -*en*) participial form of a verb, plus any modifiers. Participial phrases always function as adjectives within a sentence.

Crying uncontrollably, the senator left the podium, defeated at last.
participial phrase

b. Gerund phrases also consist of an -*ing* verb form plus any modifiers. Gerunds always function as nouns within sentences. In the following example, note that the gerund phrase (*Swimming every morning*) is actually the subject of the sentence. A gerund phrase can also serve as a direct object, an indirect object, the object of a preposition, or a subject complement.

Swimming every morning has kept me in good shape.
gerund phrase

My neighbor loves playing strip poker.
direct object

I think I'll give playing strip poker a try.
indirect object

Cards are useful for playing strip poker.
object of a preposition

His one great passion in life is playing strip poker.
subject complement

c. Infinitive phrases consist of the infinitive form of a verb (*to* + *verb*) as well as any modifiers. An infinitive can function as a noun within a sentence — as a subject, a direct object, or a subject complement, for example — and it can also function as an adjective or an adverb.

To sing is the job of the diva.
noun
(subject)

I'd like to sing.
noun
(direct object)

Her favorite activity is to sing.
noun
(subject complement)

Aruba is the place to be.
adjective

She lied to fool us.
adverb

Sentence Structure

There are four types of sentence structure: simple, compound, complex, and compound-complex.

1. Simple sentences consist of single independent clauses and therefore have no conjunctions joining clauses.

Sally has a headache.

Note that a simple sentence may have conjunctions in its subject or its predicate, but it will not have clause conjunctions, because it has no clauses that need to be joined — it has only one set of subject and verb.

<u>Sally *and* William</u> have <u>headaches *but* not toothaches.</u>
     compound subject   compound object
                      [one independent clause]

2. Compound sentences consist of two or more independent clauses and therefore have only *coordinating clause conjunctions*.

<u>Sally has a headache,</u> but <u>William feels fine.</u>
    independent clause   independent clause

3. Complex sentences consist of one independent clause and one or more dependent clauses and therefore have only *subordinating clause conjunctions*.

<u>Although she's happy,</u> <u>Sally has a headache.</u>
    dependent clause   independent clause

4. Compound-complex sentences consist of two or more independent clauses plus one or more dependent clauses and therefore have both coordinating and subordinating clause conjunctions.

<u>Although she's happy,</u> <u>Sally has a headache,</u> <u>which is unfortunate,</u>
    dependent   independent   dependent
      clause   clause   clause

but <u>William feels fine.</u>
    independent
      clause

In the example sentences in the following chart (page 458), subjects are underlined and verbs are italicized. Remember that each set of subject and verb constitutes a clause; a clause's dependence or independence is determined by whether or not it begins with a subordinating conjunction (or a relative pronoun). Use the chart to figure out whether a sentence is simple, compound, complex, or compound-complex.

Four Sentence Types

SENTENCE TYPE	Number and type of clauses	Clause conjunction	Example
Simple	one independent	none	Exhausted from staying up all night studying for his math test, Casey *overslept* and *missed* the bus.
Compound	two or more independent	coordinating only	Facts *are* stubborn things, but statistics *are* more pliable.
Complex	one independent + one or more dependent	subordinating only	If you *go* into the backyard, you *should watch* where you *step*.
Compound-complex	two or more independent + one or more dependent	both coordinating and subordinating	Climate *is* what we *expect*, but weather *is* what we *get*.

Sentence Purpose

There are also four types of sentence purpose: declarative, imperative, interrogative, and exclamatory.

1. Declarative sentences (also known as *indicative*) are the most common type of sentence. They are used for making statements. Declarative sentences end with a period.

I bought some roller skates.

2. Imperative sentences issue requests or commands and always have the implied subject *you*. These sentences also typically end with periods, although some imperatives are exclamatory.

Shut the door before we all freeze to death.

3. Interrogative sentences interrogate. In other words, they ask a question. Interrogative sentences end with question marks.

Are you going to eat all of the chocolate?

4. Exclamatory sentences are so excited that they need an exclamation point at the end.

Good heavens, Wiggins, you're on fire!

Punctuation

Punctuation marks can be sorted into three broad categories:

1. **Terminal punctuation marks** are those that indicate the end (or termination) of a sentence.

2. **Internal punctuation marks** are those that indicate structural distinctions within a sentence.

3. **Nonstructural punctuation marks** are those that are unrelated to the structure of a sentence but nevertheless communicate important information about how words and phrases are meant to be understood.

TERMINAL PUNCTUATION MARKS

Terminal punctuation marks have the strongest structural and rhythmic impact on writing. They help the reader to understand not only that a sentence has ended but also how that sentence ends. Terminal punctuation marks communicate the inflection with which a reader should end a sentence, and the writer chooses one based on the purpose of the sentence.

By far the most common piece of terminal punctuation is the **period**, which is used to end a declarative sentence (also known as an indicative sentence) as well as many, but not all, imperative sentences:

The rumba is a much simpler dance than the samba.

To begin, step back and to the left.

The **question mark** ends sentences that ask questions. Note that, fairly often, interrogative sentences aren't entire sentences at all.

Have you ever taken a tango lesson?

Really?

The **exclamation point** ends a sentence in an excited way. Exclamatory sentences are often also imperative — that is, they form a command or request. Use the exclamation point sparingly in academic writing. In the words of F. Scott Fitzgerald, "An exclamation point is like laughing at your own joke."

We won our badminton tournament yesterday!

Look out for that falling boulder!

INTERNAL PUNCTUATION MARKS

The semicolon, the colon, and the comma are used within sentences to indicate where clauses and phrases (and other structural elements) begin and end. Each mark has its own particular rules that govern its usage.

The internal punctuation marks covered in this section are arranged in order from strongest to weakest — that is, the marks as ordered suggest a progressively weaker separation between ideas. Problems with internal punctuation use are so plentiful that we've also included usage guidelines that provide examples of how to use (and how *not* to use) each punctuation mark.

The Semicolon

; The **semicolon** is generally used to join two independent clauses that are closely enough related that the writer doesn't want them in separate sentences. It is essentially as strong as a period; it links clauses that could stand alone if necessary.

So why use a semicolon instead of a period if those clauses could be their own sentences? Usually a writer will choose the semicolon to communicate that the ideas belong together. In other words, the ideas need to be understood in the context of each other. Another reason to opt for the semicolon is to avoid having too many short, choppy sentences in a paragraph. And finally, the semicolon has one other use that's rarely employed: to separate items in a list or series when those items already have internal punctuation.

Semicolon Usage Guidelines

Use a semicolon to . . .	For example (correct usage):
link closely related independent clauses not joined by a coordinating conjunction	I'd like to help you out; you've always been a good friend.
link independent clauses joined by conjunctive adverbs	It's not that difficult; however, it will take some time.
separate items in a series when each item contains internal structural punctuation (commas)	I have lived in Kalamazoo, Michigan; Tianjin, China; and Aberdeen, Washington.
Do NOT use a semicolon to . . .	**For example (incorrect usage):**
link dependent clauses to independent clauses	Although he was feeling good about the test; he hadn't studied.
link phrases to sentences	Once upon a time; dinosaurs roamed the earth.
introduce a list	We were told to bring the following; scissors, glue, and construction paper.

The Colon

Like the semicolon, the **colon** is generally used to join independent clauses — but only when the second clause explains the first, or when the second clause answers a question implied by the first. The colon is more versatile than the semicolon; its specific uses beyond the primary one are described in the following chart.

Colon Usage Guidelines

Use a colon to ...	For example (correct usage):
announce a second independent clause that explains, or answers a question implied by, the first	Now I understand why she was crying: she had heard about what Bob said.
introduce a final appositive	You've got to stop committing those crimes: theft and dishonesty.
introduce a series following an independent clause	We were told to bring our supplies: scissors, glue, and construction paper.
after "the following" or "as follows" to introduce a statement or series	The grading criteria are as follows: organization, content, and presentation.
introduce a long or formal quotation	As Hemingway says in *A Moveable Feast*: "There were no problems except where to be happiest."
separate subtitles from titles, subdivisions of time, biblical citations, and elements of bibliographic citations	In his article "Reading for Fun: Just Try It," Walker says that Ezekiel 4:12 is the perfect thing to read at 5:30 in the morning.
end a formal salutation	To Whom It May Concern:
Do NOT use a colon to ...	**For example (incorrect usage):**
separate a verb from the rest of the predicate	A colon must: be used very carefully.
separate a preposition from its object	Paul bothered Sandi by: talking too much.
introduce a series **not** preceded by a complete independent clause	We were told to bring: scissors, glue, and construction paper.

The Comma

> **,**

The **comma** is a wonderful piece of punctuation, but it gives writers more trouble than all other punctuation marks combined. Why? Well, primarily because, although there are rules for when a comma should and should not be used, many writers seem to have their own personal preferences for what to do with commas.

The comma offers a gentle pause in the flow of words and ideas. Therefore it is the weakest of the internal punctuation marks. If it's misplaced, it may annoy readers, but it won't disrupt the meaning of the sentence. However, because of its gentle nature, the comma is often misused. Too often, in our opinion. Study the list of dos and don'ts in the chart below. Then go ahead and use commas with confidence.

Comma Usage Guidelines

Use a comma to . . .	For example (correct usage):
link independent clauses joined by a coordinating conjunction	I am feeling very tired, so I will go home.
set off introductory phrases and clauses	During the long night, we were frightened.
set off nonrestrictive (but not restrictive) elements	My friend Steve, who is a vegetarian, came to dinner last night.
set off parenthetical expressions	Your mother, by the way, is very interesting.
set off mild interjections and words of direct address	Why yes, Bob, I do think the music is too loud.
separate elements in a parallel series of three or more (note that the comma preceding the final element is optional)	We have a government of the people, by the people, and for the people.
separate coordinate (but not cumulative) adjectives	She is tall, elegant, and graceful.
set off appositive phrases	My physician, the famous Dr. Huntington, gave a speech.
set off contrasting expressions and interrogatives	He's rather outspoken, isn't he?
set off speech tags	"I'm thinking of traveling," she said.

Use a comma to . . .	For example (correct usage):
separate components of numbers, dates, and place names	On November 15, 2008, he moved to Lexington, Kentucky.
prevent misunderstanding or show the omission of a word	Those who cared showed up; those who don't, didn't.

Do NOT use a comma to . . .	For example (incorrect usage):
separate a subject from its verb unless another rule requires it	Sam and Will, went to the opera.
separate a verb from its object or complement	Sam and Will went, to the opera.
separate a preposition and its object	Sam and Will went to, the opera.
separate cumulative adjectives	He lives in a dark, green house.
separate an adjective or adverb from the word it modifies	The opera was very, exciting.
separate parallel elements joined by a coordinating conjunction	The book was very long, and interesting.
set off restrictive elements	The student, who failed the test, wants to retake it.
follow "such as" or "like"	I have many books such as, those by Dickens and Twain.
precede or follow a list	Go to the store and buy, meat and potatoes, for dinner.
introduce indirect discourse	He said, that I was too vain.
precede "than" in a comparison	This class is easier, than my other class.
stand next to any other piece of structural punctuation	The book, (which was really good), took me four days to read.

Dashes and Parentheses

The **dash** is often used in place of a semicolon or colon between independent clauses. You may have noticed that we employ dashes rather than those other punctuation marks quite frequently in this book. The dash can also be used in the same way as commas are to set off nonrestrictive elements of a sentence.

( ) Writers sometimes use **parentheses** in place of commas or dashes to set off nonrestrictive elements in a sentence. The use of parentheses instead of commas or dashes typically communicates that the nonrestrictive element is truly extra information (also known as parenthetical information).

NONSTRUCTURAL PUNCTUATION MARKS

Punctuation marks that don't affect the syntax of sentences are still important. They clue readers in to how the words relate to each other and to what kind of meaning the writer intended.

The Apostrophe

' The **apostrophe** has two primary purposes: to indicate possession (when it appears between a noun or an indefinite pronoun and a final -s), and to mark the space where a letter or letters have been omitted in a contraction.

Apostrophe Usage Guidelines

Use an apostrophe . . .	For example (correct usage):
to indicate that a noun is possessive (precedes the -s)	Sylvia's new neighbor is happier than Walter's.
to indicate that an indefinite pronoun is possessive (precedes the -s)	The problem is either everyone's or no one's.
to mark omitted letters in a contraction	I'd prefer if you didn't tell him that it's over.
Do NOT use an apostrophe . . .	For example (incorrect usage):
to indicate that pronouns other than indefinite pronouns are possessive	Is that book your's or her's?
before the -s in plural nouns	The dog's are all barking.
before the -s in conjugated verbs	My aunt Rebecca sing's really well.

Quotation Marks

" " The primary function of **quotation marks** is to indicate that the exact words of another speaker or writer are being used. That function and a few other specific uses of quotation marks are described in the following chart. Use quotation marks carefully when combining them with other punctuation marks.

Quotation Marks Usage Guidelines

Use quotation marks to . . .	For example (correct usage):
enclose direct quotations from speakers or writers	Longfellow writes eloquently of "the forest primeval."
enclose words referred to as words	My essays repeat "like" and "really" far too often.
enclose titles of short works (articles, stories, poems, songs)	Frost's "The Road Not Taken" is about choices in life.
Format quotation marks . . .	**For example (correct usage):**
singly when enclosing a quote within a quote	Crane's poem begins, "A man said to the universe: / 'Sir, I exist!' "
outside periods or commas	"I'm sorry," she lied, "but you'll have to forgive me."
outside question marks when the quote itself is a question	The senator asked rhetorically, "What do we believe?"
inside question marks when the quote itself is not a question	Did she really say, "I'm leaving"?
inside colons and semicolons	He insisted he was "the best qualified"; we'll see about that.
Do NOT use quotation marks to . . .	**For example (incorrect usage):**
enclose indirectly reported speech	He said that "he wasn't hungry."
enclose items used ironically or sarcastically	My third-grade teacher was a real "sweetheart."

Appendix B

Writing and Citing Across the Curriculum

In this appendix, we'll give you some bare-bones advice about how to approach writing in the three broad areas of a liberal arts education: the humanities, the social sciences, and the natural sciences. This advice should help you to navigate the various writing tasks you're likely to encounter in classes across the disciplines.

All writing is the result of a writing process, and all writing has structure. Therefore, the writing you do in your other classes will have a lot of similarities to the writing you learn in composition class or English class. And most college writing will involve some research.

Characteristics of All Academic Writing

Process	All successful academic writing involves prewriting, drafting, and revision.
Structure	All successful academic writing has an introduction, a body, and a conclusion.
Main point	All successful academic writing has a central purpose (or thesis).
Research	All successful academic writing incorporates research (informal or formal).
Clarity	All professors expect clarity and precision of expression in student writing.

The writing process, the structure of good sentences, essays and paragraphs, the formulation of main points, the presentation of research, and the achievement of clarity in college writing are all addressed thoroughly in this book. In broad terms, professors assign writing similarly across the academic disciplines. So when you have writing assignments for other courses, everything you learn here should be relevant and useful.

College Writing Assignments

Type of writing	Sample assignment	Typical length
In-class writing	Essay exam	2–3 pages
Prepared writing	Report, essay	3–5 pages
Capstone project	Term research paper	7–10 pages

So what's different, you ask, *if so much is the same?* Ultimately, writing assignments will differ in three very important ways:

1. the **content** of the writing (i.e., *what* you're asked to write about);
2. the types of **sources** upon which you draw for your writing (i.e., what *evidence* you use); and
3. the style of acknowledging the sources of information you incorporate into your writing (i.e., the **citation style**).

Writing in the Arts and Humanities

The writing assignments you complete for classes in the arts and humanities will be similar to those you encounter in English composition classes. Arts and humanities comprise those disciplines that have to do with the creation and communication of human achievement in its broadest sense. We communicate through writing and speaking, of course, which is why composition and speech and foreign language classes are often included in the humanities.

But we also communicate through art forms, which is why classes in visual art, film, literature, theater, and music are in this area. Finally, the humanities include those subject areas that speak to the most elemental and profound creations of the human mind; thus, disciplines such as philosophy and religion are also in the humanities. Note that history is sometimes considered one of the humanities and sometimes considered a social science, which we'll discuss later.

CONTENT

Writing in the humanities usually discusses texts and other artifacts created by humans. A specific college writing assignment will often require you to demonstrate your understanding and appreciation of a particular text or artifact (e.g., a painting, a play, a photograph, or a song) and will ask you to discuss its meaning and aesthetic qualities. At its heart, most writing in the humanities is responsive, interpretive, and evaluative.

Good writing in the humanities tends to be exploratory, thoughtful, interactive, original, and courageous. In our experience, students understand the first four qualities instinctively, but when they get to the last one, they say, *Hold up. "Courageous"? Seriously?*

To which we say: *Yes!* It takes courage to say, essentially, *Here's what I believe is true about the meaning, artistry, or effectiveness of this text or artifact.* Once you've explored, thought about, interacted with, and developed original ideas about your subject matter, your task is to present your findings as findings, rather than as something that may or may not have value because, *Aw, shucks, ma'am, I'm just a student.*

The evidence you use to discuss a poem, film, painting, symphony, or philosophical treatise will typically come from two types of sources: from the artifact itself (the primary source) and sometimes from other texts by authoritative scholars in a relevant field (secondary sources such as critics, theorists, etc.).

In other words, the evidence in a paper written for a class in the arts or humanities will usually *not* involve charts, graphs, or tables full of numbers. Nor will it be based primarily on the ideas or opinions of others — it should be all about what *you* think and understand. It will be discursive. If you use secondary sources at all, you will do so to validate (or perhaps contradict) your ideas, rather than to draw original content from those sources.

A big part of your task in humanities writing assignments is figuring out how your argument, or perspective, fits together. When you're drafting — and doing all that important critical thinking — you'll need to ensure that your essay's **organization** integrates *your own* thoughts smoothly and reasonably with the ideas from the source material you use. You may be tempted to segregate your own ideas from your source material by writing your analysis and then adding source material as an afterthought, but *don't do that.* As a practical matter, you will likely have separate sets of notes that represent *your insights*, the *primary sources*, and the *secondary sources* — but by the time you've completed your working draft, those separations should disappear, and all ideas should be integrated into unified, coherent paragraphs structured around your claims.

One of the biggest pitfalls of writing in the humanities is summarizing too much and analyzing or interpreting too little. You can safely assume that your reader is familiar with the text or artifact that you're examining, so there's no need to describe or summarize the entire work. Focus on presenting and supporting clear claims about the topic you're addressing rather than writing long stretches of regurgitated facts.

SOURCES

Primary sources in the humanities are original pieces of art or communication, such as the poems, photographs, plays, songs, and other art forms that we've already mentioned in this section.

Secondary sources in the humanities tend to be scholarly articles written by qualified, authoritative experts in the relevant discipline: people such as critics, researchers, and theorists. For example, you might be assigned to explore the meaning and artistry of a photograph by consulting with experts on photography, visual art, aesthetics, and so on. Valid secondary sources might also come from qualified experts who are outside the relevant discipline, depending on the purpose and direction of your research: think of people like psychologists and sociologists. Regardless of what primary and secondary sources you use, you'll need to follow the general guidelines presented in Part 6 of this book as well as the specific guidelines about **MLA citation style**, which we present in the next section.

Remember that even when you're asked to engage in secondary source research, your professors are still mostly interested in what *you* think. So make sure that you've fully explored your own responses, interpretations, and evaluations of that photograph before checking out what the critics and other assorted scholars have to say. From there you can read what the Big Names say — and see what you think. If you find you agree with them, then your own opinion is still based on reasonable and careful analysis that you've already done. If you find that you disagree with them — excellent! Write about that! Just make sure that your disagreements are explained in light of that reasonable and careful analysis we just mentioned.

Citing Sources in the Humanities: MLA Style

The Modern Language Association (MLA) style of parenthetical citation is also called the **author-page** style. Why? Because the **in-text citation** consists of the last name of the author of the source followed by the page number that the idea or quote appears on, all enclosed in parentheses (*Smith 132*). If you are citing a Web source, include whatever information is available: page numbers, paragraph numbers, and/or section numbers. If there are no paragraph, section, or page numbers, MLA says it's okay for you to omit them, but it's always best to ask your professor what he or she would like you to do.

MLA In-Text Citation

While certain factors can predict NPS use, and the drugs are easily accessible (CDC), there are underlying reasons as to why students are taking them to begin with. Students may hold particular outcome expectations, beliefs that a certain effect will result from using NPS. Academically, students use the drugs because they help people "concentrate better," "feel more focused," and "get their work done more efficiently" (Labbe and Maisto 727). However, these are only beliefs held by students and may not be physically true. A study by McCabe, Knight, Teter, and Wechsler shows that students with lower GPAs have the highest connection to stimulant use (99). This conflicting information suggests that students have false information regarding NPS use. According to the *Journal of Addictive Diseases*, "[n]ew research has demonstrated that performance improvements related to methylphenidate administration in healthy volunteers are highly variable and might be dependent on baseline cognitive ability," suggesting that study drugs may not be effective in the first place (417). NPS use is not limited to purely academic reasons either. Not often realized, "many students use these drugs nonmedically to enhance their experience of partying and getting high on other substances" (Arria and DuPont 419), creating a hidden side of NPS use. The reasons that students use NPS are not always as benign as simple study aids.

> If your source has no author listed, cite either the entity that published it or a key word from the title.

> Parenthetical citations immediately follow ideas or direct quotes from sources.

> You can integrate the title and/or author as you introduce the source material.

> Parenthetical citations come before the final punctuation in the phrase or clause.

The list of sources at the end of an MLA-style research paper is called the **works cited** page. Entries in the list should be ordered alphabetically by the first word in the citation — usually the author's last name. Different types of publications have different bibliographic elements, so be sure to use a reliable, thorough reference, such as *Research and Documentation in the Digital Age* (Bedford/St. Martin's), to check the accuracy of each citation.

MLA List of Works Cited (a.k.a. Bibliography)

Works Cited

Arria, Amelia, and Robert DuPont. "Nonmedical Prescription Stimulant Use among College Students: Why We Need to Do Something and What We Need to Do." *Journal of Addictive Diseases*, vol. 29, no. 4, Oct. 2010, pp. 417-26.

Berry, D., et al. "Detection of Feigned ADHD in College Students." *Psychological Assessment*, vol. 22, no. 2, June 2010, p. 325.

Centers for Disease Control and Prevention. "Facts about ADHD." *Centers for Disease Control and Prevention*, Centers for Disease Control and Prevention, 16 July 2013, www.cdc.gov/ncbddd/adhd/facts.html. Accessed 8 Aug. 2013.

Labbe, Allison K., and Stephen A. Maisto. "Development of the Stimulant Medication Outcome Expectancies Questionnaire for College Students." *Addictive Behaviors*, vol. 35, no. 7, July 2010, pp. 726-29.

McCabe, Sean Esteban, et al. "Non-medical Use of Prescription Stimulants among US College Students: Prevalence and Correlates from a National Survey." *Addiction*, vol. 100, no. 1, Jan. 2005, pp. 96-106.

U.S. Drug Enforcement Administration. "Drug Scheduling." *DEA/Drug Scheduling*, U.S. Department of Justice, www.justice.gov/dea/druginfo/ds.shtml. Accessed 11 July 2013.

Annotations (right column):

Center "Works Cited" at the top.

Authors or text titles (if no author) should match in-text citations.

The order of elements depends on the type of source (book, print periodical, Web site, etc.). Follow correct formatting.

Alphabetize the list of works cited by the first word in each entry: A, B, C, etc.

Use a hanging indent for each entry.

Writing in the Social Sciences

The social sciences include those disciplines that focus on the behavior of humans, both individually and in groups: psychology, sociology, political science, anthropology, and often, but not always, history.

CONTENT

The ultimate goal of social sciences is to try to reasonably explain human behaviors and actions. As a result, writing in these areas tends to focus on both texts (descriptive and narrative ones) and data (both quantitative and qualitative data) that represent accounting and analysis of such behaviors and actions. Specific writing assignments in the social sciences often require you to demonstrate your understanding of the implications inherent in these texts and collections of data.

Good writing in the social sciences tends to be fact-based, expository, informative, even-tempered, and objective. These qualities are valued regardless of whether you've been assigned to write a literature review (that's small-*l* literature, not Big-*L* Literature), a report, an annotated bibliography or summary, a research paper, or an essay exam. Your primary focus should be to explain or describe something, and your approach should be objective. When you've got those down, you can feel free to adopt the same confident tone as you do when writing in the humanities. For most of the social sciences, your job in your writing will be to respond, to explain, and to understand. (In writing for history classes, however, you may find that your responses more closely resemble humanities-style responses: you might be making inferences that help you understand and interpret both facts and concepts.)

Evidence in the social sciences tends to lean fairly heavily toward facts and data. As such, much of the evidence you'll use to support your claims will be facts — statistics, surely, and their attendant charts and graphs — but also results of studies and experiments. Authoritative scholarship (and by that we mean *secondary sources*) is also deeply valued in the social sciences. As an undergraduate, your writing will often be about what *you* think of what the experts think. Professors may also ask you simply to demonstrate your understanding of the experts' research, rather than evaluate it.

There's often a delicate balance to figuring out how to **organize** a social science paper. On the one hand, you want to demonstrate that you understand what your sources say, so you need to do quite a bit of quoting and paraphrasing from the sources. On the other hand, you don't want your paper to be a patchwork quilt of nothing but borrowed source material. This is why it's important to quote sparingly (only when the original wording of the source is so good you can't do it justice in your own words). You can paraphrase a bit more but should still do so sparingly (only when the original idea is so important that you need to include it in its entirety, though in your own words). Then you can spend a larger portion of your time summarizing the source material — summary is the best way to demonstrate convincingly that you fully understand the concepts you've encountered in your reading.

SOURCES

Primary sources in the social sciences tend to be original scholarly research studies, public records, and historical documents.

Secondary sources in the social sciences are, as we mentioned earlier, a pretty big deal. In disciplines like anthropology, political science, psychology, and sociology, many of the texts that students are expected to read and understand are written by scholars who themselves are responding to the original research of others in their fields of study. For example, in a psychology class you might be assigned to write a paper about cognitive development in children. In all likelihood, your research will require you to begin with a primary source, such as a researcher who conducted his or her own studies in order to pose a theory — Jean Piaget, for example.

Now, depending on the level of the class, you might dive headfirst into every last one of Piaget's writings (he wrote a lot), or you might just read enough to get a sense of what one of the major theories entails and how he arrived at his conclusions. Then, in all likelihood, you'd move on to secondary sources — scholars who have come along since Piaget advanced his theories and who have agreed with, disagreed with, modified, critiqued, discredited, or reenvisioned Piaget's work. In this way, you would do sufficient research to demonstrate not only that you understand the original theory but also that you understand what subsequent scholars have seen as the strengths and weaknesses of that theory.

After you have consulted your sources, done your thinking, and drafted and revised your writing, you'll need to make sure that you have followed the appropriate set of rules for formatting your paper and citing your sources before you submit your work to your professor.

Citing Sources in the Social Sciences: APA Style

Most disciplines in the social sciences use **APA citation style**, the style of the American Psychological Association. Like all citation styles, APA involves both an in-text reference and a full bibliographic citation. And like most — but not all! — citation styles, APA uses parenthetical citations for in-text references. In other words, APA style is very similar to MLA style in most important respects. However, there are a few very important differences.

APA PARENTHETICAL IN-TEXT CITATION

The APA style of parenthetical citation is also called the **author-year** style. Why? Because the in-text citation consists of the last name of the author of the source and the year of its publication. In the social sciences — and any research- or discovery-based discipline — the year of publication is *crucial*. After all, if you're writing a paper about the latest developments in the treatment of post-traumatic stress disorder, you probably shouldn't be using a source text written in 1992 (or even in 2010, for that matter).

As with MLA style, the parenthetical citation in APA style immediately follows whatever you borrow from a source. Unlike MLA, the citation includes the author's name and the year of publication, separated by a comma (*Smith, 2014*). However, in the case of direct quotations and close paraphrases (in other words, in the case of very specific borrowings), the parenthetical citation must include the page number as well. The page number should be preceded by "p." or, for more than one page, "pp." And again, be sure to separate the elements with commas (*Smith, 2014, pp. 3-4*).

APA In-Text Citation

The Washington State Department of Health explains that information collection helps prevent and control disease by "describing disease trends, identifying and controlling the sources of infection, educating the public, and preventing disease," all while protecting patient privacy (2011, ch. 70.24).

> The author is mentioned in the sentence, so only cite the year and page number. This is a Web source, so use the chapter number instead of the page number.

With no intention of releasing sensitive information, health professionals must still follow Health Insurance Portability and Accountability Act (HIPAA) regulations. This means that if a health care professional releases patient information to anyone other than the health department by legal requirements, they face criminal and civil liability ("The Limits of Privacy," 2013, p. 57). Washington's law attempts to gain medical knowledge

> Use the title or a key word or phrase in the citation if there's no author.

and utilize information to reduce the incidence of sexually transmitted diseases, while ensuring patients' rights surrounding a sensitive topic.

While Washington's law is in good faith, it is not doing the job. A study by the Centers for Disease Control and Prevention about doctors' actions following STD diagnosis of their patients suggests that laws are not being followed. Only 44 percent to 50 percent of providers consistently reported cases to health departments (McCree et al., 2003). The study suggests that lack of knowledge regarding STD reporting laws may be one reason for the low numbers, which wouldn't be the case if laws were properly enforced. The inconsistency in STD reporting among doctors reduces the credibility of the data that is collected. For example, the study found that doctors were more likely to report syphilis than gonorrhea and chlamydia. Claiming that "the prominence of syphilis in public health is consistent with differences in post-diagnosis practices, especially higher reporting rates," data may be incorrect due to doctors' actions (McCree et al., 2003, p. 255). If syphilis is more likely to be reported than other STDs, regardless of the number of cases relative to others, it falsely inflates the incidence rates. This could overshadow the significance of other diseases, hide developing epidemics, and overall reduce efforts made to control STDs. If only 44–50 percent of doctors follow a law, it reduces credibility and consistency among STD reporting.

If you are paraphrasing a source, no page number is required.

For two authors, include both names. For more than two, list the first author only, followed by *et al.* (Latin for "and others").

Be sure to use a reliable reference source, such as *Research and Documentation in the Digital Age*, to look up the specifics for creating entries appropriate to the types of sources you're using.

APA List of References (a.k.a. Bibliography)

References	
References Cason, C., Orrock, N., Schmitt, K., & Tesoriero, J. (2002, October 1). The impact of laws on HIV and STD prevention. *Journal of Law, Medicine & Ethics.* The limits of privacy with patients with STDs. (2007). *Medical Ethics Advisor 23*(5), 56-58. McCree, D. H., Liddon, N. C., Hogben, M., & Lawrence, J. S. (2003). National survey of doctors' actions following the diagnosis of a bacterial STD. *Sexually Transmitted Infections 79*(3), 254-256. Washington State. (2011). *Control and Treatment of Sexually Transmitted Diseases*, Title 70 Washington State Legislature § Chapter 70.24 RCW.	Put "References," centered, at the top of the list. Sometimes "Bibliography" is acceptable. Alphabetize the references list by the first word in each entry (*A, B, C*, etc.). Articles (a/an/the) don't count. Use a hanging indent for each entry. Author then year generally come first. The order depends on the type of source (book, print periodical, Web site, etc.). Identify the source in the same way as you do in the text, using author, agency, or organization name. If you have none of those, use the title of the text.

Citing Sources Using *Chicago* Style

Some social sciences and humanities disciplines — notably history — use **Chicago style**, which is significantly different from either MLA or APA style: while MLA and APA both make use of in-text parenthetical citations, *Chicago* style relies on footnotes and endnotes for its citation of sources.

The general idea of footnotes is that wherever you would use parenthetical citation in MLA style (after you've used words or ideas from a source), you instead insert a footnote reference (a superscript number) that directs the reader to an entry at the bottom (or foot) of the page; that entry includes all of the reference information for the source as well as any additional notes or commentary you'd like to include. (Some people prefer to use endnotes — which appear at the very end of the paper — instead of footnotes. Check with your professor about his or her preference.) The beauty of *Chicago* citation is threefold: your reader doesn't have to flip to a bibliography to find information about your source; you can add comments or clarify a source whenever you'd like to; and your reader can easily skip any footnotes he or she isn't interested in.

Chicago-Style Footnotes

Maxine uses the stories and traditions of her culture as a way of defining herself. In this way, we see the hermeneutic circle appear once again, but on the smaller scale of creating her own identity. The use of horizons can extend further, in a way that they "encompass not only socially, culturally, and historically situated identities but also embodied ones."[1] We see this embodiment as Maxine identifies with the story of her aunt. At one point, she even calls her aunt her "forerunner,"[2] showing how much the story has affected her. This could further explain why she applied so many different imaginary contexts to her aunt's story — they may have reflected her own personal situations or dreams. It may not have really had anything to do with her aunt, but instead with the understanding of herself. The different contexts and desires of her aunt could reflect her own secret feelings or feared situations. However, she retains many conservative sexual habits of her culture as well. Maxine describes her relationship with males: "As if it came from an atavism deeper than fear, I used to add 'brother' silently to boys' names. It hexed the boys. . . . But, of course, I hexed myself also — no dates,"[3] a tendency that relates back to her mother's sexual warnings. These choices Maxine makes are evidence of her struggle to fit into multiple "embodied"[4] worlds and standards at once.

> Footnotes should appear in order in your paper from beginning to end.

---

[1] Georgia Warnke, "Sex and Gender in Context," in *Debating Sex and Gender* (New York: Oxford University Press, 2011), 104.

[2] Maxine Hong Kingston, "No Name Woman," in *The Longman Anthology of Women's Literature*, ed. Mary K. DeShazer (New York: Longman, 2001), 311.

[3] Ibid., 313.

> Use "Ibid." to refer to a previous footnote if you use the same one again immediately.

---

[4] Georgia Warnke, "Sex and Gender in Context," 104.

Once you've cited a work, shorten subsequent citations to just author, title, and page number(s).

As with other citation styles, the order of elements in the citation might vary depending on the type of source, so be sure to consult a reliable resource like *Research and Documentation in the Digital Age* for the specifics.

Ready for the good news? The citation page for a *Chicago*-style research paper looks very much like an MLA-formatted works cited page, except that the header in the *Chicago*-style paper should be "Bibliography" — and of course, individual entries may be formatted slightly differently.

Writing in the Natural Sciences

Writing assignments aren't as common in the natural sciences as they are in the humanities and social sciences. But the relative absence of these assignments doesn't necessarily mean that writing assignments in the sciences are nonexistent. Professors in the sciences are more likely to assign what we like to call *stealth writing assignments* than outright essays, papers, and research projects. These assignments tend to fly beneath the radar, pretending not to be college writing at all. Let's say you're looking at your syllabus for biology or chemistry, for example, and you see that part of your grade is based on "labs." What do you think that means? Well, we're willing to bet that at least a portion of your lab grade is based on lab reports, which are, you know, *written*. And those exams that science professors like to give? More often than not, they include essay or short-essay questions, in response to which you need to, you know, *write*. That's what we mean by stealth writing assignments.

CONTENT

At its heart, most writing in the natural sciences is expository. Its ultimate goal is to explain how and why the natural world operates. So the content of writing in these areas tends to focus on that which is observable through the scientific method of inquiry — that is, through observation, hypothesis, reasoning, experimentation, evaluation, and confirmation of findings. As a result, writing in the natural sciences is only occasionally interpretive.

Evidence in this discipline doesn't just lean on facts and data — it is made *entirely* of facts and data. In the sciences, if it isn't hard data, it isn't evidence. If it can't be observed, tested, and replicated, it doesn't exist. The notion of the "right answer" is not just accepted but expected. This doesn't mean that the natural sciences are rigid or biased, however: one of the most noble and honorable elements of science is its insistence on modifying previous conclusions when new evidence suggests that past knowledge offers an insufficient explanation.

The most important quality of scientific writing is rationality, which is the practice of drawing logical conclusions based on evidence and reason as opposed to sensation, perception, or feeling. An important component of rationality is *reasonableness*. In order to be reasonable in presenting your findings in scientific writing, you need to *think* about what you're writing and ask yourself, *Does this make sense?* We can't tell you how many times we've seen students make a simple arithmetic error (or perhaps hit the wrong key on the calculator) and end up writing something like, "In 18 of 25 trials, the solution reacted as expected; therefore, the experiment had a 1.39 percent predictability rate." It doesn't take a whole lot of thinking to realize that there's no way 18 out of 25 equals 1.39 percent. Seriously.

Errors in reasonability aren't just about numbers, though. As you know (because you've been reading this book), reasonableness is a crucial component of any argument because it guarantees the logic of that argument. Any unreasonable presentation or discussion of information is likely to result in a logical fallacy. (Remember logical fallacies? Chapter 18?) Say, for example, that you're writing about the difference between mixtures, solutions, and suspensions for a chemistry class. Most of the examples you run across in your reading are about liquids, so you casually mention in your report that because salt and sugar are two different particles that don't react to each other, then salt and sugar will create a liquid mixture when combined.

Wait, what? you may be thinking. And we don't blame you. It's not very reasonable to state that if you put sugar and salt together, they'll turn into a liquid through the magic of chemistry, is it? We realize that this is a particularly egregious example of unreasonableness, but we've seen stranger things. So keep a skeptical eye on everything you write in the sciences to ensure accuracy and precision and — most important — to avoid looking like a doofus.

SOURCES AND CITATION

Writing in the sciences tends to value **primary sources** over secondary sources. Beyond this, it tends to value original primary research over the work of others (in other words, your own work based on the scientific method is valued over what you read about your topic).

In some cases, though, you will be asked to consult both primary sources and secondary sources of other scholars in order to develop what we in the English Biz call an "actual paper." When this happens, you would be well advised to make use of the guidelines for using sources in the social sciences — with one big, notable exception: the format and citation style.

Some of the formal academic writing that happens in lower-division science classes uses APA style, which we discussed earlier in this appendix. However, formal academic writing in the higher levels of science study makes use of the **CSE style** of formatting and citing sources. CSE (Council of Science Editors) style makes use of three different systems of citation, just to be difficult. We will not discuss those systems here, but you can look them up if you need them in the excellent resource *Research and Documentation in the Digital Age*.

The Bottom Line

We think it's really important to cite your sources when you do research writing in college (did you pick up on that?). It's also important to use the right citation method, and to use it accurately. Remember back in Chapter 22 when we talked about the reasons for being an ethical writer when it comes to acknowledging your sources? Here's a quick reminder about why it's important to cite your sources well.

Three Major Reasons to Cite in Good Conscience

1. It keeps you from committing plagiarism, which is the cardinal sin of college writing.
2. It helps your reader to navigate your use of information from experts.
3. It gives proper acknowledgment to the creators of borrowed information.

In general, don't fret about memorizing the details of citation. Your primary task is to pay attention to *when* you need to cite a source. You can always look up *how* to cite that source — that's what excellent references like *Research and Documentation in the Digital Age* are for. This advice is true whether you're writing for an English class, a humanities class, a social science class, or a class in the natural and physical sciences: good writing is good writing, no matter what you're writing *about*.

Appendix C

Readings for Writers

The Gettysburg Address

Abraham Lincoln

Four score and seven years ago our fathers brought forth on this continent, a new nation, conceived in Liberty, and dedicated to the proposition that all men are created equal.

Now we are engaged in a great civil war, testing whether that nation, or any nation so conceived and so dedicated, can long endure. We are met on a great battle-field of that war. We have come to dedicate a portion of that field, as a final resting place for those who here gave their lives that that nation might live. It is altogether fitting and proper that we should do this.

But, in a larger sense, we can not dedicate — we can not consecrate — we can not hallow — this ground. The brave men, living and dead, who struggled here, have consecrated it, far above our poor power to add or detract. The world will little note, nor long remember what we say here, but it can never forget what they did here. It is for us the living, rather, to be dedicated here to the unfinished work which they who fought here have thus far so nobly advanced. It is rather for us to be here dedicated to the great task remaining before us — that from these honored dead we take increased devotion to that cause for which they gave the last full measure of devotion — that we here highly resolve that these dead shall not have died in vain — that this nation, under God, shall have a new birth of freedom — and that government of the people, by the people, for the people, shall not perish from the earth.

A Modest Proposal

Jonathan Swift

It is a melancholy object to those, who walk through this great town, or travel in the country, when they see the streets, the roads and cabin-doors crowded with beggars of the female sex, followed by three, four, or six children, all in rags, and importuning every passenger for an alms. These mothers instead of being able to work for their honest livelihood, are forced to employ all their time in strolling to beg sustenance for their helpless infants who, as they grow up, either turn thieves for want of work, or leave their dear native country, to fight for the Pretender in Spain, or sell themselves to the Barbadoes.

I think it is agreed by all parties, that this prodigious number of children in the arms, or on the backs, or at the heels of their mothers, and frequently of their fathers, is in the present deplorable state of the kingdom, a very great additional grievance; and therefore whoever could find out a fair, cheap and easy method of making these children sound and useful members of the common-wealth, would deserve so well of the public, as to have his statue set up for a preserver of the nation.

But my intention is very far from being confined to provide only for the children of professed beggars: it is of a much greater extent, and shall take in the whole number of infants at a certain age, who are born of parents in effect as little able to support them, as those who demand our charity in the streets.

As to my own part, having turned my thoughts for many years, upon this important subject, and maturely weighed the several schemes of our projectors, I have always found them grossly mistaken in their computation. It is true, a child just dropt from its dam, may be supported by her milk, for a solar year, with little other nourishment: at most not above the value of two shillings, which the mother may certainly get, or the value in scraps, by her lawful occupation of begging; and it is exactly at one year old that I propose to provide for them in such a manner, as, instead of being a charge upon their parents, or the parish, or wanting food and raiment for the rest of their lives, they shall, on the contrary, contribute to the feeding, and partly to the clothing of many thousands.

There is likewise another great advantage in my scheme, that it will prevent those voluntary abortions, and that horrid practice of women murdering their bastard children, alas! too frequent among us, sacrificing the poor innocent babes, I doubt, more to avoid the expense than the shame, which would move tears and pity in the most savage and inhuman breast.

The number of souls in this kingdom being usually reckoned one million and a half, of these I calculate there may be about two hundred thousand couple whose wives are breeders; from which number I subtract thirty thousand couple, who are able to maintain their own children, (although I apprehend there cannot be so many, under the present distresses of the kingdom) but this being granted, there will remain an hundred and seventy thousand breeders. I again subtract fifty thousand, for those women who miscarry, or whose children die by accident or disease within the year. There only remain an hundred and twenty thousand children of poor parents annually born. The question therefore is, How this number shall be reared, and provided for? which, as I have already said, under the present situation of affairs, is utterly impossible by all the methods hitherto proposed. For we can neither employ them in handicraft or agriculture; we neither build houses, (I mean in the country) nor cultivate land: they can very seldom pick up a livelihood by stealing till they arrive at six years old; except where they are of towardly parts, although I confess they learn the rudiments much earlier; during which time they can however be properly looked upon only as probationers: As I have been informed by a principal gentleman in the county of Cavan, who protested to me, that he never knew above one or two instances under the age of six, even in a part of the kingdom so renowned for the quickest proficiency in that art.

I am assured by our merchants, that a boy or a girl before twelve years old, is no saleable commodity, and even when they come to this age, they will not yield above three pounds, or three pounds and half a crown at most, on the exchange; which cannot turn to account either to the parents or kingdom, the charge of nutriments and rags having been at least four times that value.

I shall now therefore humbly propose my own thoughts, which I hope will not be liable to the least objection.

I have been assured by a very knowing American of my acquaintance in London, that a young healthy child well nursed, is, at a year old, a most delicious nourishing and wholesome food, whether stewed, roasted, baked, or boiled; and I make no doubt that it will equally serve in a fricassee, or a ragout.

I do therefore humbly offer it to public consideration, that of the hundred and twenty thousand children, already computed, twenty thousand may be reserved for breed, whereof only one fourth part to be males; which is more than we allow to sheep, black cattle, or swine, and my reason is, that these children are seldom the fruits of marriage, a circumstance not much regarded by our savages, therefore, one male will be sufficient to serve four females. That the remaining hundred thousand may, at a year old, be offered in sale to the persons of quality and fortune, through the kingdom, always advising the mother to let them suck plentifully in the last month, so as to render them plump, and fat for a good table. A child will make two dishes at an entertainment for friends, and when the family dines alone, the fore or hind quarter will make a reasonable dish, and seasoned with a little pepper or salt, will be very good boiled on the fourth day, especially in winter.

I have reckoned upon a medium, that a child just born will weigh 12 pounds, and in a solar year, if tolerably nursed, increaseth to 28 pounds.

I grant this food will be somewhat dear, and therefore very proper for landlords, who, as they have already devoured most of the parents, seem to have the best title to the children.

Infant's flesh will be in season throughout the year, but more plentiful in March, and a little before and after; for we are told by a grave author, an eminent French physician, that fish being a prolific diet, there are more children born in Roman Catholic countries about nine months after Lent, the markets will be more glutted than usual, because the number of Popish infants, is at least three to one in this kingdom, and therefore it will have one other collateral advantage, by lessening the number of Papists among us.

I have already computed the charge of nursing a beggar's child (in which list I reckon all cottagers, labourers, and four-fifths of the farmers) to be about two shillings per annum, rags included; and I believe no gentleman would repine to give ten shillings for the carcass of a good fat child, which, as I have said, will make four dishes of excellent nutritive meat, when he hath only some particular friend, or his own family to dine with him. Thus the squire will learn to be a good landlord, and grow popular among his tenants, the mother will have eight shillings neat profit, and be fit for work till she produces another child.

Those who are more thrifty (as I must confess the times require) may flea the carcass; the skin of which, artificially dressed, will make admirable gloves for ladies, and summer boots for fine gentlemen.

As to our City of Dublin, shambles may be appointed for this purpose, in the most convenient parts of it, and butchers we may be assured will not be wanting; although I rather recommend buying the children alive, and dressing them hot from the knife, as we do roasting pigs.

A very worthy person, a true lover of his country, and whose virtues I highly esteem, was lately pleased, in discoursing on this matter, to offer a refinement upon my scheme. He said, that many gentlemen of this kingdom, having of late destroyed their deer, he conceived that the want of venison might be well supply'd by the bodies of young lads and maidens, not exceeding fourteen years of age, nor under twelve; so great a number of both sexes in every country being now ready to starve for want of work and service: And these to be disposed of by their parents if alive, or otherwise by their nearest relations. But with due deference to so excellent a friend, and so deserving a patriot, I cannot be altogether in his sentiments; for as to the males, my American acquaintance assured me from frequent experience, that their flesh was generally tough and lean, like that of our school-boys, by continual exercise, and their taste disagreeable, and to fatten them would not answer the charge. Then as to the females, it would, I think, with humble submission, be a loss to the public, because they soon would become breeders themselves: And besides, it is not improbable that some scrupulous people might be apt to censure such a practice, (although indeed very unjustly) as a little bordering upon cruelty, which, I confess, hath always been with me the strongest objection against any project, how well soever intended.

But in order to justify my friend, he confessed, that this expedient was put into his head by the famous Salmanaazor, a native of the island Formosa, who came from thence to London, above twenty years ago, and in conversation told my friend, that in his country, when any young person happened to be put to death, the executioner sold the carcass to persons of quality, as a prime dainty; and that, in his time, the body of a plump girl of fifteen, who was crucified for an attempt to poison the Emperor, was sold to his imperial majesty's prime minister of state, and other great mandarins of the court in joints from the gibbet, at four hundred crowns. Neither indeed can I deny, that if the same use were made of several plump young girls in this town, who without one single groat to their fortunes, cannot stir abroad without a chair, and appear at a play-house and assemblies in foreign fineries which they never will pay for; the kingdom would not be the worse.

Some persons of a desponding spirit are in great concern about that vast number of poor people, who are aged, diseased, or maimed; and I have been desired to employ my thoughts what course may be taken, to ease the nation of so grievous an encumbrance. But I am not in the least pain upon that matter, because it is very well known, that they are every day dying, and rotting, by cold and famine, and filth, and vermin, as fast as can be reasonably expected. And as to the young laborers, they are now in almost as hopeful a condition. They cannot get work, and consequently pine away from want of nourishment, to a degree, that if at any time they are accidentally hired to common labor, they have not strength to perform it, and thus the country and themselves are happily delivered from the evils to come.

I have too long digressed, and therefore shall return to my subject. I think the advantages by the proposal which I have made are obvious and many, as well as of the highest importance.

For first, as I have already observed, it would greatly lessen the number of Papists, with whom we are yearly over-run, being the principal breeders of the nation, as well as our most dangerous enemies, and who stay at home on purpose with a design to deliver the kingdom to the Pretender, hoping to take their advantage by the absence of so many good Protestants, who have chosen rather to leave their country, than stay at home and pay tithes against their conscience to an episcopal curate.

Secondly, The poorer tenants will have something valuable of their own, which by law may be made liable to a distress, and help to pay their landlord's rent, their corn and cattle being already seized, and money a thing unknown.

Thirdly, Whereas the maintenance of an hundred thousand children, from two years old, and upwards, cannot be computed at less than ten shillings a piece per annum, the nation's stock will be thereby increased fifty thousand pounds per annum, besides the profit of a new dish, introduced to the tables of all gentlemen of fortune in the kingdom, who have any refinement in taste. And the money will circulate among ourselves, the goods being entirely of our own growth and manufacture.

Fourthly, The constant breeders, besides the gain of eight shillings sterling per annum by the sale of their children, will be rid of the charge of maintaining them after the first year.

Fifthly, This food would likewise bring great custom to taverns, where the vintners will certainly be so prudent as to procure the best receipts for dressing it to perfection; and consequently have their houses frequented by all the fine gentlemen, who justly value themselves upon their knowledge in good eating; and a skillful cook, who understands how to oblige his guests, will contrive to make it as expensive as they please.

Sixthly, This would be a great inducement to marriage, which all wise nations have either encouraged by rewards, or enforced by laws and penalties. It would increase the care and tenderness of mothers towards their children, when they were sure of a settlement for life to the poor babes, provided in some sort by the public, to their annual profit instead of expense. We should soon see an honest emulation among the married women, which of them could bring the fattest child to the market. Men would become as fond of their wives, during the time of their pregnancy, as they are now of their mares in foal, their cows in calf, or sow when they are ready to farrow; nor offer to beat or kick them (as is too frequent a practice) for fear of a miscarriage.

Many other advantages might be enumerated. For instance, the addition of some thousand carcasses in our exportation of barrel'd beef: the propagation of swine's flesh, and improvement in the art of making good bacon, so much wanted among us by the great destruction of pigs, too frequent at our tables; which are no way comparable in taste or magnificence to a well grown, fat yearly child, which roasted whole will make a considerable figure at a Lord Mayor's feast, or any other public entertainment. But this, and many others, I omit, being studious of brevity.

Supposing that one thousand families in this city, would be constant customers for infants flesh, besides others who might have it at merry meetings, particularly at weddings and christenings, I compute that Dublin would take off annually about twenty thousand carcasses; and the rest of the kingdom (where probably they will be sold somewhat cheaper) the remaining eighty thousand.

I can think of no one objection, that will possibly be raised against this proposal, unless it should be urged, that the number of people will be thereby much lessened in the kingdom. This I freely own, and 'twas indeed one principal design in offering it to the world. I desire the reader will observe, that I calculate my remedy for this one individual Kingdom of Ireland, and for no other that ever was, is, or, I think, ever can be upon Earth. Therefore let no man talk to me of other expedients: Of taxing our absentees at five shillings a pound: Of using neither cloths, nor household furniture, except what is of our own growth and manufacture: Of utterly rejecting the materials and instruments that promote foreign luxury: Of curing the expensiveness of pride, vanity, idleness, and gaming in our women: Of introducing a vein of parsimony, prudence and temperance: Of learning to love our country, wherein we differ even from Laplanders, and the inhabitants of Topinamboo: Of quitting our animosities and factions, nor acting any longer like the Jews, who were murdering one another at the very moment their city was taken: Of being a little cautious not to sell our country and consciences for nothing: Of teaching landlords to have at least one degree of mercy towards their tenants. Lastly, of putting a spirit of honesty, industry, and skill into our shop-keepers, who, if a resolution could now be taken to buy only our native goods, would immediately unite to cheat and exact upon us in the price, the measure, and the goodness, nor could ever yet be brought to make one fair proposal of just dealing, though often and earnestly invited to it.

Therefore I repeat, let no man talk to me of these and the like expedients, 'till he hath at least some glimpse of hope, that there will ever be some hearty and sincere attempt to put them into practice.

But, as to myself, having been wearied out for many years with offering vain, idle, visionary thoughts, and at length utterly despairing of success, I fortunately fell upon this proposal, which, as it is wholly new, so it hath something solid and real, of no expense and little trouble, full in our own power, and whereby we can incur no danger in disobliging England. For this kind of commodity will not bear exportation, and flesh being of too tender a consistence, to admit a long continuance in salt, although perhaps I could name a country, which would be glad to eat up our whole nation without it.

After all, I am not so violently bent upon my own opinion, as to reject any offer, proposed by wise men, which shall be found equally innocent, cheap, easy, and effectual. But before something of that kind shall be advanced in contradiction to my scheme, and offering a better, I desire the author or authors will be pleased maturely to consider two points. First, As things now stand, how they will be able to find food and raiment for a hundred thousand useless mouths and backs. And secondly, There being a round million of creatures in humane figure throughout this kingdom, whose whole subsistence put into a common stock, would leave them in debt two million of pounds sterling, adding those who are beggars by profession, to the bulk of farmers, cottagers, and laborers, with their wives and children, who are beggars in effect; I desire those politicians who dislike my overture, and may perhaps be so bold to attempt an answer, that they will first ask the parents of these mortals, whether they would not at this day think it a great happiness to have been sold for food at a year old, in the manner I prescribe, and thereby have avoided such a perpetual scene of misfortunes, as they have since gone through, by the oppression of landlords, the impossibility of paying rent without money or trade, the want of common sustenance, with neither house nor clothes to cover them from the inclemencies of the weather, and the most inevitable prospect of entailing the like, or greater miseries, upon their breed forever.

I profess, in the sincerity of my heart, that I have not the least personal interest in endeavoring to promote this necessary work, having no other motive than the public good of my country, by advancing our trade, providing for infants, relieving the poor, and giving some pleasure to the rich. I have no children, by which I can propose to get a single penny; the youngest being nine years old, and my wife past child-bearing.

The Deep Sadness of Elk That Don't Run

Michael Byrne

I don't particularly like being shy. I don't think it benefits me in any way, whether in terms of regular ol' evolutionary selection or in terms of post-nature meta-survival (broad-spectrum human fulfillment, say). Shyness in humans is undesirable to the point of pathology — you may be prescribed a medication to overcome social-anxiety, which might be (only somewhat incorrectly) considered shyness at a clinical, disabling level. I've never actually been prescribed a medication for my own extreme shyness/social-anxiety situation, and that's probably only because social-anxiety is covered pretty well by medications I consume for other things, one of which being the sort of anxiety that happens alone watching television or while walking on a nice day in the woods. Which is to say anxiety that happens anytime and anywhere for no reason, a more or less lifelong condition previewed by an '80s childhood of being the sort of shy that may cause one to fail at a great many normal childhood things.

"Being shy" is a term that has been absolutely robbed away by drug companies via intense direct marketing of social-anxiety/social phobia as a thing you are currently, certainly suffering from — you do not "suffer" from shyness, you "are" shy. Meanwhile, you *have* social-anxiety — you are afflicted by it. And you can't be treated for something you *are*, only for something that is inflicted on you, even if the source of that infliction is your own genes (you are not cancerous after all, you have cancer).

Pfizer got approval to market the SSRI paroxetine (Paxil) for social-anxiety treatment in 1999, the first such drug with the green light to ease the pain of a new condition afflicting untold numbers of humans. Sertraline (Zoloft) followed in 2003, receiving FDA approval for short-term treatment of "social phobia." The makers of such drugs proceeded to pour tens of millions of dollars into pushing SSRIs on a much wider base of potential customers than they ever could have imagined and, quite suddenly, the word "shy" made an abrupt exit from the vocabulary of suffering.

So, by the year 2012, shyness has gone from being this bad thing that might hold back a kid in school to an entry in the DSM and a powerful sales vehicle for a large industry. (Let's also acknowledge real quick the social-anxiety disorder acronym, "SAD.") Meanwhile, society has done well in establishing the gregarious extrovert, the team player, the ace communicator, as its idol. Susan Cain, author of this year's *Quiet: The Power of Introverts in a World That Can't Stop Talking*, wrote in a *New York Times* essay in March:

> Children's classroom desks are now often arranged in pods, because group par-
> ticipation supposedly leads to better learning; in one school I visited, a sign

announcing "Rules for Group Work" included, "You can't ask a teacher for help unless everyone in your group has the same question." Many adults work for organizations that now assign work in teams, in offices without walls, for supervisors who value "people skills" above all. As a society, we prefer action to contemplation, risk-taking to heed-taking, certainty to doubt. Studies show that we rank fast and frequent talkers as more competent, likable, and even smarter than slow ones. As the psychologists William Hart and Dolores Albarracin point out, phrases like "get active," "get moving," "do something," and similar calls to action surface repeatedly in recent books.

In America particularly, we find a lot of weight being put on a kind of brash individuality, a caricature that survives pretty well IRL, as we'll see in levels leagues beyond bearability in the next two months before U.S. national elections. Though brash individuality, at least within the modern American caricature, is never anything more than a means to group success. That's the selection mechanism that American group culture uses: victory to the loudest. I submit as evidence every group I've ever participated in or witnessed, save for a newspaper I used to work for that was once but no longer is led by a brilliant and quiet editor rent ineffective by the pushing and shoving of the loud and dull, who eventually won, as they have at most newspapers.

The inventors and theorists are the ones that actually practice individuality, at least insofar as that means independent thinking and doing and disinterest in conformity and *approval*. And these are the people that don't succeed in groups, either because they're not interested in group structure or group structure isn't interested in them. Cain quotes in her essay a choice line from science writer Winifred Gallagher: "The glory of the disposition that stops to consider stimuli rather than rushing to engage with them is its long association with intellectual and artistic achievement. Neither $E=mc^2$ nor 'Paradise Lost' was dashed off by a party animal."

Is it glory with which we regard them though? Or pity? Milton was friendly with kings, but wouldn't have anything to do with the group. Wasn't *Paradise Lost* about exile and alienation? And if you Google Image Search "mad scientist" right now, the first result returned that isn't a cartoon of an Einstein-looking scientist is an actual photo of Albert Einstein. We enjoy the idea of successful introverts a great deal more than we enjoy the idea of promoting them through our social structures. The shy, the introverted, the SAD don't actually get much glory, though the tech economy has arguably allowed a short-circuit of sorts between glory and the messy office full of half-finished sketches. Though, of course, for every "innovation leader" doubling as a walking media event (Steve Jobs, Larry Page), there's a great many people you will never hear of unless your hobby is patent law.

Shyness-as-error isn't universal. The Islamic prophet Ali, considered by some sects to be the first Imam, said, "God loves the shy, moderate person, and detests the lewd, demanding, forward boor," and "Shyness is a way to everything beautiful." In Islam, shyness is a means to reflection and humility, which are means to God. The Bible, at least according to gotquestions.org, one of the leading internet authorities on shame, seems to have a different perspective. Shyness is fear, and fear comes from a lack of faith, or inadequate faith. The shy should be ashamed.

Some 15 to 20 percent of humans are born shy, which roughly parallels the incidence of shyness or anxiety or whatever you chose to call it within different species of animals. Shyness is an evolutionary tactic. Someone within a society must be shy for that society to be selected for and survive. If every member of a population was gregarious and stoked to rush into vulnerable positions, that would be a population less likely to persist. In other words, it's natural and necessary for species to have shy members. Humans aren't an exception. Some of us are just like this, and that's for the good of the species, no matter how aggressively we try to medicate it away.

A new study out now in the journal *Proceedings of the Royal Society B: Biological Sciences* looks at shy elk, specifically elk that are currently being selected for by (evolving as a result of) the recreational hunting of humans. Some elk respond to threats by running faster and further. Others avoid danger in the first place, avoiding new areas and traveling less, as revealed through GPS tracking and analysis. Researchers collared 122 elk and, at the end of the study, 25 of those were dead by hunters' guns. The data revealed that the hunters were favoring bold elk, animals more likely to travel farther and faster. The shy elk were the ones more likely to survive and continue the species.

If you don't understand why that's sad, let me explain: being shy, or having "social phobia," sucks. It feels bad. It limits opportunities, by definition, to experience pleasure. This is why there's a massive market for SSRI treatment for SAD and social phobia — Pfizer isn't marketing into a void or inventing experiences. And this is why it gets really frustrating when armchair experts start going on about how it's all the drug companies making up new diagnoses for "normal" feelings. Feeling terrible and excluded — thinking here of that solitary elk lurking on well-trampled pee-snow under the same evergreen branches hiding from hunters — may be normal, but often, it's also terrible. Shouldering the persistence of a species or not, no one wants to feel that way.

Bad Feminist

Roxane Gay

My favorite definition of a feminist is one offered by Su, an Australian woman who, when interviewed for Kathy Bail's 1996 anthology *DIY Feminism*, described them simply as "women who don't want to be treated like shit." This definition is pointed and succinct, but I run into trouble when I try to expand it. I fall short as a feminist. I feel like I am not as committed as I need to be, that I am not living up to feminist ideals because of who and how I choose to be. I feel this tension constantly. As Judith Butler writes in her 1988 essay, "Performative Acts and Gender Constitution": "Performing one's gender wrong initiates a set of punishments both obvious and indirect, and performing it well provides the reassurance that there is an essentialism of gender identity after all." This tension — the idea that there is a right way to be a woman, a right way to be the most essential woman — is ongoing and pervasive.

We see this tension in socially dictated beauty standards — the right way to be a woman is to be thin, to wear makeup, to wear the right kind of clothes (not too slutty, not too prude, show a little leg, ladies), and so on. Good women are charming, polite, and unobtrusive. Good women work but are content to earn 77 percent of what men earn. Depending on whom you ask, good women bear children and stay home to raise them without complaint. Good women are modest, chaste, pious, submissive. Women who don't adhere to these standards are the fallen, the undesirable. They are bad women.

Butler's thesis could also apply to feminism. There is an essential feminism, the notion that there are right and wrong ways to be a feminist, and there are consequences for doing feminism wrong.

Essential feminism suggests anger, humorlessness, militancy, unwavering principles, and a prescribed set of rules for how to be a proper feminist woman, or at least a proper white, heterosexual, feminist woman — hate pornography, unilaterally decry the objectification of women, don't cater to the male gaze, hate men, hate sex, focus on career, don't shave. I kid, mostly, with that last one. This is nowhere near an accurate description of feminism, but the movement has been warped by misperception for so long that even people who should know better have bought into this essential image of feminism.

Consider Elizabeth Wurtzel, who, in a June 2012 *Atlantic* article, says, "Real feminists earn a living, have money and means of their own." By Wurtzel's thinking, women who don't "earn a living, have money and means of their own," are fake feminists, undeserving of the label, disappointments to the sisterhood. She takes the idea of essential feminism even further in a September 2012 *Harper's Bazaar* article where she suggests that a good feminist works hard to be beautiful. She says, "Looking great is a matter of feminism. No liberated woman would misrepresent the cause by appearing less than hale and happy." It's too easy to dissect the error of such thinking. She is suggesting that a woman's worth is, in part, determined by her beauty, which is one of the very things feminism works against.

The most significant problem with essential feminism is how it doesn't allow for the complexities of human experience or individuality. There seems to be little room for multiple or discordant points of view. Essential feminism has, for example, led to the rise of the phrase "sex-positive feminism," which creates a clear distinction between feminists who are positive about sex and feminists who aren't — and that in turn creates a self-fulfilling essentialist prophecy.

•

I sometimes cringe when someone refers to me as a feminist, as if I should be ashamed of my feminism or as if the word *feminist* is an insult. The label is rarely offered in kindness. I am generally called a feminist when I have the nerve to suggest that the misogyny deeply embedded in our culture is a real problem, requiring relentless vigilance. For example, in an essay for Salon, I wrote about Daniel Tosh and rape jokes. I try not to read comments because they can get vicious, but I couldn't help but note one commenter who told me I was an "angry blogger woman," which is simply another way of saying "angry feminist." All feminists are angry instead of passionate.

A more direct reprimand came from a man I was dating, during a heated discussion that wasn't quite an argument. He said, "Don't you raise your voice to me," which was strange because I had not raised my voice. I was stunned because no one had ever said such a thing to me. He expounded, at length, about how women should talk to men. When I dismantled his pseudo-theories, he said, "You're some kind of feminist, aren't you?" His tone made it clear that to be a feminist was undesirable. I was not being a good woman. I remained silent, stewing. I thought, "Isn't it obvious I am a feminist, albeit not a very good one?"

I'm not the only outspoken woman who shies away from the feminist label, who fears the consequences of accepting the label.

In an August 2012 interview with Salon's Andrew O'Hehir, actress Melissa Leo, known for playing groundbreaking female roles, said, "Well, I don't think of myself as a feminist at all. As soon as we start labeling and categorizing ourselves and others, that's going to shut down the world. I would never say that. Like, I just did that episode with Louis C. K."

Leo is buying into a great many essential feminist myths with her comment. We are categorized and labeled from the moment we come into this world by gender, race, size, hair color, eye color, and so forth. The older we get the more labels and categories we collect. If labeling and categorizing ourselves is going to shut the world down, it has been a long time coming. More disconcerting, though, is the assertion that a feminist wouldn't take a role on Louis C. K.'s sitcom *Louie*, or that a feminist would be unable to find C. K.'s brand of humor amusing. For Leo, there are feminists and then there are women who defy categorization and are willing to embrace career opportunities. In a July 2012 *Guardian* interview, critically acclaimed performance artist Marina Abramovic, when asked how she felt about being invited to lead a woman-only lecture, said, "I really had to think about it. I am very clear that I am not a feminist. It puts you into a category and I don't like that. An artist has no gender. All that matters is whether they make good art or bad art. So I thought about it, but then I said yes."

Again, we see this fear of categorization, this fear of being forced into a box that cannot quite accommodate a woman properly. Abramovic believes an artist has no gender, but there are many artists who would disagree, whose art is intimately shaped by their gender, such as artist and sculptor Louise Bourgeois, for whom feminism was a significant influence. In a 1982 *Time* article on Bourgeois and her Museum of Modern Art retrospective, Robert Hughes wrote, "The field to which Bourgeois's work constantly returns is female experience, located in the body, sensed from within. 'I try,' she told an interviewer, with regard to one work, 'to give a representation of a woman who is pregnant. She tries to be frightening but she is frightened. She's afraid someone is going to invade her privacy and that she won't be able to defend what she is responsible for.'"

Trailblazing female leaders in the corporate world tend to reject the feminist label, too. Marissa Mayer, who was appointed president and CEO of Yahoo! in July 2012, said in an interview,

> I don't think that I would consider myself a feminist. I think that I certainly believe in equal rights, I believe that women are just as capable, if not more so in a lot of different dimensions, but I don't, I think, have, sort of, the militant drive and the sort of, the chip on the shoulder that sometimes comes with that. And I think it's too bad, but I do think that feminism has become in many ways a more negative word. You know, there are amazing opportunities all over the world for women, and I think that there is more good that comes out of positive energy around that than negative energy.

For Mayer, even though she is a pioneering woman, feminism is associated with militancy. Despite the strides she has made through her career at Google and now Yahoo!, she'd prefer to eschew the label for the sake of so-called positive energy.

•

Audre Lorde once stated, "I am a black feminist. I mean I recognize that my power as well as my primary oppressions come as a result of my blackness as well as my womanness, and therefore my struggles on both of these fronts are inseparable."

As a woman of color, I find that some feminists don't seem terribly concerned with the issues unique to women of color — the ongoing effects of racism and post-colonialism, the status of women in the Third World, working against the trenchant archetypes black women are forced into (angry black woman, mammy, Hottentot, and the like).

White feminists often suggest that by believing there are issues unique to women of color, an unnatural division occurs, impeding solidarity, sisterhood. Other times, white feminists are simply dismissive of these issues. In 2008, prominent blogger Amanda Marcotte was accused of appropriating ideas for her article "Can a Person Be Illegal?" from the blogger "Brownfemipower," who posted a speech she gave on the same subject a few days prior to the publication of Marcotte's article. The question of where original thought ends and borrowed concepts begin was complicated significantly by the sense that a white person had yet again appropriated the creative work of a person of color.

Around the same time, feminist press Seal Press was taken to task for not devoting enough of their catalogue to women of color, which made senior editor Brooke Warner and other white feminists defensive. Warner went so far as to respond to a comment made by blogger "Blackamazon," on her eponymous blog, saying, "Seal Press here. We WANT more WOC. Not a whole lotta proposals come our way, interestingly. Seems to me it would be more effective to inform us about what you'd like to see rather than hating." In addition to assuming a defensive posture, Warner also placed the burden of her press's diversity on women of color instead of assuming that responsibility as a senior editor. To be fair, Warner was commenting on a blog and perhaps did not think her comment through before posting, but she is neither the first nor will she be the last white feminist to suggest that the responsibility for making feminism and feminist organizations more inclusive lies with women of color.

The feminist blogosphere engaged in an intense debate over these issues, at times so acrimonious that black feminists were labeled "radical black feminists" who were "playing the race card."

Such willful ignorance and disinterest in incorporating the issues and concerns of black women into the mainstream feminist project makes me disinclined to own the feminist label until it embraces people like me. Is that my way of essentializing feminism, of suggesting there's a right kind of feminism or a more inclusive feminism? Perhaps. This is all murky for me, but a continued insensitivity toward race is a serious problem in feminist circles.

•

There's also this: lately, magazines have been telling me there's something wrong with feminism or women trying to achieve a work/life balance or just women in general. The *Atlantic* has led the way in these lamentations. In the aforementioned June 2012 article, Wurtzel, author of *Prozac Nation*, wrote a searing polemic about "1 percent wives," who are hurting feminism and the progress of women by choosing to stay at home rather than enter the workplace. Wurtzel begins the essay provocatively:

When my mind gets stuck on everything that is wrong with feminism, it brings out the nineteenth century poet in me: Let me count the ways. Most of all, feminism is pretty much a nice girl who really, really wants so badly to be liked by everybody — ladies who lunch, men who hate women, all the morons who demand choice and don't understand responsibility — that it has become the easy lay of social movements.

There are problems with feminism, you see. Wurtzel says so, and she is vigorous in defending her position. Wurtzel goes on to state there is only one kind of equality, economic equality, and until women recognize that and enter the workforce *en masse*, feminists, and wealthy feminists in particular, will continue to fail. They will continue to be bad feminists, falling short of essential ideals of this movement.

The very next issue of the *Atlantic* included Anne-Marie Slaughter writing 12,000 words about the struggles of powerful, successful women to "have it all." She was speaking to a small, elite group of women — wealthy women with very successful careers — while ignoring the millions of women who don't have the privilege of, as Slaughter did, leaving a high-powered position at the State Department to spend more time with her sons. Many women who work do so because they have to. Working has little to do with having it all and much more to do with having food on the table.

Slaughter wrote, "I'd been the woman congratulating herself on her unswerving commitment to the feminist cause, chatting smugly with her dwindling number of college or law-school friends who had reached and maintained their place on the highest rungs of their profession. I'd been the one telling young women at my lectures that you can have it all and do it all, regardless of what field you are in."

The thing is, I am not at all sure that feminism has ever suggested women can have it all. This notion of being able to have it all is always misattributed to feminism when really it's human nature to want it all.

Alas, poor feminism. So much responsibility keeps getting piled on the shoulders of a movement whose primary purpose is to achieve equality, in all realms, between men and women. I keep reading these articles and getting angry and tired because these articles tell me that there's no way for women to ever get it right. These articles make it seem like there is, in fact, a right way to be a woman and a wrong way to be a woman. And the standard appears to be ever changing and unachievable.

●

Which leads me to confess: I am failing as a woman. I am failing as a feminist. To freely accept the feminist label would not be fair to good feminists. If I am, indeed, a feminist, I am a rather bad one.

I want to be independent, but I want to be taken care of and have someone to come home to. I have a job I'm pretty good at. I am in charge of things. I am on committees. People respect me and take my counsel. I want to be strong and professional, but I resent how hard I have to work to be taken seriously, to receive a fraction of the consideration I might otherwise receive. Sometimes I feel an overwhelming need to cry at work so I close my office door and lose it. I want to be in charge and respected and in control, but I want to surrender, completely, in certain aspects of my life.

When I drive to work I listen to thuggish rap at a very loud volume even though the lyrics are degrading to women and offend me to my core. The classic Ying Yang Twins song "Salt Shaker"? It's amazing. "P poppin' til you percolate / First booty on duty no time to wait / Make it work, with your wet T-shirt / Bitch you gotta shake it til your calf muscle hurts."

Poetry.
(I am mortified by my music choices.)
I care what people think.

Pink is my favorite color. I used to say my favorite color was black to be cool, but it is pink — all shades of pink. If I have an accessory, it is probably pink. I read *Vogue*, and I'm not doing it ironically though it might seem that way. I once live-tweeted the September issue. I demonstrate little outward evidence of this, but I have a very indulgent fantasy where I have a closet full of pretty shoes and purses and matching outfits. I love dresses. For years I pretended I hated them, but I don't. Maxi-dresses are one of the finest clothing items to become popular in recent memory. I have opinions on Maxi-dresses! I shave my legs! Again, this mortifies me. If I take issue with the unrealistic standards of beauty women are held to, I shouldn't have a secret fondness for fashion and smooth calves, right?

I know nothing about cars. When I take my car to the mechanic, they are speaking a foreign language. A mechanic asks what's wrong with my car, and I lose my mind. I stutter things like, "Well, there's a sound I try to drown out with my radio." The windshield wiper fluid for the rear window of my car no longer sprays the window. It just sprays the air. I don't know how to deal with this. It feels like an expensive problem. I still call my father with questions about cars and am not terribly interested in changing any of my car-related ignorance. I don't want to be good at cars. Good feminists, I assume, are independent enough to address vehicular crises on their own; they are independent enough to care.

Despite what people think based on my writing, I very much like men. They're interesting to me, and I mostly wish they would be better about how they treat women so I wouldn't have to call them out so often. And still, I put up with nonsense from unsuitable men even though *I know better* and can do better. I love diamonds and the excess of weddings. I consider certain domestic tasks as gendered, mostly all in my favor as I don't care for chores—lawn care, bug killing, and trash removal, for example, are men's work.

Sometimes — a lot of the time, honestly — I totally "fake it," because it's easier. I am a fan of orgasms, but they take time, and in many instances I don't want to waste that time. All too often I don't really like the guy enough to explain the calculus of my desire. Then I feel guilty because the sisterhood would not approve. I'm not even sure what the sisterhood is, but the idea of a sisterhood menaces me, quietly reminding me of how bad a feminist I am. Good feminists don't fear the sisterhood because they know they are comporting themselves in sisterhood-approved ways.

I love babies, and I want to have one. I am willing to make certain compromises (not sacrifices) in order to do so — namely maternity leave and slowing down at work to spend more time with my child, writing less so I can be more present in my life. I worry about dying alone, unmarried and childless because I spent so much time pursuing my career and accumulating degrees. This kind of keeps me up at night, but I pretend it doesn't because I am supposed to be evolved. My success, such as it is, is supposed to be enough if I'm a good feminist. It is not enough. It is not even close.

Because I have so many deeply held opinions about gender equality, I feel a lot of pressure to live up to certain ideals. I am supposed to be a good feminist who is having it all, doing it all. Really, though, I'm a woman in her thirties, struggling to accept herself. For so long I told myself I was not this woman — utterly human and flawed. I worked overtime to be anything but this woman, and it was exhausting and unsustainable, and even harder than simply embracing who I am.

And while I may be a bad feminist, I am deeply committed to the issues important to the feminist movement. I have strong opinions about misogyny, institutional sexism that consistently places women at a disadvantage, the inequity in pay, the cult of beauty and thinness, the repeated attacks on reproductive freedom, violence against women, and on and on. I am as committed to fighting fiercely for equality as I am committed to disrupting the notion that there is an essential feminism.

I'm the kind of feminist who is appalled by the phrase "legitimate rape" and politicians such as Missouri's Todd Akin, who reaffirmed his commitment to opposing abortion, drawing from pseudo-science and a lax cultural attitude toward rape: "If it's a legitimate rape, the female body has ways to try to shut that whole thing down. But let's assume that maybe that didn't work or something. I think there should be some punishment, but the punishment ought to be on the rapist, and not attacking the child."

Being a feminist, however, even a bad one, has also taught me that the need for feminism and advocacy also applies to seemingly less serious issues.

I'm the kind of feminist who knows it is complete hypocrisy that actress Kristen Stewart is being publicly excoriated for cheating on her boyfriend Robert Pattinson even though, if you believe the tabloid stories, Pattinson cheated on her for years. Being a bad feminist allows me to get riled up when I read that Stewart could be dropped from the *Snow White and the Huntsman* sequel while, say, Chris Brown, a known abuser with anger issues, is still performing at awards shows and selling albums, adored by a legion of ardent fans.

I'm the kind of feminist who looks at the September 2012 issue of *Vogue* with the Edith Wharton photo spread and knows there's a serious problem. Wharton is my favorite writer. I also love *Vogue* or, perhaps, hate to love *Vogue*. This photo spread would normally thrill me. But. Jeffrey Eugenides portrays Henry James, Jonathan Safran Foer portrays architect Ogden Codman, Jr., and Junot Díaz portrays diplomat Walter Van Rensselaer Berry. Wharton is portrayed by model Natalia Vodianova; she is gorgeous, and *Vogue* is a fashion magazine, but a great disservice is being done.

The editors of *Vogue* are, apparently, unaware of the famous, talented, contemporary women writers who would be excellent choices for the photo essay. Zadie Smith released a book in September. There's also Karen Russell, Jennifer Egan, Aimee Bender, Nicole Krauss, Julianna Baggott, Alicia Erian, Claire Vaye Watkins, and the list could go on forever.

This disservice rises, in part, out of a culture that assumes women writers are less relevant than their male counterparts, that women in general are simply not as important, that their writing is not as critical to arts and letters. This disservice rises out of a culture where Jonathan Franzen lost the Pulitzer rather than Jennifer Egan winning the award.

All too often, these seemingly smaller issues go unchecked because there are so many more serious issues facing women.

There's more to the problem. Too many women, particularly groundbreaking women and industry leaders, are afraid to be labeled feminists, afraid to stand up and say, "Yes, I am a feminist," for fear of what that label means, for fear of how to live up to it, for fear of feminism as something essential, for fear of the punishments — both obvious and indirect — that come with openly owning feminism or doing feminism wrong.

●

At some point, I got it into my head that a feminist was a certain kind of woman. I bought into grossly inaccurate myths about who feminists are — militant, perfect in their politics and person, man hating, humorless. I bought into these myths even though, intellectually, I *know* better. I'm not proud of this. I don't want to buy into these myths anymore. I don't want to cavalierly disavow feminism like far too many other women have done.

I also want to be myself. Bad feminism seems like the only way I can both embrace myself as a feminist and be myself.

No matter what issues I have with feminism, I am one. I cannot nor will not deny the importance and absolute necessity of feminism. Like most people, I'm full of contradictions, but I also don't want to be treated like shit for being a woman.

I am, therefore, a bad feminist. I would rather be a bad feminist than no feminist at all.

Serving Life for Surviving Abuse

Jessica Pishko

On August 3, 1995, 23-year-old Kelly Savage was making last-minute plans to leave her abusive husband, Mark Savage. A few weeks before, Kelly had contacted a battered-women's organization for advice on how to leave her husband. "Act as normal as possible," they told her, a common tactic given to women seeking to evade their abusive spouse's suspicion. For the next few weeks, Kelly quietly amassed what she needed to leave — birth certificates for her two young children (Justin, who was three, and Krystal, who was almost two), medications, and clothes — all of which she hid so that Mark would not find them. She purchased bus tickets to Los Angeles dated the next day, August 4.

That afternoon, Kelly left to cash a check and pick up a few items for their departure. While she was out, she called Mark and asked him what size vacuum bags they needed. In a sworn statement, Kelly said, "I thought that by asking about vacuum bags, Mark would think that I was planning to stick around to use them." Instead, Mark told her to come home because Justin, her three-year-old son, was not breathing. Medical experts determined that his death was caused by physical abuse.

Like many abusers, Mark had escalated in the days leading up to Kelly's planned escape. While he had always been violent — he had a habit of throwing Kelly onto the bed and choking her — he had recently tied Kelly to a couch and tried to carve his name into her ankle. Neighbors called the police twice based on the noise they heard. The night before, possibly because he knew Kelly was planning to leave, he had beaten Justin severely enough to possibly cause the brain injuries that killed him. When Kelly returned home and found Justin lifeless, Mark tackled her and threatened to kill her if she called 9-1-1. She did so anyway.

Both Kelly and Mark were tried for Justin's murder, found guilty, and sentenced to life without parole. Kelly has been in prison now for 19 years, and her pro bono attorneys have recently filed a habeas petition for a new hearing, which is being opposed by California's Attorney General Kamala Harris. Their argument: The jury never heard about Kelly's long and painful history of abuse, evidence which shows that Kelly's case was a textbook example of intimate-partner battering.

●

According to statistics provided by the California Department of Corrections and Rehabilitation, there were 186 women serving life without parole (LWOP) sentences in July 2013.[1] This represents about 3 percent of all inmates statewide. The Sentencing Project reported that same year that there are over 5,300 women nationally serving life and life without parole sentences, reflecting an increase of about 14 percent since 2008.[2] About 300 of these women were sentenced to LWOP, which means that California's prisons alone contain about half of America's female inmates serving LWOP sentences.

As Kelly's case shows, a common characteristic of women sentenced to LWOP is their history of abuse. While there's no exact count of how many women in prison have been physically or sexually abused, most place the odds around 85 to 90 percent — disproportionately high compared to men.[3] As the length of sentence increases, so do the odds that a woman has been abused. Among all women in prison, women who have been sentenced to LWOP sentences are the most likely to have been abused, more so than women serving non-life sentences and men serving life sentences, said Professor Margaret Leigey, a criminologist at The College of New Jersey who has studied LWOP sentencing.[4]

On the surface, the numbers seem overwhelmingly higher. Professor Heidi Rummel, who directs the Post-Conviction Justice Project at the University of Southern California Law School, which assists those convicted of serious crimes, said that, among the women she represented — those sentenced to life or LWOP sentences — the rate of physical and sexual abuse is "basically 100 percent."

---

[1] Department of Corrections and Rehabilitation Offender Information Services Branch, *Prison Census Data as of June 30, 2013* (Department of Corrections and Rehabilitation: Sacramento, CA, Sept. 2013), http://www.cdcr.ca.gov/Reports_Research/Offender _Information_Services_Branch/Annual/Census/CENSUSd1306.pdf.

[2] Ashley Nellis and Jean Chung, *Life Goes On: The Historic Rise in Life Sentences in America* (Washington, DC: The Sentencing Project, 2013), http://sentencingproject .org/doc/publications/inc_Life%20Goes%20On%202013.pdf.

[3] Ibid.

[4] M. E. Leigey and J. K. L. Reed, "A Woman's Life Before Serving Life: Examining the Negative Pre-incarceration Life Events of Female Life-Sentenced Inmates," *Women and Criminal Justice* 20, no. 4 (2010): 302–22, in Nellis and Chung, *Life Goes On*, 11.

●

At trial, Kelly's prosecutor painted a picture of a woman who not only tolerated abuse, but wanted it. She argued that Kelly "aided and abetted" her husband Mark, pointing to Kelly's failure to escape sooner or report Mark's behavior to the police. She told the jury that Kelly was "sadistic" and "narcissistic," arguing that Kelly helped Mark torture Justin because "she gets to please Mark so, therefore, she gets pleasure out of doing this."

A witness at Kelly's trial was her first husband, Michael Alvarado, who testified that Kelly was "strong," even though Michael beat her, raped her, and threatened to shoot her. He admitted lightly in his testimony to "slapping [Kelly] up the side of her head," which made the jury laugh.

Intimate partner battering and its effects (once commonly known as "Battered Women's Syndrome") are often described as a set of behaviors where women follow their abuser because they are afraid and traumatized.[5] Its symptoms are most similar to PTSD, according to Rummel, and less similar to mental illness, a common misconception.

Arguments like the one Kelly's prosecutor made are based on long-standing prejudices that such women who live with abusers are selfish and manipulative. In a report submitted in support of Kelly's habeas petition, Dr. Geraldine Butts Stahly pointed out that women respond to severe and prolonged physical and sexual abuse through a series of survival mechanisms, such as learned helplessness (where victims are too afraid to defend themselves) and traumatic bonding (where victims form an emotional attachment toward their abuser).

The law permits survivors of abuse to present relevant testimony at their trial to show that they may be less culpable for their actions. But many women facing criminal charges never have this opportunity, either because the attorney fails to produce a suitable expert or because the jury misinterprets evidence of abuse. In addition, criminal laws are more male-centered. "When men experience violence," said Rummel, "they react immediately. The laws are based on duress and provocation."

Women, on the other hand, often experience ongoing violence, many times from the very people who are supposed to protect them.[6] "They may not react

---

[5] Carrie Hempel, "Battered and Convicted: One State's Efforts to Provide Effective Relief," *Criminal Justice* 25, no. 4 (2011), http://www.law.uci.edu/news/in-the-news/2011/CriminalJustice_Hempel_Winter2011.pdf.

[6] Patricia Tjaden and Nancy Thoennes, *Extent, Nature, and Consequences of Intimate Partner Violence: Findings from the National Violence Against Women Survey* (Washington, DC: National Institute of Justice, 2000), https://www.ncjrs.gov/pdffiles1/nij/181867.pdf.

immediately," Rummel said. "They go about their lives. They raise their kids. They move on. Then their rage explodes."

Under most state criminal statutes, defendants can claim affirmative defenses of duress or self-defense, but these require that such acts be proximate in time and place, failing to address female-specific responses to violence. Women who kill their abusers, for example, often lash out after years of brutal violence.[7] In other instances, women are not the primary actors; they are instead intimidated by their abusive partner and appear to be a co-conspirator. As Rummel suggests, this is an area where the law has not caught up to the psychological reality.

In recognition of this dynamic, California enacted Section 1473.5 of the Penal Code in 2001, which allows women to file a writ of habeas corpus if expert testimony on abuse was not presented at trial. (A habeas corpus petition — literally meaning "you may have the body" — is filed when someone has already gone through the appeals process. It is, in many ways, a petition of last resort.) Originally, the law was intended for women who were convicted of killing their batterers; the law was amended in 2005 to include all women who may have been abused. While the law was heralded as a success by women's advocacy groups, Rummel points out that it can be difficult to prove physical and sexual abuse years — sometimes decades — after the fact.[8] She pointed out, "Witnesses may be gone, passed away, or have forgotten what they saw. Medical records might be destroyed or not available."

Savage's case is one of many that fall under Section 1473.5. Attorney General Harris is opposing Savage's petition despite her record of speaking in favor of regulations that protect women.[9] A successful habeas petition would allow Kelly to present evidence of her history of abuse that was never provided to her trial jury. (Harris's office was contacted twice for comment on Kelly's case but provided no response.)

---

[7] Mary Helen Wimberly, "Defending Victims of Domestic Violence Who Kill Their Batterers: Using the Trial Expert to Change Social Norms," American Bar Association on Domestic and Sexual Violence, Law Student Writing Competition, 2007, http://www.americanbar.org/content/dam/aba/migrated/domviol/docs/Wimberly.authcheckdam.pdf.

[8] Free From Abuse, "California's habeas law," June 2012, http://www.freefromabuse.org/wp-content/uploads/2012/06/California-habeas-law.pdf.

[9] State of California Department of Justice, "Attorney General Kamala D. Harris Calls on Congress to Reauthorize Violence Against Women Act," news release, January 11, 2012, http://oag.ca.gov/news/press-releases/attorney-general-kamala-d-harris-calls-congress-reauthorize-violence-against; Kamala Harris, Twitter post, September 9, 2014, 4:27 p.m., https://twitter.com/kamalaharris/status/509483258501804032.

One common misconception is that LWOP sentences are reserved for incorrigible offenders. But, that simply isn't the case. Kelly, like many other women serving LWOP, is a first-time offender, and they are frequently not the primary actors. LWOP sentences, particularly when given to young people, can mean that someone is serving 40 or more years in prison, and, regardless of an inmate's desire to rehabilitate, they are never leaving prison alive.

In 1995, Mary Elizabeth Stroder was sentenced to LWOP for a kidnapping and murder committed by her partner.[10] (He is on death row.) Like Kelly, Stroder was not the primary participant in the crime. In a phone interview, Stroder told me that people misunderstood what it meant to survive physical and sexual abuse and that the jury "didn't understand why I made those choices . . . people need to understand that we aren't evil or bad people." She believed that if the jurors had been allowed to hear testimony about her abuse, they would have better understood why she was present at the crime scene. Tracee Ward, another woman serving LWOP in California, was sentenced for crimes her batterer committed when she was 19. Both Stroder and Ward were first-time offenders who will now never leave prison.

●

Because Kelly's attorney never presented this evidence at trial, the jury never heard about her extensive history of abuse and neglect. Kelly's abuse began at four, and she was repeatedly raped and assaulted by family members until she ran away from home at fifteen. Then, she suffered abuse at the hands of her two husbands.

Kelly's case is far from extraordinary and represents both the problems most criminal defendants face in terms of ineffective counsel as well as the many stereotypes and prejudices against survivors. As Rummel told me, domestic abuse happens at home, away from other witnesses, and often by the very people who are supposed to love and care for you the most. "Very few women really disclose the abuse; they go through great lengths to cover it up."

Kelly's surviving daughter, Krystal, is now twenty-one; she was only about two when Kelly went to prison. Despite the fact that she may be in prison for the rest of her life, Kelly has tried to better herself during her incarceration by becoming involved in groups that work with women who have survived abuse. "I feel undeserving," she said over the phone, "because I've always been pretty much alone."

---

[10] *State of California v. Charles F. Rountree*, S048543 (Kern County Super. Ct. 2013).

The Cosmic Perspective

Neil deGrasse Tyson

> Of all the sciences cultivated by mankind, Astronomy is acknowledged to
> be, and undoubtedly is, the most sublime, the most interesting, and the most
> useful. For, by knowledge derived from this science, not only the bulk of the
> Earth is discovered . . . ; but our very faculties are enlarged with the grandeur
> of the ideas it conveys, our minds exalted above [their] low contracted
> prejudices.
>
> — James Ferguson, *Astronomy Explained upon*
> *Sir Isaac Newton's Principles, and Made Easy to*
> *Those Who Have Not Studied Mathematics*
> (1757)

Long before anyone knew that the universe had a beginning, before we knew that
the nearest large galaxy lies two and a half million light-years from Earth, before
we knew how stars work or whether atoms exist, James Ferguson's enthusiastic
introduction to his favorite science rang true. Yet his words, apart from their
eighteenth-century flourish, could have been written yesterday.

But who gets to think that way? Who gets to celebrate this cosmic view of life?
Not the migrant farmworker. Not the sweatshop worker. Certainly not the home-
less person rummaging through the trash for food. You need the luxury of time
not spent on mere survival. You need to live in a nation whose government values
the search to understand humanity's place in the universe. You need a society in
which intellectual pursuit can take you to the frontiers of discovery, and in which
news of your discoveries can be routinely disseminated. By those measures, most
citizens of industrialized nations do quite well.

Yet the cosmic view comes with a hidden cost. When I travel thousands of miles
to spend a few moments in the fast-moving shadow of the Moon during a total
solar eclipse, sometimes I lose sight of Earth.

When I pause and reflect on our expanding universe, with its galaxies hurtling
away from one another, embedded within the ever-stretching, four-dimensional
fabric of space and time, sometimes I forget that uncounted people walk this Earth
without food or shelter, and that children are disproportionately represented
among them.

When I pore over the data that establish the mysterious presence of dark matter
and dark energy throughout the universe, sometimes I forget that every day —
every twenty-four-hour rotation of Earth — people kill and get killed in the name
of someone else's conception of God, and that some people who do not kill in the
name of God kill in the name of their nation's needs or wants.

When I track the orbits of asteroids, comets, and planets, each one a pirouetting dancer in a cosmic ballet choreographed by the forces of gravity, sometimes I forget that too many people act in wanton disregard for the delicate interplay of Earth's atmosphere, oceans, and land, with consequences that our children and our children's children will witness and pay for with their health and well-being.

And sometimes I forget that powerful people rarely do all they can to help those who cannot help themselves.

I occasionally forget those things because, however big the world is — in our hearts, our minds, and our outsize atlases — the universe is even bigger. A depressing thought to some, but a liberating thought to me.

Consider an adult who tends to the traumas of a child: a broken toy, a scraped knee, a schoolyard bully. Adults know that kids have no clue what constitutes a genuine problem, because inexperience greatly limits their childhood perspective.

As grown-ups, dare we admit to ourselves that we, too, have a collective immaturity of view? Dare we admit that our thoughts and behaviors spring from a belief that the world revolves around us? Apparently not. And the evidence abounds. Part the curtains of society's racial, ethnic, religious, national, and cultural conflicts, and you find the human ego turning the knobs and pulling the levers.

Now imagine a world in which everyone, but especially people with power and influence, holds an expanded view of our place in the cosmos. With that perspective, our problems would shrink — or never arise at all — and we could celebrate our earthly differences while shunning the behavior of our predecessors who slaughtered each other because of them.

●

Back in February 2000, the newly rebuilt Hayden Planetarium featured a space show called *Passport to the Universe*, which took visitors on a virtual zoom from New York City to the edge of the cosmos. En route the audience saw Earth, then the solar system, then the 100 billion stars of the Milky Way galaxy shrink to barely visible dots on the planetarium dome.

Within a month of opening day, I received a letter from an Ivy League professor of psychology whose expertise was things that make people feel insignificant. I never knew one could specialize in such a field. The guy wanted to administer a before-and-after questionnaire to visitors, assessing the depth of their depression after viewing the show. *Passport to the Universe*, he wrote, elicited the most dramatic feelings of smallness he had ever experienced.

How could that be? Every time I see the space show (and others we've produced), I feel alive and spirited and connected. I also feel large, knowing that the goings-on within the three-pound human brain are what enabled us to figure out our place in the universe.

Allow me to suggest that it's the professor, not I, who has misread nature. His ego was too big to begin with, inflated by delusions of significance and fed by cultural assumptions that human beings are more important than everything else in the universe.

In all fairness to the fellow, powerful forces in society leave most of us susceptible. As was I . . . until the day I learned in biology class that more bacteria live and work in one centimeter of my colon than the number of people who have ever existed in the world. That kind of information makes you think twice about who — or what — is actually in charge.

From that day on, I began to think of people not as the masters of space and time but as participants in a great cosmic chain of being, with a direct genetic link across species both living and extinct, extending back nearly 4 billion years to the earliest single-celled organisms on Earth.

●

I know what you're thinking: we're smarter than bacteria.

No doubt about it, we're smarter than every other living creature that ever walked, crawled, or slithered on Earth. But how smart is that? We cook our food. We compose poetry and music. We do art and science. We're good at math. Even if you're bad at math, you're probably much better at it than the smartest chimpanzee, whose genetic identity varies in only trifling ways from ours. Try as they might, primatologists will never get a chimpanzee to learn the multiplication table or do long division.

If small genetic differences between us and our fellow apes account for our vast difference in intelligence, maybe that difference in intelligence is not so vast after all.

Imagine a life-form whose brainpower is to ours as ours is to a chimpanzee's. To such a species our highest mental achievements would be trivial. Their toddlers, instead of learning their ABCs on *Sesame Street*, would learn multivariable calculus on *Boolean Boulevard*. Our most complex theorems, our deepest philosophies, the cherished works of our most creative artists, would be projects their schoolkids bring home for Mom and Dad to display on the refrigerator door. These creatures would study Stephen Hawking (who occupies the same endowed professorship once held by Newton at the University of Cambridge) because he's slightly more clever than other humans, owing to his ability to do theoretical astrophysics and other rudimentary calculations in his head.

If a huge genetic gap separated us from our closest relative in the animal kingdom, we could justifiably celebrate our brilliance. We might be entitled to walk around thinking we're distant and distinct from our fellow creatures. But no such gap exists. Instead, we are one with the rest of nature, fitting neither above nor below, but within.

●

Need more ego softeners? Simple comparisons of quantity, size, and scale do the job well.

Take water. It's simple, common, and vital. There are more molecules of water in an eight-ounce cup of the stuff than there are cups of water in all the world's oceans. Every cup that passes through a single person and eventually rejoins the world's water supply holds enough molecules to mix 1,500 of them into every other cup of water in the world. No way around it: some of the water you just drank passed through the kidneys of Socrates, Genghis Khan, and Joan of Arc.

How about air? Also vital. A single breathful draws in more air molecules than there are breathfuls of air in Earth's entire atmosphere. That means some of the air you just breathed passed through the lungs of Napoleon, Beethoven, Lincoln, and Billy the Kid.

Time to get cosmic. There are more stars in the universe than grains of sand on any beach, more stars than seconds have passed since Earth formed, more stars than words and sounds ever uttered by all the humans who ever lived.

Want a sweeping view of the past? Our unfolding cosmic perspective takes you there. Light takes time to reach Earth's observatories from the depths of space, and so you see objects and phenomena not as they are but as they once were. That means the universe acts like a giant time machine: the farther away you look, the further back in time you see — back almost to the beginning of time itself. Within that horizon of reckoning, cosmic evolution unfolds continuously, in full view.

Want to know what we're made of? Again, the cosmic perspective offers a bigger answer than you might expect. The chemical elements of the universe are forged in the fires of high-mass stars that end their lives in stupendous explosions, enriching their host galaxies with the chemical arsenal of life as we know it. The result? The four most common chemically active elements in the universe — hydrogen, oxygen, carbon, and nitrogen — are the four most common elements of life on Earth. We are not simply in the universe. The universe is in us.

●

Yes, we are stardust. But we may not be of this Earth. Several separate lines of research, when considered together, have forced investigators to reassess who we think we are and where we think we came from.

First, computer simulations show that when a large asteroid strikes a planet, the surrounding areas can recoil from the impact energy, catapulting rocks into space. From there, they can travel to — and land on — other planetary surfaces. Second, microorganisms can be hardy. Some survive the extremes of temperature, pressure, and radiation inherent in space travel. If the rocky flotsam from an impact hails from a planet with life, microscopic fauna could have stowed away in the rocks' nooks and crannies. Third, recent evidence suggests that shortly after the formation of our solar system, Mars was wet, and perhaps fertile, even before Earth was.

Those findings mean it's conceivable that life began on Mars and later seeded life on Earth, a process known as panspermia. So all earthlings might — just might — be descendants of Martians.

Again and again across the centuries, cosmic discoveries have demoted our self-image. Earth was once assumed to be astronomically unique, until astronomers learned that Earth is just another planet orbiting the Sun. Then we presumed the Sun was unique, until we learned that the countless stars of the night sky are suns themselves. Then we presumed our galaxy, the Milky Way, was the entire known universe, until we established that the countless fuzzy things in the sky are other galaxies, dotting the landscape of our known universe.

Today, how easy it is to presume that one universe is all there is. Yet emerging theories of modern cosmology, as well as the continually reaffirmed improbability that anything is unique, require that we remain open to the latest assault on our plea for distinctiveness: multiple universes, otherwise known as the multiverse, in which ours is just one of countless bubbles bursting forth from the fabric of the cosmos.

●

The cosmic perspective flows from fundamental knowledge. But it's more than just what you know. It's also about having the wisdom and insight to apply that knowledge to assessing our place in the universe. And its attributes are clear:

▷ The cosmic perspective comes from the frontiers of science, yet it's not solely the province of the scientist. The cosmic perspective belongs to everyone.

▷ The cosmic perspective is humble.

▷ The cosmic perspective is spiritual — even redemptive — but not religious.

▷ The cosmic perspective enables us to grasp, in the same thought, the large and the small.

▷ The cosmic perspective opens our minds to extraordinary ideas but does not leave them so open that our brains spill out, making us susceptible to believing anything we're told.

▷ The cosmic perspective opens our eyes to the universe, not as a benevolent cradle designed to nurture life but as a cold, lonely, hazardous place.

▷ The cosmic perspective shows Earth to be a mote, but a precious mote and, for the moment, the only home we have.

▷ The cosmic perspective finds beauty in the images of planets, moons, stars, and nebulae but also celebrates the laws of physics that shape them.

▷ The cosmic perspective enables us to see beyond our circumstances, allowing us to transcend the primal search for food, shelter, and sex.

▷ The cosmic perspective reminds us that in space, where there is no air, a flag will not wave — an indication that perhaps flag waving and space exploration do not mix.

▷ The cosmic perspective not only embraces our genetic kinship with all life on Earth but also values our chemical kinship with any yet-to-be discovered life in the universe, as well as our atomic kinship with the universe itself.

•

At least once a week, if not once a day, we might each ponder what cosmic truths lie undiscovered before us, perhaps awaiting the arrival of a clever thinker, an ingenious experiment, or an innovative space mission to reveal them. We might further ponder how those discoveries may one day transform life on Earth.

Absent such curiosity, we are no different from the provincial farmer who expresses no need to venture beyond the county line, because his forty acres meet all his needs. Yet if all our predecessors had felt that way, the farmer would instead be a cave dweller, chasing down his dinner with a stick and a rock.

During our brief stay on planet Earth, we owe ourselves and our descendants the opportunity to explore — in part because it's fun to do. But there's a far nobler reason. The day our knowledge of the cosmos ceases to expand, we risk regressing to the childish view that the universe figuratively and literally revolves around us. In that bleak world, arms-bearing, resource-hungry people and nations would be prone to act on their "low contracted prejudices." And that would be the last gasp of human enlightenment — until the rise of a visionary new culture that could once again embrace the cosmic perspective.

Black Men and Public Space

Brent Staples

My first victim was a woman — white, well dressed, probably in her early twenties. I came upon her late one evening on a deserted street in Hyde Park, a relatively affluent neighborhood in an otherwise mean, impoverished section of Chicago. As I swung onto the avenue behind her, there seemed to be a discreet, uninflammatory distance between us. Not so. She cast back a worried glance. To her, the youngish black man — a broad six feet two inches with a beard and billowing hair, both hands shoved into the pockets of a bulky military jacket — seemed menacingly close. After a few more quick glimpses, she picked up her pace and was soon running in earnest. Within seconds she disappeared into a cross street. That was more than a decade ago. I was twenty-two years old, a graduate student newly arrived at the University of Chicago. It was in the echo of that terrified woman's footfalls that I first began to know the unwieldy inheritance I'd come into — the ability to alter public space in ugly ways. It was clear that she thought herself the quarry of a mugger, a rapist, or worse. Suffering a bout of insomnia, however, I was stalking sleep, not defenseless wayfarers. As a softy who is scarcely able to take a knife to a raw chicken — let alone hold it to a person's throat — I was surprised, embarrassed, and dismayed all at once. Her flight made me feel like an accomplice in tyranny. It also made it clear that I was indistinguishable from the muggers who occasionally seeped into the area from the surrounding ghetto. That first encounter, and those that followed, signified that a vast, unnerving gulf lay between nighttime pedestrians — particularly women — and me. And I soon gathered that being perceived as dangerous is a hazard in itself. I only needed to turn a corner into a dicey situation, or crowd some frightened, armed person in a foyer somewhere, or make an errant move after being pulled over by a policeman. Where fear and weapons meet — and they often do in urban America — there is always the possibility of death.

In that first year, my first away from my hometown, I was to become thoroughly familiar with the language of fear. At dark, shadowy intersections in Chicago, I could cross in front of a car stopped at a traffic light and elicit the *thunk, thunk, thunk, thunk* of the driver — black, white, male, or female — hammering down the door locks. On less traveled streets after dark, I grew accustomed to but never comfortable with people who crossed to the other side of the street rather than pass me. Then there were the standard unpleasantries with police, doormen, bouncers, cabdrivers, and others whose business is to screen out troublesome individuals *before* there is any nastiness.

I moved to New York nearly two years ago and I have remained an avid night walker. In central Manhattan, the near-constant crowd cover minimizes tense one-on-one street encounters. Elsewhere — visiting friends in SoHo, where sidewalks are narrow and tightly spaced buildings shut out the sky — things can get very taut indeed.

Black men have a firm place in New York mugging literature. Norman Podhoretz in his famed (or infamous) 1963 essay, "My Negro Problem — and Ours," recalls growing up in terror of black males; they "were tougher than we were, more ruthless," he writes — and as an adult on the Upper West Side of Manhattan, he continues, he cannot constrain his nervousness when he meets black men on certain streets. Similarly, a decade later, the essayist and novelist Edward Hoagland extols a New York where once "Negro bitterness bore down mainly on other Negroes." Where some see mere panhandlers, Hoagland sees "a mugger who is clearly screwing up his nerve to do more than just *ask* for money." But Hoagland has "the New Yorker's quick-hunch posture for broken-field maneuvering," and the bad guy swerves away.

I often witness that "hunch posture," from women after dark on the warrenlike streets of Brooklyn where I live. They seem to set their faces on neutral and, with their purse straps strung across their chests bandolier style, they forge ahead as though bracing themselves against being tackled. I understand, of course, that the danger they perceive is not a hallucination. Women are particularly vulnerable to street violence, and young black males are drastically overrepresented among the perpetrators of that violence. Yet these truths are no solace against the kind of alienation that comes of being ever the suspect, against being set apart, a fearsome entity with whom pedestrians avoid making eye contact.

It is not altogether clear to me how I reached the ripe old age of twenty-two without being conscious of the lethality nighttime pedestrians attributed to me. Perhaps it was because in Chester, Pennsylvania, the small, angry industrial town where I came of age in the 1960s, I was scarcely noticeable against a backdrop of gang warfare, street knifings, and murders. I grew up one of the good boys, had perhaps a half-dozen fistfights. In retrospect, my shyness of combat has clear sources.

Many things go into the making of a young thug. One of those things is the consummation of the male romance with the power to intimidate. An infant discovers that random flailings send the baby bottle flying out of the crib and crashing to the floor. Delighted, the joyful babe repeats those motions again and again, seeking to duplicate the feat. Just so, I recall the points at which some of my boyhood friends were finally seduced by the perception of themselves as tough guys. When a mark cowered and surrendered his money without resistance, myth and reality merged — and paid off. It is, after all, only manly to embrace the power to frighten and intimidate. We, as men, are not supposed to give an inch of our lane on the highway; we are to seize the fighter's edge in work and in play and even in love; we are to be valiant in the face of hostile forces.

Unfortunately, poor and powerless young men seem to take all this nonsense literally. As a boy, I saw countless tough guys locked away; I have since buried several, too. They were babies, really — a teenage cousin, a brother of twenty-two, a childhood friend in his midtwenties — all gone down in episodes of bravado played out in the streets. I came to doubt the virtues of intimidation early on. I chose, perhaps even unconsciously, to remain a shadow — timid, but a survivor.

The fearsomeness mistakenly attributed to me in public places often has a perilous flavor. The most frightening of these confusions occurred in the late 1970s and early 1980s when I worked as a journalist in Chicago. One day, rushing into the office of a magazine I was writing for with a deadline story in hand, I was mistaken for a burglar. The office manager called security and, with an ad hoc posse, pursued me through the labyrinthine halls, nearly to my editor's door. I had no way of proving who I was. I could only move briskly toward the company of someone who knew me.

Another time I was on assignment for a local paper and killing time before an interview. I entered a jewelry store on the city's affluent Near North Side. The proprietor excused herself and returned with an enormous red Doberman pinscher straining at the end of a leash. She stood, the dog extended toward me, silent to my questions, her eyes bulging nearly out of her head. I took a cursory look around, nodded, and bade her good night. Relatively speaking, however, I never fared as badly as another black male journalist. He went to nearby Waukegan, Illinois, a couple of summers ago to work on a story about a murderer who was born there. Mistaking the reporter for the killer, police hauled him from his car at gunpoint and but for his press credentials would probably have tried to book him. Such episodes are not uncommon. Black men trade tales like this all the time.

In "My Negro Problem — and Ours," Podhoretz writes that the hatred he feels for blacks makes itself known to him through a variety of avenues — one being his discomfort with that "special brand of paranoid touchiness" to which he says blacks are prone. No doubt he is speaking here of black men. In time, I learned to smother the rage I felt at so often being taken for a criminal. Not to do so would surely have led to madness — via that special "paranoid touchiness" that so annoyed Podhoretz at the time he wrote the essay.

I began to take precautions to make myself less threatening. I move about with care, particularly late in the evening. I give a wide berth to nervous people on subway platforms during the wee hours, particularly when I have exchanged business clothes for jeans. If I happen to be entering a building behind some people who appear skittish, I may walk by, letting them clear the lobby before I return, so as not to seem to be following them. I have been calm and extremely congenial on those rare occasions when I've been pulled over by the police.

And on late-evening constitutionals along streets less traveled by, I employ what has proved to be an excellent tension-reducing measure: I whistle melodies from Beethoven and Vivaldi and the more popular classical composers. Even steely New Yorkers hunching toward nighttime destinations seem to relax, and occasionally they even join in the tune. Virtually everybody seems to sense that a mugger wouldn't be warbling bright, sunny selections from Vivaldi's *Four Seasons*. It is my equivalent of the cowbell that hikers wear when they know they are in bear country.

Acknowledgements

Mick Bourbaki. "All of the Counting Numbers Are Interesting: A Theorem with a Proof." Reprinted by permission of the author.

Michael Byrne. "Deep Sadness of Elk That Don't Run." Reprinted by permission of the author.

Roxane Gay. "Bad Feminist." *The Virginia Quarterly Review*, Fall 2012, Vol. 88, #4. http://www.vqronline.org/essay/bad-feminist. Used by permission of The Virginia Quarterly Review.

Jessica Pishko. "Serving Life for Surviving Abuse." *The Atlantic*, January 26, 2015. Reprinted by permission of the author.

Brent Staples. "Black Men and Public Space." First published in *Harper's Magazine*, December 1986. Reprinted by permission of the author.

Neil deGrasse Tyson. "The Cosmic Perspective." *Natural History* Magazine, April 2007. Reprinted by permission of *Natural History* Magazine. http://www.haydenplanetarium.org/tyson/read/2007/04/02/the-cosmic-perspective

Gore Vidal, "Drugs: Case for Legalizing Marijuana." *The New York Times*/On the Web/Books, September 26, 1970. Used by permission of Janklow & Nesbit Associates Literary Agency.

Index

516

Internal Punctuation
Semicolons and colons
Commas
  and independent clauses
  and other coordinating
    conjunctions
  between subjects and verbs
  with internal phrases
  with introductory material

Practice! **Internal Punctuation**

Grammatical and Mechanical Punctuation
Hyphens vs. dashes
Quotations marks
Apostrophes

Practice! **Grammatical and Mechanical Punctuation**

Reality Check! Boxes